ISBN 978-1-330-01759-3
PIBN 10005046

1 MONTH OF
FREE
READING

at

www.ForgottenBooks.com

By purchasing this book you are
eligible for one month membership to
ForgottenBooks.com, giving you
unlimited access to our entire
collection of over 700,000 titles via
our web site and mobile apps.

To claim your free month visit:

www.forgottenbooks.com/free5046

English
Français
Deutsche
Italiano
Español
Português

www.forgottenbooks.com

Mythology Photography **Fiction**
Fishing Christianity **Art** Cooking
Essays Buddhism Freemasonry
Medicine **Biology** Music **Ancient**
Egypt Evolution Carpentry Physics
Dance Geology **Mathematics** Fitness
Shakespeare **Folklore** Yoga Marketing
Confidence Immortality Biographies
Poetry **Psychology** Witchcraft
Electronics Chemistry History **Law**
Accounting **Philosophy** Anthropology
Alchemy Drama Quantum Mechanics
Atheism Sexual Health **Ancient History**
Entrepreneurship Languages Sport
Paleontology Needlework Islam
Metaphysics Investment Archaeology
Parenting Statistics Criminology
Motivational

THE

ANCIENT CLASSICAL DRAMA

MOULTON

HENRY FROWDE, M.A.

PUBLISHER TO THE UNIVERSITY OF OXFORD

LONDON, EDINBURGH, AND NEW YORK

THE

ANCIENT CLASSICAL DRAMA

A Study in Literary Evolution

*INTENDED FOR READERS IN ENGLISH AND IN
THE ORIGINAL*

BY

RICHARD G. MOULTON

A.M. (Cantab.), Ph.D. (Penn.)

PROFESSOR OF LITERATURE IN ENGLISH IN THE UNIVERSITY OF CHICAGO, LATE
LECTURER TO CAMBRIDGE UNIVERSITY (EXTENSION), TO THE LONDON
AND TO THE AMERICAN SOCIETIES FOR THE EXTENSION
OF UNIVERSITY TEACHING

SECOND EDITION

Oxford

AT THE CLARENDON PRESS

1898

Oxford
PRINTED AT THE CLARENDON PRESS
BY HORACE HART, M.A.
PRINTER TO THE UNIVERSITY

PREFACE TO THE SECOND EDITION

—⋅⋅—

THIS second edition, except for some minute corrections of detail, is a reproduction of the first. There were temptations to make additions on certain topics, but this could not be done without enlarging the book to an extent which would have impaired its serviceableness in practical education.

In the preface to the first edition I made a plea for recognizing the study of classical literatures in translation as an element in liberal education, both for those who did and those who did not read these literatures in the original languages. The reception of my book, as shown by reviews and by letters from prominent scholars, has convinced me that there was much wider sympathy for the position I took up than I was aware of at the time. And the eight years since the first edition was published have shown a steady, if slow, advance in the prospects of the new study. Expensive and laborious stage productions of ancient dramas have afforded good evidence of popular interest in the literature of antiquity; in some cases the plays have been acted in English. Topics of classical literature and antiquities have maintained, and even improved, their position in the programmes of University Extension and private lectures. The admirable work of Mr. Arthur Way has removed what was at once a reproach to scholarship and a difficulty in practical teaching—the absence of an adequate translation of Euripides. It is an ideal illustration of the kind of study I am advocating to follow faithfully, as Mr. Way does, all the technicalities of verse-fluctuation, without the force or flow of the English poem being allowed to flag[1]. In the classical studies of universities and schools there has been during these last few years a perceptible tendency to give more emphasis to the literary element, and, I think, a diminution in the prejudice against reading translations. Partiality for my own University will excuse my instancing, as a step in the right direction, the institution by the University of Chicago of a department of 'Literature in English.' To supplement—which is part of the purpose of that department—the study of particular literatures in the original by wider reading in English versions is precisely what constitutes a leading object of the present book; and the extension of this treatment to other than Greek and Latin literatures will be so much advance towards the recognition of that unity of all literature which will make its study scientific. That the study of literature

---

[1] Mr. Way's translation is in three volumes [Macmillan]. The second volume contains a valuable Introduction to Euripides as a whole. Some of the plays can be obtained separately.

when adequately organized will hold its pre-eminence in education, the experience of the newest as well as of the older seats of learning leaves no doubt. In the conflict between 'classical' and 'modern' schemes of education it will not be the modern that will triumph: wherever classical studies are what they claim to be, and not merely the linguistic husk of a dead literary culture, the most modern mind does homage to that universality of interest which has made ancient literatures classical.

March, 1898.

PA

PREFACE TO THE FIRST EDITION

—•—

I HAVE ventured to entitle this work 'A study in Literary Evolution.' It is obvious that some of the familiar processes and results of evolution are to be traced in literature. Within the field of the Ancient Classical Drama we can see a common starting-point from which lines of development extend in various directions; the rise of new literary species, or transitional tendencies not amounting to distinction of species; developments traceable in embryo and on to maturity, with precious links preserving processes of change all but lost; unstable forms that continually originate literary changes, reversions to type, and survivals of forms long after their *raison d'être* has passed away; while the Drama as a whole will present the double process of growth in simplicity from the indefinite to the regular, and the passage from simple to complex. Thus to survey the phenomena of literary development gives a point of view distinct from that of literary history. History is concerned with the sum of individual works produced: evolution takes account only of literary varieties. History will always give prominence to the author, and tends to consider a dramatist's plays as so many steps of achievement in the life-history of the poet. Evolution concerns itself with the works more than with the author; or rather, it treats a literature as an entity in itself, of which literary works are dis- tinguishing features, and expounds it as a continuous unfolding of new phases by the operation of creative impulse on ever-changing environment.

But my book has a wider and more practical purpose than this of tracing evolution. It aims at presenting the Ancient Drama from a purely literary standpoint, and addresses itself to readers in English and in the original. Circumstances have given me an exceptional experience in this matter of teaching Ancient literature in translation. Under the Cambridge University Extension scheme I have since 1880 conducted courses of lectures on Ancient Drama in twenty-six different places, addressed to adult audiences, representing all classes of society, in which not one person in ten would know a word of Greek or Latin. Taking my experience as a whole I should rank the Ancient Classics second only to Shakespeare and Goethe as an attractive subject for lectures ; and I may add that the largest audiences I have ever myself had to deal with were in connexion with a course on Ancient Tragedy at Newcastle-on-Tyne, where they reached a weekly *average* of over seven hundred. In all these cases a considerable percentage of the audience did regular exercises in the subject of the lectures, and were tested at the end of the course in a formal examination, with results satisfactory enough to assure the position of this study as part of a general English education. I have spoken of what is within my own cognisance: I am well aware that more distinguished teachers are at work in the same field. With Mr. Arthur Sidgwick to represent it at Oxford, and Mr. Churton Collins among the teachers of London, this enterprise of opening the ancient classics to the ordinary English reader is secure of a favourable trial.

I am one of those who believe a knowledge of the ancient classical literatures to be a first requisite of a liberal education. I think it is a mistake to divert attention from these in favour of our own earlier literature. Our true literary ancestors are the Latin and Greek Classics: the old English writers have had less influence in moulding our modern literature than have Homer and Virgil and the Greek dramatists. As a practical teacher of literature I find it almost impossible to give an intelligent grasp of form in Shakespeare to those who are ignorant of Classical Drama, for the first is a multiple of which the latter is the unit. Milton and Spenser construct their poems out of details which were made into literary material by the literatures of the past. The ancient classics constitute a common stock from which the writers of all modern countries draw, and their familiar ideas are the currency in which modern literary intercourse is transacted. The educational problem of the day is to adjust the claims of classical and ' modern' systems. I believe an essential point in its solution will be a recognition of the distinction between language and literature : whatever may be ultimately found practicable with reference to the study of the Latin and Greek tongues, the leading productions of Latin and Greek literature will have to be the groundwork of all education that is not content to omit literature altogether.

I have also desired to make my book useful to those who read in the original languages, supplementing their other study with a treatment that presents the ancient drama purely as literature. Whatever may be the intention of those who direct our higher education, I believe that our study of Latin and Greek is in practice almost exclusively a study of language : the great mass of those receiving a classical education enter upon life with no knowledge of literature or taste for it, while they can be at once interested in science or art. It is of course easy to point out exceptions. But men of the intellectual calibre to make senior classics and double firsts are persons of small importance in educational discussions. It is the average man that tests the system, and with the passmen of our universities, and the still larger number who follow classical studies at school, I believe that the language element of their Classics almost entirely swallows up the element of literature. I do not see how it can be otherwise. The unit in the study of literature is the book or play that to a reader in a dead language

means a considerable course of work; an ordinary
student cannot cover the ground fast enough to get the
comparison of work with work and author with author
necessary for literary grasp. Thus Classics, to the
ordinary student, is a study terribly out of perspective,
demanding exactness in minor points yet admitting
vagueness in all that is great, tithing the mint and anise
and cummin of *oratio obliqua* and second aorist para-
digms, but omitting the weightier matters of a poet's
conceptions and literary force. It is no revolution that
I am contemplating. But where it is customary at present to set, say, two books of Homer or two Greek plays,
would it not be possible to set only one for reading in
the original, and for the time thus saved to prescribe
the whole *Odyssey*, or a group of plays, to be studied in
English, or some such course of reading in ancient and
English Classics combined as I suggest in an appendix
to this book? Or even in a course of study so elementary as to comprise no more than one Greek or Latin
work, I do not see why a definite fraction of it might
not be sufficient for study in the original, and the whole,
with one or two kindred works, be set for reading in
English; the difference between five hundred and a
thousand lines for exercise in parsing and construing is
not very serious, while the substitute for the other half
might be sufficient to at all events awaken a beginner's
taste and imagination. Such a change as I advocate
would be welcome to a large proportion of both teachers
and taught. But some of the most willing among these

teachers are from lack of experience at a loss. It is for these I have hoped my book may be useful, in suggesting what sort of questions need to be taken up and thought out in order to present the ancient drama as literature.

The arrangement of the book will, I hope, explain itself. An Appendix contains Tables intended to bring out general lines of development in ancient drama, and the structure of particular plays, more especially in regard to the variations of metrical effect. I fear these Tables have a somewhat forbidding look: but the reader must please understand that a dry appendix means so much dry matter kept out of the text. In the Appendix is also a list of suggestions for courses of reading, both in (translated) plays and in English Classics associated with the ancient drama.

In order not to break the text with a multitude of references, I express here once for all my indebtedness to the various English translators of the Ancient Classical Drama. First and foremost to Dean Plumptre, whose complete versions of Aeschylus and Sophocles (though too expensive for popular classes) are the only means by which the English reader is enabled to appreciate the delicate variations of metre in the dramatic scenes which make so important a feature in Greek tragedy. For Euripides I have had to fall back upon the last-century translation of Potter: it is to the disgrace of English scholarship that we have no verse translation of this all-important poet produced in our own day. Potter

almost always neglects stage lyrics, and it has been often
necessary to alter his lines or retranslate. Of Seneca
I know no English version except the antiquated one of
Sir Edward Sherborne. Aristophanes is the only case
in which there is the distraction of choice. Hookham
Frere's renderings of particular plays make him the
great pioneer in the opening of Comedy to modern
readers. I have drawn copiously from these and from
the translation (now out of print) by Rev. L. H. Rudd ;
the beautiful version by the latter of the Comus Song
in the *Frogs* I have quoted in full [1]. The translations by
Mr. Rogers of the *Clouds, Wasps, Peace*, and above all
the *Lysistrata*, appear to me amongst the greatest feats
in translation ever accomplished : I have used them freely,
and only regret that they are not made accessible to the
general reader. For Plautus and Terence there are only
the old translations by Bonnel Thornton and Colman :
they are of considerable literary interest, but neglect the
distinctions of metre, and it has been often necessary to
retranslate. For occasional passages in the various
poets I have borrowed from Mr. Morshead's admirable
House of Atreus, from the late Professor Kennedy's
valuable edition of the *Birds*, and a notable passage from Robert Browning's version of the *Hercules*
of Euripides. I have never used my own translation where I could get any other that served the
purpose.

---

[1] Mr. Rudd omits the Iambic Interlogue altogether : I have supplied it
(in iambic metres) as essential to my purpose.

I must also express my obligation to my friend Mr. Joseph Jacobs for reading the proof sheets, and for many suggestions made at various stages of my work. I fear, however, that there will be many errors of detail in the book of a kind that only the author can correct, and I wish I could have brought to my task a less rusty linguistic scholarship.

RICHARD G. MOULTON

December, 1890.

NOTE

₊ IT will be observed that in the stage arrangements of the various plays commented upon I have not adopted the theory of Dörpfeld, which, in the age of Sophocles and Euripides, would abolish the distinction between stage and orchestra. Without in the least underrating the value of the facts brought to light by this eminent discoverer and his coadjutors, I am unable to see that the inferences from them, whatever they may show about the material and permanency of the early stage, prove anything at all as against the separateness of stage from orchestra, while the whole weight of internal evidence from the plays themselves tells in favour of a distinct and elevated stage. On this and all other matters of theatrical antiquities I would refer the reader to Mr. Haigh's valuable work on *The Attic Theatre* [1] : his statement of the controversy and conclusions I entirely accept.

[1] Clarendon Press, 1889 : see especially pp. 142–6.

REFERENCES

THE References in this work are to the original:—to the Cambridge texts of Aeschylus, Sophocles, and Euripides, to Bergk's text of Aristophanes (which differs from Dindorf's in many points of importance to the literary student), to Fleckeisen's Plautus and Parry's edition of Terence. Difficulty arises in the case of English readers, for the English versions persistently omit any numbering of lines, and thereby greatly reduce the value of the work for purposes of study. The exceptions are the Aeschylus and Sophocles of Dean Plumptre, which adopt the sensible plan of making the numbering in the margin refer to the lines of the original, not to the translated lines. Similarly, Mr. Way's version of Euripides (above, p. vi) is practically a line for line translation. In the case of the other poets I can only leave the English reader to find the reference by guesswork, and I have been on account of this difficulty the freer in my quotations. A Table (on page 480) will somewhat facilitate references to the translations of Euripides in the Universal Library.

CONTENTS

APPENDIX

I

ORIGIN OF TRAGEDY

THE origin of Ancient Tragedy is one of the curiosities
of literary evolution. On the one hand the assertion is
made that the drama of the whole world, so far as it is
literary drama, is derived from, or at least moulded by, the
drama of Greece; while in Greece itself this form of art
reached maturity only among one people, the Athenians.
On the other hand, the process of development in this
Athenian drama can be carried back in history, by intelligible stages, to that which is the common origin of all
literary art. So defined a root has spread into such wide
ramifications : and the process of growth can be surveyed
in its completeness.

This ultimate origin to which Greek Tragedy traces up
is the Ballad-Dance, the fundamental medium out of which
all varieties of literature have been developed,—a sort of
literary protoplasm. It consists in the combination of
speech, music, and that imitative gesture which, for lack
of a better word, we are obliged to call dancing. It is very
important, however, to guard against modern associations
with this last term. Dances in which men and women
joined are almost unknown to Greek antiquity, and to say
of a guest at a banquet that he danced would suggest
intoxication. The real dancing of the Greeks is a lost art,
of which the modern ballet is a corruption, and the orator's
action a faint survival. It was an art which used bodily
motion to convey thought : as in speech the tongue articu-
lated words, so in dancing the body swayed and gesticulated
into meaning. It was perhaps the supreme art of an age

which was the great period of the world for bodily development; and the degree of perfection to which dancing
attained in Greece may be described in the enthusiastic
words of Charles Kingsley:

> A dance in which every motion was a word, and rest as eloquent as
> motion; in which every attitude was a fresh motive for a sculptor of the
> purest school, and the highest physical activity was manifested, not, as
> in coarse comic pantomimes, in fantastic bounds and unnatural dis-
> tortions, but in perpetual delicate modulations of a stately and self-
> sustaining grace.

The Bal-
lad-Dance
the common
origin of all
literature :

It is such dancing as this which united with speech and
music to make the Ballad-Dance; wherever the language
of primitive peoples raises itself to that conscious elevation
which makes it literature, it appears not alone, but supported by the sister arts of music and dance,—a story, or
poetical conception, is at one and the same time versified,
chanted, and conveyed in gesture. In the case of Miriam's
Song of Deliverance the poetical form of her words has
come down to us, while the two other elements are supplied
by the verse which tells how Miriam 'took a timbrel in her
hand, and all the women went out after her with timbrels
and dances.' It was a sacred Ballad-Dance that David
danced with all his might before the Lord. Heathen War-
Dances, chanting rude defiance with savage gestures, are
the same embryonic poetry of races which are to-day passing
through the early stage of civilisation traversed by ourselves
hundreds, and by the Hebrews thousands of years ago.

the parent
of epic,

And that such a Ballad-Dance is fitted to be the starting-
point of all literary progress will be the easier to understand
when it is recognised as the natural parent of the three
main divisions of poetry. In epic poetry, where thought
takes the form of simple narrative, the speech (Greek, *epos*)
of the Ballad-Dance triumphs over the other two elements.

lyric,

Lyric poetry consists in meditation or highly-wrought description taking such forms as odes, sonnets, hymns,—

poetry that lends itself to elaborate rhythms and other *and dra-*
devices of musical art : here the music is the element of *matic*
the Ballad-Dance which has come to the front. And the *poetry*
imitative gesture has triumphed over the speech and the
music in the case of the third branch of poetry : drama is
thought expressed in action.

But the Ballad-Dance in primitive antiquity took an *Varieties*
infinite variety of forms, as being the sole medium in *of Ballad-*
which religious ritual, military display, holiday and social *Dance: the*
festivity found expression ; this youth of the world literally *Dithy-*
danced through all phases of its happy life. Only one of *ramb*
these Ballad-Dances was destined to develop into drama.
This was the Dithyramb, the dance used in the festival
worship of the god Dionysus, better known by the name
Bacchus—his pet name, if the expression may be allowed
of a god, that is, the name used by his votaries in their
invocations. The question arises then, what was there in *Dionysiac*
the worship of Dionysus which could serve as force sufficient *worship the*
to evolve out of the universal Ballad-Dance the drama as *developing*
a special branch of art? *force of*
drama :

It must be premised that in Greek antiquity divine
worship as a whole shows traces of a dramatic character.
The ancient temple was not a place of assembly for the
worshippers, but was the dwelling of the god, of which the
worshippers occupied only the threshold. A sacrifice was
a feast in which the god and his votaries united ; the
choicest morsels were cut off and thrown into the fire, the
freshly poured wine was spilled on the ground, and the
deity was supposed to feed on the perfume of these while
the worshippers fell to on grosser viands. So the 'mysteries'
of ancient religion were mystic dramas in which the divine
story was conveyed. It is natural to suppose that the most
powerful religion would have the most dramatic ritual.
Now the worship of Bacchus was a branch of nature-
worship ; and in early civilisation nature is the great fact

and the main interest for mankind. Moreover this worship of the Wine-god was the supreme form of nature-worship. Partly this may have arisen from the circumstances of its introduction; that it was a late and therefore fashionable cult, that it came tinged with some of the oriental excess of the countries through which it had travelled to Greece. But the nature of the case is reason sufficient for explaining why this celebration of the most dazzling among the gifts of nature should become at all events the most exciting of religious functions. In modern life all the force of religion is often insufficient to control appetite for vinous excess; where religion and appetite were on the same side it is no wonder that Dionysiac festivals were orgies of wild excitement. The worship of Bacchus was a grand Intemperance Movement for the ancient world. Hence the worship of Dionysus was foremost in displaying that wildness of emotion in ancient religion which has bequeathed to *as contain-* modern language the word 'enthusiasm,' a word which in *ing the* its structure suggests how the worshipper is 'filled with the *germs of* *Passion,* god.' Enthusiasm was held as closely akin to madness; it was an inebriety of mind, a self-abandonment in which enjoyment was raised to the pitch of delirious consciousness. Like the Roman Saturnalia, the Italian Carnival, the mediæval Feasts of Unreason, these enthusiastic orgies of Bacchus were moral safety-valves, which sought to compound for general sobriety and strictness of morals by a short period of unbridled license. The chief distinction then of the Dithyramb among the Ballad-Dances was this enthusiasm of which it was the expression. In such wildness of emotion we see the germ of 'Passion,' one of the three elements of which dramatic effect is made up.

of Plot,   Again: as soon as the worship of Dionysus took the lead among the festivals of nature it became the form used to convey that which is the great point in primitive religion, sympathy with the changes of the year. Whether in early

or late civilisation the most impressive external experience
for mankind is the perpetual miracle of all nature descending into gloom in the winter, to be restored to warmth and
brightness in the spring. Modern appreciation, diluted as
it is over its myriad topics, cannot without a secret thrill
hear detailed the symptoms of the changing year :

> For, lo, the winter is past,
>   The rain is over and gone ;
> The flowers appear on the earth ;
>   The time of the singing of birds is come,
>   And the voice of the turtle is heard in our land ;
> The fig tree putteth forth her green figs,
>   And the vines are in blossom,
>   They give forth their fragrance.

The worship of Dionysus divided itself equally between
the celebration of the vine and of the changing year.   His
festivals marked the four winter months : our December
was, in the southern climate of Greece, the month for the
Rural Dionysia, a harvest-home for the vintage ; in the next
month was the Festival of the Wine-press [1]; the Feast of
Flowers [2] was the name given (in February) to the ritual
of opening the wine-casks ; while the series was brought to
a climax in March by the Greater Dionysia, which celebrated
the beginning of spring and the reopening of navigation.
Accordingly, the mythic stories of Dionysus had to accom-
modate themselves to his connexion with the changing
seasons, and became distinguished by the changes of fortune
they conveyed.   As a rule, the deities of Olympus were
loftily superior to human trouble, but in proportion as they
became nature deities their legends had to tell of gloom
mingled with brightness ; Dionysus so far surpassed them
in capacity for change of experience that the 'sufferings
of Dionysus' became a proverbial expression—sufferings
always a prelude to triumph.   Now it is precisely in such

---

[1] *Lenæa.*   [2] *Anthesteria.*

change of fortune that we have the germ of 'Plot,' the second great element of dramatic effect.

And the third is not far to seek.   One form taken by the self-abandonment to Dionysiac excitement was that the worshippers disguised themselves as followers of the god. They coloured their bodies with soot or vermilion, they made use of masks and skins of beasts.   If Dionysus stood for nature as a whole, it was easy to personify, as attendants on the deity, the special forms in which nature is known to us ; so the votaries of Bacchus arrayed themselves as Panes (or Spirits of Hunting), as Nymphs and Fauns.   Especially popular were the Satyrs, the regular attendants on Bacchus, equally ready to share his misfortunes or his sportive adventures : grotesque beings, half men, half goats, suggestive of a gross yet simple sensuality, the sensuality that belongs to a state of nature.   It was a noticeable feature of Dionysiac festivals that the worshippers thus imitated, in guise and behaviour, Satyrs and other attendants on the god : and this is nothing else than dramatic 'Characterisation.'   The answer then to the question, why the worship of Dionysus should be the developing force of drama, is that in different aspects of its ritual are latent germs of the three main elements of dramatic effect—Passion, Plot, Character.

Before these slow and universal principles of natural development could culminate in complete Drama they had to be interrupted by a distinct revolution, the work of an historical personage.   We have next to consider the Revolution of Arion, which consists in the amalgamation of the embryonic drama with fully developed lyric poetry.

The revolution is technically expressed by saying that *the Dithyramb was made choral.*   It will be noted that as music holds in the modern world the position occupied by dancing in antiquity, so it has taken over many of the technical terms of the lost art.   'Chorus' is one example amongst many of expressions that convey musical associations to us,

but are terms originally of dancing. The Chorus was the
most elaborate of the lyric Ballad-Dances,—lyric, because,
though it retained all three elements of speech, music and
gesture, yet it was moulded and leavened by music. Its
distinctions of form were three. First, its evolutions were
confined to a dancing-place or 'orchestra'—another example
of a term appropriated by music; in this the Chorus was
directly contrasted with the Dithyramb, which was a 'Comus,'
or wandering dance. Again, the Chorus was accompanied
with the lyre, a stringed instrument, unlike the Comus of
which the musical accompaniment was the flute. A third
distinction of the Chorus was that it was divided into what
we call 'stanzas.' But the Greek notion of stanzas was
different from ours. In Greek poetry stanzas ran in pairs,
Strophe and Antistrophe; the metre and evolutions for the
two stanzas of a pair were the same down to the minutest
gesture, but might be changed altogether for the next pair.
An ode was thus performed. The Chorus started from the
altar in the centre of the orchestra, and their evolutions
took them to the right. This would constitute a Strophe,
whereupon (as the word 'Strophe' implies) they turned
round and in the Antistrophe worked their way back to
the altar again, the second stanza of the pair getting its
name because in it the rhythm, gestures and metre of the
first were exactly repeated though with different words. A
second Strophe, very likely accompanied with a change of
rhythm, would take the dancers towards the left of the
orchestra, in the corresponding Antistrophe they would
retrace their steps to the altar again. The process would
be continued indefinitely; if there was an odd stanza it was
performed round the altar, and called an Epode if at the
end, or a Mesode if in the middle, of the performance.

With such characteristics of form the Chorus represents *The two*
the highest achievement of lyric art. The contrast between *amalga-*
it and the Dithyramb reflects the contrast between the two *mated by Arion*

CHAP. I national deities to whose worship the dances were consecrated—Apollo, the intellectual god of the stately Dorians,
and the passionate Dionysus, chief adoration of the excitable
Ionic peoples. Arion had connexion with both sides of
the contrast. A native of Methymna in Lesbos, which was
a great seat of Bacchic worship, he had travelled widely
among the Doric states of Greece, and he was moreover
the first lyre-player of his time; thus early associations
would root in his mind a love for the passionate freedom
of the Dithyramb, while later experience and his specialty
as an artist inclined him to the lyric Chorus. Accordingly,
when he settled down at the Ionian city of Corinth, he
accomplished the feat of amalgamating the two opposites.
The Dithyramb in his hands was confined to an orchestra,
it was made strophic, and was altogether so transformed
that henceforward it was called a Chorus[1]. On the other
hand it necessarily retained the subject-matter proper to
a festival of Dionysus, and with the subject-matter the
characterisation of the performers as Satyrs, together with
the exuberance of emotion which had given to the old
Dithyramb its chief artistic worth. This life-work of Arion
is thus no mere matter of technicalities, but constitutes one
of the most remarkable revolutions in the history of art. It
was a union between self-discipline and abandon, a marriage
of intellect with emotion ; in the history of rhythmic movement it was an amalgamation of the stationary and the
roving ; it gave to the new ritual the full artistic intricacies
and elevation of the Chorus, while leaving it to retain its
hold on the heart through the sense of sacred revel. Yet
to modern observers what Arion did is less interesting than
what he failed to do. The main art of the modern world
is music, the basis of modern music is orchestration, and

---

[1] The Dithyramb in its old form still remained, but passes out of the
line of dramatic development: it had a different history, and became
distinguished by florid music and wild verse.

the key to orchestration is the combination of stringed with
wind instruments. In the case of Arion we have, six centuries before Christ, an amalgamation effected between two
rituals, one of which had been regularly accompanied with
a stringed instrument and the other with a wind instrument :
had the acoustic knowledge of the age enabled Arion to
unite the strings with the wind in the new ritual the history
of music might have been rewritten, and Beethoven and
Wagner anticipated by centuries. As it was, a stringed
accompaniment was used for the Dithyrambic Chorus when
it was applied to serious, and a flute accompaniment
when it was applied to lighter purposes.

How far this event has brought us in our present task *Founda-*
will be seen when it is added that we now reach the word *tion of*
'Tragedy,' which is first applied in antiquity to the reformed *' Tragedy'*
Dithyramb of Arion. The word, it must be noted, has no
suggestion of drama in its signification. 'Tragi' is an old
word for Satyrs ; the three letters *-edy* are a corruption of
the Greek word which has come down to us in the form
'ode,' a leading form of lyric poetry. Thus to a Greek ear
'Tragedy' simply suggests a lyric performance by Satyrs ;
modern scholarship has endeavoured to keep up the effect
to English readers by applying the term 'Lyric Tragedy' to
this earliest outcome of Arion's reforms. Such Tragedy is *Lyric*
clearly a compound form of art. It is entirely lyric in form : *Tragedy*
a story conveyed in descriptive meditation, and with
elaboration of metre, musical accompaniment, and dancing
evolutions. It is dramatic only in spirit, distinguished
from other lyric poetry by wildness of emotion, and self-
abandonment to sympathy with the incidents described,
which continually tended to break out in actual imitation.
The remaining history of Tragedy consists simply in a *Steps of de-*
succession of steps by which the dramatic spirit struggles to *velopment*
break through the lyric form in which it is restrained. *from Lyric*
to Drama-
The first of these steps may be taken to be the splitting *tic Tragedy*

up of the Chorus into two Semi-choruses for the purpose of emphasising, by rapid and brief dialogue, some critical point in the ode.   An exact illustration of such a device in its most elementary form may be borrowed from modern music. The opening chorus of Bach's oratorio, *St. Matthew*, is a general invocation to lament, of which the words run thus :

> Come, ye daughters, weep with me;
> Behold Him, the Bridegroom!
> See Him, as like a Lamb!
> See His innocence!
> Look on our offence!

In the performance of this movement a startling effect is produced: the Chorus suddenly appears as double, and while one Chorus is singing the words in the ordinary form, the other is interrupting with short sharp interrogatories.

> Behold Him—
> *Second Chorus.*   Whom?
>   *First Chorus.*   The Bridegroom!
> See Him—
> *Second Chorus.*   How?
>   *First Chorus.*   As like a Lamb!
> See—
> *Second Chorus.*   What?
>   *First Chorus.*   His innocence!
> Look—
> *Second Chorus.*   Where?
>   *First Chorus.*   On our offence!

The effectiveness of such a device is obvious; it is equally clear how slight a departure it is from the strictest lyric form. Such bifurcation for sudden effect seems to have been the earliest change that the Dithyrambic Chorus underwent, and would fit well with the points of suspense or climaxes of excitement in which Dionysiac subject-matter abounded. The significance of such a change in the development of the drama is clear : it has introduced *dialogue* into Tragedy, and dialogue is the very essence of drama.   To the end of

Greek history the Chorus retained the power of breaking
into semichoric dialogue to express supreme emotion, full *Its use in*
choral order being resumed when the crisis was passed. *complete*
The dialogue so introduced into Tragedy would find a *Tragedy*
ready source of extension in the function of the 'Exarch,' *Second step: the*
or Leader of the Chorus : the word is related to dancing as *Episode*
the word 'precentor' is related to singing. Tradition agrees
with the nature of the case in suggesting how, the evolutions
of the dance being suspended at intervals, this leader would
hold conversation with the rest of the Chorus to bring out
special points of the story, or divide it into parts, each conversation introducing a fresh subject for choral illustration.
This represents a considerable advance on the first stage.
What was before an ode has now become a series of small
odes, separated by passages of dialogue ; the alteration of
lyric and dramatic elements gives already to Greek Tragedy
the double external form it never ceased to present. The
supremacy, however, of the lyric over the dramatic element
is reflected in the name given to these dialogues—'Episodes,'
a word exactly equivalent to our 'parentheses.' In the
completely developed drama a trace of this second stage *Traces of*
survives in the prominence of the Chorus-Leader [1], who *this stage in complete*
regularly enters into the dramatic dialogue, speaking on *Tragedy*
behalf of the Chorus as a whole. It is perhaps another
trace of this stage in which the Chorus themselves constituted the second interlocutor that, in the fully developed
Tragedy, they regularly speak of themselves in the singular
and not in the plural.
The next, and the main, stage in the development of *Revolution*
dramatic Tragedy is again connected with the name of an *of Thespis (B.C. 535)*
individual ; as the revolution of Arion had brought the
influence of lyric poetry to found Tragedy, so the revolution
of Thespis gave the chief impulse to its development by
linking it with the epic. Epic and lyric poetry had been

[1] His appellation has then changed to *Coryphæus*.

CHAP. I   developing side by side from their common origin the

Influence of   Ballad-Dance.   The Homeric epic had reached a stage in
epic poetry   which it had shaken off the influence of music, but not
on the
drama   entirely that of gesture, since the earliest reciters of such
poetry—called 'Rhapsodists'—made use of a staff to emphasise the rhythm of their verses.   All recitation has in it
an element of drama ; but there was one form of epic
recitation, obtaining at the great festival of the Panathenæa
and elsewhere, which was highly dramatic.   This consisted
in the union of two performers in one recitation.   In a
story like the one known to us as the first book of the
Iliad, when the chief reciter reached the quarrel of the
princes, a second reciter would come forward and declaim
the speeches of Agamemnon, while the other confined
himself to the part of Achilles.   In such an effect it is clear
that epic and dramatic approached very near one another ;
and the revolution of Thespis consisted simply in the introduction of such epic reciters into the episodes of Tragedy,
for the purpose of carrying on the dialogue with the Leader
of the Chorus.

Third   The importance of this step is very great.   Hitherto,
step: the   while Tragedy had consisted of alternations between dra-
Actor,   matic dialogue and lyric odes, yet the dialogue had been
a subordinate function of the lyric performers.   The work
of Thespis was to introduce an ' Actor,' separate altogether
from the Chorus ; and the first word for an actor—a word
that has come down to us in the form ' hypocrite,' one who
plays a part—is borrowed from the epic recitations, its
etymological significance being fairly translated by the term
' answering-reciter.'   Moreover this change carries with it
another.   As the Actor was not a member of the Chorus
there was no place for him in the orchestra ; hence the
and the   origin of the ' Stage,' or external platform from which the
Stage   speeches of the Actor were declaimed.   In Tragedy as
remodelled the lyric element might still predominate ; but

at all events the dramatic element had secured a place and *Chap. I*
performers of its own.

Two palpable traces of this important transitional step *Traces in*
are visible in the completely developed Drama. One is *complete*
Tragedy :
the ' Messenger's Speech,' which few Greek tragedies omit, *the Mes-*
and which is wholly unlike other dramatic speeches, resem- *senger's*
Speech,
bling rather a fragment of an epic introduced into a play.
The other is still more striking to those who read in the
original. Greece always presents itself as twofold, conti- *and the dis-*
tinction of
nental and peninsular, Peloponnesus and Attica, inhabited *dialects*
(for the most part) by strongly contrasted races, the Dorians
and the Ionians. Before Thespis the development of
Tragedy had been mainly in the hands of the Dorians, and
it was at Corinth that Arion effected his reforms. With
this last step the leadership in Greek drama removes to
Attica and Athens ; the epic recitations which gave it an
actor were the special characteristic of this country, and
Thespis himself was a villager of Attica, and made his
reforms under the countenance of the famous autocrat of
Athens, Pisistratus. This double source of the lyric and
dramatic elements in ancient Tragedy has brought it about
that, to the end of Greek literature, the choral odes are
composed in the Doric dialect, while the dramatic scenes
are in the dialect of Athens : the effect is as if the dialogue
was in Shakespearean English and the interludes in the
language of Burns. So clearly may the external form of
literature reflect the story of its origin.

From the revolution of Thespis the history of Tragedy *Fourth*
presents a continuous advance, but an advance that was *Stage : ad-*
vance, gen-
double in its character : on the one hand there was a steady *eral and*
increase in general artistic effectiveness, on the other hand *dramatic*
there was a tendency to the development of the dramatic at
the expense of the lyric element. As illustrating changes
of the first kind, it is easy to imagine how the original stage-
platform would develop into a complete Dionysiac theatre,

with its permanent scene of stonework, its narrow stage, capacious orchestra, and auditorium large enough to contain the population of a city. More complex figures for the dance enabled Tragedy to keep pace with advance in choral art. And an increased splendour of outward setting became an artistic medium for giving expression to the primitive wildness of Bacchic orgies. But the more noticeable changes in the later development of Tragedy are those which increase its dramatic capacity. By far the most

Blank Verse, and influence of Satire on the drama important of these is the adaptation to an organ of poetic expression more in harmony with dialogue than the lyric and epic metres used for it originally. This was afforded by Satire, which had, partly from the nature of the case and partly through the genius of its first great master, Archilochus, separated itself very rapidly from the original form of the Ballad-Dance, and early developed that iambic metre which may be called the 'Blank Verse' of Greek poetry[1], that is, the metre approaching most nearly to prose. As these iambic satires were, like epic poems, recited by rhapsodists, their metrical form easily found its way into

Increase in number of speaking actors the dialogues of Tragedy. Again, the successors of Thespis increased the number of actors to two, three, or even four. It must be understood that the number of actors affects only the number of personages on the stage speaking in the same scene ; each actor could take different parts in different scenes, and the number of mute personages was unlimited.

Realism in costume and scenery Once more, the costume and masks of the actors, by means of which they varied their parts, became in time more and more imitative of the character presented, and less and less

---

[1] This metre, the *Iambic Senarius*, or *Iambic Sixes*, closely resembles English Blank Verse, differing from it, indeed, only by the addition of a single Iambic foot.

How sweet | the moon- | light sleeps | up- on | this bank |
O   tek- | na tek- | na   sphon | men est- | i   dee | do- mos

As to Satire and Archilochus, see below, page 249.

mere variations in the traditional dress of Bacchic festivals. CHAP. I
When a similar imitativeness was applied to the scenery
of the stage,—chiefly owing to the invention of perspective by Agatharchus,—the Greek theatre was thoroughly
equipped for the vivid presentation of life.

One question remains : where does this process of de- *Completion*
velopment stop, and when is Tragedy, originally lyric and *of the*
process:
gradually becoming more and more dramatic, entitled to *character-*
be called drama?   The answer to this question is clear. *isation of*
the Chorus
Originally the Chorus personated worshippers of Bacchus,
Satyrs, and the like.   By historical times they have come to
take their characterisation from the story of the play ; not
that they are individual personages like the actors, but they
represent a nameless body of bystanders, friends of the
hero, or casual spectators of the events pourtrayed.   At
that point, whatever may have been the date, where the
Chorus ceased to take their characterisation from the
festival and began to take it from the story, the origin of
Tragedy was accomplished.   It continued to have a
doubleness of form, dramatic and lyric, action and meditation on the action ; but by this change the lyric performers were themselves taken into the dramatic plot, and
meditated in an assumed character.   In a word, the lyric
element was itself dramatised, and Tragedy had become
drama.

Such are the stages through which we may trace the *Summary*
evolution of Ancient Tragedy, from a form entirely lyric,
with a latent element of drama, to a form entirely dramatic,
though with a lyric chorus as its most prominent instrument
of dramatic effect.   In the process, Tragedy may be seen
to have concentrated in itself the main branches of poetic
literature : from a lyric stock it developed a dramatic
offshoot, epic poetry gave it actors, and satire furnished
the metre for its dialogues.   It will be easily understood
how Tragedy, so developed and out of such ingredients,

should come to be the main literary interest of Greece and the natural channel for its best thought.

Imaginary Illustration : Legend of Lycurgus The actual poetry in which these different stages of Tragedy could be traced has long ago perished: for illustrations we are compelled to fall back upon our imagination. Avoiding subjects of existing dramas, I select the legend of Lycurgus. Told in outline the traditional story would run thus. Lycurgus, a Thracian king, was fiercely resolved that the Bacchic worship should never be introduced into his dominions. When in his journeys to extend his worship Bacchus himself came, in mortal guise, to Lycurgus's country, the king attempted to arrest the stranger, who escaped him and leaped into the sea. Then the god sent a plague on the country, and madness on the king himself, who in his distraction slew his own son, and afterwards himself perished miserably.—I propose to trace, in imagination, this story through the principal forms assumed by Tragedy in the course of its development.

As a Lyric Tragedy While Tragedy maintains its purely lyric form, no theatre is required beyond the simple orchestra. The Chorus appear as Satyrs in honour of Dionysus, to whose glory the legend is a tribute; they maintain throughout the combination of chant, music, and dance. With the solemn rhythm and stately gestures of choral ritual they lead off to the praise of Bacchus. They sing his glorious birth from love and the lightning flash, his triumphant career through the world to establish his worship, before which all resistance went down, as Pentheus driven mad might testify, and Damascus flayed alive. With awe they meditate on the terrible thought of mortals resisting the gods, most terrible of all when the resistance seems to be successful! So it was with Lycurgus :—and the music quickens and the gestures become animated as the Chorus describe a strange portent, a god fleeing before a mortal man! In ever increasing

crescendo they depict the scene, and how the mortal gains CHAP. I
on the god; till at last the agitation becomes uncontrollable, and the Chorus breaks into two Semichoruses
which toss from side to side of the orchestra the rapid
dialogue :—What path is this he has taken ?—Is it the path
to the precipice ?—Can a god be other than omniscient ?—
Can a mortal prevail against a deity ?—So the dance whirls
on to a climax as the fugitive is pictured leaping from the
precipice into the sea below.   The Semichoruses close into
a circle again, and with the smoothest rhythms and most
flowing gestures the Chorus fancy the waves parting to
receive the god, softly lapping him round as a garment, and
gently conveying him down to the deep; there the long
train of Nereids meets him, and leads him in festal procession to the palaces of the sea : you can almost catch the
muffled sound of noisy revelry from the clear, cool, green
depths.   The music takes a sterner tone as the Chorus
go on to the thought that the god's power can act though he
be absent; and in minor cadences, and ever drearier and
drearier gestures, they paint a land smitten with barrenness,
—no clouds to break the parching heat, vegetation drooping,
and men's hearts hardening.   The dance quickens again as
the theme changes to Lycurgus's futile rage : friends interpose, but he turns his anger on them, clear omens are
given, but he reads them amiss.   More and more rapid
become the evolutions, until in thrilling movements is
painted the on-coming madness; and when, in the midst of
his mad fit, they realise Lycurgus meeting his son, again the
agitation of the Chorus becomes uncontrollable, and a
second time they break into semichoric dialogue :—What
means the drawn sword?—What the wild talk of hewing
down the vines of Bacchus ?—Is it his son he mistakes for
a vine ?—Ah, too late !—The dance subsides with the calmness that comes on the king when he awakes too late to his
deed; and from this calmness it quickens to a final climax

as it suggests the people inflamed by the god, the crowd of Bacchanals pouring in, the cries for vengeance on the king, the tearing by wild horses. Then, returning to their first strains, the Chorus repeat their reverence for the gods, whose might is irresistible !

Adapted to Tragedy in a transition stage   Taking next an early transition stage, we shall find the only variation in the performance required is the suspension of the dance at intervals to admit of dialogue between the Leader and the rest of the Chorus. These dialogues would be mainly speeches by the Leader, who would personate for the moment one or other of the characters in the legend, and thus develop new scenes for realisation by the Chorus in a lyric form. After the general opening, we can imagine a pause while the Leader assumes the part of Lycurgus, and solemnly forbids the worship of the new deity. The Chorus resume the dance with agitation at the thought of a contest between their king and their new god. The dance stops again for the Leader to speak as a messenger, answering the eager enquiries of the Chorus by relating the god's leap into the sea : whereupon this deliverance is lyrically celebrated, and the scene beneath the waves pictured. Later on the Leader might take the character of a seer ; and foretell a plague of barrenness, which the ode would lament when it resumed. Once more he might be a messenger, describing in narrative the closing scenes of the story, and the repetition of these in passionate action would make a lyrical climax.

As a complete Tragedy   If the legend is to be presented in the form of Tragedy fully developed, the theatre must include besides the orchestra a stage fitted with more or less of scenery ; the Chorus will personate Subjects of Lycurgus ; the performance will consist of alternate episodes by actors on the stage and odes by the Chorus in the orchestra : moreover, the general treatment of the story must at once maintain rational sequence of events, and show contrivance sufficient to minister to our sense of plot. By way of prologue, Lycurgus might appear upon the stage, announcing his intention of extirpating the new worship, and having the innovator who has introduced it torn by wild horses. *In agitated march a Chorus of Lycurgus's Subjects enter the orchestra, expressing their hopes that they may be in time to remonstrate with their rash king.* The lyric rhythm changes to blank verse for the first episode, when a Soldier of the Guard, speaking from the stage, tells, in answer to the enquiries of the Chorus-Leader, how the king ordered the arrest of the mysterious stranger, and how, when the guard, believing him to be a god, hesitated, Lycurgus himself advanced to make the arrest : the god escaped from him and leaped into the sea. *An ode follows, which is a burst of relief, and elaborately pictures the reception of the fugitive god by the deities of the sea.* The interest is again transferred to the stage as a Seer enters, and, calling for Lycurgus, tells a vision he has had that the land is to be smitten with famine. He is going on to tell of yet another woe, but the king will not hear him, and drives him forth as a corrupt prophet. *Left to themselves, the Chorus chant the woes of a land smitten with barrenness.* Countrymen next appear on the stage, come (by a violation of probabilities in time not uncommon in Greek Tragedy) to tell of the famine that has already begun, and how all vegetation is mysteriously withering. Lycurgus treats this as part of a general conspiracy to rebel; when his son attempts to mediate, the father turns his passion against him. Gradually it becomes evident that the king has been smitten with madness, and he chases his son from the stage to slay him. *In great agitation the Chorus divide into parties: one party is for hurrying to the rescue, the rest are irresolute. Inaction prevails, and the Chorus settling down to a regular ode develop the story of Pentheus, and similar stories of mortals who have resisted the gods and been smitten with madness.*

In the next episode Lycurgus enters, heartbroken: the fit has passed from him, and he knows the deed he has done. In his humiliation he sends for the Seer, to hear the rest of the vision. The Seer says that the woe he was hindered from revealing was the sight of Lycurgus himself torn by wild horses. This brings back the king's rage; he seizes the prophet, and declares that he shall himself die by the death he has denounced. *The Chorus are too much overawed by the clear hand of destiny to interpose: they sing the infatuation of those whom the gods are about to destroy.* This brings us to the finale, in which a messenger relates, in a long epic narrative, the scene of Lycurgus attempting to carry out his sentence on the Seer, and how the wild horses turned on the king, and tore him to pieces. While the Chorus are lamenting, Bacchus appears as a god, takes the curse of barrenness off the land, and establishes his worship as an institution for all time.

II

CHORAL TRAGEDY

The ' Story of Orestes ' in the hands of Aeschylus

II

In presenting a specimen of Ancient Tragedy as fully developed, it may be well to recall to the reader some of the more important points as to which he must divest his mind of modern associations, if he is to appreciate the Greek stage. To begin with, as the drama was not an entertainment, but a solemn national and religious festival, so the tragic plots were not invented, but, like the Miracle Plays of the Middle Ages, were founded on the traditional stories of religion. Thus the sacred legends which enter into the *Orestes* of Aeschylus would be familiar to the whole audience in outline.

They are concerned with the woes of the House of Atreus : *Memorandum of what the audience is supposed to know beforehand.* *the foundation of them laid by Atreus himself, when, to take revenge on his brother Thyestes, he served up to him at a banquet the flesh of his own sons :*

His grandsons were Agamemnon and Menelaus : Menelaus's wife, Helen, was stolen away by a guest, Paris of Troy, which caused the great Trojan War :

Agamemnon, who led the Greek nations in that war, fretting at the contrary winds which delayed the setting out of the fleet, was persuaded by the Seers to slay his own daughter, Iphigenia, to appease the Deities :

Her mother Clytæmnestra, treasured up this wrong all through the ten years' wars, and slew Agamemnon on his return, in the moment of victory, slew him while in his bath by casting a net over him and smiting him to death with her own arm :

Then she reigned in triumph with Aegisthus her paramour (himself one of the fatal house), till Orestes her son, who had been rescued as an infant when his father was slaughtered, returned at last and slew the guilty pair:

For this act of matricide, though done by the command of Apollo, Orestes was given up to the Furies, and driven over the earth, a madman, until at last in Athens, on Mars Hill they say, he was cleansed and healed.

Cassandra too was involved in the fall of Agamemnon: the Trojan princess beloved of Apollo, who bestowed on her the gift of prophecy; when she slighted his love, Apollo—since no gift of a God can be recalled—left her a prophetess, with the doom that her true forebodings should be ever disbelieved. She having thus vainly sought to save Troy, with its fall fell into captivity, and to the lot of Agamemnon, with whom she died.

The name of Orestes would carry with it a suggestion of the proverbial friendship between Orestes and Pylades, formed when Orestes was in exile and never broken.

Next, the reader should bear in mind the character of the Athenian theatre: its vast dimensions, capable of accommodating the population of a city, and admitting of spectacular effects on so grand a scale; its solid stone scene; its long and narrow stage; and its capacious orchestra, with the Thymelé or Altar of Dionysus conspicuous in the centre. Lastly, he should remember that a Greek tragedy does not so much resemble our modern drama as our modern opera, with dancing substituted for the music. Or, more definitely, it consists of dramatic scenes spoken on the stage alternating with lyric odes in the orchestra: these odes, performed with all the subtle intricacies of choral ritual—that lost art which enchained the mind by its combination of verse, chant, and imitative gesture, the poetry of words, the poetry of sound, and the poetry of motion, fused into one.

The 'Story of Orestes' is cast by Aeschylus in the form
of a trilogy—three plays developing a single series of
events. The first play, acted in early morning, is entitled

AGAMEMNON.

The permanent scene is decorated to represent the façade of
Agamemnon's palace at Argos; the side scene on the right [1]
shows the neighbouring city, that on the left suggests distance. A portion of the high balcony immediately over the
great central gates appears as a watch-tower. At intervals
along the front of the palace are statues of gods, especially
Zeus, Apollo, Hermes. The time is supposed to be night
verging on morning, which would fairly agree with the time
of representation. At the commencement, both orchestra
and stage are vacant: only a Watchman is discovered on
the tower, leaning on his elbow and gazing into the distance.
The Watchman opens the play by soliloquising on his *Prologue*
toilsome task of standing sentinel all night through and
looking for the first sight of the signal which is to tell the
capture of Troy. He has kept his post for years, until the
constellations which usher in winter and harvest-tide are his
familiar companions; he must endure weather and sleep-
lessness, and when he would sing to keep up his spirits he
is checked by the thought of his absent master's household,
in which, he darkly hints, things are 'not well.' He is
settling himself into an easier posture, when suddenly he
springs to his feet. The beacon-fire at last! He shouts
the signal agreed upon, and begins dancing for joy. Now
all will be well; a little while and his hand shall touch the
dear hand of his master; and then—ah! the weight of an
ox is on his tongue, but if the house had a voice it could
tell a tale! The Watchman disappears, to carry the tidings
to the Queen.

MORNING
PLAY:
AGAMEM-
NON

[1] The spectators' right.

As if roused by the shout, the Chorus appear in the orchestra: twelve Elders of Argos, moving in the usual processional order that combines music, chanting, and gesture-dance to a rhythm traditionally associated with marching. They enter by the right passage, as from the city, and the processional chant takes them gradually round the orchestra towards the Thymelé, or Altar of Dionysus, in the centre.

In this chorus-entry, and the ode to which it leads up, the poet is bringing before our minds the sacrifice of Iphigenia, which is the foundation on which the whole trilogy rests. They have an obscurity which is one of the artistic effects of the piece, as striking the keynote of the action,— a tone of triumph through which is ever breaking vague apprehension of evil, increasing till it finds its justification in the catastrophe. So here, the Chorus, hastening to enquire the meaning of the tumult, are swayed opposite ways, by their expectation of the triumph over Troy, which cannot be far distant now, combined with misgiving, as to misfortunes sure to come as nemesis for the dark deed connected with the setting out of the expedition. They paint the grand scene of that starting for Troy, now ten years ago: the thousand vessels in the harbour, and on shore the army shouting fiercely the cry of war,—

> E'en as vultures shriek, who hover,
> Wheeling, whirling o'er their eyrie,
> In wild sorrow for their nestlings,
> With their oars of stout wings rowing.

But this simile of birds crying to heaven suggests the vengeance this expedition was going to bring on Troy: the

> Many conflicts, men's limbs straining,
> When the knee in dust is crouching,
> And the spear-shaft in the onset
> Of the battle snaps asunder.

Already the bias of the Chorus towards misgiving leads

them to contrast that brilliant opening of the expedition CHAP. II
with the shadow of a dark deed that was so soon to plunge
it in gloom.

> But as things are now, so are they,
> So as destined, shall the end be.

At this point the song is interrupted. The Chorus,
reaching the altar, turn towards the stage. Meanwhile the
great central gate of the stage has opened, and a solemn
procession filed out, consisting of the Queen and her Attendants, bearing torches and incense and offerings for the
gods; they have during the choral procession silently advanced to the different statues along the front of the palace,
made their offerings and commenced the sacrificial rites.
When the Chorus turn towards the stage the whole scene
is ablaze with fires and trembling with clouds of incense,
rich unguents perfume the whole theatre, while a solemn
religious ritual is being celebrated in dumb show. The
Chorus break off their chant to enquire what is the meaning of these solemn rites. The Queen signifies by a gesture
that the ritual must not be interrupted by speech. The
Chorus then proceed to take their position at the altar, as
if for a choral ode : but, pausing awhile before traversing
the orchestra in their evolutions, they sing a prelude[1]— *Prelude*
restlessness before actual motion—swaying from side to
side but not as yet quitting their position at the altar.
They have been shut out from the war itself (they resume) *strophe*
but old age has left them the suasive power of song ; and
they can tell of the famous omen seen by the two kings
and the whole army as they waited to embark—two eagles
on the left, devouring a pregnant hare. ·

> Sing a strain of woe,
> But may the good prevail !

[1] We have no distinct information as to the evolutions of a prelude;
what is here suggested agrees with the necessities of the case in the
prelude of the third play (page 55).

CHAP. II And the prophet Calchas interpreted : they shall lay Troy
anti- low, but let them beware of the goddess who hates the
strophe eagle !

> Sing a strain of woe,
> But may the good prevail !

epode May some healer avert her wrath, lest she send delays on
the impatient host, and irritate them to some dread deed,
some sacrifice of children that might haunt the house for
ever !

> Sing a strain of woe,
> But may the good prevail !

Entry-Ode This description of splendid spectacle so soon eclipsed by
dark forebodings has accentuated the conflict of emotions
in the breasts of the Chorus, until they cast off restraint,
and break into a full choral ode : sweeping with the evolutions of each strophe to the right or left of the altar, and in
each antistrophe measuring back their way step for step
and rhythm for rhythm. This change marks a change of
1 strophe thought. It must be Zeus—the Supreme, before whom all
and anti-
strophe other gods gave way—it must be Zeus alone who shall lift
2 strophe from their mind this cloud of anxiety. Zeus leads men to
wisdom by his fixed law, that pain is gain ; instilling secret
care into their hearts, it may be in sleep, he forces the unwilling to yield to wiser thoughts. So this anxiety of theirs
may be from the irresistible gods, the way they are being
led, through pain, to a wise knowledge of justice. As if
relieved by this burst of prayer the Chorus resume the
and anti- history : how Agamemnon, not repining but tempering
strophe
himself to the fate which smote him, waited amidst delay
3 strophe and failing stores ; and the contrary winds kept sweeping
down from the Strymon, and the host was being worn out
with frettings, and the prophet began to speak of one more
charm against the wrath of Artemis, though a bitter one to
and anti- the Chiefs. At last the king spoke : great woe to disobey
strophe
the prophet, yet great woe to slay my child ! how shed a

maiden's blood? yet how lose my expedition, my allies? CHAP. II
The Chorus have now reached their fourth strophe, and ₄ *strophe*
the full power of Aeschylus is felt as they describe the
steps of fatal resolution forming in the distracted father's
breast: he feels himself harnessed to a yoke of unbending
fate—a blast of strange new feeling sweeps over his heart
and spirit—his thoughts and purpose alter to full measure
of all daring—base counsel becomes a fatal frenzy—he
hardens his heart to slay.

All her prayers and eager callings *and anti-*
On the tender name of father, *strophe*
All her young and maiden freshness
They but set at nought, those rulers,
In their passion for the battle.
And her father gave commandment
To the servants of the goddess,
When the prayer was o'er, to lift her,
Like a kid, above the altar,
In her garments wrapt, face downward,—
Yea, to seize with all their courage,
And that o'er her lips of beauty
Should be set a watch to hinder
Words of curse against the houses,
With the gag's strength silence-working.

And she upon the ground ₅ *strophe*
Pouring rich folds of veil in saffron dyed,
Cast at each one of those that sacrificed
A piteous glance that pierced,
Fair as a pictured form,
And wishing,—all in vain,—
To speak, for oftentimes
In those her father's hospitable halls
She sang, a maiden pure with chastest song,
And her dear father's life
That poured its three-fold cup of praise to God,
Crowned with all choicest good,
She with a daughter's love
Was wont to celebrate.

The Chorus will pursue the scene no further. But their *and anti-*
anxious doubt has now found a resting-place on their faith *strophe*

CHAP. II   in Zeus. There must be no shrinking from suspense ; they must wait for and face whatever issue shall appear when Justice shall turn the scale : so, through pain, will at last come the gain of wisdom.

Episode I   The ritual on the stage being now concluded, Clytæmnestra advances to the front. At the same moment the choral ode is finished, and the Chorus take up their usual position in episodes, drawn up in two lines between the altar and the stage ; they speak only through their Leader, and use blank verse. In answer to the enquiries of the Chorus, Clytæmnestra announces that Troy has been taken this last night. The Chorus cannot understand how the news could travel so rapidly.

> *Cho.* What herald could arrive with speed like this?
> *Clyt.* Hephæstus flashing forth bright flames from Ida :
> > Beacon to beacon from that courier-fire
> > Sent on its tidings ; Ida to the rock
> > Hermæan named, in Lemnos : from the isle
> > The height of Athos, dear to Zeus, received ˜
> > A third great torch of flame, and lifted up,
> > So as to skim on high the broad sea's back,
> > The stalwart fire rejoicing went its way ;
> > The pine wood, like a sun, sent forth its light
> > Of golden radiance to Makistos' watch ;

and so from Euripus' straits to Messapion, across Asopus' plain to Kithæron's rock, over the lake of Gorgopis to Mount Aegiplanctus, until the light swooped upon this palace of the Atreidæ.

> > Such is the order of my torch-race games ;
> > One from another taking up the course,
> > But here the winner is both first and last.

While the Chorus are still overcome with amazement, Clytæmnestra triumphs over the condition of Troy on that morning : like a vessel containing oil and vinegar, the conquered bewailing their first day of captivity over the corpses of husbands and sons, the victors enjoying their first rest free from the chill dews of night and the sentry's call,—and

all will be well *if*, in their exultation, they forget not that
they have the return voyage to make ! Clytæmnestra, thus
darkly harping upon her secret hope that vengeance may
even yet overtake her husband, returns with her Attendants
into the palace, while the Chorus give expression to their
joy in a choral ode.

It is the hand of Zeus they trace in all that has happened. *Choral In-*
Now what will they say who contend that the gods care not *terlude I*
when mortals trample under foot the inviolable? Wealthy *1 strophe*
Troy knows better, which has found its wealth no bulwark
to those who in wantonness have spurned the altar of
right. Paris knows better, who came to the sons of Atreus *and anti-*
and stole a queen away, leaving shame where he had sat *strophe*
as guest.

> And many a wailing cry   *2 strophe*
> They raised, the minstrel prophets of the house,
>   ' Woe for that kingly home!
> Woe for that kingly home and for its chiefs!
> Woe for the marriage bed and traces left
>   Of wife who loved her lord!'
> There stands he silent; foully wronged and yet
>   Uttering no word of scorn,
> In deepest woe perceiving she is gone;
>   And in his yearning love
>   For one beyond the sea,
> A ghost shall seem to queen it o'er the house;
>   The grace of sculptured forms
>   Is loathèd by her lord,
> And in the penury of life's bright eyes
>   All Aphrodite's charm
>   To utter wreck has gone.
> And phantom shades that hover round in dreams   *and anti-*
> Come full of sorrow, bringing vain delight;   *strophe*
>   For vain it is, when one
>   Sees seeming shows of good,
> And gliding through his hands the dream is gone,
>   After a moment's space,
>   On wings that follow still
> Upon the path where sleep goes to and fro.

CHAP. II Such are the woes in the palace : but what among the

3 strophe homes of the people, as they bring to each man's home the
ashes of his dead? War is a trafficker; in the rush of battle
he holds scales, and for the golden coin you spend on him
he sends you back lifeless shapes of men, well-smoothed
ashes from the funeral pyre. And as the people sing the
heroic fall of their kin, they think how it is all for another's

and anti- wife! So sullen discontent is doing the work of a people's
strophe curse. Thus, in their last antistrophe, the thoughts of the
Chorus have come back to foreboding; and, as they
subside into the concluding epode round the altar, their
swayings to one side and another figure their distracting

epode doubts : the courier flame has brought good news—but
who knows if it be true? Yet it is childish to be turned
from the glow of joy by ever-changing rumour—yet it is the
nature of woman to believe too soon.

Episode II Suddenly, through the distance-entrance on the extreme
left of the stage, enters a Herald, crowned with olive in token
of victory. The Chorus immediately fall into their episode
positions to receive him, the leader giving words to their
anticipations while the Herald is traversing the long stage.
The Herald solemnly salutes the statues of the gods (now
bright with the morning sun), and in rapid dialogue with
the Chorus confirms the joyful news. He tells how he
yearned for his native land, and the Chorus reply that they
too have yearned in gloom of heart : when the Herald seeks
to learn the source of their trouble he is met with significant silence. The Herald, misunderstanding this hesitation
on the part of the Chorus, says that all human success has
its mixture of trouble : the army had to encounter tossings
on the sea and exposure to the night dews till their hair is
shaggy as beasts' hair. But why remember this now? Our
toils are over!—He starts, as with a Greek's sensitiveness
to omen he perceives that he has used a phrase consecrated
to the dead ; but forces himself to shake off the weight of

foreboding. The Queen appears from the palace for a CHAP. II
moment to triumph over the Chorus, who had said that
a woman believed too soon. She exults in the thought of
her husband's near return to witness her fidelity, stainless 'as
a piece of bronze.' The strange phrase leaves an uncomfort-
able sensation, which the Chorus seek to cover by enquiring
further news from the Herald, and naturally ask first as to
Menelaus. The Herald in vain stops them, shrinking from
the dread of mingling bad news with good; he is compelled
to describe the terrible storm in which the sea blossomed
with wrecks and Achæan corpses, and the ship of Menelaus
disappeared. Thus the forebodings of the Chorus are
strengthened by the tidings that already one of the sons of
Atreus has been overtaken by fate.

But for the present the thought is of triumph, and the *Choral In-*
Chorus give vent to it in another choral ode. *Helen* has *terlude II*
proved a *hell*[1] to men, and ships, and towers. She came out
from her bowers of gorgeous curtains; at once Zephyr breezes
strong· as Titans wafted her to the leafy banks of the
Simois: and yet bloodshed was in her train, and shielded
hunters followed on her track. Verily, there is a wrath that *and anti-*
worketh after long waiting. Then were there shouts of *strophe*
'Paris' in the bridal song, now in a wedding of death
'Paris' has been shouted in other tones. They tell of *2 strophe*
a lion's cub reared in a house, fondled by young and old,

> With eyes that brightened to the hand that stroked,
> And fawning at the hest of hunger keen;

and yet when full-grown it showed the nature of its sires, *and anti-*
and repaid hospitality with a banquet of slain sheep. *strophe*

> So would I tell that thus to Ilium came *3 strophe*
> Mood as of calm when all the air is still,
> The gentle pride and joy of kingly state,
> A tender glance of eye,

---

[1] A Greek pun represented by a different English pun: 'Helen'
resembles Greek roots signifying 'captivity,' or 'slaying.'

> The full-blown blossom of a passionate love,
>   Thrilling the very soul ;
>   And yet she turned aside,
> And wrought a bitter end of marriage feast,
>   Coming to Priam's race
>   Ill sojourner, ill friend,
> Sent by great Zeus, the god of host and guest,—
> Erinnys, for whom wives weep many tears.

and anti-strophe

The saying is, that prosperity grown big will not die child-less, its offspring will be a woe unsatiable. Nay, it is not prosperity, it is an impious deed that begets impious deeds

4 strophe

like to the parent stock. Recklessness begets recklessness, this is parent to full-flushed lust and god-forgetting daring.

and anti-strophe

Justice will dwell in smoke-stained houses where life is lived by law, yet averts her eyes from golden mansions that har-bour defilement : and it is Justice which is directing the course of things to its appointed goal.

Episode III

All eyes turn to the distance-side of the theatre, where there appears the grand procession of the warriors return-ing from Troy. One line of soldiers, bending under the weight of the trophies they are carrying, march along the stage ; through the passage into the orchestra Agamemnon himself enters in his chariot, followed in another chariot by Cassandra, a captive, yet still in the garb of a prophetess ; more soldiers bring up the rear, leading captive women of Troy. The greater part of the procession traverse the theatre, and pass out on the right into the city ; Agamemnon, and his immediate followers, stop at the centre. The Chorus, falling into marching rhythm while the procession is in motion, long to pour out their welcome to their lord ; yet, from very excess of love, avoid that tone of untempered triumph, which to a Greek mind would seem the opportunity a mocking fate would choose for a change of fortune. They speak of their former fear, when, in a single strange deed, their master seemed to them like a face limned by an unskilful artist. But now,—and even as they speak, they

are checked by the recollection of the palace secrets: and
they can only say that he, the king, will soon know who has
served him well and who ill. Agamemnon, rising in his
chariot, bends first in adoration towards the statues of the
gods who have given him victory; then turns to the Chorus
and approves their cautious tone, so well has he learned
by experience the difference between professing and true
friends. He will deliberate in full council as to the
diseases of his state: but first he must offer thanksgiving
at his own hearth. Here the central gate of the stage
opens, and Clytæmnestra appears to welcome her lord, followed by Attendants bearing rich draperies of purple and
dazzling colours. The rhetorical exaggeration of her speech
suggests that tone of untempered exultation which the
Chorus had been so careful to avoid. She details her
fears and longings, and hails Agamemnon

> as watch-dog of the fold,
> The stay that saves the ship, of lofty roof
> Main column-prop, a father's only child,
> Land that beyond all hope the sailor sees,
> Morn of great brightness following after storm,
> Clear-flowing fount to thirsty traveller.

The bare ground is not fit for the foot that has trampled
upon Ilium: she bids the Attendants strew tapestry on the
floor as the conqueror alights from his car. The Attendants
commence to lay their draperies along the stage and down
the staircase into the orchestra: Agamemnon hastens to
stop them, and rebukes Clytæmnestra for the excessive
tone of her welcome, and the presumption of her triumph.
Clytæmnestra persists, and a strange contest goes on, in
which the wife is seeking to entangle her husband in an act
of infatuation, which might make him in the eyes of heaven
a fit subject for the vengeance she is meditating. At last
Agamemnon yields, but removes the shoe from his foot in
sign of humility; and in this strange guise he enters the

CHAP. II　palace, Clytæmnestra's last words being a prayer that heaven
———　may accomplish 'all that is in her heart!'

Choral In-　Such a scene has strengthened the forebodings of the
terlude III　Chorus until they seem like bodily sensations : woeful strains
in two pairs
of stanzas　haunting their ears, pulses of impending fate beating at
their heart.　They are plunged in gloom, with little hope
ever to unravel their soul, that burns with its hot thoughts.

Exodus, or　The finale of the play is marked by a notable dramatic
Finale :　device.　It was a fixed custom of the Greek Drama that no
marked by
transitions　deed of violence could be enacted on the stage ; the
between
blank verse　dramatist must find some method of making it known
and lyrics　indirectly.　The device employed in this case is the prophetic art of Cassandra, which enables her to see all that is
going on behind·the·scenes ; with the further effect that her
doom to be disbelieved forces her to depict the vision with
ever increasing vehemence.　During the preceding ode
Cassandra had remained in her chariot ; at its conclusion
the Queen returns to invite her, with forced moderation, to
join the family sacrifice of her new home.　Cassandra gives
no answer, but remains gazing into vacancy.　Clytæmnestra
says that if Cassandra cannot speak Greek she might give
some sign of assent.　At the word 'sign' a shudder con-
vulses the frame of the prophetess, and the Queen hastily
returns into the palace.　With a cry of horror from Cassandra
the crisis of the play begins.　Her words fall into the form
of strophes and antistrophes, like waves of lyric rhythm, as
the prophetic vision comes upon her.　She sees all the old
woes of this bloodstained house ; she sees the deed of the
present—the bath filling, the entangling net, the axe standing
ready ; then her wailings wax yet louder as she becomes
aware that she is herself to be included in the sacrifice.
Meanwhile, her excitement gradually passes over to the
Chorus.　At first they had mistaken her cries for the
customary lamentations of captives (and borne their part in
the dialogue in ordinary blank verse) ; then their emotions

are aroused (and their speech falls into lyrics) as they
recognise the old woes of the family history, and remember
Cassandra's prophetic fame. When she passes on to the
deed in preparation at that moment they feel a thrill of
horror, but only half understand, and take her words for
prophecy of distant events, which they connect with their
own forebodings: thus in her struggles to get her words
believed Cassandra becomes more and more graphic, and
the excitement crescendoes.

Suddenly a change comes, and the dialogue settles down
into blank verse—the calmness of an issue that has been
decided. Cassandra has passed from her chariot to the
stage, and, turning to the Chorus at the top of the steps, she
says she will no more speak veiled prophecy, her words
shall surge clear as wave against the sunlight. Then all
the woes of the House of Atreus pass before us in a single
tableau. Her vision shows a house given over to the
spirits of vengeance, a choral band never absent since the
primal woe that brought defilement. Phantom children
loom on her sight, their palms filled full with meat of their
own flesh. In revenge for that deed another crime is to
bring fresh stain on the house: and Cassandra sees Clytæmnestra as a two-headed serpent, Aegisthus lurking in the
house as a lion in his lair, while a brave man is being
murdered by a woman. The Chorus, in their perplexity, ask
WHO is being murdered: Cassandra NAMES Agamemnon—
the Chorus too late seeking to stop the shock of omen which,
to a Greek mind, made the naming of a dread event seem
like the first step to its fulfilment. Then Cassandra goes
on to tell how she also must be joined with her new master
in the sacrifice, a victim to the jealous murderers. Bitterly
she reproaches her guardian god Apollo, tearing from her
head the sacred wreath, and breaking the prophetic wand:
in place of her father's altar a butcher's block is awaiting
her. Suddenly a new wave of vision breaks over her:

> But the gods will not slight us when we're dead;
> Another yet shall come as champion for us,
> A son who slays his mother, to avenge
> His father; and the exiled wanderer
> Far from his home, shall one day come again
> Upon these woes to set the coping-stone.

Yielding to inevitable fate, she begins to move towards the palace, praying only for

> blow that bringeth death at once,
> That so with no fierce spasm, while the blood
> Flows in calm death, I then may close my eyes.

As she nears the palace it would seem as if her very physical senses caught the prophetic instinct : brightly as that palace is gleaming in the sunlight, she shrinks in disgust from it, tainted to her with the scent of blood. Arrived at the gate, she turns to gaze for the last time on the loved rays of the sun.

> Ah, life of man! when most it prospereth,
> It is but limned in outline; and when brought
> To low estate, then doth the sponge, full soaked,
> Wipe out the picture with its frequent touch!

Cassandra passes through the gate into the palace.

The Chorus are wondering what all Agamemnon's glory will avail him if he be in truth destined to an evil fate at the last,—when a loud cry is heard from the palace. The Chorus recognise the king's voice, and for the first time it dawns upon them that it is a *present doom* which has been foreseen. In great excitement they break out of their choral rank, and each individual urges rescue or doubts : at last they recollect that they have no certain knowledge of what has happened,—and in this hesitation once more the doom of Cassandra to be doubted is fulfilled. Suddenly, by the machinery of the roller-stage, the interior of the palace is discovered : Clytæmnestra is seen standing in blood-stained robes, and before her the corpse of Cassandra, and the corpse of Agamemnon in a silver bath covered with a net. In

calm blank verse Clytæmnestra avows her act. Standing
where she did the deed, she glories in it : glories in the net
by which she entangled and rendered him powerless, in the
blows—one, two, three, like a libation—which she struck,
glories in the gush of life-blood which has bespattered
her. She had waited long : behold the handiwork of her
artist hand !

Then a wild scene follows. The Chorus (in lyrics) are
denouncing the murderess and passionately mourning over
their lord : Clytæmnestra gradually falls into the rhythm
of the Chorus as she meets the passion of bereavement with
the excitement of triumph.

> *Chorus.* Ah me! Ah me!
> My king, my king, how shall I weep for thee?
> What shall I say from heart that truly loves?
> And now thou liest there, breathing out thy life,
>> In impious deed of death,
>> In this fell spider's web!
>> Yes woe is me! woe, woe!
> Woe for this couch of thine unhonourable!
>> Slain by a subtle death,
> With sword two-edged which her right hand did wield.

Clytæmnestra maintains that not herself, but the Avenger of
Blood in her shape, has done this deed : and the Chorus,
guilty as they know the queen to be, cannot deny that an
avenging doom is here. He slew my daughter, the Queen
reiterates, slain himself in recompense he was gone to hell
with nothing to boast over ! But the Chorus cry for escape
from the pelting shower of blood that is pouring upon the
house. Who is to chant the dirge for their lord, and
perform his funeral rites? That, answers Clytæmnestra,
shall be cared for, and as mourner he may find Iphigenia
by the banks of the Styx ! Again the Chorus are unable to
deny the justice of blood for blood : but where is the tale
of curses begotten of curses to come to an end? My hand,
the Queen proudly replies, has freed the house from its

frenzy of murder. Thus all seems to be going wrong in the action of the drama: Clytæmnestra is triumphant and the Chorus are cowed. But this is only the Greek idea of infatuation: the spiritual darkening which like a mist hides from the sinner his doom until he has been driven to the extremity of his crime.

The infatuation deepens as Aegisthus enters (through one of the inferior doors of the palace) from his place of concealment. He salutes the happy day which has brought vengeance for his own wrongs, as well as the wrongs of Clytæmnestra. The Chorus note that he confesses the deed: he shall die by stones hurled with the curses of the people. Aegisthus haughtily bids the old men know their weakness, and contemptuous defiances are interchanged. In the heat of their scorn the Chorus suddenly remember the destined future as hinted by Cassandra, the meaning of which now breaks upon them: with a new tone in their defiance, they remind Aegisthus that the light of life yet shines upon ORESTES! At that word the whole mist of infatuation dissolves in a moment: the *name* of the fate-appointed avenger has been spoken, and already vengeance seems near. Clytæmnestra realises her doom to perish at the hands of her own son; the audience catch the drift of the remaining plays of the trilogy; Aegisthus is maddened by the reflection that the natural avenger of Agamemnon is out of his power. Enraged he gives the signal, at which through all the entrances come pouring out of the palace the soldiers of his body-guard; they line the long stage from end to end, their helmets, spears, and shields gleaming bright in the noonday sun. The Chorus—who represent the legitimate authority of the city now Agamemnon is dead—are nothing daunted by numbers, and press forward to ascend the stage. A contest of force seems inevitable, and the metre of the play breaks into a rhythm of excitement. But the tide has too surely turned: Clytæmnestra throws herself between the

contending parties, and urges that enough ill has already CHAP. II
been done ; she beseeches Aegisthus, and hurls alternately
warning and scorn at the Chorus. With difficulty the two
bodies, exchanging defiances, and each resting on the future,
are induced sullenly to separate. Aegisthus allows himself
to be forced by Clytæmnestra into the palace, the body-guard
filing after him ; the Chorus slowly retire through the right
passage into the city, and the first play of the trilogy terminates.

THE SEPULCHRAL RITES[1]

In the second play of the trilogy the permanent scene[2] MIDDAY
again stands for the palace of Agamemnon at Argos, the PLAY:
THE SE-
PULCHRAL
RITES

[1] Greek: *Choephori*, or bearers of urns for pouring libations.
[2] The modern reader must understand that the manuscripts of Greek
plays contain only the speeches, without stage directions : these, and
sometimes the divisions of the speeches, have to be inferred from the text,
with the occasional assistance of notes by ' scholiasts,' or ancient commentators. Thus it will often happen that totally different arrangements
of *mise-en-scène* are reconcilable with the same text. For the present
play there are two different theories, between which the evidence seems
to me almost equally balanced. One arrangement (given in Donaldson's
Theatre of the Greeks) assumes a change of scene at the end of the first
Choral Interlude : the earlier part of the play centering round the tomb
of Agamemnon, the latter part taking place in front of the palace. This
agrees well with the prominence of the tomb in the earlier part, and the
total ignoring of it after line 709; also the anapæsts of the Chorus,
706-16, suit well with a choral re-entry. On the whole, I have preferred
the arrangement in a single scene (as in Plumptre's translation, &c.).
(1) The burden of proof seems to rest with those who suppose a change ;
(2) Choral Interlude I suits excellently with the filling up of an interval
for Orestes to go out and return, while it fits awkwardly with the other
arrangement ; (3) the address to the tomb, 709-11, is strongly in favour
of its continued presence ; (4) the whole effect of the crisis caused by
Clytæmnestra's dim suspicions of the stranger is lost if the Chorus have
been absent ; (5) there are little touches, such as lines 257, 545, which
suggest the vicinity of the palace in the earlier part. In adopting the
single scene arrangement I have myself made a variation from (e. g.)
Plumptre by supposing the tomb of Agamemnon to take the place of the
Thymele. (1) There is the undoubted analogy of the *Persians*, a drama

only difference being that the altar in the middle of the orchestra is now changed for a mound representing Agamemnon's sepulchre. The entrances on either side of the central gates are approaches to the Strangers' Wing of the palace and to the Women's Quarters. The side-scenes represent on the left the valley of the Inachus, on the right,

Prologue Argos. The prologue commences with the appearance of Orestes and Pylades, and the audience know that the day of vengeance has arrived. As they advance from the distance-entrance Orestes solemnly cuts off two locks of his hair; one he casts in the direction of the river, the thank-offering to the genius of his native valley that should have been presented when he came of age; the other is a grief-offering which exile prevented his paying at his father's funeral. Descending to the orchestra he lays this lock on the tomb: he has no sooner returned to the stage than he hears a burst of wailing from within the palace, and the two friends hasten to conceal themselves.

Sepulchral Ode as Chorus-entry From the Women's Quarters appears a melancholy train of Trojan captive maidens, in attendance on the princess Electra, all with dishevelled hair and wild gestures, and bearing in their hands the urns used for funeral libations. With the exception of Electra, who brings up the rear, they all descend the staircase into the orchestra, and perform a funeral ode round the tomb of Agamemnon.

in three paired stanzas and epode The words of this ode simply describe the tearings of cheeks, rending of garments, with groanings, which are actually the gestures of the dance, and are proper to such a sepulchral rite as the Chorus have been sent to perform. The Queen

which much resembles the present play; (2) in line 98 the Chorus seem to lay their hands on the tomb; (3) the title of the play and prominence of sepulchral rites fit well with such a centre. No doubt this arrangement causes some little difficulties as to the actors who lay offerings on the tomb, but I hope I have got over these by the arrangements I suggest, and we need go no further than the third play of the trilogy to find authority for passing from stage to orchestra and vice versa.

has sent them, terrified by a dream signifying how the Dead were wroth with their slayers. But the Chorus like not this graceless act of grace : what can atone for the slaughter of a hero? With him awe has been overthrown, and success reigns in its stead.

> Yet stroke of vengeance swift
> Smites some in life's clear day;
> For some who tarry long their sorrows wait
> In twilight dim, on darkness' borderland;
> And some an endless night
> Of nothingness holds fast.

Through this ode Electra, who ought to have taken the *Episode I:* lead, has remained standing on the stage irresolute : she *including* now addresses the Chorus, who fall into their episode positions to converse with her. Electra's difficulty is, how can she use the customary formulas of such rites :— 'I bring from loving wife to husband loved gifts,' or 'Good recompense make thou to those who bring these garlands'? Or shall she, dumb with ignominy like that with which He perished, pour libations as if they were lustral filth, looking not behind her? The Chorus move to the altar, lay their hands on it in sign of fidelity, and so advise Electra to cast off all disguise and pray boldly for friend and against foe. Electra offers prayer in this sense for Orestes and vengeance ; then calling on the Chorus for another funeral song she *short pæan* descends in her turn to the tomb. When she returns to the stage after the short pæan of the Chorus, her whole manner is changed: as if the prayer had already been answered she has found on the sepulchre mysterious locks of hair, which, bit by bit, she lets out must be those of Orestes. When, in addition, she has discovered the footprints on the stage, Orestes and his friend come forward and make themselves known. The Chorus are alarmed lest the noisy joy of this meeting may be overheard in the palace. But Orestes has no fears of failure in his task, so strong were the sanctions with which Apollo bade him do the deed :—leprosy, madness, exile, wasting death should over-take him if he hung back. With Apollo on their side, the Chorus feel certainty of near retribution; and the play *and elabo-* resolves itself at this point into an elaborate dirge, by the *rate Lyric* brother and sister on the stage and the Chorus in the *Concerto* *in twenty* orchestra, in highly intricate and interwoven [1] strophes and *interwoven* antistrophes, with funeral gestures. The jaws of flame, they *stanzas* sing, do not reduce the corpse to senselessness : the dead can hear this our rite and will send answer. They sing the sad fate of Agamemnon : not that of the warrior who dies leaving high fame and laying strong and sure his children's paths in life, but to be struck down by his own kin. But there is a sense of vengeance at hand : and the dirge crescendoes till it breaks into the Arian Rhythm, a foreign ritual with violent gestures, proper to the Chorus as Asiatics ; from this it reaches a climax by dividing into two semi-choruses, one of which sings of woe, the other of vengeance.

By a favourite Greek effect, the passion of this lyrical dirge repeats itself in a calmer form in blank verse; the duett between Orestes and Electra is a sort of Litany to the Dead. Orestes promises banquets to the departed : Electra will be the first to pour the libations.

> *Orestes.* Set free my Sire, O Earth, to watch the battle.
> *Electra.* O Persephassa, goodly victory grant.
> *Orestes.* Remember, Sire, the bath in which they slew thee !
> *Electra.* Remember thou the net they handselled so.

They appeal to him to save his children, the voices that preserve a man's memory when he dies.

Their minds composed by these devotional exercises, Orestes and Electra turn to the means of carrying out vengeance. Orestes enquires as to the purpose of these sepulchral rites, and the dream is narrated in parallel verse.

[1] See below, page 314.

Orestes. And have ye learnt the dream to tell it right?
Chorus. As she doth say, she thought she bare a snake.
Orestes. How ends the tale, and what its outcome then?
Chorus. She nursed it, like a child, in swaddling clothes.
Orestes. What food did that young monster crave for then?
Chorus. She, in her dream, her bosom gave to it.
Orestes. How 'scaped her breast by that dread beast unhurt?
Chorus. Nay, with the milk it sucked out clots of blood.
Orestes. Ah, not in vain comes this dream from her lord.
Chorus. She, roused from sleep, cries out all terrified,
       And many torches that were quenched in gloom
       Blazed for our mistress' sake within the house.
       Then these libations for the dead she sends,
       Hoping they'll prove good medicine of ills.
Orestes. Now to Earth here, and my sire's tomb I pray,
       They leave not this strange vision unfulfilled.
       So I expound it that it all coheres;
       For if, the self-same spot that I left leaving,
       The snake was then wrapt in my swaddling clothes,
       And sucked the very breast which nourished me,
       And mixed the sweet milk with a clot of blood,
       And she in terror wailed the dread event,
       So must she, as that monster dread she nourished,
       Die cruel death: and I, thus serpentised,
       Am here to slay her, as this dream portends.

They rapidly arrange their plans to get admission to the
palace as foreigners, Electra returning to the Women's
Quarters to keep watch within.

The Chorus fill up the interval with an ode, which sings *Choral In-*
the most monstrous of all monsters, a passion-driven woman: *terlude I*
such as Thestias, who burnt out the mystic brand that *in four pair-*
measured her son's life; Scylla, who stole her father's *ed stanzas*
life-charm. They hint of another who slew a warrior-king,
a deed which might compare with the Lemnian deed, foremost of crimes. But the anvil-block of vengeance is firm
set, and Fate is the sword-smith hammering.

The action of the play recommences with the appearance *Episode II*
of Orestes advancing a second time through the distance-
entrance, followed by Pylades and Attendants. Arrived at

CHAP. II the central gate of the palace, he calls loudly for admission, telling the Porter that he is a traveller, and must do his message before night falls. Clytæmnestra, who enters from the Women's Quarters, is cold in her offer of hospitality, having heard Orestes' phrase, that he desires the lord or the lady of the house, though a lord is the seemlier ruler. Orestes bluffly delivers to her a message he professes to have received from a fellow-traveller, who begged him to seek out the kinsmen of Orestes at Argos, and say Orestes was dead. Clytæmnestra affects a burst of grief, which the traveller interrupts by remarking that he cannot expect the reception of one who brings good news. Orestes is over-acting his part, and the Queen, with a dim feeling of suspicion, answers that he shall lack nothing of that which befits; she then motions the porter to conduct Orestes through the central gates, but signs other Attendants to take his companions into the Strangers' Wing[1]: she herself retires into the Women's Quarters, saying that the master of the house, with no lack of friends, shall share the news. The Chorus catch the critical condition of their project, and, breaking into marching rhythm, invoke Hermes and the Spirit of Persuasion to sit upon the lips of Orestes.

The Nurse of Orestes comes out from the Women's Quarters, sent by Clytæmnestra to summon Aegisthus. She is dissolved in tears at the sad news which has arrived, and details all her petty cares over the boy's infancy, now rendered fruitless. The Chorus give mysterious hints of consolation; and, enquiring the exact terms of the message to Aegisthus, bid her alter them, and beg him to come

---

[1] This separation of Orestes from his companions is not very clear in Clytæmnestra's own words, though the *de* of line 700, assisted by a gesture, might be sufficient. The fact of his separation is clear from line 851, and gives point to the speech of the Chorus that follows, especially their reference to persuasion, which must now do the work of force.

alone and come at once. Somewhat reassured, the Nurse CHAP. II
proceeds through the right entrance into the city.

The Chorus again fill up an interval of waiting with an *Choral In-*
ode, in which they invoke the various gods worshipped *terlude II*
by the family—as Zeus, Apollo, Hermes—to hold back the *in eight interwoven*
rapid course of calamity for the dear son of the house. *stanzas with mesode*
Like Perseus, he must look not on the deed while he does
it ; as she utters the name of Mother, he must hurl back the
cry of Father !

Aegisthus now enters from Argos : as he passes the *Episode*
Chorus, he speaks of a summons he has received ; it may *III*
after all be but women's fears, that leap up high and die
away to nought. The Chorus answer that there is nothing
like enquiring. Aegisthus will do so : they will not cheat
a man with his eyes open. Speaking these words he disappears through the central gate to his doom.

The Chorus, in a short lyrical burst, express the critical
moment that gives success or failure. Then cries are heard
from within, and the Porter rushes from the central gate
to the door of the Women's Quarters, loudly summoning
Clytæmnestra : when she appears, he informs her that the
'dead are slaying the living.' She sees in a moment the
truth, and is hurriedly looking for aid, when Orestes appears
from the central door and confronts her, while Pylades and
his Attendants rush out from the Strangers' Wing to support
him.

> *Orestes.* 'Tis thee I seek : he there has had enough.
> *Clytaemnestra.* Ah me ! my loved Aegisthus ! art thou dead ?
> *Orestes.* Lov'st thou the man ? Then in the self-same tomb
> Shalt thou now lie, nor in his death desert him.

The mother bares her breast and appeals to filial instinct,
and Orestes' courage all but fails : Pylades speaks (for this
one time only in the whole play), reminding his friend that
a god had bidden him do the deed, and Orestes rallies to his
task, forcing the guilty Queen—now realising the meaning
of her dream—to go within and suffer death.

E

Choral In-
terlude III
in six
interwoven
stanzas

As the gate closes on the son and his mother the Chorus sing how vengeance has come, though late; on a lover of guile retribution has descended subtle-souled.

> The will of gods is strangely over-ruled,
> It may not help the vile.

At last they see the light : all-working Time, with cleansing rites, will purify the house; Fortune's throws shall fall with gladsome cast : at last they see the light.

Exodus or
Finale

Once more the central gate opens, and Orestes solemnly advances to the front, his Attendants bearing the corpses of Aegisthus and Clytæmnestra, bearing also the net in which Agamemnon had been murdered : the hero bids them spread the net in the full light of the Sun, the great purifier, while he testifies before its brightness that the dread deed he has done is a deed of necessary vengeance. He dwells on the cruel device of Clytæmnestra—a deed of one who, had she been a viper, with touch alone would have made a festering sore. But the Chorus, seeing side by side that fatal net and the ghastly slaughter with which it has just been avenged, by unhappy chance can think of nothing but the growth of evil out of evil, which the avenger in his turn will have to prove. Orestes, strung already by the task he has performed to the highest pitch of nervous excitement, staggers under the shock of this untimely utterance. He recounts again the crime of which this deed is the nemesis : the Chorus cannot help repeating the unhappy omen. At this moment Orestes feels his brain giving way.

> Like chariot-driver with his steeds I'm dragged
> Out of my course ; for passion's moods uncurbed
> Bear me their victim headlong. At my heart
> Stands terror ready or to sing or dance
> In burst of frenzy.

While reason yet stays with him he reiterates his innocence, and puts on the suppliant's fillet; with this he will go to

Delphi, and challenge the god who sent him on his mission CHAP. II
to free him from its dire consequences. The madness
increases: he can see the Furies in bodily shape, dark-
robed, and all their tresses entwined with serpents . . . they
swarm, they swarm, and from their eyes is dropping loathsome blood . . . they drive him on, and he can bear no
more!—Orestes rushes through the distance-entrance to
commence his long career of wanderings, while the Chorus
cry that a third storm has burst upon the house of their
king: when will the dread doom be lulled into slumber?

THE GENTLE GODDESSES [1]

It is the third play of the trilogy which presents the AFTER-
greatest difficulties to modern appreciation. One of these PLAY:
difficulties is connected with the national character of a THE
Greek tragic celebration, which made it possible for a GENTLE
dramatist to substitute political sentiment, and even appeals DESSES
to party feeling, in the place of strictly dramatic effect.
The 'Story of Orestes' was brought on the stage in March
of 458 B.C., during the excitement caused by the popular
attack on the aristocratic court of the Areopagus: it is a
leading purpose of the poet to assist the defenders of that
institution by associating it with the legendary glories of
Athens. To appreciate portions of the final play, the reader
must be able to sympathise with the spirit of conflicts
between the party of conservatism and the party of reform.

But the play presents an even greater difficulty on the
side of art, from the fact that it deals with the supreme
horror of ancient mythology, that terror which was a background for all other terrors—the beings called by us the
Furies, termed by the Greeks 'Erinnyes' or Destroyers,
where they did not avoid altogether uttering the name of
dread, and speak of the 'Gentle Goddesses,' using a similar

[1] Greek: *Eumenides.*

E 2

euphemism to that by which in Scotland mischievous fairies are called the 'Good Neighbours.' These Furies were personifications of remorse, or of those unnatural crimes that separate the criminal for ever from his fellows. Accordingly, they are represented as dwelling apart from all the gods ; sprung from darkness, they remain in the lowest depths of hell till the curses of the victim summon them to earth. Their appearance is too terrible to be otherwise than dimly defined : when they grow visible it is as black forms with serpent hair, they breathe out fire and blood, and foulness drops from their eyes. They were to be worshipped in places which none might approach ; the victims offered to them were black ; and wine—the symbol of comradeship —was banished from their festivals. And of all the details of dread associated with the Furies none was more weird than their mode of attack :—no outward blow or plague, but unremitting pursuit, the stroke of madness, the secret power of their presence to drain the victim of energy and life. These loathly creatures—the supreme effort of creative melancholy—are in the third play of the trilogy brought actually before our eyes. Such an attempt would on the modern stage be doomed to failure, but it must be recollected that Ancient Tragedy possessed a weapon we have lost in the choral art, which could reach the mind by three distinct avenues, all producing their separate impressions in harmony. It is necessary then to string up the imagination to the conception of these beings, for they form the central interest of the play. This is clear from the choral and poetic devices the author has lavished on their part ; especially striking is the effect of their gradual disclosure, from the first dim sight we catch of them in the background of the dark shrine, up to the point where they actually perform their spell on a victim before our eyes.

The opening scene represents the Temple of Apollo at Delphi : the central gates are the richly adorned entrance to the oracular cave, the side-scenes suggest the landscape of CHAP. II the locality famous in song. From her dwelling, on the left of the central gates, the Priestess of the oracle advances *Prologue* towards the cave, offering the morning prayer ; she enumerates the various deities who have shared with Apollo the guardianship of the sacred oracle, and prays that her divinations that day may excel all she has given before. Inviting pilgrims to come forward, she passes into the cave. In a moment she returns, pale and disordered, flinging wide open the central gates, through which can dimly be discerned dreadful forms in the darkness. She can hardly stand, for the terror of the sight she has seen : the sacred shrine has been polluted by the presence of a suppliant, his sword yet dripping with bloodshed ; and, sitting round him, she saw a yet more dread sight—a troop of women, or gorgons, or wingless harpies, swarth and everyway abominable.

> They snort with breath that none may dare approach,
> And from their eyes a loathsome humour pours,
> And such their garb as neither to the shrine
> Of gods is meet to bring, nor mortal roof.

She can only appeal to the god to protect his own, and hurries back to her dwelling.

At her word, a bright vision breaks out of the gloom : two deities appear—all the resources of tragic splendour lavished on their figures—leading out of the cave the dejected Orestes. Apollo pledges himself never to desert his trusting suppliant : it is himself who has sent sleep upon these loathly beings, born out of evils, and he bids Orestes seize the momentary respite to make his way to Athens, where a means of escape shall be found. Committing the fugitive to his brother deity, Hermes, the god of escort, Apollo disappears in the cave, while Hermes and his charge pass through the distance-entrance to their journey.

The stage being vacant, the machinery of the roller-stage [1]

---

[1] I understand the *deutera phantasia* of the scholiast's note to mean, not (as Donaldson) a twofold evolution of the eccyclema, but an ordinary

CHAP. II brings the interior of the cave to the front, giving a nearer view of the sleeping Furies, poured confusedly over the floor in uncouth attitudes. The Ghost of Clytæmnestra rises from beneath the earth, and towering over the recumbent sleepers she taunts them with their defeat. They are sleeping, while she remains in disgrace among the shades beneath, reproached as a murderess, yet none will do vengeance on him who murdered her. She shows her heart-wounds and taxes the Furies with ingratitude.

> Many a gift of mine
> Have ye lapped up, libations pure from wine,
> And soothing rites that shut out drunken mirth;
> And I dread banquets of the night would offer
> On altar-hearth, at hour no god might share.
> And lo! all this is trampled under foot.
> He is escaped, and flees, like fawn, away,
> And even from the midst of all your toils
> Has nimbly slipped, and draws wide mouth at you.
> Hear ye, for I have spoken for my life:
> Give heed, ye dark, earth-dwelling goddesses,
> I, Clytæmnestra's phantom, call on you.

The Furies moan in their sleep.

> Moan on, the man is gone, and flees far off:
> My kindred find protectors; I find none.

The moaning of the Furies grows louder and nearer the waking point as Clytæmnestra presses them with her reproaches, until at last they wake with a yell, and sit up in various postures of horror, still drowsy with their charmed sleep. The Ghost passes amongst them, seeking to rouse each individual: one she praises as a hound that never

use of it at this point, which would constitute the second (and nearer) discovery of the Furies, the first having been the dim vision of them through the central gates left open by the priestess. There remain further stages in their display: (1) where they wake in sitting postures, (2) where they start to their feet, and perform a prelude (on the roller-stage); besides their further appearance on the stage proper, and finally in the orchestra.

rests from toil, another she reproaches as losing in sleep all CHAP. II
sense of loss, a third she urges with vehemence :

> Breathe on him with thy blood-flecked breath,
> And with thy vapour, thy maw's fire, consume him ;
> Chase him, and wither with a fresh pursuit.

The Furies at last start to their feet, fully revealed, and *Prelude*
break into a prelude : crowded into a single tangled group
by the narrow dimensions of the roller-stage, they sway to
right and left with successive stanzas into fresh varieties of
hideousness. Their prey, they sing, is gone ! Apollo has
shown himself again as a robber-god ! Earth's central
shrine has been polluted ! But not even with a god to help
him shall the victim escape.

Apollo reappears from the darkness shrouding the in-
most parts of the cave, driving before him with his
threatening bow the Furies, who retreat on to the floor of
the stage and stand defying him. He bids them begone
from his sacred precincts, and seek scenes more fitted to
their nature ;

> There, where heads upon the scaffold lie,
> And eyes are gouged and throats of men are cut,
> Where men are maimed and stoned to death, and groan
> With bitter wailing 'neath the spine impaled.

A contest ensues in parallel verse. The Furies reproach
Apollo with taking the part of a matricide ; Apollo urges
that the mother had first slain her husband ; the Furies
retort that the husband is not kin to the wife, which Apollo
treats as a reflection on Zeus and Hera and the sanctity of
marriage. Neither party will give way, and the Furies fling
themselves on the footprints of Orestes and track them
through the distance-entrance towards Athens.

· At this point, stage and orchestra being empty, a change *Change of*
of scene is effected. The central gate is now the porch of *scene*
an Athenian temple—that of Athene, Guardian of the

City: the side-scene on the left gives a view of the road to Argos, the other displays the city of Athens. Orestes enters from the Argos road, no longer a blood-stained wanderer, but with tragic dignity of mien, and clad in the gorgeous vestments of Bacchic ritual. Advancing to the temple porch he clasps the statue, of Athene, and tells how, in his long wanderings, the stain of his deed has been by due rites washed away. Suddenly, by the same entrance, the Furies make their appearance on the stage, their faces to the ground and tracking Orestes' steps. At last the dumb informer is clear again, already they catch the loved scent of blood. They see their victim praying, and silently spread themselves along the stage behind him to bar escape; in low voices they mock his hopes of staking all on one trial, they will keep him to his doom of suspense, sucking his blood from his living members, and when they have had their fill of this drink undrinkable, they will drag him down alive to Hades, a matricide still. Orestes continues his prayer: details the cleansing rites he has undergone, vindicates the pureness of the hand he lays on the statue of the pure goddess. The Furies start up: Not Apollo nor Athene can save thee from thy doom! Orestes clings convulsively to the statue of Athene.—Thou resistest? Then feel our spell!

Parode, leading to   They fling themselves exultingly down the steps into the orchestra, chanting in marching rhythm, and summoning one another to their dance of hate, their office of witnesses for the dead against the sinner: then they form about the altar, and the audience feel a vague thrill of terror as they

Choral Spell   watch the Chorus moving with no sound of musical accompaniment through the spell-dance of the Furies, clustering in ghastly groups, weaving weird paces, and with gestures of incantation strangely writhing their shadowy shapes.

1 strophe   They appeal to Night, their mother, whose sway like theirs is over living and dead alike; they appeal against the despite Apollo is doing them in robbing them of their cowering victim—

> And over him as slain
> We raise this chant of madness, frenzy-working,
> The hymn the Erinnyes love,
> A spell upon the soul, a lyreless strain
> That withers up men's strength.

The Destiny that spun the web of all things spun as one *and anti-strophe* thread of it that they should haunt the slayer of kin, their victim, till death, and after death their victim yet more :—

> And over him as slain
> We raise this chant of madness, frenzy-working,
> The hymn the Erinnyes love,
> A spell upon the soul, a lyreless strain
> That withers up men's strength.

They tell of their birth-lot : to be sundered for ever from *2 strophe* the deathless gods, from social joys and garments of white : for them was the overthrow of homes in which love and slaughter have met—

> Ha! hunting after him,
> Strong though he be, 'tis ours
> To wear the newness of his young blood down—

they are jealous for the task they have taken over from *and anti-strophe* all others : heaven must stop the prayer before it reaches them, since, their work once begun, no gods may draw near to strive with them, unapproachable beings of blood and hate—

> For leaping down as from the topmost height
> I on my victim bring
> The crushing force of feet,
> Limbs that o'erthrow e'en those that swiftly run,
> An Até hard to bear.

So far the Furies have alternated between dejection at their isolated lot and frantic joy in their task ; for a pair of stanzas they give themselves up to unmingled exultation in

3 strophe

and anti-strophe

4 strophe

and anti-strophe

Episode I

the sure secrecy of their attack. They laugh at the glory of man, towering so high in the blessed sunlight, and all the while beneath the earth its foundation has been wasting away and dwindling to dishonour, as they have been approaching and retreating with the dancings of their loathly feet. His guilt reaches the frenzy of ignorance, that gathers round him a cloudy mist hiding that which is coming, even while rumour has begun to sigh all around and tell the fall of the house. In the final pair of stanzas, the Furies fall back into unrelieved gloom, with nothing to vary the irresistible horror of their motions. For ever! ever finding means, never missing the goal, never forgetting, never appeased, lacking honour, lacking reverence, in no company of gods, in no light of sun, in life, in dim death, pursuing their uphill task, the law imposed on them, given them to fulfil, the law that none may hear and fear not, the task of old which it is their high prerogative to work out, dwellers though they be beneath the earth in the sunless world of shadows.

The spell is broken by a shock of surprise when Athene herself appears aloft in the air, floating as in a chariot of clouds along the balcony of the permanent scene. She has heard the cry of Orestes, and now enquires what is this strange presence in her own city? The Chorus explain who they are, and seek to enlist Athene against the matricide. The goddess answers that she has heard only one side. The Chorus rejoin that their adversary dares not rest his case on oath for oath. We can understand these words producing a stir through the vast Athenian audience, as trenching on current politics: the exchange of oaths was a feature of procedure in ordinary Athenian courts, from which the threatened Court of Areopagus claimed separate jurisdiction. When Athene answers that such a device is a poor way of getting at truth, a burst of applause from the aristocratic party welcomes this as

a distinct declaration in their favour. Orestes proceeds to CHAP. II
put his case, saying how Apollo sent him on his mission.
Athene pauses: murder stirred by wrath (that is, homicide
as distinguished from murder, the peculiar province of the
Areopagus Court) is too hard a matter for mortal or god
to determine; she will, therefore, appoint jurors on oath
as a perpetual institution for dealing with such cases. Let
the parties prepare, while she seeks citizens of the best for
jurors. Athene in her cloudy chariot floats onward in the
direction of the city, amid the long and loud applause of
the aristocratic party, who henceforward excitedly turn the
whole performance into a political demonstration.

The choral ode that fills up the interval assists this effect, *Choral In-*
being a glorification of the spirit of conservatism. Unless *terlude I*
the right side wins here, the Furies sing, there will be an *in four paired*
outbreak of new customs and general recklessness. Awe *stanzas*
is the watchman of the soul, the calm wisdom gained by
sorrow: he who dares all and transgresses all will perforce,
as time wears on, have to take in sail, while each yard-arm
shivers with the blast; in vain he struggles amid the
whirling waves, ever failing to weather round the perilous
promontory, till he is wrecked on the reefs of vengeance.

The political effect reaches its climax as another change *Change of*
of scene reveals Mars Hill itself: the centre masonry indi- *scene and Finale, or*
cating the very spot in which the Court of Areopagus held *Exodus*
its sittings, while one of the side-scenes displays a portion
of the hill—rocky steps, and a wide long chasm, at the
bottom of which were the Caves of the Eumenides.
Athene enters on foot from the city with her jury of
aristocratic citizens. Dramatic effect may be considered
to be suspended, and the interest now lies in reproducing
exactly the procedure of the Court of Areopagus, with
Athene for president, Orestes for prisoner, Apollo as his
counsel, and the Chorus to prosecute in person. The spirit
of the scene is adapted to gratify the peculiar Athenian

love of legal hair-splitting. Instead of deep arguments, founded on morals or religion, we have the Chorus resting their case on the plea that the murder of a husband is a lesser crime than the murder of a parent, affinity being violated and not relationship. This is met by a counter-plea of a similar type : that the mother is not even a relative, but only an instrument of child-bearing :

> The mother is not parent of the child
> That is called hers, but nurse of embryo sown ;
> He that begets is parent.

Apollo puts this his plea with a personal appeal to the judge as one born of father without mother, while no myth tells of a child sprung from no father. This at once wins Athene to his side, and she calls upon the jurors to vote, in a speech which, as an inauguration for the Court of Areopagus, makes the safety of the Athenian state rest upon this court to the end of time. Amid an accompaniment of threats and promises from the contending parties, the jurors advance one by one and cast their votes in the urns. Last of all the goddess gives her personal voice in favour of Orestes, thus affording a mythical basis for a technical term of Areopagitic procedure, by which, where a jury was evenly divided, the prisoner was said to be acquitted by the 'vote of Athene.' This proves to be the case on the present occasion, and Orestes, being thus solemnly discharged, after pouring out his gratitude to Athene, and pledging a firm alliance between Athens and his native Argos, quits the scene with his patron Apollo, and the trial is at an end.

Lyric Concerto   The political purposes of the play being now secured, its dramatic character is resumed, and it rises to the full height of tragic effect in an elaborate choral finale. The Chorus (breaking into strophic lyrics) vow vengeance and a long train of ills on the city for this their defeat : black venom shall drop on the land, which shall smite the earth with

barrenness, blight shall come upon the leaves and murrain
on the flocks.   Between each strophe and antistrophe
Athene (in blank verse) seeks to propitiate the angry deities.
Their cause has been fairly tried, she urges; moreover,
in their wrath they will lose all the good things the city
would do for them if friendly: they should have shining
thrones in the dark homes they love, the citizens would
bring them the first-fruits of a wide champaign, and the
offerings of births and wedlocks.   Gradually the Chorus
calm down, and (their lyrics subsiding into parallel verse)
they, as it were, demand reiteration of the pledge article by
article.

> *Chorus.*   Athene, queen, what seat assign'st thou me?
> *Athene.*   One void of touch of evil; take thou it.
> *Chorus.*   Say I accept, what honour then is mine?
> *Athene.*   That no one house apart from thee shall prosper.
> *Chorus.*   And wilt thou work that I such might may have?
> *Athene.*   His lot who worships thee we'll guide aright.
> *Chorus.*   And wilt thou give thy warrant for all time?
> *Athene.*   What I work not I might refrain from speaking.
> *Chorus.*   It seems thou sooth'st me; I relax my wrath.

The lyrics break out again as the Chorus recall their curse.
There shall be no tree-blighting canker, no blaze of scorch-
ing heat, no plague of barrenness nor dust drinking the
blood of citizens: but the earth shall feed fair flocks and
bear rich produce for the Higher Powers.   Athene makes
acknowledgment for the city (in marching rhythm as signifying exultation); she then offers to conduct the now friendly
deities to their homes.   At her word, torches are seen on
the stage, lighting up the dull March afternoon, and there
enters from the city an array of highborn matrons and girls,
in vestments of purple, some carrying urns for libations,
others graceful baskets, thus providing for the final spectacle
of the trilogy the favourite festival of the Eumenidea.   The
worshippers file down the steps into the orchestra and
mingle their brightness with the dark forms of the Chorus:

then—all winding round the orchestra in the long line which Greek art so loves, and raising the festival hymn, while the vast audience of thirty thousand join to shout the burden till the neighbouring hills ring again—the procession passes out towards the Caves of the Eumenides, and the trilogy is concluded.

III

CHORAL TRAGEDY AS A DRAMATIC SPECIES

III

1 Structure of Choral Tragedy

THE form of drama, the origin of which was traced in the first chapter of this work, while in the chapter immediately preceding an illustration of it has been presented from the spectator's point of view, is best described by the term Choral Tragedy: its distinctive mark, as a species of the universal drama, being the combination in it of a lyric with the dramatic element.

Greek Tragedy was not pure drama, but a union[1] of Lyric Odes by the Chorus in the Orchestra in Strophic form, and Dramatic Episodes by Actors on the Stage in what may be called Blank Verse. The Chorus was the bond between the lyric and dramatic elements: having connection with the dramatic plot as the hero's confidants, and taking part (through their Coryphæus or Leader) in

---

[1] The structural parts of a tragedy are five :—(1.) The Prologue includes everything (acted scene or explanatory speech) that precedes the first appearance of the Chorus. (2) Parode, or Chorus-entry, the speech of the Chorus on entering before they take part in an Episode: it often includes a Choral Ode and sometimes (see below, page 178) becomes a scene of dialogue. (3) Episode is the technical name for a dramatic scene upon the stage, the Chorus being present and taking part through their Leader. (4) Choral Interludes are by the Chorus alone, with no action taking place on the stage, and in strict strophic form. The Greek name *stasimon* describes such a performance as 'stationary' to distinguish it from the Parode and Exode. The bulk of a tragedy consists in Episodes and Choral Interludes, alternating to any number of each. (5) The Exodus or Exode includes all the action subsequent to the last Choral Interlude.—Note: The words *Parode, Episode, Exode* have no etymological connection with *ode*, but are connected with a Greek word *hodos* applied to entrance and exit.

F

CHAP. III the dialogue of the episodes, while the lyric parts they had wholly to themselves

The Chorus as 'ideal spectators' The Chorus are able to harmonise their double functions by their peculiar position as 'ideal spectators.' This happy description is true only if it be understood in the fullest sense: the Chorus are spectators *in* the drama, and they are spectators *of* the drama.

The Chorus as specta-tor's in the drama As spectators in the drama, the Chorus serve the purpose of the crowds[1] which Shakespeare and other dramatists sometimes introduce into their plays to supplement individual personages[2]. Again, two institutions of the modern stage, the soliloquy and the confidant—channels by which a poet can convey matter to his audience more directly than by acted representation—were unnecessary in the Greek Drama, where a hero had always a recognised body of confidential friends to whom he could unfold his train of meditations more naturally than in a soliloquy[3]. The function of by-standers as distinguished from actors is well illustrated in the *Agamemnon*[4]. The Chorus here are well adapted for their part: shut out by old age from the war

---

[1] E. g. the Roman mob in *Julius Cæsar*.

[2] In the technical sense of the term, there can of course be only one Chorus in a tragedy. The term is loosely applied to companies of mute personages on the stage, such as the body-guard of Aegisthus. In two cases, words have been written for such 'Secondary Choruses': the Ritual Hymn at the close of the trilogy, and the Huntsmen's Chorus in *Hippolytus*.

[3] A near approach to an ancient Chorus is found in Ben Jonson's play, *Every Man out of his Humour*, where he utilises his prologue to bring upon the stage (that is, upon that portion of the stage reserved in his day for fashionable spectators) two persons of a critical disposition who remain all through the piece and assist the audience with their passing comments.—Note also the school of modern fiction, of which George Eliot is the most prominent type: here, while the main points of the story are developed in dialogue, the action can be suspended at any point for the purpose of making philosophic comments, which are a prose analogue to the lyric meditations of the Chorus.

[4] Another excellent illustration is in *Oedipus at Colonus*, 823–86.

itself they are yet Senators, to whom the formal announce- CHAP. III
ment of the news received would naturally be made. They
are so situated as to take the deepest interest in the
incidents that occur without being themselves actually
involved in them. Clytæmnestra's announcement they
receive in the most ordinary manner possible : at first with
amazement, which gives opportunity for the chain of beacons
to be described, then with lyric exclamation in an ode which,
free from any fixed method of thought, passes from reflection by insensible stages to narration. Like by-standers
they receive the Herald, and exchange with him gossip-
ing news. But this passive attitude of the Chorus is most
strikingly exhibited in the finale, where, in contact with the
catastrophe of the piece, they are again and again carried
to the verge of active interference, yet always stop short.
They are directly told by Cassandra that their beloved
master is to be murdered within the palace : but the mystic
doom of Cassandra to be for ever doubted operates to
produce irresolution till the moment for action is past.
Shortly afterwards they have the crime and the criminal
before their eyes : but as the violence of their emotions
encounters the calm triumph of Clytæmnestra her infatuation seems to become infectious, and again action is para-
lysed. When at last they have shaken themselves free of
their doubts and foreseen vengeance, then they advance,
reckless of odds, to arrest Aegisthus : even here they allow
themselves to be restrained by irresistible force and the
certainty of future retribution.

But the Chorus are also spectators *of* the drama ; they *The Chorus*
are made, in a peculiar manner, to stand for the public *as specta-*
tors of the
present in the theatre. The very impression which the *drama :*
dramatist wishes to leave in the minds of his hearers he
outwardly embodies in the words and action of the Chorus :
the Chorus are the audience thinking aloud. This appears
in various ways. For one thing, a tragedy was a religious

catching
religious
lessons,
(hence con-
ventional
style)

celebration, and the Chorus are, from time to time, made to
catch the religious bearing of the action, just as the chorales
of a modern oratorio draw a devotional lesson from the
point of the sacred history at which they occur. In connection with this religious function an explanation may be
found for that which is a stumbling-block to many a modern
reader of Greek Tragedy,—the preternatural feebleness of
expression which the Chorus so often affect. One form
taken by the devotional spirit among the Greeks was a
striving after the normal state of mind amidst a tumult of
emotions. It is in accordance with this conception of
devotion that the Chorus make themselves the moderators
in every dispute, and damp every outburst; they reprove
vice and discourage enterprise with equal gentleness; there
is no restraint to their lyric passion in dealing with things
divine, but they enter into human emotions—as in the
welcome to Agamemnon—only with chilling qualifications.
They have, in fact, contributed a new style to poetic

celebrating
incidents
that cannot
be acted,

expression—idealised commonplace. Again, the Chorus
are treated as representatives of the audience when the
poet utilises their odes for the purpose of bringing out any
features in his story which he wishes the audience to have
in their minds during the play, but which are outside the
field of action. The crime of Helen and the sacrifice of
Iphigenia—one the cause of the expedition which is keeping
Agamemnon absent, the other the motive of the vengeance
prepared for him on his return—are both of them incidents
which occurred many years before the action of the play
commences. Aeschylus can lead the Chorus, and through
them the audience, to meditate upon these scenes, and
realise them with all the emphasis imaginative poetry can
afford, precisely at those points of the plot where they will
be most effective.

expressing
the feelings
intended to

But more than all this, the Chorus reflect the audience in
the way they are made to meet successive incidents of the

drama with just the changes of feeling which the play is CHAP. III
intended to produce in the spectators themselves. Nowhere *be aroused*
is this function fulfilled with more force and subtlety than in *in the*
the *Agamemnon*. The whole play is the dramatisation of *audience*
a doubt, and the Chorus sway between triumph and misgiving until the doubt is for ever solved in the catastrophe.
Odes setting out to celebrate vengeance mysteriously come
round to fear ; scenes in which the Chorus receive good
news lead them, by natural changes, to presentiments of
doom ; the anxious caution of the Chorus to avoid in themselves the most accidental touch of presumption is at once
neutralised when presumption is acted by Clytæmnestra's
contrivance before their eyes. The peculiar excitement an
audience naturally feel in face of a crisis they must witness
while they may not interfere is magnified in the Chorus,
who are plainly told of the coming crime, and yet are
forced by the spell of Apollo to disbelieve Cassandra until
too late. And the total transformation that comes over
the Chorus upon the sudden thought of the future avenger
fitly conveys the passage of the audience in a drama from
the distraction of suspense and pity to the dramatic satisfaction which serves as a final position of rest. We sometimes speak of ' transporting our minds ' to a distant scene :
the operation was literally accomplished in a Greek tragedy,
where the Chorus were ambassadors from the audience
projected into the midst of the story, identifying themselves
with the incidents represented without ceasing to be
identified with the public witnessing the play.

2 The Lyric Element in Ancient Tragedy

The lyric element—or, as it may fairly be called, the *The lyric*
operatic element—in Ancient Tragedy centres around the *element in*
Tragedy
Chorus, and is two-fold : the odes separating or introducing *two-fold*

CHAP. III the dramatic scenes the Chorus have to themselves; again,
——   when they take part in the episodes they sometimes give
these a lyric character. These two functions of the Chorus
may be considered separately.

1   The Choral Odes of the ancient drama introduce us
Choral Odes directly to the lyric poetry of Greece. The lyric poetry
Compared most familiar to modern readers will be the Psalms of the
with Bibli- Bible : it is interesting to compare these with the odes of
cal Psalms Tragedy, so far as literary form is concerned. Two funda-
Odes not mental differences at once reveal themselves. The choral
indepen- odes are not separate poems composed on particular subjects,
dent poems, but arise out of situations springing up from time to time in
the course of the plot. A Biblical psalm may of course be
a description of a situation, just as it may treat any other
subject, but it will be an independent poem, complete in
and always itself and self-explaining. Again : the associations of
character- oratorio lead us to think of a ' chorus ' as an abstract
ised musical form, not bound down to any particular performers ;
a Greek Chorus never loses its characterisation, but is
a definite band of performers— Argive Women, or Elders
of Thebes—whose personality enters into all they sing.
No doubt many of our Hebrew psalms were composed for
priests, or for the king : but characterisation is not essential
to this form of composition.

Side by side with these differences there is one striking
resemblance of form between Hebrew and Greek lyrics,
which resemblance, however, is at the same time a
contrast. Both are highly antiphonal: but the antiphonal treatment is differently applied in each. In the
Psalms Biblical psalm the parallelism relates to the structure of
antiphonal each individual verse[1]. That which makes a ' verse '
in clauses: in Hebrew poetry is not, as with us, metre, nor, as with
the Greek and Latin languages, syllabic quantity, but

---

[1] The ' verse ' in Hebrew and Classical poetry corresponds to the 'line '
of English poetry and not to the stanza.

simply parallelism of clauses. Each verse must consist Chap. III
of two members—

> The Lord of Hosts is with us ;
> The God of Jacob is our refuge :

or of three—

> He maketh wars to cease unto the end of the earth :
> He breaketh the bow, and cutteth the spear in sunder ;
> He burneth the chariots in the fire :

while various modes of combination extend these fundamental forms into a variety of figures [1], all of them retaining the
effect of parallelism and inviting antiphonal rendering [2].   In *Odes antiphonal
in stanzas*

---

[1] Thus there may be a quatrain :—

> With the merciful
>   Thou wilt show Thyself merciful ;
> With the perfect man
>   Thou wilt show Thyself perfect.

Or a quatrain reversed :—

> Have mercy upon me, O God,
>   According to Thy lovingkindness,
>   And according unto the multitude of Thy tender mercies
> Blot out my transgressions.

An example of a triplet reversed is Isaiah vi. 10. Another figure
may be made by a couplet of triplets, or even a triplet of triplets, as in
the first verse of the first psalm, which speaks of the man

> that walketh not
>   in the counsel
>   of the ungodly,
> nor standeth
>   in the way
>   of sinners,
> nor sitteth
>   in the seat
>   of the scornful.

Parallelism, as distinguished from strict metre, is highly elastic, and
the same passage will admit of several different arrangements.

[2] Modern chaunting of the psalms is arbitrary, and by no means
corresponds to their real structure. I am not aware that any attempt

CHAP. III .Greek there is no such parallelism of clauses, its verses being determined by syllabic quantity.   On the other hand, the choral ode is characterised by the strictest parallelism of stanzas, the antistrophe reproducing the measure of the strophe ; and this, it has been pointed out [1] connected itself directly with antiphonal rendering in the dance.   How far such strophic form characterises Hebrew poetry it is difficult to determine.   The psalms fall naturally into divisions, to which modern commentators apply the term 'strophes'; but the question of the parallelism of such divisions leads to differences of interpretation.   Occasionally the antiphonal effect in the psalms is very strong.   In the latter part of the twenty-fourth psalm the summons to the everlasting doors to open is, as it were, met by a challenge from within :

> Who is the King of Glory?

to which there is the response—

> The Lord, strong and mighty;
> The Lord, mighty in battle.

Again—in a manner suggesting the withholding of an expected watchword—the summons is repeated, and once more the challenge follows : the watchword of the Divine name then brings the climax—

> THE LORD OF HOSTS,
> He is the King of Glory.

Such antiphonal effect has analogy with the breaking up

has been made to mark the difference between couplet and triplet verses, though it is obvious that musical devices for this purpose would be easy. Attention has been turned of late years to the matter of conveying musically the 'strophic' structure of the psalms : see Bishop Westcott's *Paragraph Psalter* (Deighton, Bell & Co.), *The Golden Treasury Psalter* (Macmillan), and Dr. Naylor's musical rendering of Psalms lxxviii and civ (Novello).—For the whole subject of Biblical Parallelism see my *Literary Study of the Bible* (D. C. Heath & Co., Isbister & Co.)

[1] See above, page 9.

of a Greek Chorus into semichoruses, as well as with the Chap. III
response of an antistrophe to its strophe.

To pass from form to matter, the choral odes of Tragedy *Classifica-*
admit of a simple classification. By far the larger number *tion of*
will be Odes of Situation, conveying the state of affairs in *Odes*
the play as between the situation just concluded and the *Odes of*
scene which is to follow. All the odes in *Oedipus King* are *Situation*
good examples of this class, being clear expressions of the
several stages in the action of that play. The prologue having
been occupied with a suppliant procession to Oedipus, be-
seeching him to become a deliverer from the plague as he
had formerly been a deliverer from the Sphinx, the first ode
paints the city crushed beneath its affliction, and the heaps
of corpses unburied with none to lament ; while they call
on every god for assistance the hopes of the Chorus are in
the oracle, which messengers have been sent to bring from
golden Delphi. In an episode this response is brought,
bidding Oedipus discover the murderer of the late king.
The Chorus at once give themselves up to wondering
where in the whole world the wretched murderer can be,
flying the wrath of heaven, with immortal hate pursuing him
and the snares of destiny spreading him round. In the
next episode the investigation is commenced, and it seems
to cast doubts on the trustworthiness of the oracle itself :
Oedipus cries out that the oracle is doubly false. The
Chorus, shocked at this defiance, pray for themselves that
they may be kept ever in the paths of virtue, in unbroken
obedience to eternal law. Again, the investigation becomes
distracted from its main purpose by the light it seems to be
throwing upon another mystery—the doubtful question of
the king's birth : the chain of evidence is made complete
except for one link, and the herdsman is sent for who will
supply this. The Chorus fill up the interval with an ode
in which they catch the hope that by to-morrow the whole
stain will be purged from the origin of their beloved ruler.

CHAP. III But this missing link is found to reconcile the apparent discrepancies in the oracle, and to pronounce Oedipus at once
the son and the murderer of Laius.   Accordingly the Chorus
in their final ode fall back from hope to the lowest de-
spondency, and see the fleeting state of all human glory
instanced in the change of Oedipus the supremely blest into
Oedipus the parricide.

*Special use
for em-
phasising
a situation,* An ode of this type is a powerful weapon in the hands of
a dramatist who has occasion for making a particular situation
emphatic.   In *Antigone* the opening situation is the victory
of the preceding day.   It is a victory in which are latent all
the elements whose conflict is to make up the play : there
is the patriotic death of one brother, the fall of the traitor
which unlocks again for him the affection of his sister, and
the infatuation of the victor which is to carry him beyond
humanity and plunge him in a crushing reverse.   Accordingly, Sophocles concentrates his powers upon a morning
song of triumph [1].   The sun which the Chorus of Thebans
see rising before them is the same sun which yesterday was
advancing his quiet course over the current of Dircé, while
beneath he watched the headlong flight of the foe : that foe
which had come from Argos in such proud array, a flight
of eagles lured on by a traitor, their wing-shields aloft like
snow, their mane-crested helms hanging over the city's seven
portals.   But eagle was encountered by dragon ; and Zeus,
that never relents to haughty speech, smote the foe even
with victory on his lips.

> Death-struck, he lies on the earth in an instant down-dashed;
> Dark is the torch that he flourished in hostile fury ;
>   He rushed, snorting with rage,
>   Pressing onward first to engage,
>   Scaled the wall
>   But to fall !
>   All, soon or late,
>   Bow to their fate !

[1] *Antigone*, 100.

They continue to tell how in every gate man met man in
deadly strife : but most dread was the meeting of the two
who owned one sire and one mother, who thrust and fell
and were together in their death. Then came victory and
fame for Thebes : and the Chorus will waken the revel until
every shrine is shaking with the dance and hymn of joy.

A situation will occasionally arise in a drama which is *or for a*
lyrical in its nature, and so lends itself in a special *situation*
lyric in its
degree to choral treatment. In the *Rhesus*, one of the *nature*
odes embodies a military evolution, a change of the watch.
The words of the strophe may very well have been set to the
actual motions of a soldiers' dance, with clash of weapons
to bring out the rhythm.

> Who now before the camp keeps guard?
> Who to relieve me is prepared?
> The stars are sinking from the skies,
> The rising Pleiads show the approach of day;
> High in mid-heaven the eagle flies:
> Awake, arise: why this delay?
> Awake, the watch forbids repose:
> See, the pale moon a fainter lustre throws;
> The dawn is nigh, the dawn appears.
> See you yon star the heavens adorn?
> 'Tis the bright harbinger of morn,
> New risen, his gold-encircled head he rears.

Breaking into two halves, the Chorus in rough dialogue run
over the order of the watches, and find that the Lycians are
due to succeed them. They close again into a chorus
and work through the antistrophe, with softer motions (we
may suppose) to express the exquisite moment when the
sounds of night have not ceased and the sounds of day are
beginning.

> Where silver Simois winds along,
> I hear the sweet bird's mournful song:
> High-seated on some waving spray
> To varying chords the warbling nightingale
> Attempers her melodious lay,
> And pours her sorrows through the vale.

> The flocks now feed on Ida's height,
> Loud shrills the pastoral pipe, and charms the night.
> O sleep, I feel thy soothing pow'r:
> Gently it creeps my eyes to close,
> And seal them in a calm repose;
> Sweet thy approach in morn's o'erlaboured hour.

Once more falling out of rank, the Chorus exchange fears with one another at the continued absence of their spy; then they march out in a body to rouse the Lycians, and leave the scene unprotected for the critical moment of the play [1].

Odes of Nature   A second class of choral odes will be the Odes of Nature. It must be understood, however, that the influence of nature

---

[1] *Rhesus*, 527.—Other Odes of Situation are: *Choephori*, 770, Prayer at a Crisis and (921) Exultation when the Crisis is past; *Seven against Thebes*, 78, a Panic Ode; *Phœnissæ*, 202, Travellers to Delphi detained in Thebes by the siege. A peculiar case is *Hercules*, 874, where the Chorus, having been miraculously granted a vision of Madness on her way to smite the hero, fall into an ode of lamentation which in reality depicts the scene actually going on within. Sometimes the situation is more distinctly moralised upon, as in *Eumenides*, 468, Glorification of the conservative spirit; *Antigone*, 584, A house under the curse of heaven; *Iph. Aul.* 544, Moderation in love; *Hippolytus*, 1102, Longing for a humble lot in life.

Analogous in Biblical poetry are Deborah's Song of Triumph (Judges, chapter v), or David's lament over Jonathan (2 Samuel i. 19-27). Psalm xviii is put in the Authorised Version as A Song of Deliverance, and a very close parallel to an Ode of Situation is suggested by the heading of Psalm lix, 'When Saul sent and they watched the house to kill David.' But as a rule Biblical psalms of this nature convey a double situation, a transition taking place in the course of the poem ; e.g. Psalm lvi, and especially Psalm lvii, where the change comes in the middle of the middle verse.—Note an interesting parallel between the thought of Psalm lv, verses 1-8, and *Hippolytus*, lines 732-751.

Sometimes it is the General Situation of affairs in the play as a whole, rather than a particular situation, that is conveyed: *Prometheus*, 406, The world mourning for Prometheus and his brother; *Seven against Thebes*, 276, Horrors of war sung by women ; *Helena*, 1107, The whole story of Helen and Troy ; *Iph. Aul.* 164, Sightseers describing the Grecian fleet.

over the mind of classic antiquity was different from that
which dominates modern and Hebrew poetry. We do not
find Greek literature celebrating the phenomena of nature
for their own sake, as in the twenty-ninth psalm, which, with
the words 'the Voice of the Lord' running through it as a
burden, is simply a lyric realisation of a thunderstorm in all
its stages, from its first rumble on the waters of the north,
through its full majesty overhead amid cedars breaking and
cleaving flames of fire, till it passes away over the wilderness
to the south, and the fresh gleam that follows makes the
whole landscape a temple in which everything is crying,
Glory. Still less does the ancient mind conceive the unity
of nature, which in the hundred-and-fourth psalm gathers up
the sights and sounds of the external and human universe—
from the curtains of heaven and the messenger winds down
to the wild asses quenching their thirst—into one symphony
of nature, and presents the whole as waiting upon God : as
satisfied, troubled, returning to dust, renewing the face of the
earth, according to the varying operations of His Spirit.
In classic poetry, on the other hand, the attraction is to
particular spots and landscape. Euripides describes his
fellow-citizens of Athens as moving through purest air
in motion of delight, with the clearest of skies above
them and an unconquered soil below. And Sophocles
in extreme old age immortalised the scenery of his native
village :—

> Our home, Colonus, gleaming fair and white ;
> The nightingale still haunteth all our woods
>   Green with the flush of spring,
>   And sweet melodious floods
> Of softest song through grove and thicket ring ;
>   She dwelleth in the shade
> Of glossy ivy, dark as purpling wine,
>   And the untrodden glade
> Of trees that hang their myriad fruits divine
>   Unscathed by blast of storm ;
> Here Dionysus finds his dear-loved home,

Here, revel-flushed, his form
Is wont with those his fair nurse-nymphs to roam.
Here, as Heaven drops its dew,
Narcissus grows with fresh bells clustered o'er,
Wreath to the Dread Ones due,
The Mighty Goddesses whom we adore ;
And here is seen the crocus, golden-eyed ;
The sleepless streams ne'er fail ;
Still wandering on they glide,
And clear Kephisus waters all the vale ;
Daily each night and morn
It winds through all the wide and fair champaign,
And pours its flood new-born
From the clear freshets of the fallen rain.
The Muses scorn it not ;
But here, rejoicing, their high feast-days hold,
And here, in this blest spot,
Dwells Aphrodite in her car of gold [1].

National Odes

National Odes constitute a small but striking section. The parode of the *Persians* includes a sort of national anthem, celebrating the Persians, the people stout-hearted, and their god-given task of wars, with the crash of towers, and the surge of horsemen, and the fierce sack. It is soon succeeded by an ode of national humiliation, emphasised with all the reiterations of oriental mourning :—

'Twas Xerxes led them forth, woe! woe!
'Twas Xerxes lost them all, woe! woe!
'Twas Xerxes who with evil counsels sped
Their course in sea-borne barques.

Their own ships bore them on, woe! woe!
Their own ships lost them all, woe! woe!
Their own ships, in the crash of ruin urged,
And by Ionian hands [2].

---

[1] *Medea*, 824; *Oedipus at Colonus*, 668.—Other examples of this class are *Hecuba*, 444, or *Troades*, 197, Captives wondering to what regions of Greece they will be carried; *Iph. Taur.*, 1089, Greek exiles fancying the voyage homewards.

[2] *Persians*, 106 and 260.—Another example of this class is the Patriotic Appeal in the *Suppliants* (of Euripides), 365. National Psalms in Scripture are such as Ps. xliv, cxiv, lxxx.

No lyrics in Ancient Tragedy are more striking than the CHAP. III
Odes of Human Life. The Chorus in *Prometheus* take Odes of
occasion by the sufferings of Io to deprecate unequal Human
marriages : love is the theme of many odes ; old age is Life
celebrated in the *Oedipus at Colonus*, in the *Hercules* it is
contrasted with youth ; if the woes of parentage are detailed
in the *Medea*, its joys are sung in the *Ion*. But the great type
of this class is the ode which, in *Antigone*, presents man as
the chief wonder of nature. The rapidity of invention in
modern times is àpt to make us forget that the greatest
marvels of all are the familiar things of every-day life : that
the electric telegraph is no more than a slight extension to
the grand invention of writing, while this writing in its turn
must yield in mystery to the foundation-step in all human
intercourse, the invention of speech ; that steam, and the
latest triumph of machinery, are insignificant beside the
invention of fire or the discovery of iron. The Greeks lived
near enough to the infancy of the world to gaze with awe
upon the primal mysteries of human civilisation. Accordingly, the Chorus in *Antigone* can inflame our sense
òf wonder by merely mentioning one after another the
earliest achievements of humanity :—the seafarer's great
experiment, the hard-won victory over the brutes and the
violence of nature, the agricultural miracle of the buried seed
returning in increase, the mystery of speech, of thought, of
the social bond, the mystery of death, the marvels of the
arts, the mystery of religion, and as a climax the mystery of
sin. .

> Wonders in nature we see and scan,
> But the greatest of all is Man[1] !

Hymns and Ritual Odes are natural interludes in a form of *Hymns*
composition which is an outgrowth of religious ceremonial. *and Ritual*
Odes

[1] *Prometheus*, 906 ; *Oedipus at Colonus*, 1211 ; *Hercules*, 637 ; *Medea*,
1081 ; *Ion*, 452 ; *Antigone*, 332. In the Bible, Psalms xc, viii, cxxvii,
cxxviii, may be called Psalms of Life.

CHAP. III We have already noticed the Spell of the Furies in the third,
and the Sepulchral Rites in the second play of Aeschylus's
trilogy; in other plays we find an Ode for the Dying, and
an Ode over the Dead [1]. The *Antigone* contains a Hymn to
Bacchus, and the *Ajax* a Dance to Pan ; one of the odes in
the *Ion* opens as a prayer to the goddess of poison. And
when the Chorus seek to soothe Admetus in his bereavement their consolation takes the form of a Hymn to
Necessity.

> Of all the Powers Divine,
> Alone none dares to approach Her shrine ;
> To Her no hallowed 'image stands,
> No altar She commands.
> In vain the victim's blood would flow,
> She never deigns to hear the suppliant's vow [2].

Narrative Odes : One more class remains to be mentioned : the Narrative
Odes, embodying traditionary legends, the point at which
the epic and lyric modes of poetry approach nearest to one
embodying a single legend, another. Sometimes an ode is entirely given up to a single
story : we have seen how the first three odes in *Agamemnon*
present the legends of Iphigenia, of Paris, and of Helen
respectively. In other cases a situation arises in a play
embodying a string of legends which suggests to the Chorus a series of similar situations
in traditional lore. Thus when Antigone, so noble in race
and in the deed for which she is to suffer, is led forth to the
rock which is to be her prison and her tomb, the Chorus recall other great ones who have suffered the same cruel fate.
They think of Danae, whose brazen tower was to her a cell
of death parting her from mankind : yet she was of high
lineage, and destined to receive Zeus himself in a golden
shower.

---

[1] *Oedipus at Colonus*, 1557, and *Alcestis*, 435.
[2] *Antigone*, 1115; *Ajax*, 693; *Ion*, 1048; *Alcestis*, 962. In the Bible,
Psalms xlv and lxviii are examples of Festival Hymns, and No. cxviii
may be interpreted as a Ritual Psalm.

> What can withstand thy will, O Fate,
> The gold, the ship, the shield, the gate?
> Ah no! o'er all thou art triumphant.

They think of the monarch of Thrace, who impiously sought to check the revels of the Wine-god, and in retribution wasted drop by drop away in the mountain cavern. And the rough shores of the Bosporus, with their rougher hordes of men, saw the cruel deed of blinding done on the sons of Phineus, while their mother perished in a cave, daughter though she was of the boisterous North-wind:

> Yet the lot which Fate had decreed
> She could not escape, it caught her[1].

So far we have been concerned with those parts of a tragedy in which the Chorus are alone. But they also enter as a body of actors into the dramatic episodes; from their first appearance they are regularly present to the end of the play, and all that happens is addressed to them. Now the action of these episodes will often include matter of a lyric nature—public mourning, passionate contests, and the like: hence interaction takes place between the lyric and dramatic elements, the metres and style of lyric poetry passing over at suitable points to include the actors. We thus get two new literary forms in Tragedy: the Lyric Solo (or Monody) by an actor alone, and the Lyric Concerto (or Commos) by an actor (or pair of actors) and the Chorus alternately.

2
Choral Work in Episodes

Both may be illustrated from the play of Sophocles which covers the same ground as the middle play in Aeschylus's

The Lyric Solo (or Monody)

---

[1] *Antigone*, 944.—Compare *Choephori*, 576, Dread deeds of Women; *Alcestis*, 568, Story of Apollo as a slave on earth; *Iph. Taur.* 1234, the infant Apollo's triumph over Dreams [a parallel to the play itself, in which a prophecy has come true and a dream proved false]; *Iph. Aul.* 1036, Nuptials of Peleus and Thetis; *Hercules*, 348, Labours of Hercules; *Troades*, 511, or *Hecuba*, 905, The night of Troy's capture. The second, third, and fourth odes in the *Phœnissæ* carry on the local legendary lore of Thebes.—There are similar Narrative Psalms in the Bible, e. g. lxxviii, cv, cvi.

CHAP. III trilogy. At the point where (according to both versions)
Orestes has made his appearance and again retired, Electra
comes (in the version of Sophocles) alone from the palace
to breathe the morning prayer by which she daily testifies
against the deed her oppressors would fain bury in oblivion.
The lyric style of a Monody is the natural medium in which
to clothe so formal an act of lamentation.   Electra appeals
to the holy morning light, and the air which wraps the whole
world round, to be witnesses of her nightly vigils and daily
mourning in memory of the father who fell, not by honour-
able war, but by a traitor's stroke :—

> As they who timber hew
> Cut down a mighty oak, so him they slew ;
> And from none else but me
> Comes touch of sympathy,
> Though thou wast doomed to die,
> My father, with such shame and foulest ignominy.

Electra protests how she will outdo the nightingale, and
pour out her sorrows by day as well as by night.   Then she
calls on the Powers beneath for vengeance :—

> O house of Hades and Persephone !
> O Hermes ! guide of dwellers in the gloom,
> Thou awful Curse, and ye,
> Erinnyes, daughters of the gods, most dread,
> Whose eyes for ever see
> Men foully slain, and those whose marriage bed
> The lust of evil guile
> Doth stealthily defile,
> Come, come avengers of my father's fate !
> Come, send my brother back !
> For I the courage lack
> Alone to bear the burden of this evil weight.

The Lyric Concerto (or Com- mos)   The Lyric Solo passes into a Lyric Concerto[1] as the
Chorus silently enter the orchestra, and advancing towards
the altar hail Electra as daughter of ill-fated mother : they
gently reproach her for her unceasing lamentations, cursed

---

[1] The Monody commences at line 86, the Concerto at line 121.

though the deed be for which she weeps. Electra from CHAP. III
the stage carries on the rhythm of their strophe as she
hails the Chorus by the name 'daughters of the brave and
true,' recognises how they fulfil every office of friendship, yet
begs they will leave her to waste in sorrow alone. The
Chorus, passing to the other side of the altar, respond in
antistrophe :—

> And yet thou canst not raise
> Thy father, nor with wailing nor with prayer,
> From Hades' darkling ways,
> And gloomy lake where all who die repair ;

meanwhile, the ceaseless lamentation is sinking the mourner
herself from woe to deeper and unbearable woe. Electra
again responds : —

> Ah, weak as infant he who can forget
> His parents that have perished wretchedly ;
> Far more she pleaseth me that mourneth yet,
> And ' Itys, Itys,' wails unceasingly,
> The bird heart-broken, messenger of Heaven.
> Ah, Niobe, most sad !
> To thee, I deem, high fate divine was given,
> For thou in cavern grot,
> Still weeping, ceasest not.

With a change of posture and movements the Chorus in
a second strophe remind Electra that she is not the only
one who has such a fate to mourn : there is Iphianassa and
Chrysothemis, there is another — happier in that he is
destined to return as his home's avenger. But Electra
sees in Orestes fresh matter for trouble : he mocks all her
messages, yearning for home yet coming not. The Chorus
pass back to the other side of the altar again, and in their
antistrophe strike a note of hope :—

> Take heart, my child, take heart ;
> Still mighty in the heavens Zeus doth reign,
> Who sees the whole world, rules its every part :
> To Him do thou commit thy bitter pain.

They bid Electra trust to the kind god Time, for neither

CHAP. III Orestes will forget, nor the Powers of the world beneath. But Electra complains that the larger half of life is gone and hope fails : no parent, no fond husband to guard her, she is an alien and slave in her own father's home. The Chorus cannot resist the infection of her grief, and, changing for their third strophe to gestures of despair, they paint the scene of Agamemnon's return, and the stern keen blow devised by guile and wielded by lust. Electra, from the stage, out-wails their wailing :—

> O day, of all the days that ever came
> Most hateful unto me!
> O night! O woes of banquets none may name,
> Which he, my sire, did see!

For the foul deed which thus destroyed her father and herself together she invokes a curse from heaven, eternal grievings with guilt-avenging groans. The Chorus—according to the wont of Choruses—take alarm at this violence, and, passing to the other side of the altar, bid Electra remember how she has already fallen from prosperity to desolate sorrow, and shrink from further conflict with the mighty. Electra (carrying on the antistrophe) is not blind in her wrath : she would fain be left to her weepings, which shall be endless. The Chorus, pausing in front of the altar, repeat that with all a mother's affection they counsel moderation. Electra heatedly cries, What moderation was there in the deed? All honour and good forsake her, if she ever consents to clip the wings of her grief :—

> If he who dies be but as dust and nought,
> And poor and helpless lie,
> And these no vengeance meet for what they wrought,
> Then truly Awe will die,
> And all men lose their natural piety.

With this epode the Concerto ends.

The term 'Stage Lyrics' is the generic name for these lyric solos and concertos, and a great variety of action finds

appropriate expression in this medium. We have already
noticed the sepulchral rites carried on between Electra and
Orestes and the Chorus in the trilogy. The return from
the funeral of Alcestis gives opportunity for a concerto
between the bereaved Admetus and his faithful subjects;
the finale of the *Seven against Thebes* is given up to the
public mourning after the battle. In the *Ion* the Chorus
enter the orchestra as sightseers, and in concerto with the
priest on the stage have pointed out to them the beauties of
the temple. Just as the parode to *Electra* is a visit of condolence, so the parode to *Orestes* is a scene of visiting the
sick, Electra from the stage hushing the voices and foot-
steps of the Chorus, and the Chorus at one point performing
a sleeping spell. Later in the same play another concerto
illustrates the degree to which stage lyrics enable the Chorus
to be taken up into the action of the play. Electra opens
her plan of seizing Hermione as a hostage, and spreads the
Chorus through the orchestra to watch for the victim.

Electra.	Divide, divide! with careful view
	Watch you the street, the entrance you.

The Chorus at once separate :

1 *Semicho.*	Haste, to your stations quickly run :
	My watch be towards the rising sun.
2 *Semicho.*	Be mine, with cautious care addrest,
	To where he sinks him in the west.
Electra.	Now here, now there, now far, now nigh,
	Quickly glancing dart th' observant eye.
1 *Semicho.*	With fond affection we obey,
	Our eyes quick glancing every way.
Electra.	Glance through that length of hair, which flows
	Light waving o'er your shaded brows.
1 *Semicho.*	This way a man comes hast'ning down;
	His garb bespeaks some simple clown.
Electra.	Undone, undone, should he disclose
	These couched, armed lions to their foes.
1 *Semicho.*	He passes on, suppress thy fear,
	And all this way again is clear.

> *Electra.* And that way doth no footstep rude
>   Disturb the wished-for solitude?
> *2 Semicho.* This way no rude step beats the ground.
>   But all is still, all safe around.

The concerto continues all through the excitement of the supposed murder within, until Hermione arrives and falls into the snare [1].

Metrical Structure of Greek Tragedy

When to the regular combination of odes with episodes there is added this power of changing in the course of an episode to stage lyrics, it will appear that Greek Tragedy possesses as a distinctive feature a very wide variety of metres for the purpose of conveying variations of feeling and movement. Six metrical styles may be enumerated.

Six metrical styles: Blank Verse,

1. There is Blank Verse [2], which, it has already been remarked, differs from English Blank Verse only by the addition of a single foot.

Parallel (or Stichomuthic) Verse,

2. A distinct variety of style is produced when in dialogue remark and answer are identical in length. In the present work this will be called Parallel Verse; the Greek term is Stichomuthic—literally, rows of speech. Parallel Verse usually is made up of speeches each one line in length, and in this form it is, in Euripides, sustained without a break sometimes for more than a hundred lines together [3]. In other cases the speeches are each a line and a half, or half a line long: all three kinds of parallelism are illustrated in the following extracts from the recognition scene in the *Electra* of Sophocles :—

> *Orestes.* Is this Electra's noble form, I see?
> *Electra.* That self-same form indeed, in piteous case.
> *Orestes.* Alas, alas, for this sad lot of thine.
> *Electra.* Surely, thou dost not wail, O friend, for me!
> *Orestes.* O form most basely, godlessly misused!

---

[1] *Alcestis*, 861; *Seven against Thebes*, 818-1007 ; *Ion*, 184; *Electra* (of Sophocles), 121 ; *Orestes*, 140 and 174 ; 1246.

[2] See above, page 16 (note).

[3] An example is *Ion*, 264-368; compare in the same play 934-1028.

Electra. Thy words, ill-omened, fall, O friend, on none
     But me alone.
Orestes.   Alas, for this thy state,
     Unwedded, hopeless!
Electra.   Why, O friend, on me
     With such fixed glance still gazing dost thou groan?

It is as the scene reaches its crisis that the lines become shorter.

    Orestes. Of those that live there is no sepulchre.
    Electra. What say'st thou, boy?
    Orestes.   No falsehood what I say.
    Electra. And does he live?
    Orestes.   He lives if I have life.
    Electra. What, art thou he[1]?

3. A third metrical style, founded on the trochaic foot, *Accelerated* may be called Accelerated Rhythm[2]; it is used for sudden *Rhythm,* outbursts in dramatic episodes, and may be almost exactly reproduced in English :—

Nay, enough, enough, my champion! we will smite and slay no more.
Already we have heaped enough the harvest-field of guilt;
Enough of wrong and murder, let no other blood be spilt!
Peace, old men, and pass away into the homes by Fate decreed,
Lest ill valour meet our vengeance—'twas a necessary deed.
But enough of toils and troubles—be the end, if ever, now,
Ere the wrath of the Avenger deal another deadly blow.

4. Midway between blank verse and the full lyrics of *Marching* a choral ode comes Marching Rhythm, distinguished by the *Rhythm,* prominence of anapæstic feet, which are banished from the metrical system of choral odes. The name suggests how

---

[1] A curious example of Parallel Verse is in the *Alcestis* (387), where, as the Queen sinks, the responses become shorter and shorter :—

    Alcestis. As one that is no more, I now am nothing.
    Admetus. Ah, raise thy face! forsake not thus thy children!
    Alcestis. It must be so perforce; farewell, my children.
    Admetus. Look on them, but a look.
    Alcestis.   I am no more.
    Admetus. How dost thou? Wilt thou leave us so?
    Alcestis.   Farewell.

Parallel Verse is much affected by Shakespeare in his earlier plays; see *Richard III*, 1. 2 and 4. 4.

[2] Trochaic Tetrameter Catalectic.

CHAP. III this is the regular rhythm for a Chorus-entry; it is also used to convey any passing excitement in the course of a play. The metre does not suit the English language; some idea of it may be given by the following attempt to imitate the opening lines of the parode to *Agamemnon* :—

> 'Tis the tenth weary year since the warfare began,
>> The great vengeance on Troy:
> Menelaus the king, and his comrade in rank,
> Agamemnon, the two who from Heaven derive,
> Great yoke-fellows both, their sway over men,—
> These aroused vast hosts with their myriad ships,
>> From this country to sail,
>> In war irresistible helpers.

Anti-phonal Lyrics,

5. Lyrics, chiefly Antiphonal (with strophe answered by antistrophe), are the regular measure for choral odes, and have been sufficiently illustrated. There remains (6) the *Semichoric Excite-ment* variety of these which may be called Semichoric Excitement, where the Chorus breaks up into halves, or more numerous subdivisions, to express excitement or anxiety in dialogue.

Metrical transitions reflecting transitions of feeling:

The literary importance of these metrical styles lies, not in the metres themselves (the analysis of which belongs wholly to the science of language), but in the transitions from one to another as a means of conveying transitions of mood and feeling. One delicate example of such transitions has already been mentioned, the variation in the movements of the Chorus itself between marching rhythm and antiphonal

between marching rhythm and anti-phonal lyrics,

lyrics. When a Chorus is entering or quitting the orchestra, or when it is irresolute or merely excited, the language falls into anapæsts; as soon as it gives itself up to set emotion, such as is proper to an ode, the strophic arrangement prevails. This may be further illustrated from the parode to *Alcestis*. The Chorus, old men of Pheræ, come to the palace to enquire for the Queen on this the day fated for her death. They enter the orchestra in two loosely formed bodies, scanning the outside of the palace for signs whether the dreaded event has taken place:

1 *Semicho.* What a silence encloses the palace!
What a hush in the house of Admetus!

2 *Semicho.* Not a soul is at hand of the household
To answer our friendly enquiry—
Is it over, all over but weeping?
Or sees she the light awhile longer,
Our Queen, brightest pattern of women
The wide world through,
Most devoted of wives, our Alcestis?

For a moment they give themselves up to a strophe of woe :—

Listen for the heavy groan,   *strophe*
Smitten breast and piercing moan,
Ringing out that life is gone.
The house forgets its royal state,
And not a slave attends the gate.
Our sea of woe runs high :—ah, mid the waves
Appear, Great Healer, Apollo!

They fall out of rank, and exchange doubts in marching rhythm.

1 *Semicho.* Were she dead, could they keep such a silence?
2 *Semicho.* May it be—she is gone from the palace?
1 *Semicho* Never!
2 *Semicho.*   Nay, why so confident answer?
1 *Semicho.* To so precious a corpse could Admetus
Give burial bare of its honours?

They unite again in a set antistrophe :—

Lo, no bath the porch below,   *antistrophe*
Nor the cleansing fountain's flow,
Gloomy rite for house of woe.
The threshold lacks its locks of hair,
Clipped for the dead in death's despair.
Who hears the wailing voice and thud of hands,
The seemly woe of the women?

Once more they break into two bodies, and the anapæsts recommence :—

2 *Semicho.* Yet to-day is the dread day appointed—
1 *Semicho.* Speak not the word!
2 *Semicho.* The day she must pass into Hades—
1 *Semicho.* I am cut to the heart! I am cut to the soul!
2 *Semicho.* When the righteous endure tribulation,
Avails nought long-tried love,
Nought is left to the friendly—but mourning!

CHAP. III Accordingly they settle finally into rank and perform a full
ode which concludes the parode.

between lyrics and blank verse,   The transitions thus traced are between one lyric form
and another: the interchange of lyrics and blank verse
within the same episode forms a still more powerful dramatic
weapon for conveying variations of tone [1]. Attention has
been drawn in a former chapter to the typical example of
this effect—the finale to *Agamemnon*, in which so many
and rapid changes of passion reflect themselves in varying
rhythms: in particular, it has been noticed how, as the
prophetic vision comes upon Cassandra, the versification
bursts into strophes, the Chorus being more slowly drawn
into the current of excitement, until, when the vision is
complete, the whole returns to blank verse as into the
calmness of despair. Electra, in the version of Sophocles,
after spending her emotion in the lyric solo and concerto,
tells over again more collectedly her story in blank verse:
and this is a type of many similar situations [2]. The *Ajax*
gives an example of a subtle transition: in a scene of lyric
lamentation over the hero's malady there is a sudden change
to blank verse after the novel suggestion of Tecmessa, that
his recovery of consciousness may prove a greater evil. The
dying scene in *Alcestis* is naturally in lyric metre: when the
heroine rallies to make a last request for her children a
change is made to ordinary verse. Once more, in the
Orestes, the scene of watching by the hero's sick bed is
conveyed in a lyric concerto: the sudden ceasing of the
delirium, followed by the awaking of the patient, is indicated by blank verse [3].

between blank verse and accelerated rhythm   Especially powerful is the transition from blank verse to

[1] Unfortunately, this effect is almost wholly lost in the cheap translations, which as a rule translate everything outside the choral odes
in blank verse.

[2] *Electra* (of Sophocles), 254; compare in *Antigone*, 806-82 with
891-928.   [3] *Ajax*, 263; *Alcestis*, 280; *Orestes*, 207.

accentuated rhythm, as handled by Euripides. The typical example in his *Hercules* may be appreciated by the English reader with peculiar force in the translation of Robert Browning. The scene represents the personification of Madness reluctantly dragged by the messenger of heaven to the task of afflicting the hero. As long as Madness hesitates, she speaks blank verse; when at last she yields, and abandons herself to her awful work, the metre bounds into the rapid rhythm, which is made still wilder in the translation.

Madness. This man, the house of whom ye bound me to,
　　　　Is not unfamed on earth, nor gods among;
　　　　Since, having quelled waste land and savage sea,
　　　　He alone raised again the falling rights
　　　　Of gods—gone ruinous through impious men.
　　　　Desire no mighty mischief, I advise!

Iris. Give thou no thought to Here's faulty schemes!

Madness. Changing her step from faulty to fault-free!

Iris. Not to be wise did Zeus' wife send thee here!

Madness. Sun, thee I cite to witness—doing what I loathe to do!
　　　　But since indeed to Here and thyself I must subserve,
　　　　And follow you quick, with a whizz, as the hounds a-hunt
　　　　　　with the huntsman,
　　　　Go I will! and neither the sea, as it groans with its waves
　　　　　　so furiously,
　　　　Nor earthquake, no, nor the bolt of thunder gasping out
　　　　　　earth's labour-throe
　　　　Shall cover the ground as I, at a bound, rush into the
　　　　　　bosom of Herakles.
　　　　And home I scatter, and house I batter,
　　　　Having first of all made the children fall,—
　　　　And he who felled them is never to know
　　　　He gave birth to each child that received the blow,
　　　　Till the Madness I am have let him go!
　　　　Ha, behold, already he rocks his head—he is off from the
　　　　　　starting-place!
　　　　Not a word, as he rolls his frightful orbs, from their sockets
　　　　　　wrenched in the ghastly race!
　　　　And the breathings of him he tempers and times no more
　　　　　　than a bull in the act to toss,
　　　　And hideously he bellows, invoking the Keres, daughters
　　　　　　of Tartaros.

> Ay, and I soon will dance thee madder, and pipe thee quite
>   out of thy mind with fear!
> So, up with the famous foot, thou Iris, march to Olumpos,
>   leave me here!
> Me and mine, who now combine, in the dreadful shape no
>   mortal sees,
> And now are about to pass, from without, inside of the
>   home of Herakles [1].

Analogous devices in Modern Drama   The question will suggest itself, whether this use of metrical changes to convey variations of tone has descended to the modern stage. There are traces of such effects in the early plays of Shakespeare: the rhymed lines in *Midsummer Night's Dream* seem a sort of lyric contrast to the blank verse of the play as a whole. But this usage was soon abandoned by Shakespeare in favour of the more powerful interchange between verse and prose, which is a fixed feature of his style. In the late Romantic Dramas, such as Goethe's *Faust*, every possible variety of metre occurs, including prose. But a closer analogue to the ancient practice is suggested by Mendelssohn's treatment of *Antigone* [2]. The passages of stage lyrics in that play he has left to be spoken by the actor, but he maintains throughout their recital a low orchestral accompaniment; and such incidental music to highly emotional scenes is a recognised device in a well-appointed theatre. With all this, it must be remembered that the Modern Drama is only to a partial extent the representative of Ancient Tragedy. Music is the lyric art of the modern world: and in our Opera all possible transitions of feeling, alike the boldest and the most subtle, can be adequately expressed without going outside the ductile medium of music.

---

[1] It will be observed, of course, that Browning does not use the exact metre of the original, but the literary effect of the transition is maintained and enhanced.

[2] A portion of the play so treated is the concerto between Antigone and the Chorus, when she first appears on her way to her tomb (806–82).

3 Motives in Ancient Tragedy

Tragedy is a mode of thought, as well as a form of art : CHAP. III
not only will serious poetry naturally be thoughtful, but it is *Dramatic*
impossible to construct a story on any considerable scale *Motives in*
without its reflecting conceptions of the social framework, *Ancient Tragedy*
and speculations as to the principles on which the world
is governed.   Ancient Tragedy is, perhaps, in a degree
beyond any other form of drama a vehicle of thought :
its representation was connected with religious and political
festivals ; it included, moreover, a lyric element which gave
it the power of direct meditation in the choral odes, to supplement the more indirect embodiment of ideas in plot.
There is thus in the case of Greek literature a special
importance in that department of Dramatic Criticism which
reviews the thoughts, feelings, and interests underlying
plays : at least, so far as these exercise a real influence
on the conduct of a drama, inspiring it or, so to speak,
carrying its incidents along.   It is to these 'motive' forces
in Ancient Tragedy that the present section is devoted.

Destiny is the main idea inspiring Ancient Drama : what- *Destiny*
ever may have been the religion of Greek life, the religion
reflected in Greek Tragedy is the worship of Destiny.   This
word embodies the feeling which ancient thinkers carried
away from their speculations into the mysteries of the
universe ; if they formed different conceptions as to these
mysteries, the conceptions are found to be different aspects
of Destiny.   First, it is to be noted that Destiny appears as *Destiny as*
an abstract Power or Force, not clearly coloured with *an abstract Force*
purpose :—Necessity (Anangké), the Irresistible (Adrasteia).
In the *Prometheus* of Aeschylus this aspect of Destiny is the *Prome-*
master thought ; the personages of the drama have signifi- *theus*
cance as they group themselves around the idea of Power.
This great play seems to fall at a point where two streams of
poetic thought meet—allegory and mythology, and ideas of

CHAP. III universal interest associate themselves with familiar legendary figures as they are handled in this plot. Prometheus himself includes a host of lofty conceptions. In contrast to the rest, he is the Wisdom that sees the end from the beginning; he is the Art that contrives and evolves; Foresight is the suggestion of his name. He is immortal: denied the deliverance of death, he is omnipotent in suffering. He embodies universal sympathy, and is the helper of gods and men: having already succoured the gods against the rude powers that preceded them, he is the only one who in the crisis of the far future can give to Zeus the secret of deliverance; while to men, when Zeus disregarded their feebleness, Prometheus gave fire—the first step which, once gained, makes progress irresistible. Himself is the sole thing outside the sphere of his sympathy: the taunt hurled at him by Strength is only another rendering of the taunt—He saved others, himself he cannot save. Zeus appears before us as the Power that Is: to most this seems Adrasteia, but Prometheus sees further, knowing the older Powers that Zeus overthrew, and the Power that is to come hereafter. Zeus represents an advance on the forces of the universe that had preceded him; yet his action is all for self and his own reign, and he would have blotted out man in his impotence. Strength and the messenger god Hermes are the agents of Power, with no horizon wider than the system of which they are the limbs; zeal in executing is their highest wisdom, scorn of opposition their noblest emotion. Hephæstus too is on the side of Power, for he shares the dynasty of Zeus. But his scope is wider: he is not a mere official, but contriving genius; he remembers his kinship with Prometheus and how Prometheus saved the gods; moreover he vaguely catches the possibility of change in the order of things so surely established—

Not yet is born who shall release thee.

We have Ocean—the ever-changing Ocean—standing for the

'trimmer.' As nearer to mankind, he has had a share in the
work of Prometheus for men, and has been drawn to him ;
even now he comes to sympathise, and offers counsels of
submission couched in the form of a wisdom other than that
of Prometheus—the wise maxim, Know thyself, which in his
mouth means to know our limitations. Yet he yields easily
to the advice of Prometheus that he should save himself,
and crowns his part in the drama with an unheroic close.
In compensation for the father we have the Daughters of
Ocean for Chorus—pure womanly sympathy drawn to the
side of suffering, their hearts won to the noble work of
Prometheus for man. Yet they are unable to reach so far
as the daring thought of resisting Zeus : twice they speak of
the 'sin' of Prometheus, and their devout ideal is never to
set their strength against the strength of Heaven, nor fail in
the service of feasts and offerings, so sweet do they feel life
with its strong hope and cheering joy. None the less when
Prometheus stands firm, and Hermes bids the Chorus consider their own safety, they without hesitation take sides with
Prometheus, and are prepared to face all the terrors Zeus is
about to send. One more figure appears in the play : Io,
the victim of Power, learning from Prometheus the long
array of inevitable woes that are to descend upon her from
the pitiless gods, learning also the equally inevitable consolation, that from her progeny alone can come the shadowy
Power that in the far future may overthrow Zeus. Thus in
this play the human drama of Power is reflected in all
its phases on the colossal scale of allegoric mythology.
And all the while there is looming dim in the background
The Irresistible—the march of events that must be : foresight into this makes the helpless Prometheus the real power,
before which the omnipotence of Zeus promises and tortures
in vain, while for the rest their highest mental act is to bow
in blind submission —

Wisdom is theirs who Adrasteia worship.

When this abstract force of Destiny makes itself felt in human affairs the 'Irony of Fate' appears as a measure of its irresistibility :—a march of Destiny, relentless and mocking, through means and hindrances alike, never so sure as when it is opposed, using the very obstacles in its path as stepping-stones by which it travels forward. The *Oedipus King* is a play devoted to this Irony of Fate. The city, overwhelmed with the plague, is bidden by the oracle to discover the murderer of its late king. Oedipus leads the search, vehement in his curses :—the audience catching the irony, for they know that he is denouncing himself. The Chorus in their ode wonder in what distant secret spot the malefactor can be hiding, unconscious of the irony that they have him before them in the king they serve. The Seer, wishing for Oedipus's sake to conceal the truth he has been sent for to reveal, is by the taunts of Oedipus stung to a sudden outburst :—

Thou art the plague-spot of the accursed land !

But here irony is encountered by irony, for all receive this plain truth as some mystic metaphor of prophecy. There is irony again in the way Oedipus gets plausibly on to the wrong track, seeing a possible motive for the Seer, that he may be making common cause with Creon ; and Oedipus goes on to press home this suspicion against his colleague in the sovereignty, adding fresh force to the overthrow he is preparing for himself. Jocasta, seeking to pacify, begins to cast doubts upon oracles in general ; telling how her husband Laius was doomed to die by the hands of his son, yet the son himself perished as an infant, and Laius was slain by robbers at the meeting of three roads. Her effort is mocked as a single phrase she has used takes hold of Oedipus : he too had slain a man at the meeting of three roads, and he tremblingly tells how the oracle had forewarned him he should slay his father, and how, to avert the doom, he would not return to Polybus, but avoiding Corinth

fell in with a traveller whom, in a quarrel, he killed at a turn Chap. III
in the road to Thebes. Jocasta would restrain further
enquiry, but Oedipus must search into the story of the
robbers; before this can be accomplished, a messenger
arrives with fair tidings how the Corinthians have chosen
Oedipus for their king, in the room of Polybus who is
dead—not dead through any violence, but departed in
painless old age. Now the oracles are completely discredited, so that Oedipus has courage to speak of the one
mystery yet uncleared, how he was to be wedded to his
mother as well as to murder his father. But that fear the
messenger can himself remove, now that it is safe to speak
out: the Merope who still lives at Corinth is no mother
of Oedipus, nor was Polybus his father; Oedipus is a foundling, whom the messenger himself gave to his queen. In
spite of Jocasta's remonstrance, Oedipus—stung with frenzy
of curiosity—will follow up this link until he draws out the
whole truth that makes him the overthrower at once of his
father, his mother, and his kingdom. Thus saturated has
the story been with irony in all its stages. It was the
casting out of the infant to perish which caused the ignorance in which this infant grew up to slay its father; it was
the doubting the prediction of the oracle that made Oedipus
take the road on which he walked to fulfil it. No effort
throughout the play is made to hide the truth but it
adds another touch of discovery. The oracles, that became
more and more discredited as more and more evidence
came in, lead on to the final bit of evidence which harmonises all discrepancies in one ghastly truth. And when
good fortune was complete but for one small doubt, the
reopening of this doubt plunges the whole in irretrievable
ruin.

 This root idea of Destiny passes readily into two other *Destiny*
ideas: where, on the one hand, design emerges in the *passes*
governing force of the universe, Destiny becomes Providence;

H

where, on the other hand, the absence of design in fate is more prominent even than its irresistibility we get Fortune, or the motiveless control of events [1]. Two plays well bring out these two aspects of Destiny. The *Ion* is pre-eminently a drama of Providence. Its plot is a weaving together of incidents that are to restore a lost son to his mother through a tangle of fate in which the mother all but takes the life of her son, the audience looking on with calm faith, since they know from the prologue the god's purpose that day to undo an old wrong. The force of providential control is measured by the slightness of the circumstance that can restore the course of events when all is going wrong; and never did greater issue turn upon slighter accident than in this story. The banquet in honour of the hero is in full course, the guests are standing to drink, the goblets are charged with wine and the poison adroitly slipped into the goblet of Ion : just at that moment a single word is overheard from the crowd of servants in the background and deemed by the fastidious ear of the young priest ill-omened. He bids the guests pour out the wine upon the ground, and ere the cups can be refilled a flock of temple doves flit about sipping the

spilt liquor; and the bird drinking where Ion stands dies instantly in convulsive agonies, and reveals the deadly plot. The *Iphigenia among the Tauri*, in its earlier part, might well seem a drama of Providence too. Here the audience— though in this case with no divinely revealed purpose to reassure them—have to watch a perplexed scene in which a brother is all but offered up in sacrifice by his own sister, the terrible deed being averted at the last moment by the slight accident of reading the address of a letter delivered to the victim's companion. Again the interest of the audience is fixed upon the long-drawn intrigue of escape, in which, by the finesse of Iphigenia, the barbarian king himself is made

---

[1] It will be seen in the next section of this chapter that one form of tragic plot is founded on the conception of Destiny as Fortune.

to bear a chief part in furthering the flight of his prisoners. CHAP. III
But when all that contrivance can do has succeeded, at that
moment—without suggestion of reason or purpose—by sheer
accident a contrary wind springs up impetuous, and, in
spite of straining oars and struggling mariners and praying
priestess, by dead force rolls back the ship to the shore,
until the fugitives are seized by their foes again, and deliverance is quenched in ruin. The two plays embody the two
alternatives of the ancient doubters —

> O supreme of heav'n,
> What shall we say? that thy firm providence
> Regards mankind? or vain the thoughts which deem
> That the just gods are rulers in the sky,
> Since tyrant Fortune lords it o'er the world!

The fundamental notion of Destiny combines with other
ideas that lie at the root of religion. It appears as the *Destiny as*
great moral sanction, and is identified with retribution. *the Moral*
Sanction:
The Greeks formed two distinct conceptions of retribution
—though these were conceptions that could easily coalesce.
On the one hand, there was what might almost be styled
artistic retribution, the 'Nemesis,' which seems to be a *artistic*
reaction in the drift of things against excess, even though it *retribution,*
or Nem-
be an excess of that which is not in itself evil. Just as in *esis;*
one legend Polycrates perished simply because he was too
prosperous, so the general impression left by the *Hippolytus*
is that no man can carry the virtue of temperance to such
a height as it is carried by the hero of that play without
drawing down upon himself ruin from a jealous heaven [1].
On the other hand, Ancient Tragedy is full of the moral *moral re-*
retribution which identifies the governing power of the *tribution,*
or Justice;
universe with Justice (Diké); in particular, an ode in
Agamemnon directly declares for such Justice as against

---

[1] The case is somewhat difficult to state, because Destiny is in this
play so clearly identified with Deity (see next paragraph).

CHAP. III   Nemesis, denying the old saw that prosperity grown big brings forth woe as its offspring, and contending that it is impiety which brings forth fresh impiety like to the parent *the two* stock[1]. But the form of retributive destiny which is most *combined in Infatu-* prominent in Greek Tragedy is that which is viewed from *ation or* the standpoint of the victim. This is the leading dramatic *Judicial Blindness* interest of Judicial Blindness.

> Full well spake one of old,
> That evil ever seems to be as good
> To those whose thoughts of heart
> God leadeth unto woe.

Judicial Blindness includes both the aspects of retribution just distinguished: it is an Infatuation, or haughty Insolence (Hybris), that is the natural precursor of Nemesis; while, as a means of moral retribution, it is claimed by the Furies as their leading weapon in visiting crime—the frenzy born of guilt that hides from the sinner like a mist what sighing rumour is telling all around[2]. Such Infatuation dominates the *Agamemnon*, the *Oedipus King*, and the part of Creon in *Antigone*; scarcely any play is without example of it, and the constant shrinking from such high-mindedness, even in its faintest form, seems to constitute the 'conscience' of a Greek Chorus.

Destiny   Of course, among the root ideas of religion must be the *inter-* conception of Deity; and if the devotion of the tragic *changing with* thinker was chiefly to Destiny, ordinary life in Greece was *Deity* permeated with the worship of the different deities. Accordingly, we find in the drama a continual interchange between Deity and Destiny as the controlling force of the

---

[1] *Agamemnon,* 727.
[2] *Eumenides,* 355.—Although such Judicial Blindness or Infatuation is specially prominent in Greek Tragedy, yet in some form the idea is universal; it even enters into the metaphorical language of Scripture (e. g. Isaiah vi. 10; Exodus x. 1).

universe [1].   The wavering between the two is exactly ex- CHAP. III
pressed by Hecuba when facing a great and unexpected
vindication of justice :—

> O Jove! who rulest the rolling of the earth,
> And o'er it hast thy throne, whoe'er thou art,
> *The ruling mind, or the necessity*
> *Of nature,* I adore thee: dark thy ways,
> And silent are thy steps; to mortal man
> Yet thou with justice all things dost ordain.

Often in Aeschylus, and notably in the *Prometheus,* Destiny
appears as a power beyond Deity, to which Deity itself is
subject :—

> *Chorus.*   Who guides the helm, then, of Necessity?
> *Prometheus.* Fates triple-formed, Erinnyes unforgetting.
> *Chorus.*   Is Zeus, then, weaker in his might than these?
> *Prometheus.* Not even He can scape the thing decreed.

In the trilogy, on the other hand, it is a leading motive to
identify Destiny and Zeus.   The ode of triumph over Troy,
starting with the thought that it is Zeus whose blow the
conquered city is feeling, goes on to set forth the steps in
the process of retribution on the familiar lines of infatuation :— impulse, secret and resistless, child of far-scheming
Até, leading on the evil-doer.   And similarly the creed
of the Chorus, as it appears in an earlier ode, while in
the main fixing faith on Zeus, is equally inspired by simple
fatalism :—

> For our future fate,
> Since help for it is none,
> Good-bye to it before it comes: and this
> Has the same end as wailing premature [2].

But if this notion of Deity as the supreme power could *Deity*
pass into the abstract idea of Destiny, it could also sink *sinking*
into
Humanity
enlarged :

[1] The element of plot known as Divine Intervention (below, page 191)
is an identification of Deity with Destiny.

[2] Hecuba in the *Troades,* 884 ; *Prometheus,* 523 ; *Agamemnon.* 358–
389 and 241–248.

CHAP. III into the concrete idea of humanity.   Humanity enlarged is
the Homeric conception of Deity, and it is extensively
(though rebelliously) followed by Euripides[1].   The great
study for it is his *Rhesus*, which is simply an incident from
the *Iliad* dramatised.   Here Artemis is associated with the
game of war as a backer with contempt for fair play :
bursting upon Ulysses and Diomede to scold them for
giving up their venture, detailing straight out all the information they are seeking, and then, in order to allow her
protégés to pillage undisturbed, diverting the attention of
Paris, for which purpose she borrows, with a touch of
feminine spite, the form of her sister Deity, Paris's pro-

hence
Rational-
ism or
Criticism
of Deity

tectress Aphrodité.   From such presentation of divine
personages we get as an inevitable consequence another
dramatic motive—Rationalism, or criticism of Deity.
Theseus n the *Hercules* enquires as to the gods :—

> Have they not formed connubial ties to which
> No law assents? Have they not galled with chains
> Their parents through ambition? Yet they hold
> Their mansions on Olympus, and their wrongs
> With patience bear.

Still more direct is the criticism of Amphitryon in the same
play :

> Mortal as I am,
> In virtue·I exceed thee, though a god
> Of mighty pow'r : for I have not betrayed
> The sons of Hercules . . . thou art a god
> In wisdom or in justice little versed.

---

[1] Compare the general treatment of his Prologues and Divine Interven-
tions, especially in the *Ion* and *Hippolytus*.   Illustrations in Aeschylus
are the parts of Athene and Apollo in the *Eumenides*.   Compare also
Athene in the *Ajax* of Sophocles.   It is true she does not inspire
the malice of Ajax, but only intervenes to divert his rage into harmless
madness : but the general impression left by Odysseus and Athene in
relation to their common foe is that the deity differs from the mortal
mainly in pitilessness.

It must be carefully noted, however, that the rationalism of C<small>HAP.</small> III
Euripides is always open to the interpretation that it is not
the gods themselves, but the accepted ideas about them,
which are condemned. And this is expressly said by the
speaker who answers Theseus :—

> I deem not of the gods as having formed
> Connubial ties to which no law assents,
> Nor as oppressed with chains. . . .
> *These are the wretched fables of the bards* [1].

Another fundamental notion connected with religion is *Revelation:*
Revelation: the question will arise, how does Revelation *Destiny revealed*
stand in reference to the religion of Destiny? Destiny *(1) through*
reveals itself in many ways, above all in the form of oracles. *Deity—the Oracle*
Fate being a thing of mystery, its revelation is naturally a
mystic glorification of curiosity : oracles present an inevitable future in terms that are dim, ambiguous, equivocal,
ironical ; the dimness lessens as the issue advances, but the
clear meaning or true rendering is only apparent when the
fulfilment is entirely accomplished. Accordingly, what may
be called the ' Oracular Action,' that is, a train of events
including an oracle and its fulfilment, and in which destiny
is seen working gradually out of mystery into clearness, is
one of the most common and most powerful dramatic
motives.

Two tragedies are special studies of this oracular action, *The*
the *Maidens of Trachis* and the *Oedipus King.* The *Maidens of Trachis*
peculiarity of the former is the number of different oracles
that are gathered up in fulfilment as the plot moves on.

---

[1] *Hercules,* 1316, 342, 1341.—The *Ion* is a remarkable study of
rationalism : doubts of Apollo are sown in the mind of his own priest,
producing as the plot progresses bursts of censure (436, 1312), while
the audience know that the incidents calling forth such censures are
transitional steps in a process that is to vindicate Apollo's watchful
care over Ion himself. Was Euripides dramatically expressing some
dream of reconciliation between the thought and the religious tradition
of his age?

The opening situation is the anxiety of Deianeira for her absent husband. When she hears that he is in Eubœa, she bethinks her of true oracles Hercules had left her touching that same land—that he must either end his life there, or, his labours finished, rejoice all the rest of his days. This fatal indication as to place soon recalls a fatal indication as to time : the oracle of Dodona which Hercules had told his wife, when on parting he gave her his will,—that an absence of a whole year and three months more would bring the crisis moment, when he must die or henceforth live unvexed. The two predictions unite in the immediate issue, and make the announcement that soon follows of Hercules returning in victory seem a pledge of final security. Accordingly, when the wife's joy in the victory is marred by the sight of the youthful captive who is to be her rival, no thought of possible danger for her husband occurs to interrupt the natural suggestion that this is the time to try the force of her love-charm. Now this love-charm is itself an oracle : the Centaur, slain by Hercules for insulting his bride, had with dying breath bidden her treasure up the clotted blood which oozed from his wound, for she should find it a charm over the soul of Hercules—

> That he shall never look on woman fair,
> And love her more than thee.

So she anoints a garment with this chrism, and sends it to the hero for a robe of triumph. This oracle begins to pass out of mystery into clearness when, after the robe is sent, Deianeira sees with horror the tuft of wool which she had used in anointing the garment burn in the sunlight to tinder. And the Chorus, their minds quickened by this awful incident, recollect (too late) a still earlier oracle—that the twelfth earing-tide should bring the son of Zeus a rest from toil : is it death that is to be his rest, and is Fate working out a subtle, great calamity ? The whole catastrophe follows : the hero by his triumph-robe is in a moment

converted into a mass of burning agonies, and the wife CHAP. III
at the news slays herself on her marriage-bed. When Hercules, breathing curses against Deianeira, is at last made to
understand the terrible mistake she had made, and hears
the source from which she had obtained the chrism, in
an instant the recognition is flashed into his· mind of
the last oracle he knows, the secret trust of his whole life,
given to him by Zeus himself :—

> That I should die by hand of none that live,
> But one, who dead, had dwelt in Hades dark.

So, as the story has moved on, five separate oracles have
successively appeared, all· pointing to the same event, all
mystic and perplexing, yet all reconciled'and made clear by
the event.

It will be noticed that these various oracles are brought to
fulfilment in different ways : the prediction of the love-charm
is fulfilled by Deianeira's seeking to obey it, the oracle as to
the twelfth earing-tide comes to pass by the fact of its being
ignored and forgotten. But the oracular action reaches
perhaps its most intense interest when an oracle is brought
to fulfilment by the very act of opposing it. This is re-
markably the case in the *Oedipus King*. Laius receives an *Oedipus*
oracle that his son is to slay him : he casts out the infant *King*
to perish, and as a result the child grows up in ignorance
of his father and comes to kill him. Oedipus in his turn
hears from the oracle that he is to cause his father's death :
in avoiding his supposed father, he falls in with Laius and
slays him. The two parties involved in a prediction,
by the very course they severally take to frustrate the
oracle, are in fact combining to fulfil it.

In the case of oracles, the Revelation of Destiny is made
by means of Deity [1]. There is a second form of Revelation

---

[1] In the same category may be placed (1) Madness, which was
conceived as a species of inspiration. Compare Cassandra in the

CHAP. III
(2) *Destiny revealed through trained men–Sooth-saying*
(3) *Destiny self-re-vealed by accident–the Omen* through an order of specially trained men—Prophecy, Sooth-saying. Teiresias holds the same place of prophetic emi-nence in tragedy as that held by Calchas in epic. But perhaps the most striking conception of Revelation is that of the Omen, in which Destiny is self-revealed by accident. We have already seen in the trilogy the dread with which the Chorus seek to stop Cassandra from naming Agamem-non as the victim to be murdered, and how later the mere naming of the avenger is sufficient to transform the tone of the finale from despair to triumph ; how again in the *Ion* the chance word of a bystander, spoken too loud, vitiates an act of ceremony and thereby averts a catastrophe. It is only by the strongest effort that we can realise the power of such omens over the sensitively superstitious minds of anti-quity, so fully have we lost all sense of the mysterious properties of words, on which much of magic rested, which kept the Jews from writing the name of Jehovah, and led the Greeks to call the ' Furies' the ' Blessed God-desses': an idea of some mystic bond between a word and the thing it signifies, so that to name a dread event would seem to have already brought it nearer. The verbal omen, however, is only a single one in a class of things, the common point between which is awe of the accidental. The casual flitting to and fro of birds, the exact appearance of the intestines in a newly-slain victim, the fitful play of a sacrificial flame,—all these were eagerly questioned by ancient superstition for signs of events to come. Things governed by law might even in the religion of Destiny be left to the calmer interpretation of reason ; in the domain of chance, there seemed to be the direct control of Destiny itself.

Agamemnon. (2) Dreams: how these act as oracles may be clearly illustrated from Clytæmnestra's dream in the trilogy and the similar play of Sophocles. The dream in this case comes from Agamemnon, who after death is in some measure treated as a deity.

One more point is important for our survey of the dra- CHAP. III
matic motives connected with Destiny. Strange as it may *Destiny*
seem, this Destiny can be set in motion, or even controlled, *set in*
by man. In the 'Erinnyes' and 'Até,' the idea of which so *motion by man:*
permeates Ancient Tragedy, we seem to get objective and *Erinnyes*
subjective conceptions of Destiny as called into operation by *and Até,*
human crime. In the Spell of the Erinnyes they pronounce
themselves an eternal outcome of all-pervading Destiny;
they are the 'registrars of crime,' called into action by home-
bred slaughter. That they have an objective existence is
clear from the description of them as dwelling in thick
darkness, apart from the gods, and sundered from all
comradeship and rejoicing. On the other hand, their mode
of attack—called in one line 'An Até hard to bear'—is
presented as something purely internal and subjective, with
no suggestion of external force: it is a 'chant of madness
frenzy-working,' 'a spell upon the soul withering up the
strength,' a 'frenzy born of guilt' and acting through
ignorance of danger. Where the language approaches
nearest to the idea of violence it still conveys the notion of
a spiritual violence: it is a 'driving up hill' through this
world and the next—suggestive of unresting impulse
to flight or fresh crime, it is a 'crushing force of feet
o'errunning' the victim—the perpetual presence of his
crime from which he can never escape. The whole amounts
to a sort of *haunting* by fate, and such fate-haunting is in
the trilogy extended to an entire household for generation
after generation, the outcome of a single crime. In this
case, Destiny is set in motion by human deeds: it could be
aroused by human will in the Curse, as we see in the *the Curse*
Oedipus at Colonus :—
> Once before
> I breathed these Curses deep upon you both,
> And now I bid them come as my allies. . . .
> These Curses sway thy prayers, thy sovereignty!

The curses on the sons of Oedipus, uttered in this play,

CHAP. III become a part of Destiny itself, and are seen to sway the
fate of their victims in the *Antigone*[1]. Where Destiny comes

Destiny controlled by man to be identified with Deity it is easier to understand the influence upon it of man. Orestes even threatens the oracle
that he will pollute it with his corpse if his prayer is not
heard. But the most remarkable example of humanity controlling Destiny is in an incident of the *Helena*, which shows
that the difficulty of conceiving foresight into futurity without
its implying predestination of the future is a difficulty not
confined to modern theology, but attaching equally to
ancient prophecy. The fugitives are about to ask aid of the
prophetess : before they can appeal to her she comes to
offer help.

> A council of the gods.
> Will this day round the throne of Jove be held
> With no small strife on thee.

She explains what the issues are, and continues :—

> *On me the event depends*, should I inform,
> As Venus wills, thy brother that thou here
> Art present, and destroy; or, taking part
> With Juno, save thy life.

She elects to save them, and from the sequel we are to
suppose that heaven follows the prophetess[2].

Such is Destiny, as reflected in Ancient Tragedy. We
conceive of the Athenians as a people of joy, living in a
brilliant atmosphere, entering with fervour into religious
orgies, weaving an imaginary world out of nature details
etherealised. But all this must be viewed against a sombre
background. They lived and moved and breathed in an
atmosphere of fatalism : reaching beyond the gods, yet
ready to emerge in the most trifling detail of experience ;

[1] *Oedipus at Colonus*, 1375-96.—The Oath seems in a somewhat
similar fashion to pass into a binding Destiny. Its whole ritual is
given in *Medea* (731-758).
[2] Orestes in *Iph. Taur.* 970; *Helena*, 878.

wavering between kind Providence and reckless Fortune ;
the eternal sanction of right, yet wearing at times the form
of human passions ; revealing itself only in delusive mystery ;
set in motion by a human cry, yet once aroused needing
only opposition to draw out its malignant irresistibility.

I pass on to other dramatic motives, which are not *Other*
Dramatic
specially connected with Destiny. A prominent place must *Motives*
be given to the Interest of Horror. The terrors of the *Interest of*
supernatural world were introduced upon the Greek stage : *Horror:*
ghosts frequently appear, Death is a personage in the *Alcestis*,
and in the trilogy even the Furies are brought before the
audience in visible shape. Still more terrible are the
unnatural horrors of the real world. A banquet of human
flesh is the foundation of the tragic legend with which the
Sons of Atreus are connected. Incest and matricide, on
which such great tragedies turn, are a sore trial to the
modern reader ; only it should be remembered that the
remoteness of the mythic stories from ordinary life tends
to neutralise the grossness of such ideas. Madness and
delirium possessed a strong hold on the ancient imagination.
The ravings of Cassandra, and of Phædra in the *Hippolytus*,
besides their importance to the plot, are powerful subjects
for stage lyrics ; while Euripides, usually the great master
of pathos, shows how he can handle the terrible in the drama
in which he uses a moment's madness to transform Hercules
from the deliverer of his children into their destroyer. For
the violent passions Tragedy is the natural field ; and the
types for all time of gloating revenge will be the Clytæmnestra
of Aeschylus, and Medea holding up her slaughtered children
to the father who has slighted her. Even Human Sacrifices *especially,*
Human
can enter into early Tragedy, and the offering of Iphigenia, *Sacrifices,*
besides being vividly pourtrayed in a choral ode of the
Agamemnon, is in thought present throughout the whole
trilogy. Euripides seizes upon this extinct barbarity in order

to found on it a new moral interest: human sacrifices in
his plays take the form of voluntary self-sacrifice, and in no
less than four [1] of his plays a human being voluntarily and
in cold blood gives his life for others.
In the *Iphigenia in Aulis* the sacrifice comes as the
solution to a tangle of fate that has drawn closer and closer
with the movement of the play. The deed had been
secretly planned, and Iphigenia summoned on the pretext
of being wedded to Achilles. At the opening of the play
the father is recalling the summons:—his letter is inter-
cepted by Menelaus. A fierce quarrel rages between the
brother chiefs:—it is interrupted by the announcement that
Iphigenia is on her way. By the shock of this announcement
Menelaus is most unexpectedly brought round, and he will
not allow his cause to be saved by so dread a deed; Agamemnon, still more unexpectedly, is turned in the opposite
direction, and he dares not, once his daughter has been seen
in the camp, rob the army of their sacrifice. When Iphigenia
arrives she is accompanied by her mother, who refuses all
proposals to separate the two; moreover, a chance meeting
with the designated bridegroom reveals the whole deception.
Agamemnon has to face the pleading of his family, and he—
so inclined to relent at the commencement of the play—is
now hard as adamant, while from Achilles comes the unexpected offer of help. Thus perplexed have become the
threads of safety and ruin in the web of the maiden's
destiny, when suddenly the action of the play quickens
(a quickening reflected in the accelerated verse): a tumult
is heard without, the army have got scent of the chance that
they may lose their victim, and are approaching on all sides
the royal tent—in an instant the decision must be made.

---

[1] Besides the plays of *Alcestis* and *Iphigenia in Aulis* there is the
case of Macaria in the *Heraclidæ* (381–627), and Menœceus in the
Phœnissæ (834–1018). Perhaps Polyxena (in *Hecuba*, 100–443) may
be reckoned a fifth case.

Then it is that Iphigenia is suddenly inspired with the CHAP. III
heroic resolution that solves the whole perplexity.

> To be too fond of life
> Becomes not me; not for thyself alone,
> But to all Greece a blessing didst thou bear me.
> Shall thousands, when their country suffers, lift
> Their shields, shall thousands grasp the oar, and dare
> Advancing bravely 'gainst the foe to die
> For Greece? And shall my life, my single life,
> Obstruct all this? . . . I give my life for Greece.
> Slay me, and lay Troy low: my monument
> Shall be its ruins; for my nuptial bliss
> And mother's joys, I take my country's glory!

So, while all others are dissolved in agony, the maiden
herself gives the directions for the ceremony, restraining her
tears lest she mar the perfectness of the rite; she moves to
the place of sacrifice in full lyric state, singing farewell to her
country and hymning the cruel deity to whom she is to be
offered. Allowing none of the attendants to touch her,
she holds out her own throat to the knife:—then, as all
breathless turn aside their eyes, the miracle is wrought
which substitutes a bleeding hind for the human victim,
while the virgin has been snatched away by the virgin
goddess to whom she had given herself, and hidden in
the viewless realms of the gods.

Not less prominent than the Interest of Horror is the *Interest of*
Interest of Splendour. This centres around Apollo, who *Splendour*
deifies brightness in all its forms: physical brightness is his,
and the sun's rays are arrows from his bow; he is the fountain of creative genius and artistic elevation, and of prophecy
—as it were flashes of insight into the future. Apollo is
a figure in various plays, but the drama which most needs
consideration in the present connection is the *Alcestis*. No *Alcestis:*
play of antiquity is so popular with modern readers: I *misreading*
venture to add, none is so much misunderstood. The story *of Ad-*
is read in the light of modern family life—how when a hus- *character*

band obtained from Fate permission to die by substitute, and when no other substitute was forthcoming, the wife gave herself to die for Admetus: and the reader's chief thought is the mean-spiritedness of Admetus in accepting such a sacrifice. But not only is this impression inconsistent with the treatment of Euripides, who exalts Admetus as a man supreme in moral elevation, it further diverts attention from a more beautiful moral that does underlie the play.

The play founded on a Greek sentiment—the worship of bright-ness   The mistakes arise from ignoring this difficult, and eminently Greek, sentiment—the worship of brightness and splendour. It takes many forms: two aspects of it are important for our present purpose. One is the supremacy of youth. Our reverence is for age and its wisdom; we almost apologise for enjoyment, and consider youth a synonym for folly. With the Greeks it was youth and its joys that gave value to life; and for age to claim equality with youth seemed 'unnatural' baseness. This view appears again and again throughout the *Alcestis*. To the personages in the play the question is not of Admetus's accepting a substitute: that they take for granted,—no one thinks of his doing otherwise, except the rightful substitute who is finding a miserable plea for his own cowardice. To them the meanness lies in the fact that the youthful Alcestis is the one allowed to die. The whole point of the terrible episode in which the son reproaches his father with cowardice may be summed up in a single line :—

> Is death alike, then, to the old and young?

In the prologue Death is asked why he does not choose ripe lingering age for his victims: he answers—

> Greater my glory when the youthful die!

And the Chorus—who, it must be remembered, are the embodiment of the impression to be left on the audience—put the whole matter on this footing :—

When, to avert his doom,
His mother in the earth refused to lie ;
Nor would his ancient father die
To save his son from an untimely tomb;
Though the hand of time had spread
Hoar hairs on each agèd head :
In youth's fresh bloom, in beauty's radiant glow,
The darksome way thou daredst to go,
And for thy youthful lord's to give thy life.

Again, a second side to the worship of brightness is the dignity of hospitality. With us hospitality is no more than one of the lighter graces of life ; in antiquity it was one of the loftiest motives, on a par with patriotism, or with the dominant sentiments of special ages, such as chivalry and liberty ; to the Greeks hospitality was a form of worship. Now this religion of hospitality, and the whole worship of brightness, finds in Admetus its supreme type. He is not only a type for his age and for the whole earth, but heaven itself recognises his glory, and Apollo, the very deity of brightness, has chosen Admetus's home in which to abide while on earth ; he still regards Admetus as his dearest friend, and 'holy' is the epithet he applies to him. The Chorus—with their function of keeping prominent the central ideas of the story—are at a crisis of the play reminded, by a fresh act of hospitable reverence coming from Admetus, of the glories that attended Apollo's sojourn with their king: how at the sound of his lyre beasts forgot their fury and flocked round the divine shepherd, the lion looking on while the dappled hinds came from the mountain forests to dance ; how as a consequence plenty flowed in from all sides, and made the splendid domain that stretches unbroken from lake to sea.

This identification of Admetus with the religion of bright- *Identifi-* ness and hospitality is no mere accessory to the story, it is *cation of* made the key to all the action of the drama. The opening *Admetus* situation rests entirely on this foundation : it is Apollo's *with the worship of brightness*

interest in the great pattern of hospitality that has forced

the key to the whole action of the play

the Fates to give way and allow a vicarious death. Similarly, at the turning-point of the plot, the new triumph of hospitable duty and repression of personal grief in the reception of Hercules rouses the Chorus to enthusiasm, and brings the first gleam of hope into the play. And, as a fact, it is the discovery of this hospitable self-sacrifice which inspires Hercules to work the deliverance of Alcestis.

> His hospitable heart
> Received me in his house, nor made excuse,
> Though pierced with such a grief; this he concealed
> Through generous thought and reverence to his friend.
> Who in Thessalia bears a warmer love
> To strangers? Who, through all the realms of Greece?
> It never shall be said this generous man
> Received in me a base and worthless wretch.

Thus the origin, the crisis, and the consummation of the plot are all founded on the splendid hospitality of Admetus[1].

Now what difference will this connection of Admetus with the worship of brightness—if we force ourselves to view it as the Greeks viewed it—make to our sympathies

The play is a contrast of ideals, not of individuals

in the story? It gives just the salt which takes from Admetus's deed the flavour of personal selfishness. Every one must feel what a difference it would make if the sacrifice of Alcestis was undertaken for a cause and not for a man. But to the Greek mind the religion of hospitable splendour is precisely such a cause as is needed. The case then becomes that of a general who must see soldiers interposing between him and danger, or of the Scottish Chieftain, for whom the seven sons of Torquil went as a matter of course to their deaths, winning eternal glory for themselves without disgracing him for whom they died. And yet Euripides is nearer to modern sentiment than this argument

[1] *Alcestis*: prologue and 568, 603.

suggests. As a fact, he alone of ancient writers catches this modern feeling as to the supremacy of love and the family life, and he is anticipating it in this drama. Only it is an essential point in such treatment that Admetus should be exalted, and it adds a fresh beauty to the sacrifice of Alcestis if the husband for whom she gives herself is worthy. It is two causes, not two individuals, that Euripides is contrasting: the simple human emotions of love and bereavement are brought into conflict with a lofty ideal of splendour, and are made to triumph over it in the end.

With this contrast of pathos and splendour for our clue *The move-* we may see the whole movement of the drama fall into *ment of the play* place. Euripides only gradually allows the emotion of *presents the* realism to insinuate itself into the midst of the ideal. At *religion of brightness* the commencement of the play the only thought is of *yielding to* the king's deliverance. Alcestis has arrayed herself in *the religion of love* radiant attire, and, in the spirit of the cult for which she is giving her life, treats as a triumph day the day of her doom, taking stately farewell of each altar in the palace:

> Nor sigh nor tear
> Came from her, neither did the approaching ill
> Change the fresh beauty of her vermeil cheek.

She breaks down at the sight of the marriage chamber, and here first comes in the simplicity of human love. The humble Attendant is the next to display it, and she catches the doubt whether after all Admetus will gain by his exchange.

> So stands it with Admetus. Had he died,
> His woes were over; now he lives to bear
> A weight of pain no moment shall forget.

In the death scene this doubt has seized Admetus himself, and he renounces for ever the brightness to save which Alcestis is dying, and which seems cold beside the attraction

CHAP. III of life-long mourning over her memory. Still stronger is this feeling in the final episode; and when the Chorus bid Admetus remember what he has *gained*, the word grates upon him:

> My friends, I deem the fortune of my wife
> Happier than mine, though otherwise it seems!

Love has won its way to supremacy, and the dramatist may now restore the splendour again, as, by the deliverance which Hercules has worked out, Alcestis is in all her living and breathing beauty unveiled before her husband. Well may the feasts break out again, and the altars be decked more richly than ever before; and well may Admetus say—

> I rise to higher life!

But this is not the rise of the sinner out of his sin: it is the whole religion of brightness rising into the higher religion of love.

To this same heading, the interest of splendour, is to be referred that most startling feature of ancient life—the elevation of self-abandonment and wild revelry into a sacred duty in connection with the worship of Bacchus, and which *The Bac-* is portrayed in Euripides' strangely brilliant play, *The* *chanals* *Bacchanals*. The god himself is a personage in this drama, and Bacchanal women are the Chorus, each bearing the thyrsus, or ivy-clad staff which is the symbol of their faith: at its touch age forgets its weariness and returns to fresh youth, serpents lose their venom and wolves their wildness, streams of pure water flow from the bare rock, and milk out of the earth, while from the ivy-wreath itself drops dulcet honey. The new rite makes its appearance as in triumphal procession through the fairest regions of the earth, and comes to Greece with the air of a Reformation movement. The odes are pitched in the elevated tone of religious ecstasy, celebrating the bliss of the man who has seen into the mysteries of heaven, and the sanctity of mind that links

men with the gods. The plot of the play illustrates, in the CHAP. III
unhappy fate of Pentheus, how those who oppose the ——
worship of the vine are opposing a hidden omnipotence: if
the votaries are imprisoned an earthquake overturns the
prison, chains drop off spontaneous, and a fire breaks out that
men strive to quench in vain; or the Mænads themselves
with supernatural might overturn trees and scatter the limbs
of oxen with their bare hands. And the sacred passion, if
not embraced as a mode of worship, none the less seizes the
impious miscreant in the form of madness, making him rush
with fierce joy to his own destruction. Intoxication idealised into a religion—that is the poetical presentation of the
Bacchanal worship.

Human sentiments and human bonds constitute a per- *Human*
petual interest for all branches of literature. The family tie *Sentiments*
and P° nds:
and its rupture are the basis of several tragedies; perhaps
the most notable is the *Antigone*, which brings the claims of *the family*
the family into conflict with the claims of the state. The *tie,*
heroine has to choose between the decree of Creon and
the obligations of sisterhood: challenged with the question
whether she will not obey the laws she answers by contrasting them with the higher and eternal laws of heaven—

> The unwritten laws of God, that know not change:
> They are not of to-day nor yesterday,
> But live for ever, nor can man assign
> When first they sprang to being.

The same play brings out how, in connection with the worship of ancestors, family attachment extends beyond death:

> Longer lasts the time
> To enjoy the favour of the eternal dead
> Than to please short-lived monarchs.

The suppliant bond is a purely ancient sentiment. The *the*
suppliant's prayer for protection might be rejected by the *suppliant*
bond,
ruler to whom it is addressed, but once the prayer is accepted
the tie between protector and protected is of peculiar

CHAP. III strength, and indeed is placed under the immediate protection of Zeus himself. Three plays are motived by this
relationship of the suppliant to his protector—the *Suppliants*
of Aeschylus and of Euripides, and the latter poet's *Children*
friendship, *of Hercules.* Friendship is chiefly represented in the ideal
attachment of Pylades and Orestes ; this appears conven-
tionally in several plays, and is by Euripides expanded into
a motive, not indeed of a whole play, but of important
episodes in two plays—the incident in the *Orestes* in which
Pylades refuses to quit his friends in their misfortunes, and
the still more beautiful scene in *Iphigenia among the Tauri*,
where the two friends struggle which shall die for the other [1].
celibacy The sentiment of celibacy—purity elevated into a passion—
is the motive of the *Hippolytus*. The story is repulsive, for
it involves a (false) charge of incest. But the purity and
loftiness with which Euripides has treated it are best seen
when his play is compared with the ordinary legend as
embodied, for example, in the tragedy of Seneca. Euripides
from his very prologue rests the whole complication on
miracle. It is by Aphrodité that Phædra is smitten with
unholy love, which she resists to the death, when the
betrayal of her secret brings about the situation that
domestic purity is miraculously plunged into impurity and
thrown into conflict with passionate celibacy. The reaction
from such a situation is a tragic accumulation of woe :
one dies by suicide, the other by a violent, inexorable,
divinely-wrought cruelty, called down on him through the
agency of the being he loves best. When the cloud of error
is dissipated there is left the pure memory to all time of the
unhappy Phædra and Hippolytus, together with the presentation of humanity as on a higher level than the gods,
besides a plea for the simple satisfaction of love in the
purity of family life.

---

[1] *Orestes,* 1069-1245 ; *Iph. Taur.* 578-724.

Again, it is very important, if we seek to analyse the CHAP. III
perspective of plays and understand the relative proportion *The Ideali-*
of their parts, to remember that the Idealisation of Life is *sation of*
a constant motive in ancient drama, side by side with the *Life,*
more distinctly dramatic interests of character and plot.
The size of the ancient stage gave scope for the display of
religious, military, and civil pomp on the grandest scale.
Within the limits of Aeschylus's trilogy we have seen the
ceremonial rites of Clytæmnestra's thanksgiving for triumph,
the pageant of the return from Troy, the sudden apparition
of Aegisthus's bodyguard pouring out of their hiding-places,
the ritual of the sepulchre that gives its name to the second
play of the three, the majestic procedure of the Court of
Areopagus sitting under divine presidency, the torchlight
festival of the Eumenidea—all successively filling the stage
and appealing to the sense of spectacle. On the other hand,
it is equally a purpose with the masters of Tragedy to cast
a poetic glow over the lesser things of life. In the *Hippolytus*
we have a hunting chorus, there is a scene of sick-bed
watching in *Orestes* transacted in lyrics, and in the *Iphigenia
among the Tauri* a sudden attack of illness presented in blank
verse. Even washing-day can be glorified.

> There is a rock from whose deep base
>   Fountains distilled from ocean flow,
> And from the ridge we drop the vase
>   To catch the wave below :
> A friend I have, who thither brought
> Her vests, of radiant purple wrought,
>   To bathe them in the crystal dews,
>   Then on the rock's warm face their hues
> Spread to the sun's fair rays [1].

Under this head may be cited the beauties of landscape, *and*
which in later plays [2] entered partly into the scenery of the *external*
Nature

---

[1] *Hippolytus,* 62 ; *Orestes,* 140; *Iph. Taur.* 281; *Hippolytus,* 121.
So bleaching (*Helena,* 179), and wool work (*Iph. Taur.* 222, 814).
[2] E.g. *Daughters of Troy* : compare final ode and conclusion.

CHAP. III stage, in other cases are celebrated in description. The
Nature Odes have been reviewed in a previous section.
Among the passing bits of nature-painting none is more
famous than the appeal of Prometheus to the elements when
he is cast out by the gods.

> Brightness divine of heaven, swift-winged winds,
> Ye river-wells, and ocean's wavy face
> Restless with countless-rippling smiles of light:
> O Earth that hast borne all, and thee I call,
> Thou Sun, whose eye doth ever all command.

The sacred haunts of deity would specially call out the imagination of a poet, like the spot on which the weary Oedipus
rests, full of laurel, olive, vine, and singing nightingales, or
the voiceless grass-grown grove of the Furies—

> Where blends with rivulet of honeyed stream
>   The cup of water clear.

More elaborate is the description of the meadow sacred to
Artemis:

> The unshorn mead, where never shepherd dared
> To feed his flock, and the scythe never came,
> But o'er its vernal sweets unshorn the bee
> Ranges at will, and hushed in reverence glides
> Th' irriguous streamlet: garish art hath there
> No place.

The terrible in nature is painted, as well as its fairness.

> As a wave
> Of ocean's billowing surge
> (Where Thrakian storm-winds rave,
> And floods of darkness from the depths emerge,)
> Rolls the black sand from out the lowest deep,
> And shores re-echoing wail, as rough blasts o'er them sweep.

Or again the Chorus in *Iphigenia*, detained in Taurica while
their leader is delivered, delight to picture the journey home ;
earlier in the play their imagination has been fired by the
voyage of the newly arrived strangers, whose bark has been
now threading dangerous passages, now ploughing its way

past bird-haunted cliffs, with whispering zephyrs swelling its Chap. III
sails or southern gales piping through its tackling, while ——
beneath the ringed Nereids were weaving the light dance in
the high-arched caves of the sea [1].

Another motive in ancient dramatic poetry will be easily *Prose*
distinguishable when it is recollected that, at so early a point *Topics :*
in literary development, poetry has in great part to do the
work of prose. In all literatures poetry is at the outset the
sole medium of expression; with the advance of scientific
thought a second medium is elaborated, but the transference
of topics from poetry to prose is only gradual. Before the
end of ancient Tragedy the prose literature of Greece was
in full course; but in the earlier days of Aeschylus it is quite
clear that, for example, the topic of geography had not *geography,*
passed outside the range of poetry, and that it was not
inconsistent with tragic interest to enlarge on geographical
detail. It is true that to all poetry belongs the beauty of
enumeration, by which a poet like Milton can impart
a charm. even to a list of proper names : and this might
explain such a passage as the chain of beacons in *Agamem-*
non. But the episode of Io in *Prometheus* is expanded out
of all proportion to its dramatic bearing, clearly because of
the interest felt in her wanderings as suggesting the migra-
tions of the Ionic race. A similar argument applies to *mythology,*
mythological interest in Tragedy. It is true that myth is
the raw material of tragic plot. But in prologues like that
of the *Eumenides,* or those of Euripides generally, mythological discussion is expanded to an extent suggestive of
scientific rather than dramatic interest. Again, the national *politics*
character of tragic celebrations made politics a theme on
which it was always possible to enlarge. The glorification
of Athens is a visible motive in the *Oedipus at Colonus* and
the *Ion* ; and in *Medea* the mere mechanical necessity of

[1] *Prometheus,* 88 ; *Oedipus at Colonus,* 16, 157 ; *Hippolytus,* 73 ;
Antigone, 586 ; *Iph. Taur.* 1123, 399.

CHAP. III finding some refuge for the murderess expands into the episode of Aegeus the Athenian, and the subsequent ode to Athens. Burning questions of the hour find their representation in Tragedy, such as the plea for the Court of Areopagus in the trilogy, and the bitter attack on Sparta in *Andromache*. Even the general division of parties between Aristocracy and Democracy makes itself felt from time to time. In the *Suppliants* of Euripides a scene is devoted to a set contest between the Herald from monarchical Thebes and the leader of a free state. The Herald pours official scorn on popular institutions :

> Shall they who lack the skill
> To form their speech have skill to form the state?

Theseus in his reply puts the very essence of the democratic ideal :—personal liberty, freedom of speech, land nationalisation.

> The weak, the rich, have here one equal right,
> And penury with justice on its side
> Triumphs o'er riches ; this is to be free.
> Is there a mind that teems with noble thought
> And useful to the state? He speaks his thought,
> And is illustrious. When a people, free,
> Are sovereigns of their land, the state stands firm [1].

Social Topics, especially woman

One more dramatic motive may be mentioned : that of social topics, especially woman. Shakespeare's ' merry war ' of the sexes has become a very bitter war in the poetry of Euripides. At the same time I must confess to a feeling of amazement that so many distinguished commentators can *Euripides no woman-hater* accept the tradition that Euripides is a woman-hater. It is true that as much bitterness on this topic can be collected from the pages of Euripides as from any other writer. In particular, every one is familiar with the declamation of

---

[1] *Medea*, 663-865 ; *Andromache*, 445; *Suppliants* (of Euripides), 399-464. Compare the exaltation of the agricultural as contrasted with the city life ; *Orestes*, 902-922.

Hippolytus[1], in which he reproaches heaven for placing
beneath the fair sun the specious evil, woman—a thing that
the very father who begat her gives large dowry to be rid of,
while the deluded husband receives her as a plague that
must infect his household, unless her reason is too weak to
frame a plot, or unless she could associate only with dumb
animals so that neither could corrupt the other. He longs
for a world in which the human race might multiply
without the aid of woman ; otherwise, happiest he whose
bride—

> Inactive through simplicity, and mild,
> To his abode is like a statue fixed.

But it is obvious that in dramatic literature words must be
interpreted in the light of the person who speaks them ; and
all this rhodomontade only proves that the poet is capable
of painting misogyny—in this case a marked and blatant
misogyny that brings Hippolytus to a violent end. It
is perhaps more remarkable that in the *Medea*[2] sentiments
as strong are put into the mouth of a woman. But here
again it may be urged that, as a fact, pessimism exists
among women as among men, and an artist may be drawn
to its portrayal, not at all by sympathy with the sentiment,
but just because he takes woman seriously, and chafes at
narrowing conventions and low social standards. To judge
fairly a dramatist's conception of woman it is necessary, not
only to note the expressions of opinion he attributes to his
imaginary speakers, but still more to see what sort of women
he has himself created. Tried by this test will Euripides
yield to any poet in the elevation to which he has raised the
standard of female excellence? It is a significant fact that
of the four personages who in this writer's plays give their
lives for others, three are women. The sex may easily forgive
Euripides the hard sayings about them of which he has acted
as reporter, in consideration of the additions he has himself

---

[1] *Hippolytus*, 616.　　　　　　　[2] *Medea*, 406.

CHAP. III made to the world's worthy women—in consideration of his
Iphigenia, his Macaria, his Polyxena, above all his perfect
wife and mother, Alcestis.

4 The Dramatic Element in Ancient Tragedy

The Chorus and the Theatre the determining forces in Ancient Tragedy   The lyric element in Ancient Tragedy, and the general
matter which inspired it, have been reviewed : in the present
section we confine ourselves to Tragedy considered as
drama. The forces which determined Ancient Tragedy as
a branch of the universal drama were chiefly two :—the
Chorus, and the Theatre. It will be convenient briefly to
indicate what effect each of these had in conditioning
Tragedy as a literary species, and then to survey the dramatic
features of the literature so conditioned.

Function of the Chorus to embody the unity   The Chorus had a direct and most important influence :
it was the great unity bond in Ancient Tragedy. Not only
was the Chorus the common point between the lyric and
dramatic elements, it was further the agency for binding together the details of a play into that singleness of impression
which constitutes 'unity' in a work of art. This Chorus,
on the one hand, stands regularly for the ideal spectator ; on
the other hand it has its sympathies in regard to the course
of incidents definitely assigned to it by its characterisation,
whether as confidants of the hero or otherwise: this double
relation to the audience and the personages represented
makes the Chorus an arrangement for embodying in the
drama itself the general impression of the whole, or 'unity.'
Further, as the Chorus never quits the scene [1], it is provided,
negatively, that no part of the action shall be outside the
unity ; and as everything is addressed to the Chorus, and
the Chorus is expected to comment on it, it is provided,
positively, that the sense of unity shall be brought to bear

---

[1] Apparent exceptions will be found (below, page 185) to confirm the
principle.

upon every detail. The Chorus is complete machinery for CHAP. III
at once representing and securing the unity of an ancient ———
play ; and in this respect there is nothing to compare with
the Chorus in any other branch of drama.

The unity so secured to Greek Tragedy is of a kind much *The Three*
stricter than that which exists in other species of drama : it *Unities :*
has been expressed in the famous critical principles known
as the ' Three Unities.' The first is the Unity of Action. *Unity of*
As a term of the universal drama this means no more than *Action,*
the subordination of details to the impression of the whole :
when used of Greek Tragedy the Unity of Action amounts
to a *oneness* of story, as distinguished from the harmony of
different stories which constitutes the unity of most Shakespearean dramas. In *The Merchant of Venice* we have.
(besides underplots) two tales already familiar in earlier
literature, the Story of the Cruel Jew and the Story of the
Caskets, borrowed from different sources and combined
into a single plot. Greek Drama was confined to a single
story : to have introduced more than one hero would, to a
Greek mind, have involved more than one Chorus. The
oneness is carried to the extent of presenting the matter
entirely from the side on which are the sympathies of the
Chorus. If Shakespeare has to develop the story of Shylock
he will, besides taking us into the confidence of Shylock
himself, give us some scenes which we view from the side of
Shylock's enemy Antonio ; in others we hear how Tubal and
the Jews, or how Gratiano and the gossips of Venice, look
at the matter. The ancient tragedian introduced no scenes
but such as could happen in the presence of the Chorus.
Thus for the tragedies of the Greek stage Unity of Action
implies a single story presented from a single point of
view.

The other two unities relate to changes of scene. In an *Unity of*
Elizabethan drama there may be as many as fifty changes *Place and*
of scene, the stage being varied backwards and forwards to *Unity of*
Time

CHAP. III represent some eight or ten different places; between successive scenes long intervals of time may be supposed to elapse, that between the fourth and fifth acts of *The Winter's Tale*, for example, being sufficient to admit of Perdita's growing up from a baby into a marriageable girl. In the Greek drama, on the contrary, the Unity of Place and the Unity of Time imply the arrangement of the story so that only those incidents are selected for acting which may be represented as happening in one single place at one single time: any other necessary incidents must be narrated, or made known by some means other than that of acting [1]. For these two principles the Chorus is mainly responsible. The fact that it remained in the orchestra during the interval between one episode and another made a whole tragedy one continuous scene, without any breaks such as could be utilised for changes of place and time. The combined effect of the two principles may be expressed by a single term—Scenic Unity.

The Three Unities, then, are critical features of Ancient Tragedy arising out of its connection with the Chorus. In conformity with the first of these principles the matter

---

[1] There are various devices for dealing with incidents that are outside these unities. (1) They can be narrated in Choral Odes, or (2) in the 'Messenger's Speech.' (3) Interiors can be suddenly disclosed by the Roller-Stage (an example in *Agamemnon*, above, page 40). In many cases it is doubtful whether this was used, or whether the opening of the Central Gates was not sufficient. (4) There are some special and highly dramatic devices: Cassandra's clairvoyance (in the trilogy) paints in vision the scene actually going on inside the palace; similarly in *Hercules* (above, page 91), the apparition of Madness paints beforehand the effect she is going to produce behind the scenes. (5) Compressions of time in the course of a play come to almost the same as intervals between scenes. The return of the army in *Agamemnon* could not in actual life have happened till many days after the reception of the telegraphic message by means of the beacons. In the *Suppliants* of Euripides an expedition, a battle, and a triumphant return take place in the interval covered by a single choral ode (598–633).

included in a tragedy was confined to a single story, and by CHAP. III
the operation of the other two this story was, in representation, further cut down to its crisis.

The influence on Ancient Tragedy of the Theatre and *The*
theatrical representation* rests mainly on the fact that *Theatre as*
a deter-

---

* On this subject the student must distinguish between what is essential for following the drama and its development, and that which has
only an antiquarian interest. The following note sums up the salient
points: see also note at end of preface.

1. The Theatre was open, and large enough to contain the whole
population of a city. The Stage and Scene were ultimately of stone :
but there is some doubt how early this was substituted for the primitive
wooden structure. This permanent Scene represented an elaborate
façade of a palace, in which there was a Central and Inferior doors;
the whole could however be concealed behind Moveable Scenery. The
Stage was a narrow platform running the whole length of the Scene :
of the two entrances at each end the one on the spectators' left indicated an entrance from a distance, the other an entrance from the
immediate neighbourhood. Considerably lower than the Stage [see
note on page xv] was the huge Orchestra, with the Altar of Dionysus
(*Thymele*) in the centre, and two Entrances (*Parodi*), as with the Stage.
A flight of steps connected the Stage and Orchestra, and was continued
out of sight in the 'Steps of Charon,' used for ghosts and apparitions
from the underworld. There was very little machinery. Turn-scenes
(*Periacti*) were prism-shaped side-scenes fixed at both ends of the Stage,
and turning on a pivot to produce the (rare) changes of scene. The
Roller-Stage (*Eccyclema*) was a contrivance by which an interior scene
could be rolled out from the Central Door to the front of the stage. To
these add the *Machina*, which has given rise to the proverbial *Deus ex
machina*,—a crane-like contrivance for swinging out a deity, who would
thus appear in mid air.

2. The number of Actors was confined to two, later to three [called
Protagonist, Deuteragonist, Tritagonist], and in a few plays there is an
appearance of a fourth. But this merely means that there could not be
more than that number of speaking personages on the stage together at
any one time. Each of the Actors would take several different parts in
different scenes ; and the number of mute personages on the stage was
unlimited.

3. The Costume maintained a Bacchic brilliance and dignity of proportions, especially the Buskin (*Cothurnus*), a thick shoe for increasing
the height of the actor, and which has become a synonym for Tragedy.
The costume included Masks for the Actors and Chorus : the latter of

CHAP. III   Tragedy never ceased to be a solemn religious and national
mining   festival, celebrated in a building which was regarded as the
force in   temple of Dionysus, whose altar was the most prominent
Ancient   object in the orchestra, and in presence of what may fairly
Tragedy :   be described as the whole 'public' of Athens and Attica.
Such surroundings, in the first place, gave encouragement
spectacular   to spectacular display.   I have before noticed the grand
display,   pageants with which Aeschylus fills his stage ; Euripides in
some of his plays—notably in the *Daughters of Troy*—has left
great scope for mise-en-scène, which in his time no doubt
advanced with the general advance in the art of painting.
One effect flowing from the religious associations of Tragedy
limitation   was limitation of subject-matter, which was confined to the
of subject-   sacred myths, progress towards real life being slow.   Surprise
matter,   as a dramatic effect was eliminated where all knew the end
of the story.   On the other hand, great scope was given for
irony,   Irony—ignorance of the sequel on the part of the personages
represented clashing with knowledge of it on the part of the
audience.   A third point to note is that the use of masks
would be a great limit on individuality, tending to make the
personages of an ancient play fall into classes and types.
conven-   But the general influence of representation in Ancient
tionality   Tragedy may be best summed up in the word 'conven-

course never wore the buskin.   These Masks were not individual, but
indicated types, such as a king, a priest, a slave, a young man, an old
woman, &c.
    4. The Delivery was conventional, not realistic.   Choral Odes and
Stage Lyrics were sung, Blank Verse was declaimed ;   and there
was an intermediate 'recitative' (*paracataloge*) about which little is
known.
    5. The mode of bringing out tragedies assisted to maintain the
spectacular character of the whole performance.   This was by *Choregi,*
or Chorus-providers, wealthy Athenians to whom the lot assigned the
duty of providing the magistrates with the expenses of so many Choruses.
The magistrates then assigned these to the poets who made application.
With the Chorus went other expenses of a dramatic exhibition.   There
was much competition in display between these Choregi.

tionality.' This and the antithetical term, 'realism,' are the two poles of dramatic effect, all acting having reference to both and varying between the two : the latter aims directly at the imitation of life, conventionality is for ever falling into recognised positions of beauty. Not only did the ancient drama lean to the conventional, but the conception of beauty underlying it was different from the spirited movement and picturesque situations of the modern stage, and approached nearer to the foremost art of antiquity—statuary. The acting of an ancient scene is best regarded as a passage from one piece of statuesque grouping to another, in which motion is reduced to a minimum and positions of rest expanded to a maximum :—a view which accounts for the great length of speeches in Greek drama. The episodes of Ancient Tragedy were displays of animated statuary, just as the choral odes were feats of expressive dancing; and the total performance laid down the lines of conventional acting for the universal drama.

We have now to survey the general dramatic charac- *Plot in* teristics of Ancient Tragedy, thus moulded by its connection *Ancient Tragedy* with the Chorus, and by its theatrical surroundings. Our main concern will be with that reduction of human experience to artistic form which is called plot : as a painter applies design to colours, as a musician brings sounds and rhythms into order and harmony, so a dramatist is an artist in human life, who can discover a pattern in a course of events or a combination of human relationships. There are two varieties of plot. In the first the interest lies in the accumulation of passion which is brought about in some part of the story as it progresses ; in the other variety the impression of form is given mainly by the progress and movement of the story itself. I shall consider separately these Plots of Passion and Plots of Action [1].

[1] This fundamental distinction has in modern drama come to be expressed by the misleading terms ' Tragedy ' and ' Comedy.' These

K

In Plots of Passion we may distinguish four forms of dramatic movement, which however differ very little from one another: all turn mainly upon a situation or situations, on which the dramatist concentrates attention, and in which he elaborates and accumulates a display of passion. A plot of the first form consists in an Opening Situation developed to a Climax. In the *Agamemnon* Aeschylus elaborates and emphasises the opening situation, working upon our awe by its strange mingling of triumph and foreboding. The Watchman has scarcely shouted the signal of the beacon when 'the weight of an ox upon his tongue' checks his rejoicings. Then the Chorus-Entry—so elaborate in itself, and performed against a background of mysterious ritual on the stage—is one long swaying between anxiety and faith in Zeus the Accomplisher. And this doubleness of impression is continued and carried forward by each subsequent phase of the movement. When the Queen explains her ritual as a sacrifice of triumph she qualifies her confidence with an *if.* The Chorus, in their ode of victory, by so naturally turning their thoughts to the price of victory—the bloodshed which comes back in a curse—fall again into

terms were naturally used in Greek literature, where the distinction they imply between sombre and amusing tones described two wholly separate forms of literature. But seeing that a main feature of Romantic Drama is the 'mixture of tones,' or continual interchange between grave and gay in the same drama and even in the same scene, the continued use of 'Tragedy' and 'Comedy' is most awkward, and is a relic of the discarded critical temperament which applied to all literature the single standpoint of the Ancient Classical literatures. Every one feels the absurdity of calling *Measure for Measure* or *The Merchant of Venice* a comedy, and it is difficult to describe as tragedies plays so full of comic matter as *Lear* and *Othello*. I have elsewhere (*Shakespeare as a Dramatic Artist*, page 323) suggested the terms 'Passion-Drama' and 'Action-Drama.' In action-dramas like *The Merchant of Venice* the unity of the whole play lies in entanglement and solution. In passion-dramas (tragedies) there is no restoration of happiness after the distraction of the plot, but the emotion of agitation is relieved only by the emotion of pathos or despair.

doubt. The Herald who enters with the crown of triumph Chap. III
on his head stumbles, in giving his news, upon the unhappy
omen of Menelaus; and the ode which takes Paris's crime
as a text for infatuation introduces a scene in which infatuation is fastened upon Agamemnon. So the distraction of
the opening situation has been continually developing until
the climax, when from the cloud of Cassandra's mistaken
prophecy breaks the clear light which brings a terrible
harmony to resolve the discord, and displays Agamemnon's
triumph-sacrifice selected as the sweet moment for vengeance on his forgotten crime[1].

The second form differs very little from the first. In it **II** *Develop-ment of a Final Situation* the situation on which attention is to be fastened has to be
produced in the play itself: such a plot may be described
as the Development of a Final Situation. In the *Oedipus
as King* the opening situation is not one that rests upon an
accomplished fact, but is a situation of expectancy pointing
to the future: the safety of the state depends upon discovering the murderer of Laius. With each scene the
investigation advances, not without perplexity, and with
alternate fear and hope for the hero. Three fourths of the
poem is exhausted before the discovery is accomplished.

> Woe! woe! woe! woe! all cometh clear at last!
> O light, may this my last glance be on thee,
> Who now am seen owing my birth to those
> To whom I ought not, and with whom I ought not
> In wedlock living, whom I ought not slaying.

---

[1] Another clear example will be the *Prometheus*. Our attention is
arrested by the opening situation—the agents of the gods nailing
Prometheus to the mountain as a rebel against Zeus. There is
throughout no change in the situation so opened: but subsequent
scenes develop its different elements—Prometheus's work for mankind,
his resistance to omnipotence, his insight into future doom both for the
strong (Zeus) and the weak (Io), the effect of his passion on beholders
(Ocean and the Chorus). Then, as the climax, fresh tortures descend
in the storm and tempest with which the play concludes.

CHAP. III This makes the final situation which dramatic and lyric effects unite to elaborate, displaying the self-blinding of Oedipus, the self-slaughter of Jocasta, the king driven forth as pollution from his state, and, as acutest woe of all, his separation from his children[1].

The two remaining varieties of passion-drama differ from the preceding in the fact that they involve two situations of equal prominence, the plot lying in the development from the one to the other. The distinction between these two is slight: in the first there is Development from one Situation to another, in the other an Opening Situation is developed to its Reversal. What distinction there is cannot be better illustrated than by comparing the way in which the story of Electra is handled by Aeschylus and by Sophocles. Both dramatists agree in making the misery of Electra the opening situation upon which attention is concentrated. Emphasis is given to this in the *Sepulchral Rites* by the chorus-entry and following episode, in which Electra is displayed as forlorn and deserted, chief of her mother's slaves, and driven to offer sacrifice against her own cause: a strong interest of irony being cast over the whole scene by the fact that it is overheard by the avenger who, as shown by the prologue[2], is already secretly at hand. From the moment that Orestes makes himself known the movement of the plot begins: the ritual at the tomb is turned

III
Develop-
ment from
one Situa-
tion to
another

---

[1] The *Medea* is another example of a plot in which all is working towards a final situation. Medea's purpose is at first but dimly conceived; it grows clearer and clearer, and wins the victory over her maternal tenderness; incentives multiply in successive scenes and difficulties vanish [compare the incident of Aegeus]: finally, in the messenger's speech and finale the ghastly deed is fully displayed, and crowned with the miraculous escape in the chariot of air.

[2] It often happens in Ancient Tragedy that the chorus-entry is the real opening situation from which development starts: the prologue (though of course earlier in time) belongs by dramatic connection to the subsequent plot, the starting point of which is thrown into the prologue to secure absence of the Chorus. [See below, page 184.]

against those who devised it, and the intrigue is set on foot CHAP. III
against the life of the two tyrants, and developed through
scene after scene to complete victory. Yet even at its
height the victory is transformed into ruin, as the visitation
of madness comes down upon Orestes even while he is
appealing to heaven to witness his innocence. This madness makes the final situation, and the misery of Orestes at
the end of the play balances the misery of Electra at the
beginning. In the version of Sophocles also the unhappy   IV
condition of Electra is set forth, and both lyric and dramatic *An Opening Situa-*
devices are employed to elaborate this opening situation, *tion devel-*
which culminates in the altercation between the heroine and *oped to its
Reversal*
the sister who has yielded to the pressure of unhappy
circumstances. The development of the plot commences
with the first gleam of hope in the mention of the queen's
evil dream, and amid fluctuations of emotion (which will
be traced in a future chapter) the recognition of brother and
sister is brought about, and the intrigue against Clytæmnestra and Aegisthus is carried forward. But in this case
the intrigue is crowned with a triumph in which there is
no discordant note : the misery of Electra is converted into
happiness, and the opening situation has been developed to
its reversal.

Examples may be multiplied. The *Ajax* is a striking
illustration of the third form of movement. The early part
of the play is a succession of scenes displaying Ajax in his
madness. Development begins where the opened tent displays to the Chorus the hero now restored to his senses,
and incident following incident carries him on to the
achievement of his fatal purpose. With the suicide of Ajax
the final situation commences and is elaborated through
more than five hundred lines, bringing out the accumulation of tragic emotions which gather around such a death.
There is the discovery of the corpse, the piteous lamentations, the ruin to wife, child, family, and followers ; with

CHAP. III the appearance of Menelaus is added the contest over the
body which threatens to carry enmity beyond the grave,
calls out the heroism of Teucrus, and, as Teucrus bitterly
remarks, shows the short credit of dead greatness when an
Agamemnon can insult the memory of an Ajax. As a final
and strangely mixed emotion, it is the same Odysseus in
antagonism against whom Ajax had lost his reason that now
by his calm moderation secures for his rival the melancholy
honours of burial. It is this form of plot—development
from an initial to a final situation, from Ajax mad to Ajax
dead—that accounts for the otherwise strange arrangement
by which one third of the whole play follows the death of
the hero.

Similarly, the *Antigone* is a clear example of a plot in
which an opening situation is developed to its reversal.
The chorus-entry in this play is an ode of victory,—a
victory so great that, as the subsequent episode shows, it
encourages insults to the corpse of the vanquished. The
movement commences as the tender affection of the sister
towards her fallen brother sets itself against the haughty
power of the state, and it is developed step by step until in
the end four tragedies meet, and the heroine herself, the
king's son, the queen, and the king himself are all plunged
in one common ruin.

Plots of Action

v

Complica-tion and Resolution

Ion

I pass on to the Plots of Action, which rest not so much
upon the power of individual situations as on the form
taken by the general course of the story. Of these the
most prominent type is that which consists in Complication and Resolution: a train of interest is conducted
through entanglement to clearness—the embarrassments in
which it is involved being a necessary preliminary to the
final satisfaction of unloosening and restoration. The *Ion*
of Euripides is a beautiful illustration. This story goes
back to the mythic remoteness of time when the gods
ranged the earth and mingled with the daughters of men.

Apollo has thus had a secret amour with a noble Athenian maiden; and their offspring, Ion, cast out to save his mother's good name, has been preserved by the care of the god, and conveyed a foundling to the great temple of Apollo at Delphi. The opening of the play is all serenity: in lyric monody the youthful priest appears absorbed in the rapturous service of the temple; he glories in the obscurity that hangs over his birth, and, freeing him from human ties, has dedicated him wholly to the god. The complication begins as, amid the crowd of worshippers, his own mother stands before Ion, unrecognising and unrecognised; she has been brought to the temple by the Athenian husband to whom she is now married, and who has entered the oracle to enquire what hope there is of escape from his long fate of childlessness. A strange attraction draws Ion and Creusa into mutual confidences; they exchange stories, and as the wrongs of Creusa are told, Ion for the first time feels his simple faith in Apollo disturbed by doubts. Meanwhile Xuthus has been bidden by the oracle to ac-knowledge for his son the first man he should meet: this is Ion, and Xuthus gladly accepts him, and the feast of installation is arranged for the same day. But Creusa, disdaining this substitution of a stranger for a son, thinks bitterly of the different measure dealt out to her husband and to herself by the god—how Xuthus has obtained at once all he asked, while, when she herself had given all to Apollo, he had allowed their infant child to be torn by vultures, carelessly attuning his harp amid the gods to songs of joy. An evil counsellor works upon her in this bitter mood, and she resolves upon taking the life of Ion ere he can come as heir to their home. An elaborate description is given by a messenger of the scene to which I have in an earlier section drawn attention: how the poi-soned goblet is in the hands of Ion when a chance word of ill omen disturbs the libation, and a flock of doves drinking the wine thus cast away reveal the attempt to kill. A hue and cry is raised, and Creusa is seized by Ion himself and dragged to the place of death. The entanglement of the complication is now at its height: Ion himself has been all but murdered by his own mother, and his zeal for Apollo has been wholly eclipsed by sceptical questionings; Xuthus has all but lost the heir that day given him, and lost him by the hands of his own wife; the mother is just about to perish for an attempt on the life of the child she mourns as dead. At this very point the resolution comes to disentangle the complication at a stroke. The priestess of the temple, foster-mother to Ion, meets the procession hurrying to the traitors' rock, and seeks to turn Ion to gentler thoughts by handing him the memorials of his birth—the casket containing the linen clothes with which as an infant he had been wrapped, and which in his new home of Athens may be a means of discovering friends. Creusa from the verge of death sees hope: she recognises the casket, and describes the memorials before it is opened. By this recognition the whole situation is reversed, and all is restored to peace: the son and mother are united, Xuthus finds an heir in his wife's divinely born son, and the god, instead of appearing as a careless sporter with human frailty, is now seen to be a Providence that by the smallest accidents can guide events to great issues.

Such interchange of complication and resolution is the standard form of dramatic action for modern plays, where these are not distinctly tragedies; it is one of the many points in which Euripides is the anticipator of the modern drama. But in Ancient Tragedy an extension of this form appears in a kind of plot not familiar to the modern stage, in which the resolution is not the termination of the play, but is itself re-resolved into a new complication. I have already had occasion to sketch a play which illustrates this—the *Iphigenia among the Tauri*. In this plot the long-drawn

.omplication brings a sister—unwilling priestess of cruel CHAP. III
\rtemis—to the very verge of offering her own brother
n sacrifice; an accident discovering the identity resolves
his complication, and the resolution takes the form of a
)rotracted intrigue for escape; this intrigue progresses with
success that makes the schemers light-hearted, until they
an even press the king their enemy into their service, and
)ffer their hands to be bound in ironical security. The
listinguishing feature of the plot comes when the escape is
ctually accomplished and the ship is out of reach: I have
)ointed out how, by a pure stroke of ill-fortune, the wind
hen changes, and amid struggle and excitement forces the
ugitives back into the hands of their foes. The resolution
s hopelessly complicated again, and for issue from this strait
he dramatist has to fall back upon miracle, and the interven-
ion of the omnipotent gods.

This passage from complication to resolution and back
gain to complication may be described as a Plot of Fortune-
Turns. It rests upon the conception of Destiny as blind
'ortune, overthrowing without design or motive the finest-
lrawn schemes:—indeed, the more breathlessly interesting
he issue that is changed, the more impressive is the heedless
rresistibility of Fortune. It is to be noted, however, that a *Pendulum*
imilar form extends outside Destiny to the sway of events *Plot*
within the region of human will: here also the attraction is
elt of the Pendulum Action—the swinging backwards and
)rwards in the drift of events. The most striking illustration
f this occurs, not in Euripides, but in a play of Sophocles
elonging to a period when he may well have felt the influ-
nce of Euripides. The *Philoctetes* is a masterpiece of plot. *Philoctetes*
iewed as a whole it has the highest moral interest: a
rofound intrigue is encountered by simple trust which com-
letely shatters it. In detail the play exhibits a constant
iterchange of complication and resolution. Two oracles
nite in forecasting the fall of Troy: it can be taken only by

the son of Achilles ; it must fall by the miraculous arrows of
Philoctetes, of which the aim means certain death.   But this
Philoctetes is a man bitterly injured by the chieftains of the
besieging army ; he had sailed with them as one of their
comrades, and, when smitten through a viper's bite with a
foul and loathsome disease, had been abandoned in the
desolate island of Lemnos.   At the opening of the play
*action
advancing* Odysseus—mythic master of all guile—has brought the
youthful son of Achilles to Lemnos, and is heard distilling
into his unwilling ear the fraud by which he is to gain
possession of the archer and his arrows.   Neoptolemus is to
commence the plot which Odysseus will supplement : as
unknown in person to Philoctetes he is to encounter him by
apparent accident, and to win his confidence by simulating
injuries received from the sons of Atreus, and still more from
Odysseus, chief object of the sufferer's wrath.   In regular
and interesting stages this intrigue is worked out : the lonely
Philoctetes is seen in his misery, the sympathy of Neoptolemus and the Chorus his followers wins the hero's trust,
and the two make common cause against the Greek chieftains and agree to sail to their homes together.   Here a new
impetus is given to the plot by the finesse of Odysseus, who
sends an attendant affecting to be a messenger of warning,
with news that Odysseus and his colleagues are about to
seize Neoptolemus and Philoctetes, and force them to take
part in the capture of Troy :—surely never did intrigue sail
nearer to the wind than when Odysseus thus announces
clearly his secret scheme as a means of hastening its
accomplishment.   The trick succeeds, and Philoctetes is
for sailing without delay.   The very crisis of the intrigue is
reached as Neoptolemus, now on terms of comradeship with
Philoctetes, approaches cautiously the object of his anxious
hope, the far-famed bow :

> And may I have a nearer view of it,
> And hold it, and salute it, as a God?

Not only does Philoctetes promise this, but, by strange
irony of fate, is visited suddenly by an attack of his
hideous disease, and himself places the miraculous weapons
in the hands of Neoptolemus, that they may not be lost
while the sufferer is helpless.   Then he falls back in agony,
followed by heavy torpor : the Chorus wavering between
slumber-spells sung over the unconscious Philoctetes, and
whispered appeals to their leader to seize the moment and
bear off the bow.   For nine hundred lines the intrigue has
been making unbroken progress : now the turn in the
action begins.   When Philoctetes wakes in peace, and is *action reversed*
overpowered with gratitude to the new comrade who has
not, like all others, deserted him in his affliction, the pure
heart of Neoptolemus is touched : he confesses the whole
plot, and seems to be casting all the gains of the intrigue
away when the torrent of reproaches and picture of the
sufferer's helplessness bring him to the verge of yielding.
But the original course of the story is suddenly restored *action advancing*
as Odysseus springs from behind a rock : he daunts the
youthful Neoptolemus with the authority of the Greek
hosts, nay with the authority of Zeus himself, since the
oracles seem to give the sanction of heaven to the task 'of
bringing the miraculous arrows to Troy.   So firmly established does the intrigue appear by this intervention that
Philoctetes in despair is casting himself from the rock,
when he is seized and bound ; and the success of Odysseus
seems to attain yet a further stage when he changes his
mind and bids unbind the archer—they can do without
him now they have obtained his arrows.   But at this *action reversed*
height of success the intrigue is dashed to the ground :
the reproaches have worked upon the heart of Neoptolemus,
and, after an interval, he returns and places again the bow
in the hands of Philoctetes, freely and without conditions,
while Odysseus after vain resistance finally retires.   Even *action advancing*
here the action of the play is not entirely exhausted, but

CHAP. III seems to take a turn in its first direction as Neoptolemus
essays to substitute persuasion for force, and builds up a
plea which to the reader seems irresistible : in which in-
dications from heaven, chances of healing, hope of glory,

*action
reversed* all point in one direction.   But even this line of expectation
is reversed as Philoctetes, contrary to duty, interest, and
gratitude, persists in his enmity to the Grecian leaders, and
insists on Neoptolemus's pledge to carry him home.   Neoptolemus obeys, and they are turning their steps to the ship,
when the intervention of heaven arrests them, and Hercules
descending in glory from the sky bids his arrows be used
for their heaven-destined purpose, and works out for his son
peace and healing.   Thus perfect is the play as an illustration of the Pendulum Plot, with its action swaying from
complication to resolution, and back again and yet again
forward, until the tangle of circumstances can be resolved
only by miracle.

Such are the six varieties of tragic plot in Greek literature [1].   My survey of the dramatic element in Ancient

---

[1] Students accustomed to algebraic signs may note the expression of
these different species of plot by formulæ. S is used for a Situation
(that is, if treatment is applied to elaborating it ; if merely introduced it
might be expressed by small s).   The sign + is used for development
by action or progress.   In the case of Complication and Resolution the
algebraic sign for multiplication is used ($\times$), because the play does
not pass from its complication to its resolution through any intermediate stage of progress, but the resolution directly destroys the complication.   The six plot forms may be thus tabulated :—

Plots of Passion.

1. An Opening Situation developed to a Climax [$S+$].
Examples : *Agamemnon, Prometheus.*

2. Development of a Final Situation [$+S$].   Examples :
Oedipus as King, Medea.

3. Development from one Situation to another [$S+S$].
Examples : *The Sepulchral Rites, Ajax.*

4. An Opening Situation developed to its Reversal [$S+S'$].
Examples : *Antigone, Electra* of Sophocles.

Tragedy does not extend beyond this treatment of plot: CHAP. III
the present chapter is concerned with Greek Tragedy as a
species of the universal drama, and it is in tragic action—
the conception of unity which limited it, and the varieties
of form it assumed—that its specific features are to be
found. In the other elements of dramatic art—in Character, Situation, Effect—the characteristics of Greek
drama have descended bodily to the drama of modern
times; and if some few effects, such as Irony and Dissimulation, are specially Greek, these will be most con-
veniently treated in connection with examples of them
which will from time to time occur.

5 Extraneous Elements in Ancient Tragedy

The survey of Ancient Tragedy as a species of the *Disturbing*
universal drama would not be complete without some *forces in*
Ancient
reference to the disturbing—that is, non-dramatic—in- *Tragedy*
fluences which affected Greek Drama, mingled with the
purely dramatic element in it, and left traces on its form.
Two of these disturbing forces are worthy of mention.
The first is the influence of Rhetoric. The Athenian   I
people were distinguished by a peculiar idiosyncrasy—a *Rhetoric:*
morbid rage for forensic proceedings. The principle of
trial by jury permeated their judicial system, and as juries
might be large, and the free population of Athens was
small, every citizen was frequently called upon to serve in
this capacity, and the poorer classes made a good income
from such service. The national mind thus became familiar
with the minutiæ of legal procedure, and the taste formed

Plots of Action.
  5. Complication and Resolution [$C \times R$, or CR]. Example
     Ion.
  6. The Pendulum Plot, or Plot of Fortune-Turns [CRC].
     Examples: *Iphigenia among the Tauri, Hercules Mad.*
     The plot of *Philoctetes* might be expressed as $\dot{C}\dot{R}$.

CHAP. III in business hours for the embellishments of forensic
eloquence extended to the whole of the national literature,
and could at any time become a substitute for dramatic
effect.   The influence of Rhetoric on Tragedy appears in
Rheses, three points.   First, Rheses or set rhetorical speeches
abound: they differ from other speeches in a drama by
their length and their distance from the characteristics of
dialogue.   It is perhaps worth while to distinguish Rheses
of Thought, which are expositions of a distinct theme suggested by the scene,—as where Prometheus elaborates a
whole philosophy of evolution in his account of his good
works for man,—and Rheses of Situation, such as the
famous speech of Ajax on the verge of suicide, or the
lament of Hecuba over the mangled corpse of the infant
Astyanax[1].   To the same source may be referred the
Parallel Parallel, or 'Stichomuthic,' Dialogue, already treated as a
Verse, variety of tragic style: its equality of remark and answer
rests upon the balancing of sentences which is a main
device of Rhetoric.   Both these traces of rhetorical in-
the Foren- fluence are combined in the third—the Forensic Contest.
sic Contest In the plays of Euripides, and less markedly in those of
Sophocles, there is regularly a scene answering to this title,
in which representatives of the hero and of his opponents
are brought together, and discuss their respective cases with
a degree of formality which is felt to be forensic rather than
dramatic.   Such a scene regularly contains one elaborate
rhesis on each side of the dispute, like advocates' speeches;
and the resemblance extends so far that often (as Paley has
pointed out) the two orations are identical in length, just as
in the law-courts of Athens speeches were equalised by the
water-clock.   The part of the Chorus in the scene is that of
moderators: and the elaborate speeches are usually succeeded by a spell of parallel dialogue suggestive of cross-
examination.

[1] *Prometheus,* 444; *Ajax,* 815; *Daughters of Troy,* 1156.

An illustration of such a Forensic Contest may be taken
from the *Alcestis*. Admetus, heading the procession to the
grave, is encountered by his father and mother coming to
bring their funeral offerings. According to the peculiar
conception of the play discussed in an earlier section, these
parents must be regarded as the opponents of the hero,
since they embody the selfish old age which has shrunk
from its duty and allowed the youthful queen to die for
Admetus. Accordingly when the attendants advance to
receive the offerings Admetus waves them back, and stands
coldly confronting his father. At last he speaks. His
father is an uninvited guest at this funeral feast, and un-
welcome. Then was the time to show kindness when' a life
was demanded : yet the father could stand aloof and see a
younger life perish.

> At such an age, just trembling on the verge
> Of life, thou couldst not, nay thou daredst not die
> For thine own son ; but thou couldst suffer *her*,
> Though sprung from foreign blood : with justice then
> Her only as my father must I deem,
> Her only as my mother.

Yet Pheres (he continues) had already enjoyed his share
of all that makes life happy : youth spent amid royal luxury,
a prosperous reign, a son to inherit his state and who ever
did him honour. But now let him beget new sons to cherish
his age !—The Chorus interpose :

> Forbear ! enough the present weight of woe :
> My son, exasperate not a father's mind.

To the long rhesis of Admetus Pheres replies in a speech
of similar length. Is he a slave, to be so rated by his own
son ? And for what ? He has given his son birth and nurture,
he has already handed over to him a kingdom, and will be-
queath him yet more wide lands : all that fathers owe to
sons he gives. What new obligation is this that fathers
should die for their children ?

<pre>
                              Is it a joy to thee
To view the light of heav'n, and dost thou think
Thy father joys not in it ? Long I deem
Our time in death's dark regions: short the space
Of life, yet sweet! So thought thy coward heart
And struggled not to die: and thou dost live
By killing *her !* My mean and abject spirit
Dost thou rebuke, O timidest of all,
Vanquished ev'n by a woman, her who gave
For thee, her young fair husband, her young life ?
A fine device, that thou mightst never die,
Couldst thou persuade—who at the time might be
Thy wife—to die for thee !
</pre>

After the Chorus have again essayed to check the unseemly altercation, it settles down into an exchange of stichomuthic defiance.

Pher. Had I died for thee greater were the wrong.
Adm. Is death alike then to the young and old?
Pher. Man's due is one life, not to borrow more.
Adm. Thine drag thou on, and out-tire heaven's age!
Pher. Darest thou to curse thy parents, nothing wronged?
Adm. Parents—in dotage lusting still to live!
Pher. And thou, what else but life—with this corpse—buyest?
Adm. This corpse—the symbol of thy infamy!
Pher. For us she died not : that thou canst not say.
Adm. Ah! mayst thou some time come to need my aid!
Pher. Wed many wives that more may die for thee.
Adm. On thee rests this reproach—thou daredst not die.
Pher. Sweet is this light of heav'n! sweet is this light!
Adm. Base is thy thought, unworthy of a man!
Pher. The triumph is not thine to entomb mine age.
Adm. Die when thou wilt, inglorious thou wilt die.
Pher. Thy ill report will not affect me dead.
Adm. Alas, that age should out-live sense of shame!
Pher. But lack of age's wisdom slew *her* youth.
Adm. Begone, and suffer me to entomb my dead.
Pher. I go: no fitter burier than thyself,
    Her murderer! Look for reckoning from her friends:
    Acastus is no man, if his hand fails
    Dearly to avenge on thee his sister's blood.
Adm. Why, get you gone, thou and thy worthy wife:
    Grow old in consort—that is now your lot—

The childless parents of a living son:
For never more under one common roof
Come you and I together: had it needed,
By herald I your hearth would have renounced.

The parents withdraw, and the forensic contest is concluded[1].

The second of the disturbing forces in Ancient Tragedy is Epic Poetry. The part played by this in the early development of the drama has been traced in the opening chapter: it left its mark on the fully developed Tragedy in the Messenger's Speech. This is a device by which one of the incidents in the story, occurring outside the unity of place, and thus incapable of being acted, is instead presented in description, and treated with a vividness and fullness of narration that is an equivalent for realisation on the stage. Such speeches (like the rheses) have the distinction of length, often exceeding one hundred lines; they give the impression that for a time dramatic effect is suspended, and, as a substitute, the recognised features of Epic Poetry supply a new interest. These Messengers' Speeches are interesting to read by themselves, as pictures of ancient life[2].

(margin: 11 — Epic Poetry — The Messenger's Speech)

---

[1] The most elaborate forensic contest is that in the *Phœnician Women* (446-637) between the hostile brothers. It has the peculiarity that their mother acts as moderator instead of the Chorus (so that we get three rheses instead of two); the whole climaxes in parallel verse of accelerated rhythm.

[2] The following is a list:—A Battle under the walls of Thebes (*Suppliants* of Euripides, 650). A Battle with a miraculous incident (*Heraclidæ*, 799). A Night Surprise (*Rhesus*, 756). A Siege Battle with challenge and single combat (*Phœnician Women*, 1090-1199, 1217-1263, 1356-1424, 1427-1479). Naval Battle of Salamis (*Persians*, 251: with interruptions to 516). An Escape by sea and fight on shipboard (*Helena*, 1526). The same, with a fight on shore (*Iph. Taur.* 1327). Suicides: *Oedipus the King*, 1237; *Antigone*, 1192; *Maidens of Trachis*, 899. Mystic Death (*Oedipus at Colonus*, 1586). Sacrifice of Polyxena (*Hecuba*, 518), of Iphigenia (*Iph. Aul.* 1540). Fire-poison: *Medea*, 1136; *Maidens of Trachis*, 749. Attempted poisoning at a banquet (*Ion*,

CHAP. III Battles, sieges, surprises, escapes, ambushes, suicides, death
in a chariot race, assassination at a sacrifice, death by poison
and fire, miraculous rescues, public meetings, orgies of
Bacchanal women—the whole range of sensational incident
finds representation in these fragmentary epics. Representation on the ancient stage was limited both by the infancy
of mechanic art, and by the conventional spirit of a religious
festival: the power of transferring the more elaborate scenes
to narrative presentation was a valuable addition to the
sources of tragic effect.

1122). Hippolytus and the Sea-Monster (*Hip.* 1173). Hercules
slaying his children (*Hercules Mad*, 922, or page 279 in Browning's
Aristophanes' Apology).   Death in a chariot race (*Electra*
of Sophocles, 680). An Ambush and murder at the shrine of Delphi
(*Andromache*, 1085). . A Murder at a Sacrifice (*Electra* of Euripides,
774). Miraculous rescue of Helen (*Orestes*, 1395 : solitary example of
a Messenger's Speech in lyrics, as suited to a Phrygian narrator). A
capture by herdsmen (*Iph. Taur.* 260).   A Public Meeting
(*Orestes*, 866). Last Day of Alcestis's life (*Alcestis*, 152). The
Mænades on the Mountains (*Bacchanals*, 677); their assassination of
Pentheus (1043).—It must be understood, of course, that the epic
character of a Messenger's Speech does not exclude dramatic effects:
epic and dramatic form have much in common. For illustration see
below, page 169.

IV

ANCIENT TRAGEDY IN TRANSITION

IV

1 The Story of Orestes in the hands of Sophocles and Euripides

THE origin of Ancient Tragedy has been traced, and CHAP. IV
Choral Tragedy has been both illustrated by an example
and reviewed as a species of the universal drama. In the *Transi-tional*
present chapter I propose to trace the commencement of *Tragedy*
changes—and they never went beyond a commencement—
which carried on the development of Greek Tragedy in the
direction of modern drama.

It will be a convenient arrangement, before formally *illustrated*
gathering up the characteristics of Tragedy in its transition
state, to prepare the way by a more general account of two
plays in which the two later masters of Tragedy, Sophocles
and Euripides, are handling the Story of Orestes, Aeschylus's
version of which was the trilogy considered in the second
chapter. One change is obvious at the outset—the change THE
from trilogy to single plays: the *Electra* of Sophocles, and ELECTRA
the play of the same name by Euripides, cover the ground OF SOPH(-
of the middle play in Aeschylus's version. The titles of *Change*
the poems also suggest how the point of view is shifted *from
trilogy to*
from Orestes to Electra. Orestes was the natural centre *indepen-*
for the trilogy, since, besides his part in the *Sepulchral* *dent plays*
Rites, he stands to the first play of the three in the relation
of avenger, and to the third in the relation of victim. But
in the more confined field of the single play, Electra is
the natural representative of the situation from which is

CHAP. IV to be wrought the deliverance that is the subject of the
————   action.

Four stages   In all three versions the action falls naturally into the
of the   same four stages, which are thus convenient for purposes
action
common   of comparison. First, the arrival of Orestes gives the
to all   key-note to the play: then there is the elaboration of the
versions
         situation out of which Electra is to be delivered; then
         follows the recognition between brother and sister; finally,
         the conspiracy against Clytæmnestra and Aegisthus.

First   The prologue to the *Electra* of Sophocles introduces
Stage: Orestes in company with the aged Attendant who, accord-
Return of
Orestes   ing to this version, received the infant son of Agamemnon
         from the hands of Electra, and has watched over him in
         exile. Orestes is heard explaining to this old man how he
         has undertaken the expedition by command of Apollo. In
         this point the versions of Aeschylus and Sophocles agree:
         but there is significant difference between the form taken
The   by the oracular command in each. Aeschylus details the
oracular
command   terrible penalties which made the sanction of the divine
         mandate. Sophocles says nothing of these, but makes the
         oracle a more specific duty:

> That I myself unarmed with shield or host
> Should subtly work the righteous deed of blood.

Here we see the whole difference of spirit between the two
versions. In Aeschylus the dramatic effect is overpowered
by the religious sentiment, devout brooding over man in
relation to fate; Sophocles, equally religious in his writing,
is yet supremely a dramatist. Aeschylus emphasises the
terrible consequences of disobedience in order to use them
as a balance to the horror of matricide incurred by obeying,
and so presents the religious situation of a mortal placed
between two irresistible fates. Sophocles uses the oracle
to sketch a dramatic plot, and makes Apollo, so to speak,
set Orestes an intrigue as a task. The prologue goes

on to map out in detail Orestes' scheme. The Attendant
is to seek admission to the palace as a messenger from a
friend of Clytæmnestra's, employed by her to watch Orestes ;
he is to bring news that the exile is dead. The suspicions
of the foe will thus be quieted when, later, Orestes shall
in person appear, affecting to be the bearer of his own
ashes.

A wail heard from within the palace hastens the conspira- *Second*
tors to their respective tasks ; and the play passes into its *Stage :*
second stage, in which some four hundred lines are devoted *Elabora-*
to elaborating the situation out of which Electra is to be *situation*
delivered. This portion of the drama I have anticipated in *by lyrics,*
a former chapter, when discussing the use of stage lyrics
for expressing and emphasising emotions like those of
Electra in her distress ; I have described the monody in
which she pours forth her daily testimony against her father's
murder, and how in lengthy concerto with maidens from
Argos she refuses to be comforted. By an effect common *by rhetoric,*
in later Tragedy, when the influence of rhetoric was strong,
the story already conveyed in lyrics is told over again in
a long rhesis, as Electra, struck at last with compunction
for the petulant impatience with which she has met the
attempts of the Chorus to console her, calms herself, and
in blank verse sums up the weight of woes she has to bear.
Hated by her mother, housemate with her father's murderers, she must see Aegisthus sitting on her father's throne
and pouring libations on the hearth he violated ; her mother
living in no fear of doom, but making a feast of the day
her husband perished ; Electra alone keeps his birthday
in solitary festival, chidden for weeping, and threatened
whenever news comes of Orestes.

And the situation thus lyrically and rhetorically expressed *and by*
is further brought out by the dramatic effect of contrast as *dramatic*
Chrysothemis passes along the stage. She is a younger *contrast*
sister of Electra, good but weak, cherishing her father's

CHAP. IV memory in secret, but outwardly yielding to superior force.
——   We may suppose the contrast extending to external appearances : Chrysothemis may be fancied with golden locks
and attire fitting her condition as a princess, and with the
beauty of youth, whereas for Electra 'the larger half of life
is gone,' and her raiment is tattered as part of her testimony
to the memory of the murdered Agamemnon. The dialogue
between the sisters is of temporising and resisting, the Chorus
(as ever) endeavouring to bring each disputant to learn from
the other. The conversation is flavoured moreover with an
irritable bitterness, product of many similar altercations in
the past, when the close intercourse of family life has
brought the weaker and comfortable life into continual
contact with the stronger and heroic.

Dream,   As Chrysothemis is withdrawing, the errand comes out on
and transi- which she is bent : she has been sent by her mother with
tion to
following libations to the tomb of Agamemnon, as propitiation against
stage   a dream by which the queen has been disturbed. The
dream is another point of comparison with the version of
Aeschylus, and again the differences of detail are significant.
In Aeschylus the vision prophesied destruction—the snake
drawing blood from the breast which nourished it. But the
present story of Electra is one of restoration to happiness,
and the dream points in that direction :—the presence of
Agamemnon appeared again on his hearth and planted
there his old sceptre,

> And from it sprang a sucker fresh and strong,
> And all Mycenæ rested in its shade.

What Chrysothemis tells so simply, Electra snatches at as
a message from beyond the grave.

> Gods of my fathers ! be ye with me now !

She adjures her sister to turn her errand to a different
purpose. Never let such unholy offerings reach their
destination :—

No! cast them to the rivers, hide them deep
In dust, where never aught of them shall come
To where my father sleeps; but when she dies
Let them be stored below as gifts for her.

Instead, let Chrysothemis lay on the tomb offerings from
herself, and Electra too will give from her withered locks
and fringeless girdle : and let the prayer be for Orestes and
vengeance. Chrysothemis catches something of her sister's
spirit, and with this new purpose departs for the tomb.

The Chorus mark a turning-point in the story, and in
a choral ode celebrate the change that has come over the
spirit of the play with this gleam of hope. If our minds do
not deceive us (they sing) Vengeance is coming, and her
shadow is cast before her: like the springing up of a
favourable gale, a new courage courses through our veins
at these propitious dreams, an assurance that Agamemnon
will not forget for ever, nor has the two-edged axe forgotten
beneath the rust of all these years. She too will be here,
with tramp of many a foot and clash of many a sword,
Erinnys, with her iron march, already hiding in dread
ambush. If ever vision was true, this dream will not come
harmless to the murderess and her mate.

This birth of hope makes the transition to the third stage *Third*
of the play. The recognition between Orestes and Electra *Stage:*
is the pièce de résistance in the version of Sophocles. By *Develop-*
Aeschylus it is thrown away; so far as any effect is drawn *ment of*
from it, it is a religious effect, the meeting being made to *the Recog-*
appear an immediate answer to prayer. Sophocles concentrates the resources of dramatic workmanship on the
recognition, drawing it out to its utmost extent, and illustrating with a splendid example that moulding of successive
incidents so as to combine in one common effect which so *Prepara-*
distinguishes his treatment of plot. As a first and distant *tory scenes*
preparation for the arrival of Orestes, Sophocles contrives to *in the*
bring Clytæmnestra and Electra together. In the deadly *forensic*
contest,

CHAP. IV feud between the two, the last hope of the helpless Electra
is in Orestes, and Orestes is the only fear of the powerful
queen : these emotions of hope and fear, which give significance to the coming recognition scene, are inflamed to
the utmost by the contest between mother and daughter.
The Queen is coming to dispel, in prayer to the Sun-god,
the fear of her dream, when the unexpected sight of Electra,
whose presence is a constant reminder of her sin, checks
her purpose ; the shock finds vent in reviling, and the scene
settles down into the regular forensic contest. The dramatist
does advocate's duty in making out a case for Clytæmnestra.
Her defence is, of course, based upon the sacrifice of Iphigenia : thus Justice exacted the blood of Agamemnon and
her hand was only the instrument. If the gods demanded
human sacrifices were there not other maidens among the
Greeks—had not Menelaus a daughter, he for whom the
war was waged ? or had Hades a special lust for Clytæmnestra's children ? Electra, with bitter formality, solicits
permission to reply ; and then, with the steady force of a
forensic pleader, marshals her arguments. She takes note
of the admitted fact that her mother did the monstrous
deed, and exposes her omission of the real motive and her
base connexion with a paramour ; she points out the well-
known circumstance that it was Agamemnon who had
offended Artemis, and from his family alone could repara-
tion come. With all an advocate's enjoyment, Electra turns
her mother's plea of blood for blood against herself, and
concludes with a peroration of untempered defiance. The
altercation continues, and the Queen, forgetting the permission she had given, upbraids her daughter with interrupting her prayers. At that Electra stands aside, but
Clytæmnestra still feels that her prayer will not be in
friendly presence ; she darkly hints her meaning, which
Phœbus, as a god, will understand. Thus the prayer
against the dream terror has, after all, not been offered.

At this point, the Attendant of Orestes enters to bear his
part in the plot. When he announces the death of Orestes
the emotions of the recognition are instantly changed into *the mes-*
their opposites : Clytæmnestra's dread becomes security, *speech,*
Electra's hope sinks into blank despair. In an elaborate
and most graphic messenger's speech the Attendant tells
the feigned story of the fatal chariot race : at the end even
Clytæmnestra is for a moment overpowered by maternal
passion.

> O Zeus ! What means this . . . shall I say, good news?
> Or fearful, yet most gainful ? Still 'tis sad
> If by my sorrows I must save my life.

A moment's candour lifts the veil of feigned triumph which
had concealed the terrors of remorse :—

> nor day nor night
> I knew sweet sleep, but still the sway of Time
> Led on my life, as one condemned to death.

But one single moment has freed her from all her fear:

> We shall live on, and pass our days in peace.

Clytæmnestra takes the Attendant into the palace, with a
parting scoff at Electra, who is left to wail her despair in
concerto with the Chorus.

But even this despair can be accentuated, and a further *and the*
incident serves this purpose. Chrysothemis returns from *incident of*
the tomb, radiant: she has discovered upon it flowing *themis's*
streams of milk, and a garland of all the flowers that deck *return*
the field, with a freshly severed tress that can be from none
but Orestes ! Bit by bit Electra has to damp her youthful
and sanguine confidence, and break to her the tidings that
their brother has perished: despair is enhanced by the
pathos of mocked hope. There is yet a new emotional
departure when, from the lowest depth of despair, Electra
fetches heroic resolution : now all friends are gone let the
two children do the deed of vengeance by themselves,

CHAP. IV and be called the sisters twain that saved their father's
———   house. But Chrysothemis shrinks before the very proposal :

> Lo, thou wast born a woman, not a man.

Instead of feeling reproach, she herself reproaches her
sister with lack of ' cautious reverence,' and the bickering
breaks out again, until the younger sister takes her departure
and Electra is left alone to meditate revenge. But she
has won the Chorus, and the ode which follows celebrates
Electra as emulating the piety of the stork and the faithful
melancholy of the nightingale, invoking all success for the
best and wisest of daughters.

All this is so much preparation for the coming recognition
scene. The dramatist has been playing with the emotions
that enter into it : first the bitterness of the forensic contest
was a measure of the hopes and fears bound up with the
expectation of Orestes, then the false news changed hope
and fear into despair and blind security in order to make
the shock of meeting the greater ; despair then in the light
of a moment's false hope seemed the more despairing, and
finally Electra's undertaking the impossible task herself
meant her abandoning the very thought of Orestes.   Then

Actual   it is that Orestes comes. But though the meeting has
meeting :   taken place, the recognition is still delayed until the despair
recognition
still   of Electra shall be at its deepest.   Orestes enters bearing
delayed   an urn, and he announces, as if to by-standers, that it contains the ashes of Orestes.   Electra begs leave to clasp the
urn in her arms, and pours over it a flood of grief. Here is
nothingness to represent the dear child she sent out in the
bloom of youth, and all her forethought has perished ! And
he died among strangers, without her to take part in the
funeral rites ! All her sweet toil in nursing him with more
than a mother's love is gone ! All is gone—father, mother,
brother ! She would go too ; they ever shared an equal lot,
now let her go to him, ashes to ashes !

This outburst conveys to Orestes that in the dishevelled

and faded figure before him he sees his princess sister CHAP. IV
Electra, who saved him from death, the thought of whom
has been the ideal of his life. His emotion delays the recognition on its very threshold: he can only tremble, and
amazedly question.

> *Orest.* What shall I say? Ah, whither find my way,
>   In words that have no issue!
> *Elec.*   What sorrow now
>   Disturbs thee? Wherefore art thou speaking thus?
> *Orest.* Is this Electra's noble form I see?
> *Elec.* That self-same form indeed, in piteous case.
> *Orest.* Alas, alas, for this sad lot of thine.
> *Elec.* Surely thou dost not wail, O friend, for me!

The force of parallel verse is illustrated as, detail by detail,
Orestes extracts from the unconscious Electra the full
account of her sad condition. When this is all told, and
when the Chorus are discovered to be friends, even then
the mutual recognition is hindered a moment by the very
mode in which Orestes seeks to make the announcement.
He bids Electra put away the urn, but she clings to the
'tomb of Orestes'; he cries out at the ill omen of this
phrase, but she understands some dishonour that sunders
her from her loved one's relics. At last comes the plain
truth—

> Of those that live there is no sepulchre,

and the speaker shows the well-known seal. In verses
broken by embraces the wild joy finds vent. But even now
the full effect of the recognition is not exhausted. The *Addition of*
noisy emotion brings from the palace the Attendant of *a second*
recognition
Orestes, who reproaches his master with the risk he is *effect*
running of being overheard. This gives opportunity for
pointing out to Electra the faithful old friend to whom
she had committed the precious child; fresh embraces take
place, and so by a final touch of artistic handling the main
recognition is linked on to a second effect of the same kind.
    The way is now clear for the fourth stage of the action,

CHAP. IV

Fourth Stage: Assassination of Clytæmnestra,

the conspiracy against Clytæmnestra and Aegisthus. In this part of the story the difference between the versions of Aeschylus and Sophocles is just what we should expect. Aeschylus dismisses with brief treatment the assassination of Aegisthus, and gives prominence to the matricide which was to be the foundation of the following play. Sophocles, with no such consideration to hamper him, naturally throws into the background the unpleasant topic of matricide, and reserves for his climax the murder of Aegisthus, which he makes a masterpiece of the irony for which he is so famous. Orestes and Pylades are taken by the Attendant within the palace, and the Chorus, in a brief ode, mark the critical moment when the avengers pass beneath the roof-tree of their victim. Electra rushes out to stand guard in case Aegisthus should arrive, not before she has had a glimpse of Clytæmnestra preparing a burial urn with 'those two' by her side. Cries from within tell the accomplishment of the deed, and for a moment Orestes is seen, red-handed :

> Thy mother's sin shall shame thee never more !

and of Aegisthus: irony of the finale

Aegisthus is now seen approaching, and the irony begins : irony permeates the whole situation, and even penetrates to the very words of the speakers, sentence after sentence being, whether consciously to the speakers or not, true in a double sense. The usurper has caught from slaves some rumour of the visitors, and so eager is he on his entrance that he questions even his enemy Electra.

> *Aeg.* Where are the strangers, then ? Tell this to me.
> *Elec.* Within ; for they have found a loving hostess.
> *Aeg.* And did they say distinctly he was dead?
> *Elec.* Ah no ! they showed it, not in words alone.
> *Aeg.* And is it here, that we may see it plain ?
> *Elec.* 'Tis here, a sight most pitiful to see.
> *Aeg.* Against thy wont thou giv'st me cause for joy.
> *Elec.* Thou mayst rejoice, if this be ground for joy.

Aegisthus bids the gates be thrown wide, that all Argos and

Mycenæ may view a corpse that shall teach them whom to
obey for the future. Electra replies that the lesson has
been learnt by her, and she casts in her lot with those
who are stronger than she. Then the central gates open, and
disclose a corpse covered by a winding-sheet ; Orestes and
Pylades standing behind in the shadow of the threshold.

> *Aeg.*   Lo, I see,
> O Zeus, a sight that comes right well for me—

As he speaks, even over his blinded heart comes the touch
of dread that haunts the moment of unmeasured triumph,
and he seeks, too late, to soften his boast :—

> (Without offence I say it; should it move
> The wrath divine, I wish it all unsaid)—
> Withdraw the veil that hides the face, that I
> To kindred blood may pay the meed of tears.

A voice from the depths of the threshold replies :—

> Do thou uplift it. 'Tis thy task, not mine,
> To look on this, and kindly words to speak.
> *Aeg.* Thou giv'st good counsel, and I list to thee,
> And thou, if yet she tarries in the house,
> Call Clytæmnestra.

As Aegisthus lifts the veil the same voice responds :—

> Here she lies before thee,
> Seek her not elsewhere.
> *Aeg.*   Oh, what sight is this!

Orestes stalks forth from the threshold and plants himself
full in the face of Aegisthus :

> Whom fearest thou? Who is it thou dost not know?
> *Aeg.* Into whose snares, whose closely-tangled mesh
> Have I, poor victim, fallen!
> *Orest.*   Saw'st thou not
> Long since that thou didst speak to them that LIVE
> As they were dead?
> *Aeg.*   Ah me, I catch thy words.
> It needs must be that he who speaks to me
> Is named Orestes.

Orest.   Wert thou then deceived,
                    Thou excellent diviner ?

Aegisthus struggles to get a hearing, but even Electra's
feminine pity cries out not to prolong the agony. With
a mixture of terror, sullen dignity, taunts, and bitterness,
the murderer is forced within that he may meet his doom
on the spot where he did the sin.   The gates close on the

Unmixed vengeance, and the Chorus—in contrast to the conclusion
triumph of of Aeschylus's play—give expression to the unmingled
the con-
clusion   triumph of their cause.

> O seed of Atreus, after many woes
> Thou hast come forth, thy freedom hardly won,
> By this emprise made perfect!

Euripides :   We come now to Euripides.   Next to Shakespeare, Euri-
his special
connection pides has been the best abused poet in the history of litera-
with devel- ture.   And the reason is the same in both cases : each has
opment
            been associated prominently with a dramatic revolution vast
enough to draw out the fundamental difference between two
classes of minds—those that incline to a simple ideal perfectly attained, and those that sympathise rather with a more
complex purpose which can be reached only through conflict.   The changes in ancient drama promoted by this third
of the three great masters are all in the direction of modern
variety and human power : from the confined standpoint of
Attic Tragedy they may represent decay, in the evolution
of the universal drama they are advance and development.
Euripides laid the foundation for an edifice of which the
coping-stone is Shakespeare.

His   One distinctive feature attracts notice in the most cursory
Realism   study of Euripides. He is pre-eminently the poet of realism.
Not that he is less ideal in his treatment of the mythic
stories than his predecessors.   But he loves to disturb
the stately harmony of tragic style by some discordant note
taken straight from the every-day realities of life, and appealing to the elementary sympathies of our common humanity.

> Our Euripides the human
>   With his droppings of warm tears,
> And his touchings of things common
>   Till they rose to touch the spheres.

This conflict of real and ideal he constantly maintains : it is so much addition to the totality of dramatic impressiveness, and is ever bringing home to us how deeply the ideal penetrates the commonplaces of life. Euripides is in this respect the forerunner of the modern Romantic Drama, in which—without any sense of conflict—homely touches and tragic grandeur are so completely harmonised that, in application to Shakespeare, the antithesis of real and ideal ceases to have any meaning.

No better illustration could be desired for the realism of Euripides than the 'Peasant' he has added to the Story of Electra. In all three versions it is a point to emphasise the woful situation of Electra : Aeschylus and Sophocles represent her as neglected, chidden, threatened : in the version of Euripides a new torture has been contrived for her by the fiendish malignity of Aegisthus. He has forced her into a marriage with a baseborn peasant, thus at once inflicting on herself the suffering of social degradation, and providing against the risk of some other alliance that might bring power to back Electra's vengeance. But Aegisthus has overreached himself. Unwittingly he has selected as the instrument of his malice one of those noble souls that are independent of outward rank : in condition a peasant and poor, yet as proud of his pure Mycenæan blood as Aegisthus of his royal state. He has a simple instinct of fidelity to the family of his native prince as against the foreign usurper, and a quiet exterior that can veil the sustained purpose by which he cheats the tyrant, and acts only as pretended husband to Electra, offering the shelter of his humble roof until better times shall come. At once we have secured the union of the homely and the noble, so

M

dear to Euripides, and the introduction of this Peasant carries a thread of realism through the whole story, to interweave with its most ideal effects.

Scene and opening of the play At the outset the realism appears in the very scene of the play. In place of the traditional palace, we have the Peasant's cottage occupying the centre of a broken and mountainous country : on the one side is the fountain-head of the river Inachus, on the other the road to Mycenæ lined with pastures. The prologue opens with a picture of every-day work, elevated by an exquisite glimpse of the relations between Electra and her reputed husband. The stars are still shining when the Peasant enters from the cottage on his way to his day's work. He offers his morning prayer to the River, and as he prays his thoughts wander to the scenes that River has looked upon : the mighty host marching to Troy, the dread deeds that the return from Troy ushered in. He thinks then of the share he himself has been called to bear in this history of the great, and the reverent distance at which he keeps himself from his princess-wife. At this moment Electra appears, holding a water-pot in her hand : not seeing the Peasant at first, she too commences a morning prayer, addressed to 'dark-browed Night, nurse of the golden stars.' The Peasant goes to her, and gently remonstrates against the domestic labour indicated by the water-pot, for which her royal birth is so unfitting. Electra turns lovingly to him :

> Thee equal to the gods I deem my friend !

When all else was hostile he alone has been to her a gentle power, lenient of grief, mighty source of consolations. Shall she then suffer him to lack the comradeship in toil, the sweet ordering of home by woman's hand, which he has sacrificed for her sake? The Peasant gives way with a simplicity of acceptance as graceful as Electra's condescension ; and the idyl terminates as Electra descends to the

river, and the Peasant, with a few cheerful words of zest for CHAP. IV
work, disappears up the road to the mountain.

The play falls into the same four stages as the other *First*
versions. When the preliminary scene, opening out the new *Stage:*
Return of
element added to the story, has taken place by starlight, the *Orestes*
way is clear for the first stage—the arrival of Orestes, with
Pylades and Attendants, just as grey morn is opening its
radiant eye. He has come by divine command to avenge *The ora-*
his father's death. The first charge of the god—that he *cular*
command
should present offerings on his father's tomb—he has already
fulfilled by night. The second charge is mysterious, that
he should not enter the walls of the city: and on this
he would fain consult his sister, now living, he hears, a
wedded wife in the country. The party step aside, and
conceal themselves amongst the rocks as they hear a foot-
step and see 'some female slave' approaching. The step is *Second*
that of Electra returning from the river with her water-pot *Stage:*
Elabora-
filled, and the play reaches its second stage in the lyric *tion of the*
elaboration of the opening situation, which Euripides, as *Situation,*
Sophocles, disposes in a monody followed by a concerto.
First Electra herself, in rhythmic movements which no
doubt would carry her through various poses of vase-bearing,
such as are the delight of Greek art, laments for her slain
father, her exiled and suffering brother, calling upon her
father's spirit for vengeance. Then a Chorus of Maidens
from Mycenæ enter, excited with great news : the city is to
celebrate a special festival in honour of Herè, and the
Chorus wish their old playmate and princess to lead them
once more in the dance. Electra bitterly points to her rags,
and replies that she is fit only for tears. They bid her try
the effect of festal vows on the gods who have lost their ear
for the wretched, and as to fitting attire that shall be their
care. Here we have another example of Euripides' realism
interposed amid lyric stateliness : to be stopped from a
festival by not having clothes fit to go in may be a very

M 2

CHAP. IV prosaic calamity, but it would be in real life just such a
——   reminder of descent in social scale as might well be the
          bitterest ingredient in the flavour of Electra's misfortunes.
          The lyric dialogue is interrupted by a sob from the con-
interwoven cealed Orestes : Electra, who lives the life of a hunted thing,
with the
third stage is instantly taking to flight, when the strangers come forward
          and with difficulty reassure the women. The play then
          enters upon its third stage.

Plot   This stage, the meeting of brother and sister, is treated
treatment
of Sopho- by Euripides with no less elaboration than by Sophocles,
cles and   but with a difference of purpose that illustrates a second
Euripides
compared   special tendency of the younger poet. In Sophocles we
          have the sustained deepening of a single interest ; Euripides,
          on the contrary, exhibits a striving after complexity and
          the multiplication of emotional interests. Sophocles heaps
          together incidents that all work visibly towards a common
          climax, which is delayed only that it may be accentuated.
          In Euripides there is again and again a diversion in order
          to take in new trains of emotion, and the attention has to
          be distracted before it is allowed its final satisfaction. The
          movement in a play of Sophocles is a simple spiral, that
          goes round and round only to ascend the more gradually.
          For Euripides the best illustration—and if it is a homely
          illustration it would have suited the poet the better—would
          be the figure known to children as the 'cat's cradle.' A plain
          loop is held round the extended hands : the right hand
          catches up from the left and the left from the right and the
          loop becomes double, the process is repeated and the loop
          is seen to be treble, quadruple ; but the complexity is de-
          pendent only on the performer's will, for a smart pull brings
          the whole back to the simple loop as at first. So the progress
          of events in a play of Euripides multiplies at every turn
          the varying interests that are at last seen to combine in
The Recog- a common goal.
nition in   The portion of the play that deals with the meeting of

brother and sister is complex at its very outset. Orestes
has in the previous stage overheard his sister's story, and
knows who she is; but in the hurry of recalling the
startled women, and not knowing if the Chorus are to be
trusted, he has taken up the difficult rôle of a messenger
from himself. In this way he has to draw from Electra the
whole tale of her troubles without letting his emotions
betray his assumed disguise.

*Euripides
complex at
the outset*

> *Orest.* Why here thy dwelling, from the city far?
> *Elec.* O stranger, in base nuptials I am joined—
> *Orest.* (*sobbing*). I feel thy brother's grief!—To one of rank?
> *Elec.* Not as my father once to place me hoped!—
> *Orest.* That hearing I may tell thy brother, speak.

For seventy lines of parallel verse without a break this
dialogue is continued, Orestes prolonging his enquiries to
test how his sister would behave should her brother return.
When the truth has thus been drawn out in scattered fragments, it is, according to custom, gathered into a full stream
of denunciation in a rhesis of Electra. She paints her
degraded and servile condition, her mother's splendour, the
tyrant riding on the same car as the king he murdered, and
pouring offerings upon the hearth he violated, while the
hero's tomb is insulted, and all things are calling on
Orestes. The situation is just ripe for the denouement,
when the unexpected return of the Peasant from the fields
not only causes a diversion, but introduces an entirely
fresh element into the plot.

The Peasant is astonished at seeing a party of strangers
conversing with Electra : when he hears of them as messengers from Orestes he instantly calls for refreshments, and
begs the travellers to delay no longer to enter his cottage :—
poverty is no excuse for not offering what entertainment he
can give. I have before insisted on the necessity of re-
membering that in Greek life hospitality was not one of
the lighter sentiments, but one of the loftiest passions ; and

*Diversion
and new
interest of
hospitality*

CHAP. IV this triumph of hospitable instinct over paucity of means
——   moves Orestes to an eloquent rhesis on the contrasts left
by nature between heart and outward conditions :—

> Meanness oft grovelling in the rich man's mind,
> And oft exalted spirits in the poor.

But this heroic aspect of hospitality is at once linked to its
more prosaic side when the visitors have entered the cottage,
and Electra—in a way that will appeal to every house-
keeper—is left fuming at her thoughtless man of the house,
who has invited guests altogether beyond his means of
entertaining, and in the embarrassment he is causing has
no more practical suggestion to make than this :—

> If they are noble, as their port
> Denotes them, will they not alike enjoy
> Contentment, be their viands mean or rich?

The only device Electra can think of is to send for assistance to her one friend, her father's old servant who preserved Orestes on the fatal day, and has ever since had
to hide himself in obscurity, a herdsman almost as poor
as Electra herself. The Peasant goes to find him. Meanwhile, not only is the recognition delayed, but there are
now two distinct emotions aroused in our minds, family
affection and humble hospitality, drifting apparently to a
common satisfaction when Orestes shall crown the rustic
feast with his secret that he is the long-expected brother.

Another   But this is not to be : Euripides has a third train of
diversion : interest to interweave before he will allow the knot to be
interest of
faithful   untied. After an interval, filled up by a choral ode, the
old age   Old Servant is seen painfully toiling up the steep ascent to
the cottage under the weight of a kid and other viands he
is bringing. As guardian to Agamemnon he is necessarily
a man on the extreme verge of life, and a new interest
comes with him into the play—the pathos of faithful old
age. When Electra goes to his assistance she finds him in
tears. His road has brought him past his dear master's

tomb, and turning aside to do it reverence he found it CHAP. IV
strewn with signs of sepulchral honours—a victim's blood,
tresses freshly shorn, and fragments of vesture.

> Perchance with secret step thy brother came,
> And paid these honours to his father's tomb.

It is easy for Electra to show the unlikeliness of this, but the
old man persists : he wants Electra to compare the tresses
with her own hair, to measure by her own foot the foot-
steps at the tomb. When these suggestions have been
dismissed with gentle contempt, still the old man maintains
his point :—

> But had thy brother, should he come, no vest
> Which thou wouldst know, the texture of thy hands,
> In which when snatched from death he was arrayed ?

This is of course the absurdest suggestion of all : were the
fact so, Electra naturally replies, how could he be now
dressed in the same, 'unless his vests grew with his person's
growth.' But it is precisely in the absurdity that the pathos
of the scene lies : it is second childhood clinging, in defiance
of reason and common sense, to the one hope of a lifetime.
And this realistic detail of senility rises to the tragic dignity
of an inspiration when the old man is proved to have been
right : admitted to a sight of the strangers, he moves like a
dog round and round Orestes and forces the recognition
which the hero was reserving for some appropriate moment.
So Euripides' handling of the recognition incidents is com- *Recog-*
pleted ; it has been, not the measured march of Sophocles *nition*
to a goal well in sight, but a beautiful confusion of pas- *effected and*
sionate details only seen in the end to be a harmony. *interests*
Electra's sufferings for herself and her exiled brother have *harmon-*
been detailed in the exile's hearing, her messages of appeal *ised*
have been unconsciously addressed to himself; the new
interest of hospitable poverty has interposed an obstacle to
the recognition, and yet a new diversion has added the

spectacle of faithful love surviving intellect : until all three trains of emotion have been harmonised together when the faithful old man, in his hospitable mission at the cottage door, brings about the discovery of the brother who will put an end to the troubles of all.

Fourth Stage treated for complexity

The play now passes to its fourth stage, the conspiracy against Aegisthus and Clytæmnestra. Here may again be seen the tendency of Euripides to multiply emotional situations ; unlike both Aeschylus and Sophocles he provides a separate plot against each of the tyrants, an arrangement which has the effect of furnishing four distinct scenes, all highly charged with passion. Aegisthus, it appears, is expected at a rustic festival in a neighbouring pasture ; Orestes and his companions agree to seek admission as travellers, and kill the usurper while he is in the very act of sacrifice. Clytæmnestra is to be enticed to the cottage by a report that Electra has given birth to a child, and desires her mother's presence at the ten days' rite. The conspirators separate for their allotted parts, and the Chorus fill up the period of waiting with an ode.

The Interludes

It may be pointed out that this ode, like another earlier in the play, illustrates a tendency observable in the later development of Tragedy to reduce the closeness of connexion between an ode and the matter of the episodes between which it stands. When the Chorus had to fill up the interval during which the Old Servant was being fetched, they plunged suddenly into the glories of the fleet that sailed for Troy, dwelt upon the details in the shield of Achilles, and only at the end connected their theme with the plot of the play—it was one commanding heroes like these that the accursed wife dared to slay. So now, when there is again a pause in the action, the legendary history of Mycenæ furnishes a story of a Golden Fleece, presented in a series of pictures—the marvel of it, the festival that was to celebrate its disposal, the awful crime by which Thyestes

(father of Aegisthus) secured it, the convulsion of all nature CHAP. IV
at the horror of the deed. In the final lines the ode is made
relevant:

> She, this noble pair who bore,
> Dared to murder—deed abhorred—
> This forgot, her royal lord.

The assassination of Aegisthus is presented in the form of *Messen-*
a messenger's speech: it may well be reckoned amongst the *ger's*
Speech:
scenes of the play, so dramatic is the spirit infused into its *Assassina-*
graphic details. As an epic picture, its main interest lies in *tion of*
Aegisthus
the fulness with which it displays sacrificial ceremonial. The
speech paints the locality—gardens fresh with myrtle trees
and watercourses, the busy preparations for the feast, the
invitation to the travellers as they pass along the road to
stay and partake; how these, announcing themselves as
Thessalians—noted connoisseurs in matters of sacrificial
ritual—obtain a foremost place at the ceremony, and
skilfully evade the lustral rites that might make their intended deed a violation of hospitality. Irony comes into
the scene as Aegisthus is heard praying that his own fortune
and his dreaded enemy's may ever be 'as now'; still more
when, in friendly challenge, he hands his murderer the
knife and axe with which to slay him. Orestes thus holding
the situation in his hands prolongs it, working through his
manipulation of the victim with Thessalian regularity, until
it is possible for the tyrant, as master of the ceremonies, to
inspect the omens.

> In the entrails was no lobe;
> The valves and cells the gall containing showed
> Dreadful events to him that viewed them near.
> Gloomy, his visage darkened.

With a jest at the idea of fearing an exile, Orestes proceeds
to the final step, and cleaves the bullock's breast.

> Aegisthus, yet intent,
> Parted the entrails; and, as low he bowed
> His head, thy brother, rising to the stroke,

CHAP. IV
———

> Drave through his back the ponderous axe, and rived
> The spinal joints: the heaving body writhed
> And quivered, struggling in the pangs of death.

There is a critical moment of tumult, then an appeal from Orestes to his father's retainers, a recognition, and universal shouts of triumph.

Electra's rhesis of denuncia- tion

A second scene of passion ensues when the corpse is brought upon the stage, and over it Electra—not without falterings of womanly pity at seeing the tokens of mortal suffering—gives vent to a life's hatred in a denunciation of the fallen tyrant. She speaks of the crimes he had done against their house; of his shameful union with her mother, with its wretchedness, where each partner was conscious of the other's guilt; of his trust in fleeting riches, his beauty fit only for the dance: not omitting the thought which ever haunted a Greek mind—that none may be counted fortunate till he has attained the goal of death.

The Forensic Contest

At this moment Clytæmnestra ˙ is seen approaching. Orestes is hurried into the cottage, distracted at the thought of the deed he is to do. The Queen comes riding into the orchestra in a car of gold, attended by a long train of Trojan captives. The Chorus play their part by receiving her with tones of adulation. Clytæmnestra calls her slaves to assist her to alight. Electra, in her rags, rushes forward and begs that she may assist her mother. Clytæmnestra is shocked at the change which years of poverty have worked in her daughter, and her words fall into an apologetic tone. The scene settles down into the conventional forensic contest ; but, placed where Euripides has placed it, this ordinarily formal scene receives a glow of passion reflected on to it from the incident that precedes and the catastrophe which is to follow. Clytæmnestra makes good capital of her wrongs : her Iphigenia, like a blooming flower, was mown down by Agamemnon, not for the public weal, but in a quarrel over the wanton Helen. If to avenge the deed she united herself

with another, was this more than fair requital for her CHAP. IV
husband's shame in bringing back from Troy the beauteous
Cassandra? Electra, conscious of the doom impending
over her adversary, is bitterly humble in craving permission
to reply. Accorded it, she gazes on her mother's beauty,
and speaks of the two fatal sisters, Helen whose beauty laid
Troy low, and the other who brought down Troy's conqueror.
With an advocate's steady skill she fills into Clytæmnestra's
story the details she had omitted :—how before the loss of
Iphigenia she adorned herself to please Aegisthus, how
throughout the war she alone rejoiced when the enemy
prevailed, how she still lets her paramour persecute the
innocent children of her husband. Amid her pleas are
interspersed stately moral maxims—appeals to an audience
of forensic experts. Whether from conscience or pity,
Clytæmnestra begins to feel compunction : she has been
harsh, but *for the future* she will be kinder, and so shall
Aegisthus. She speaks these words almost in the hearing
of those who have already done vengeance on Aegisthus and
are waiting to slay her ; and in speaking them she lets slip the
secret—which not even Electra has suspected before—that
it was she who urged Aegisthus to his harshness. Upon this,
Electra can only let the plot take its course. Clytæmnestra
prepares to enter the cottage, bidding her slaves return for
her when they think she will have paid these rites to the gods.
Electra ceremoniously ushers her in, bidding her see that her
vestments be not defiled by the smoke : then turns before
following her mother to speak words of terrible triumph :—

> There shalt thou sacrifice, as to the gods
> Behoves thee sacrifice ! The basket there
> Is for the rites prepared, and the keen blade
> Which struck the bull; beside him thou shalt fall
> By a like blow; in Pluto's courts his bride
> He shall receive, with whom in heaven's fair light
> Thy couch was shared: to thee this grace I give,
> Thou vengeance for my father shalt give me.

CHAP. IV

Crisis and Reaction:

A moment of dreadful suspense is covered by the Chorus, who sing how the waves of mischief are flowing back, the gale of violence is veering. Then shouts from within proclaim the deed done. But the scene that ensues comes upon us as a surprise. Orestes rushes from the cottage sword in hand, Electra following: instead of the expected triumph, we see them crushed and horror-stricken. The high-wrought spirit and trust in the divine .mission of vengeance which had supported them so long has deserted them as soon as the deed was accomplished; a revulsion of feeling has come over them, and they realise the full guilt and shame of matricide. The details of the horrible scene press upon their memory :—

> *Orestes.* Holding my robe before mine eyes I raised
> The sword and plunged it in my MOTHER'S breast!
> *Electra.* I urged thee to it! I, too, touched the sword!

plot recom-plicated,

All this is true to nature, and adds a new emotional study to a drama already full of passion. But meanwhile, this way of feeling after emotional situations has brought the plot into confusion : by such a backward swing of the action at the last moment despair has taken the place of triumph, and, with the details of the story all exhausted, how is the plot to be extricated and a position of rest found?

resolved by the Divine Interven-tion

This difficulty is met by a device dear to Euripides, the name of which has passed into a proverb—the *Deus ex machina*. The plot is not extricated at all, but is concluded by a non-dramatic method—in a word, by a miracle. The 'Divine Intervention' was the sudden apparition of a god, or other supernatural being, and the 'machina' was a piece of stage machinery which gave him the appearance of speaking from the sky. He would take the tangled incidents of a story into his own hands, away from the region of human causes and effects with which dramatic plot concerns itself, and settle them by his own supernatural fiat. In this case

it is Castor and Pollux, deities of the family, whose sudden CHAP. IV
splendour draws all thoughts from the scene beneath : they
have come from heaven—and the waves have grown calmer
as they passed along—to speak words of fate. The deed
done is justified, not without hints of blame for their fellow-
god Apollo ; the secret history of Atreus's family, both past
and future, is prophetically unfolded ; Electra is to be united
to Pylades, the Peasant is to share the prosperity of the
family he has served so well, and Orestes, after years of
wandering and persecution by the Furies, is to find purifi-
cation at the hands of the Athenian Areopagus. The scene
is prolonged by the awe of the mortals who for the first time
find themselves in converse with deity, and by the tearful
embraces of brother and sister, so soon torn from the intercourse of love they had awaited so long. Then the various
personages withdraw to their allotted lives, and the deities
return to heaven, bidding men note that it is only the just
and reverent in life whom they come down the tract of æther
to assist. It only remains for the Chorus, spectators in a
story that has been so hurled from emotion to emotion, to
conclude with their favourite prayer for an even course of
life.

> Blessed be ye in heaven ! and blest on earth
> They only who, nor tossed on waves of pride,
> Nor in afflictions sunk, their voyage end.

2   Nature and Range of Transition Influences

I now proceed from single plays to development as a
whole in Ancient Tragedy.

Develop-
It will be observed that there is a difference between *ment con-*
writing the history of literature and tracing literary develop- *cerned*
ment. History will take note of all additions made to the *varieties,*
mass of literary production : the field of development will be *not sum,*
confined to such progress as exhibits itself in varieties of form *duction*

CHAP. IV and matter.   In physical science it makes no difference to the evolutionist whether the number of rose-trees in the world belonging to a particular type can be reckoned by the score or by the million; but he will concern himself with the smallest variation of type.   So in the ordinary way literary development consists in the multiplication of literary species.

Range of the transition Ancient Tragedy is, however, to a certain extent an exception : the period of literary activity in Greece was so short, and the force of conservatism and conventionality so strong, that nothing amounting to a second species of Greek Tragedy has come down to us.   The whole range of the transition we are to consider is confined to certain tendencies towards change within the limits of a single species.

Order of development not the same as chronological succession The treatment proper for our purpose will not be an attempt to divide Greek drama into periods such that the later would be developments out of the earlier.   For one thing, order of development does not necessarily follow chronological succession.   Of course, a later form of development cannot precede in time an earlier form.   But the converse is not true : earlier forms once developed are established as models and can be reproduced side by side with later forms.   Geologists have settled the order of the strata composing the crust of our earth, and have placed granite low, sedimentary rocks like limestone many places higher; but this principle is not inconsistent with the appearance, owing to some upheaval, of granite and limestone side by side on the surface of adjacent districts.   So in the history of Greek literature, forms described developmentally as early and late may be found in the same work and at any date.   Moreover, the three masters of Ancient Tragedy were in part contemporary with one another.   When Aeschylus died, Euripides had been before the public for six years, Sophocles had been in the front rank of poets for double that time ; and Sophocles and Euripides died in the same year.   It is thus quite possible that Aeschylus was feeling

the influence of Sophocles when he gave so much more pro- CHAP. IV
minence to plot in his later plays, and it seems highly
probable that in one drama Sophocles is accepting innovations from Euripides[1]. Thus, while literary history, in *Ancient*
discussing the individualities of the three tragic poets, might *Tragedy*
a single
describe them roughly as constituting three separate stages, *species*
yet for our purpose it will be better to look upon the whole
as one single period, in which symptoms of transition become
visible. Development in reference to such a period will *its develop-*
consist in variations from the type—a type determined by *ment*
consists in
induction from a survey of the whole. Such variations, *variations*
visible in the works of all three, will appear least in *from the*
type
Aeschylus, and be very prominent in Euripides. Yet even
in the earliest of the three there will be found a few very
wide differences from the normal form, while some return to
the Aeschylean manner is to be traced in plays so late as the
Hercules and *Bacchanals* of Euripides.

Before the details of this development are examined, it may *Develop-*
be convenient to enquire what were the forces by which it *ing forces :*
was brought about. The influences on Greek Tragedy of
its age and social surroundings tended mainly towards fixity
of form ; the forces making for progress belonged chiefly to
the natural order of things. In distinguishing them, two may
be named together : they are specific decay and natural *specific*
expansion. A species in literature will be constituted by the *decay,*
exceptional prominence of some important form, or set of
characteristics, which give an impulse to imitation ; when
the attraction of these forms and characteristics declines the
impulse to exactness of imitation weakens, and, while the
species may continue, its specific distinctiveness becomes less
marked. Again, one tendency of literature, as of all art, *natural*
expansion,

---

[1] The *Philoctetes*, usually considered one of the latest productions of
Sophocles, appears to me to follow Euripidean method in (1) what I
have called the 'pendulum action' (above, page 137) and (2) the Divine
Intervention : neither of which occurs elsewhere outside Euripides.

CHAP. IV under free conditions is to become fuller, more various,
—————   more complex. A third developmental influence has to be
struggle of   added to these. Literature is not art merely, it is also a
matter and
form   medium for thought: the balance of matter and form becomes sometimes disturbed, and types appear in which now
one now the other is dominant. Greek Tragedy was pre-
eminently a medium for thought: it was the pulpit and press
of its age, in which religious, political, and social topics were
freely discussed. It gave admittance, moreover, to two non-
dramatic elements—epic poetry introduced by the accidents
of its origin, rhetoric forced upon it by the tastes of its
audience. It was natural that there should arise at times
a struggle between thought and form in Ancient Tragedy,
between what was intrinsic and what was extraneous, and
this struggle will be seen to form a third disturbing force in
dramatic history.

Under such influences as these, an element of transition
appears in Greek Tragedy ; it falls into certain well-marked
lines of development, which it will be the object of the
following sections to trace.

3 Instability of the Chorus

Choral in-   The technical name for the tragic poetry of Greece is
stability a
first line Choral Tragedy, its distinctiveness as a species of the
of develop- universal drama lying in the union of a lyric element with
ment
drama : if this union by any cause becomes weakened,
specific decay sets in. Now, this amalgamation of lyric and
dramatic in Greek Tragedy was a highly artificial union ; the
lyric Chorus had not only evolved a separate dramatic
element, but itself entered into the dramatic just so far as to
adopt a slender characterisation, which it maintained through
odes and episodes. Such artificial combinations are highly
unstable. They may be compared to the unstable equilibrium
of the pyramid nicely balanced on its apex, liable to change

at any moment to a position of rest; or they resemble CHAP. IV
chemical compounds, some of the elements in which have
less affinity for one another than for surrounding things,
and are continually feeling after new combinations. So the
instability of the Chorus is the foundation for the first line
of development in Ancient Tragedy, which may be thus
formulated:—*The Chorus, occupying an unstable position
between lyric and dramatic functions, tends to give way in
both directions.* On the one hand it tends to become more *Two*
dramatic, and pass into the play as a body of actors; on *opposing*
tendencies
the other hand there is a tendency for the choral part to
become more strictly lyrical, and lose connexion with plot
and characters.

First, the Chorus is more and more drawn into the ¹
dramatic action. In the type, the Chorus are just within *The*
Chorus
the story as spectators. They are dependants of the hero: *drawn into*
senators of Agamemnon, or sailors who have followed the *the drama-*
tic action:
lead of Ajax to Troy. Or they are friends coming to
sympathise, like the Argive maidens who pay a visit of
condolence to Electra, or the Chorus in *Prometheus* and in
Ion, who at distinct points in the action take sides with the
suffering hero and the persecuted Creusa. Or they are still
more strictly by-standers: in *Oedipus at Colonus* the Chorus
is made up of passers-by, called together by the cries of
one who is shocked to see the sacred grove violated by
a traveller; in a play of Euripides the Chorus are themselves
travellers—'Women from Phœnicia' detained in Thebes by
the war, who look on the whole action with foreign eyes.
But there are a few plays in which the Chorus are unmis- *as secon-*
takably actors in the story. An early play of Euripides, *dary*
actors,
the *Rhesus*, dramatises a single night of the Trojan war.
The Chorus are the night watch: it is they who give the
alarm as to movements in the Grecian camp; they take
their full share in the council of war which follows; their
momentary absence from their post gives opportunity for

N

CHAP. IV the enemy to commit his depredations, and on their return they actually arrest Odysseus, but have to release him; in the discovery that follows, they are the first to be suspected. The Chorus have here acted a part second only to that of Aeneas and the Grecian leaders. But in two plays— *as primary* both of them plays by Aeschylus—the Chorus are more *actors* than secondary actors. In the third part of the trilogy the Chorus of Furies serve as motive force for the whole drama : their action is divided between the stage and the orchestra, their persecution of the hero makes the plot, and their pacification is its disentanglement. And in the *Suppliants*, the Chorus are in the fullest sense of the term the heroines of the play : they enter in full flight from their enemies, their safety is the sole matter for religious supplication and dramatic contrivance, their threat of suicide is the turning-point of the action, actual violence is offered to them and repulsed, and with their divided feelings at the issue the poem concludes [1].

Lyric Even the peculiarly lyric function of the Chorus, the *Interludes* entr'-acte, shows a tendency to become dramatic. An ode, *approach* *dramatisa-* especially an entrance-ode, comes to be addressed to an *tion* actor : in *Agamemnon* the Chorus, in the middle of their parode, notice Clytæmnestra's ritual on the stage and make enquiries of her ; in *Hecuba* and *Andromache* the Chorus, who come to bring news of evil, address the whole of their entrance-song to the heroines of the play. A step nearer to the dramatic is taken when the parode or some entr'-acte is shared with an actor in the form of a concerto ; the choral portion of *Prometheus* and the two *Electras* opens

[1] In the *Suppliants* of Euripides the position of the Chorus is theoretically the same as in Aeschylus's play, but a difference is made by the fact that *Aethra* speaks for them in the episodes. In three plays of Euripides, the *Hecuba, Daughters of Troy, Iphigenia amongst the Tauri,* the Chorus are captives, whose fortunes are bound up with those of the personages in the plot.

with such duetts of sympathy[1]. Finally, we have a case in Chap. IV which an interlude is wholly surrendered to an actor, and Electra's monody (in *Orestes*) over the ruin of her house serves exactly the same purpose as the ode on the same subject by the Chorus in a previous part of the play[2].

One more symptom of reduced lyric activity on the part *Strophic* of the Chorus may be seen in the separation of a strophe *dichotomy a symptom* from its antistrophe. The correlation of these two stanzas *of lyric* of a pair is the essence of choral form : their separation by *decline* an interval arises from the utilisation of lyrics for dramatic purposes. In a case taken from the *Rhesus* the purpose is to mark stages in the development of an intrigue ; as soon as Aeneas has started his suggestion of sending a spy to the Grecian camp the Chorus express approval in a strophe, which finds its antistrophe when an agent has been found in Dolon to accept the dangerous mission[3]. It is more remarkable to find such strophic dichotomy affecting parts of a play widely sundered from one another, and in fact belonging to different episodes. In *Hippolytus*, when Phædra has just made her terrible disclosure, the Chorus give lyric expression to the shock which all feel, before the subsequent conversation plants in the Nurse's mind the thought of her wicked device for rescue. When, in a later part of the play, the fatal consequences of the Nurse's action burst upon the women in the bitter denunciations of Hippolytus the agitation falls into the same rhythm as in the former outburst : these two supreme shocks standing out from the

---

[1] In *Medea* the Chorus, attracted by the cries of the Queen, enter into a duett of enquiry with the Nurse, and the delirious ravings of Medea behind the scenes make this a concerto of three.

[2] See Structure of the *Orestes*, in Table on page 438.

[3] *Rhesus*, 131 and 195.—Compare the elaborate use of this form in the *Seven against Thebes* (370-716) : description of the hostile forces and disposition of the Theban army in successive passages of blank verse interposed between strophes and antistrophes of comment.—Another example in *Philoctetes*, 391 and 507.

CHAP. IV rest of the action, bound together by antistrophic corre-
spondence [1]. In this way divided odes obtain a footing
in Tragedy: at last we find the separate halves usurping
the place of full odes in the function of the entr'-acte [2].

In all these ways—by increased activity in the episodes,
by the attraction of the interludes to dialogue, and by the
modification of the strophic form itself for purposes of dramatic effect—we trace the instability of the Chorus on this
one side of tending to pass from lyric to dramatic. I may
just anticipate a future chapter to point out here that this
tendency is still further developed after the close of Greek
Tragedy. The power of ignoring the Chorus throughout
whole scenes of Seneca is a sign that it has lost its function
of giving lyric embodiment to the unity of the whole play;
so far as it has any place in the action, it is there in the
same category with the rest of the actors.

II
*Counter
tendency:
dedrama-
tisation of
the Chorus
Their
function
of modera-
tors*

We have now to notice the counter tendency of the
Chorus to fall back into the purely lyric, and lose connexion with dramatic plot and characterisation. At the full,
their normal position is slight enough—that of spectators.
But with the forensic contest another function for the
Chorus came in, which may be described by calling them
'moderators': as if they were presiding at a public meeting,
their duty in such cases is formally to receive the personages who appear, and break up the length of a debate by
interposing a brief conventional remark as they turn from
one speaker to another. In some plays of Euripides [3]

---

[1] *Hippolytus*, 362 and 669.—A less marked example is in the *Rhesus*,
454 and 820.

[2] A case of this occurs in the *Orestes*: the effect of this divided ode
near the end of the play is like that of an *accelerando* in music, as suggesting the hurry of exciting events to the nearing climax. The whole
play is a good example of the degree to which the lyric element can be
drawn within the dramatic action. [See Tabular Analysis, page 438.]

[3] E. g. *Hecuba* and *The Daughters of Troy*.

this function is extended to a considerable portion of the CHAP. IV
action: in *Andromache*, it seems to describe all that the
Chorus do outside lyrical passages [1].

In the odes this dedramatisation of the Chorus is again *Interludes*
suggested by the practice of Euripides, in some of his plays, *disconnect-*
ed from
to dissociate the choral interludes from the point of the plot *adjacent*
at which they occur, and connect their matter with the *episodes:*
wh°lly,
subject of the story as a whole. In the *Hecuba* and
Daughters of Troy all the odes (after the parode) are of
this description; the captive women, awaiting the moment
when they will be borne from Troy, sing the lands of their
coming captivity, the fatal deed of Paris, the awful night
of their city's fall: but ignore the particular scenes which
each ode follows or precedes [2]. As a transitional step to *or in part*
this complete disconnection between odes and episodes
we have the interludes in which Euripides leads off with
some distant theme, but at the close of the ode formally
connects it with the course of the action. Examples have,
in a previous section, been cited from the *Electra*. But
the classic illustration of this treatment is a famous ode in
the *Helena* [3]. It occurs just where the intrigue of the play *Helena*
is to all appearance completely successful, and the disguised Menelaus has carried off Helen from the barbarian
king, her captor, upon the pretext of celebrating his own
death at sea. The Chorus, instead of expressing congratu-
lation or relief, start upon the theme of the Mountain
Mother inconsolable for her lost Daughter of the Mysteries.
How in wild search she traversed thick-entangled forests
and valleys of streaming floods, with loud clashing cymbals,

---

[1] It might be remarked that this play seems largely made up of
forensic contests.

[2] In the *Women from Phœnicia* the legendary glory of Thebes (where
the scene is laid) is resumed (sometimes abruptly) and carried on
through several odes, with occasional reference to the situation of affairs
in the play.

[3] *Helena*, 1301.

Chap. IV and in her train the Virgins of Heaven, Artemis of the
silver bow and Pallas with her Gorgon: but Jove had set
the fates against them all. How, foiled, she threw herself
into solitudes beyond the eternal snows of Ida, amid damp
weeds and rocky rudeness; without her to bless them the
plains, bare of the faintest green, wasted the generation
of men, and for lack of juicy tendrils the flocks failed and
there were no victims for the altar; the very fountains,
unfreshened by dews, told of inconsolable grief for a lost
child. How at last all heaven was roused to interpose, and
at Jove's own bidding they went on a mission of consolation—holy Graces, and Muses with chanted dances, Cypris,
fairest of the blessed, leading the way with brass and drum:
till at last joy again touched the Mother's heart and she
took in her hand the sounding flute. It is now that the
relevancy is made apparent. It is a point of this play that
Euripides is here singing his palinode to Helen, and arranging the legend so as to make her innocent. On this theory
the seizure of Helen against her will, which has plunged the
nations in the turmoil of the Trojan War, can find a parallel
in nothing less than the great Rape of Proserpine, for which
all heaven and earth had to mourn. Accordingly, in their
final antistrophe, the Chorus suggest that Helen may have
slighted the Great Mother, and therefore unholy violence
has met her in her own marriage chamber; now that deliverance has come they bid her remember the due honours
of heaven, and give herself to the profitable joys of the
spotted fawn-skin and ivy-wreathed thyrsus, her vestments
waving and hair streaming in the ring of the Bacchic dance.

4 Other Lines of Development

*Decompo-
sition
of dra-
matic*   It has been shown in a former chapter that when, by the
fusion of Chorus and Drama, Ancient Tragedy was constituted a distinct species, one of the most important effects

of this fusion was to stamp upon its action a very peculiar type of unity. It is natural, then, that the changes which exhibit Greek Tragedy as losing its specific distinctiveness should include a wavering in the unity of action as conceived by the ancients. Here we get another line of development, which may be described as the *Decomposition* of *Dramatic Unity*. Now the term 'unity' has two senses, singleness and completeness; it is antithetical to variety and fragmentariness. Hence the decomposition in question covers two cross tendencies: one towards the variety and multiplicity of modern treatment, the other towards a kind of action which is, dramatically, imperfect.

First, we are to trace a tendency towards variety and multiplicity of action. It may be well to repeat how very strict the Greek conception of unity was. A modern dramatist may weave many stories into one, and will naturally place his readers in touch with many aspects of the matter with which he deals. But Choral Tragedy could admit only one story in a play, since only one Chorus could be common to the audience and the plot; this one story, moreover, Choral Tragedy could present only from a single side, since the Chorus, through whose eyes the audience would look, had their sympathies fixed by their characterisation. This is what unity was in the type: nevertheless, means were found to present occasional scenes otherwise than from the standpoint of the Chorus, and an approach was even made towards the admission of additional stories into the plot.

Three devices introduced a measure of variety into the mode of presenting a story, all tending in the direction of admitting the audience to see events with other eyes than those of the Chorus. One of these is the forensic contest, which has been described at length in a previous chapter. It was that point in a tragedy where the dramatic spirit yielded for a time to the forensic spirit, so strangely

CHAP. IV

unity as a line of development

Two cross tendencies

1
Towards variety and multiplication of action

Encroachments on unity of standpoint: the Forensic Contest,

CHAP. IV characteristic of the Athenians; in form the scene remains
——   an incident of the play, but in tone it is a judicial proceeding,
in which two personages drawn from opposing sides of the
story put their respective cases with formal completeness,
the Chorus posing as judicial moderators. It is an approach
to variety of standpoint for viewing the incidents of the
play, in the sense that it gives to opposing sympathies just
that degree of free expression that is implied in a fair trial.
A modern dramatist would take us almost as deeply into
the confidence of Clytæmnestra as into that of his heroine
Electra.   An ordinary scene in a Greek Tragedy could
display Clytæmnestra only as she would appear to the hostile
Chorus.   But in the forensic contest the dramatist passes
into the advocate for both parties in succession, and makes
a fair case for each; while the Chorus drop from sympa-
thisers into arbitrators, and can even urge that each might
learn of the other.

the Pro-   The other two devices go further.   The Prologue[1] of
logue,   a Greek Tragedy by definition includes all that precedes the
entrance of the Chorus, and may amount to one or more
scenes, in the modern sense of the word 'scene.'   Here we
have, as a regular thing, a section of the story not controlled
by the presence of the Chorus.   It may or may not amount
to a breach in the unity of standpoint.   The *Prometheus* is
an example of a play in which the prologue, representing
the act of nailing the hero to the rock, contains nothing
that could not be transacted in the presence of the Chorus,
though as a fact they do not enter till later.   It is different
with such plays as the three versions of *Electra*; here the
prologue introduces the arrival of Orestes, while the working
of the plot mainly rests upon the ignorance of this fact on
the part of Electra and her Argive friends.   In fact, the

[1] That is, the Prologue Proper, or 'Dramatic Prologue' as it may be
called to distinguish it from the 'Formal Prologue,' introduced by
Euripides (below, page 191).

prologue will often start the story on the opposite side from CHAP. IV
that which is fixed by the Chorus for the rest of the play;
in the dialogue between Antigone and Ismene we see
planned a deed of devotion, which in the rest of the play
will appear—viewed through the eyes of Creon and his
Senators—as an act of rebellion against the State.

The prologue, then, gives opportunity at the commence- *and the*
ment of a play for a scene outside the standpoint of the *Stage*
Chorus: by another device, such a scene may occur at a *Episode*
later place in the action. In some dramas the Chorus are
made to quit the orchestra in the course of the story, and
before their return an incident has taken place confined to
the stage. Such a 'Stage Episode' is clearly a scene outside
the choral unity. An example occurs in the *Ajax*. News
having arrived that the oracle makes the hero's safety depend
upon his keeping his tent that day, all disperse to find their
leader and bring him home; the Chorus dividing and
hurrying in opposite directions to join in the search. Then
(the scene having changed [1]) Ajax himself appears alone,
takes leave of life, and falls upon his sword. Soon after
the Chorus re-enter, as if brought by their search to this
new spot; after a brief delay, the corpse is discovered by
Tecmessa. The whole incident of the hero's suicide has
been presented directly to the audience without the intervening medium of the Chorus. The significance of this
particular case is small, as the discovery is so quickly made.
It is very different with the *Alcestis*. Here the Chorus
accompany Admetus to the tomb. In their absence Hercules, left refreshing himself in a separate wing of the palace,
appears on the stage, and wrings from the Steward the secret
of his gloomy looks; he learns the pious fraud put upon him
by his self-repressing friend, and is fired to attempt the

---

[1] Changes of scene in themselves only affect the unity of place:
in the *Blessed Goddesses* (e. g.) no action takes place in the absence of
the Chorus, and change between Delphi and Athens.

CHAP. IV deliverance of Alcestis from death to prove himself the equal
of Admetus in generosity.   Accordingly, when Admetus
and the Chorus return from the funeral and give themselves
up to mourning and consoling, the audience hold in their
hand the clue to the disentanglement of the plot which is
lacking to the Chorus, and a totally new dramatic effect is
thus given to the long-drawn finale, in which the recovered
wife is slowly made known to her husband [1].

Prologue and Stage Episode combined in Helena   By each of these devices, the prologue and the stage
episode, the audience can be admitted to a point of view
from which the Chorus are excluded, so far as a single
scene is concerned.   In one play, the *Helena*, the two
devices are combined.   It is part of the plot to bring
Helen and Menelaus together.   In the prologue Helen, in a
long soliloquy, opens out her forlorn situation, miraculously
banished to a barbarian country, while the deceived Greeks
and Trojans are fighting over her supposed crime.   A
dialogue that follows intensifies the situation: Teucer, just
landed, shows abhorrence of one who even resembles
Helen, and tells the rumour that Menelaus is lost at sea.
The Chorus enter, and long scenes of lamentation ensue,
but at last they bid their mistress not to despair until she
has certain knowledge of her lord's death, and accompany
her to enquire of the prophetess.   The orchestra being thus
vacant, a stage episode follows.   Menelaus enters, escaped
from shipwreck, and in soliloquy describes his forlornness.
In his case also the situation is deepened by a dialogue
with the first person to whom he can apply for succour;
this Attendant tells the cruel customs of the country to slay
all Greeks, and mystifies Menelaus by speaking of Helen—
whom he thinks he has left by the shore—as long resident

---

[1] Compare the *Rhesus* : by the Chorus (the Watch) quitting their post,
opportunity is given for the Greek spies to do their work ; the audience
see the raid, and hear the result of Dolon's expedition, and the designs
against Rhesus, of all which the Chorus are ignorant on their return.

in the country. At this point Helen and the Chorus return, CHAP. IV
the mystification is soon cleared and the recognition effected.
Thus, by complete parity of handling, the audience has been
(without the aid of the Chorus) introduced separately into
the confidence of the two personages, whose union is the
fiist stage of the plot. The treatment differs only in degree
from the modern variety of presentation.

These devices, then, amount to a breach, not in the *Encroach-*
unity of the story, but only in the singleness of the stand- *ments on unity of*
point from which it is viewed. We have now to see how, *story*
in the latest of the three masters, there is at all events
an approach to the actual multiplication of actions. The
natural expansion of the drama tended more and more to
fulness of personality and incident. The natural outlet
for such increase of matter is the multiplication of plots,
such as in Shakespearean treatment can bring within the
limits of the same play a tragedy in the family of Lear and
a tragedy in the family of Gloucester, developed together
side by side. But thus to multiply centres of interest would,
in Greek Drama, have run counter to the influence of
the Chorus for unifying the sympathies of the audience.
Accordingly, the tendency to multiplication of actions, barred *Plot com-*
in one direction, finds an outlet in another, and we get plot *pounded by agglu-*
compounded by *agglutination* : the additional matter being, *tination*
not a companion story interweaving with the main plot, but
an extension of the main plot added at the end, and centering around the same personages and chorus. No illustration
can be better than the *Electra* of Euripides, already analysed
in this chapter. It is clear that completeness of plot would
be abundantly satisfied if this play had come to an end
with the recognition of brother and sister, what remained of
Orestes' mission being despatched formally and the assassination of the tyrants being made to appear—as it does
appear in the versions by Sophocles and Aeschylus—the
final detail in the return of the avenger. Instead of this,

CHAP. IV the version of Euripides starts a new and complex intrigue
for the accomplishment of vengeance, an intrigue which is
carried through four distinct scenes to an unexpected denouement, and which of itself would suffice for the plot of
a separate drama, with the meeting of Orestes and Electra
a formal detail at its commencement. Here then we have
two plots in a Greek tragedy, referred to the same personages
and Chorus, the second beginning where the first leaves
off[1]. Compared with the organic unity of a modern complex drama, such agglutinated plots resemble certain lower
organisms in nature: these can be chopped into sections,
and each section becomes itself a distinct organism with a
vitality of its own. The natural impulse to multiplication
of actions has made itself felt, but been adapted to the
unifying influence of the Chorus.

Rise of   But Greek Tragedy can go further even than this, and we
the Second- find an approach to the Secondary Plot that is developed
ary Plot: side by side with the main story. There was only one way
in which this could possibly have come about :—not by the
importation of a new story into the play, but by a rise of
subordinate personages in the scale of dramatic interest
until they became a distinct interest in themselves. This
important chapter of dramatic development we are able
to trace in two well-marked stages, corresponding to
Sophocles and Euripides. Chrysothemis in the *Electra* of

[1] The case of the *Electra* is particularly clear, because the two plots
are distinct in kind: the first is an example of Complication and
Resolution, in the second an Opening Situation is developed by intrigue
to its Reversal. [According to the scheme on page 140, the plot formula
for this play might be $S\ C\ R\ +\ S'$.] Compare the *Helena*. But the
same analysis applies substantially to all cases of what has in this work
been called the 'Pendulum Plot.' This involves a complication and resolution, after which the action is recomplicated. One plot is complete
with the resolution; a second plot commences with this resolution, which
may be regarded as a complication finding its resolution in that which is
the recomplication of the play. The two plots overlap, that which
stands as resolution to the first serves as complication for the second.

Sophocles, Ismene in his *Antigone*, do something more than CHAP. IV
bring out by contrast the characters of their respective ——
heroines: each has a little drama of her own. Chryso- *embryonic*
in Sopho-
themis appears at first as an element in the surroundings *cles,*
hostile to heroism; she is gradually won to an interest in
Electra's hopes of retribution, returns in triumph from the
sepulchre, is damped by the sad news of Orestes, and falls
finally into an acquiescence in evil lower than before. So
Ismene, having resisted in the prologue Antigone's bold purpose, returns repentant at the crisis and insists on sharing
the rebel's fate. In each case there is a rise and fall of
incident that attaches distinct plot interest to the younger
sisters. But it is remarkable that Sophocles entirely drops
these personages in the very middle of his drama: not only
are they absent from subsequent scenes, but in all the wide
spreading woe of the catastrophe there is no hint how they
are affected by it. It is clear that in Sophocles there is no
sense of underplot, such as would have led this great master
of dramatic movement to find at least a formal connexion
for such centres of interest with the conclusion of the action.
In Sophocles, then, the underplot is no more than an em- *complete in*
Euripides
bryo: in Euripides, it has developed further. In his *Orestes*
the drama as a whole is a story of family affection: Pylades
appears in it to represent the allied interest of friendship.
In the similar plays of Aeschylus and Sophocles, Pylades is
little more than a tacit symbol for the proverbial friendship;
in the version of Euripides he takes an active part in the
story. It is he who comes to tell, in rhythm of excitement,
the new plot to banish Orestes; he accompanies his friend
to the assembly and gives him his support. When Orestes
is condemned, and all is despair, attention is diverted for a
time from the main theme by the episode in which Pylades
insists on sharing death, as he has shared life, with his
comrade. To him is given the turning-point in the action,
when out of the despair he evolves desperate counsels

CHAP. IV of rescue. He has a share only subordinate to that of Orestes in the incidents by which the conspiracy is carried out, and the recognition of him throughout these scenes is perhaps the more marked because it has at one time to be maintained against the stage convention limiting the number of speakers in a scene.

> *Menelaus.* And art thou, Pylades, accomplice with him?
> *Orestes.* His silence speaks: sufficient my reply.

Finally, in the Divine Intervention that sets all straight, provision is made for Pylades, and he is assigned Electra for a wife. Faint as such an underplot may seem in comparison with the elaborate multiple action of modern drama, it is technically complete; and this is one among the many cases in which Euripides has laid the foundation for dramatic treatment which has reached its culmination in Shakespeare [1].

11
Counter tendency to imperfect unity

So far, any decomposition of dramatic unity which we have traced has been in the direction of including in a play more than a single story. We have now to see how, on the other hand, encroachment can be made upon the unity of a drama in the opposite direction, more and more of the story being, by certain devices, withdrawn from dramatic treatment. The disturbing force which set up this line of development was mainly the struggle of dramatic interest with the extraneous elements of rhetoric and epic; and three devices of treatment illustrate how these could supersede plot at certain points of a play.

[1] Another example of Secondary Plot is that of the Peasant in *Electra*, who plays such an important part in the earlier half of the play, importing into it the interest of humble hospitality, disappears with only a slight part in the intrigue of the second part, but is recognised and provided for in the Divine Intervention. In the *Iph. Taur.* the friendship of Pylades is a secondary interest in a way precisely parallel to the case of the *Orestes*; only here there is no allusion to Pylades in the Divine Intervention, seeing that he is already wedded to Electra.

The first of these is the Formal Prologue, which is not, CHAP. IV
like the usual tragic prologue[1], a dramatic scene, but *The*
resembles the prologue of the modern drama in being a *Formal*
speech outside the action. Sometimes it takes the form *Prologue*
of a soliloquy by one of the personages in the play, as the
famous speech of Electra[2] in the *Orestes*, in which, starting
with a general meditation on human misery, she traces this
misery through her mythic ancestral history down to her
own desperate condition, her sole hope being in the rumoured
arrival of Menelaus. Or, as in the *Suppliants* and *Electra*,
a prayer to a deity may be the form in which the situation
of affairs is made known. Or again, the prologue may
be spoken by a god possessed of supernatural knowledge.
It is so in the *Ion*. Hermes starts abruptly with his own
divine genealogy and his arrival at the scene of the play. He
proceeds to tell methodically the whole story of the amour
between Apollo and Creusa, and the subsequent history of
the mortal maiden and the child up to the moment of the
play opening. Having to mention that the child was
'exposed' by its mother, the god digresses to explain the
origin of rites observed in exposure, and he digresses a
second time to explain how Creusa came to marry a
foreigner. He concludes with a glance at the future, in
which he puts the end, though not the successive steps, of
the plot. The general style of such a speech, and especially
its digressions, show how entirely external it is to dramatic
form; its interest is the rhetorical interest of a formal and
logical explanation, whereas the essence of drama is that
events must explain themselves.

As this Formal Prologue is a non-dramatic introduction, *The Mirac-*
so the Miraculous Close is a non-dramatic conclusion. *ulous close:*
This usually takes the form of a Divine Intervention, like *tervention*

[1] The two are frequently combined : e. g. in *Orestes*, &c.
[2] This is said to be the portion of classical poetry most largely
quoted in antiquity.

CHAP. IV

*or Final
Oracles*

*The Mes-
senger's
Speech*

that already described in the *Electra* : a god from the sky
arrests the course of the story, and declares the sequel by
his supernatural knowledge and will.   In some plays which
lack this, there is an approach to the same effect in the
oracular prophecies of the future uttered at the end by the
victim of the play.   In the *Hecuba*, nemesis has come upon
Polymestor in the form of blinding; similarly in the
Children of Hercules, Eurystheus has been given up to those
he has persecuted to be put to death.   In each case the
sufferer suddenly pours out oracles he has learned, painting
the future destiny of those who are now triumphant over
him ; these are accepted by all as revelation, and have the
effect of giving a back-turn of fate at the last moment[1].
The point in common between this and the Divine Intervention is that in both cases the plot is wound up by
miracle : now, where miracle intervenes, dramatic interest,
which rests upon the working out of cause and effect, at
once ceases.   For it is substituted a different interest, akin
to the rhetorical and epic satisfaction that belongs to a story
completely wound up[2].

To these two devices—the special invention of Euripides
—must be added the Messenger's Speech, the use of which
he has greatly extended, and which substitutes epic narrative

---

[1] An approach to the ' pendulum form of action.'

[2] The *Daughters of Troy*—in all respects one of the most masterly
and characteristic productions of Euripides—has the structural peculiarity that a Formal Prologue and a species of Miraculous Close are put
together at the commencement of the play.   Neptune's speech opens
the state of affairs, the subsequent dialogue with Pallas, and the plot
concerted by the two deities against the victorious Greeks, convey to
the audience the idea of an ultimate back-stroke of fate outside the
dramatic action and made known by supernatural machinery.   The
effect is to reduce the whole body of the play to a single pregnant
situation : plot has been absorbed into passion, and the line of action
become a point.   The episodes are various phases of this situation :
fates of various captives bound into a unity by Hecuba, who, as queen
and mother, feels over again all that the rest feel.

for dramatic presentation in the case of one incident or CHAP. IV
more of the story. The example described at length in the
Electra illustrates how highly dramatic some points of such
a speech can be ; for in fact drama and epic have much in
common. But the Messenger's Speech may diverge very
widely from the spirit of drama. This is well seen in the
Ion, where the Messenger's Speech describes, to the alarmed
and impatient Chorus, the attempt to poison the hero at a
banquet ; not only does the narration take over a hundred
lines, but one-third of the length is devoted to technically
describing the proportions of the banqueting-tent, and
explaining in detail the subjects represented in the
tapestry.

> Meanwhile, with reverent heed, the son gan rear
> On firm supporters the wide tent, whose sides
> No masonry require, yet framed to exclude
> The mid-day sun's hot beams, or his last rays
> When sinking in the west : the lengthened lines
> Equally distant comprehend a square
> Of twice five thousand feet, the skilful thus
> Compute it, space to feast—for so he willed—
> All Delphi. From the treasures of the god
> He took the sacred tapestry, and around
> Hung the rich shade on which the admiring eye
> Gazes with fixed delight. First over head
> Like a broad pennon spread the extended woof,
> Which from the Amazonian spoils the son
> Of Jove, Alcides, hallowed to the god :
> In its bright texture interwoven a sky
> Gathering the stars in its ethereal round,
> Whilst downward to the western wave the sun
> His steeds declines, and to his station high
> Draws up the radiant flame of Hesperus.
> Meanwhile the Night, robed in her sable stole,
> Her unreined car advances: on her state
> The stars attend; the Pleiads mounting high,
> And with his glittering sword Orion armed ;
> Above, Arcturus to the golden pole
> Inclines ; full-orbed the month-dividing moon
> Takes her bright station, and the Hyades

> Marked by the sailor; distant in the rear
> Aurora, ready to illume the day
> And put the stars to flight. The sides were graced
> With various textures of th' historic woof,
> Barbaric arguments; in gallant trim
> Against the fleet of Greece the hostile fleet
> Rides proudly on ; here, monstrous forms pourtrayed,
> Human and brutal mixed ; the Thracian steeds
> Are seized, the hinds and the adventurous chase
> Of savage lions ; figured near the doors
> Cecrops, attended by his daughters, rolled
> His serpent train.

Such laborious expansion of description, in the midst of a situation full of peril, is clear evidence that the sense of dramatic propriety is for the time suspended, and is replaced by interest of an epic order.

These three devices, the Formal Prologue, the Miraculous Close, and the Messenger's Speech, are encroachments on the unity of action, in the sense that they abstract certain portions of the story from the plot and deal with them by *Three* methods extraneous to drama.   Now, as these devices are, *stages of* two of them wholly and one mainly, confined to Euripides, *diminish-* *ing unity* while in his plays they are of almost universal application, *in the* we get, when we compare the three masters, three stages of *three* *masters* diminishing unity.   Aeschylus produces trilogies[1]: here the dramatic unity may embrace three plays.   In Sophocles, the dramatic unity is conterminous with a single play.   In Euripides, the dramatic unity is less than the play, the beginning of the story, the end, and portion of the middle being cut off by non-dramatic treatment.   The three stages differ as a group, a full-length portrait, and a vignette.   And after Euripides the decomposition—as a future chapter will show—is carried further still, the unity of action sinking

---

[1] The term ' trilogies ' applies to all the dramatists : Aeschylus alone made the three tragedies, which each competitor was expected to produce, continuous in matter.

into a formal bond of plot, which serves as a frame to bind CHAP. IV
together situations contrived for effects which are more often
than not extraneous to drama.

Passing from action to more general elements of dramatic *Other lines*
effect, we notice as another line of development in Ancient *of development :*
Tragedy *a gradual widening of field and characterisation,* *Widening*
and of tone. Originally the matter of tragic story was con- *of Characterisation*
nected with Dionysiac myths, soon it came to include all *and field*
sacred legend. Under Aeschylus the dramatic field appears
to be confined to heroic life, and deities move amongst his
personages without any sense of incongruity. Sophocles
widens the field to human nature, but it is human nature
in the type: his character-sketching shows power in
idealising the type rather than subtlety in inventing
variations. In the characterisation of Euripides there is
a strong flavour of individuality. Thus the Clytæmnestra of
Aeschylus is demonic : a conscious inspiration of retributive
justice gives dignity to her crimes. The Clytæmnestra of
Sophocles is created out of the story : the wrong done to
her as a mother has turned strong love into strong hate,
of which her devotion to Aegisthus is a symptom and an
instrument. The personage corresponding to these in the
Electra of Euripides is distinguished by a strain of pettiness
as an addition to the traditional character. Luxury and
display seem to be her master motives : the splendour of
her car and retinue is an effect in the play, we hear of her
adorning herself for Aegisthus before Agamemnon did the
wrong against Iphigenia, the wealth she had amassed was
the attraction that brought Aegisthus to her, and his
effeminate beauty made him a fitting partner. The pettiness appears again in the social degradation she contrived
for her daughter, working secretly through her paramour.
There is pettiness even in the compunction she shows at
the last, seeing that this is aroused only by the offensive
details of poverty she finds in her daughter's rustic home,

CHAP. IV and that it may be cheaply indulged now her object is
secured by the (supposed) birth of Electra's child. Such
individuality of character belongs to the general realism of
Euripides. It extended the field of the drama to domestic
life, and the degree to which the poet introduces women
and children into his plays was a scandal to the critics of
his age. But Tragedy was brought into conflict with the
mythic stories, from which its materials had still to be
drawn, the attempt of a contemporary poet, Agathon, to
break away from these in favour of invented personages
having been resisted. Once more the developing tendency
of Euripides needed the free play of modern literature to
give it full scope.

*Widening
of Tone*   We may trace a similar widening of tone. The term
'tragic' covers many meanings. The tone of Aeschylus is
tragic of the religious order, resting upon such ideas as
fate, hereditary curse, resistance to omnipotence, sanctity
of the suppliant bond. Sophocles leans to tragic in the
purely dramatic sense, resting upon the working out of
plot: his writing is deeply religious, but he chooses the
dramatic aspects of religion—nemesis, and oracular revelation. Under Euripides the tone widens to all that can be
included in the word 'tragic'; he has a special leaning to
the pathetic side of tragedy, and his treatment extends
beyond this to the serious tone which is distinguished from
tragic by the happy ending of the story. This appears in
the *Ion* by natural causes; in many plays it is brought
about by the Divine Intervention.

*Especially
the Mix-
ture of
Tones,*   But in this connexion there is one piece of development
worthy of special notice: the approach, under Euripides, to
the modern *Mixture of Tones*—the union of serious and
light in the same play—by which the Romantic literature of
modern times has won some of its greatest triumphs. It is
not correct to describe this as the union of tragedy and
comedy: these were, in Greece, entirely distinct rituals.

But there was another dramatic species which tended to amalgamate with tragedy, and so favour the mixture of tones. This was the Satyric Drama. To understand the term[1] the reader must carry his thoughts back to the ultimate beginning of tragedy in the dance of satyrs. At this period (it has been remarked) 'tragi' was another name for satyrs : so that Tragedy and Satyric Drama would then be synonymous terms. Out of this Satyr dance, it has been shown in the opening chapter, was step by step developed dramatic poetry ; the old form however was not discarded, but existed side by side with the developing drama. By a process familiar to the student of etymology the two terms, which at first were identical in meaning, became in time differentiated with the differentiation of that to which they were applied : Tragedy became the name of the developing drama, while Satyric Drama was applied to the unreformed dithyramb. In process of time even this Satyric Drama began to follow in the steps of Tragedy, and adopted its form of alternating odes and episodes, while retaining the boisterous tone of the satyric dance. In historical times the two species are found side by side, the Satyric Drama using the same mythic stories as Tragedy, but treating them for burlesque. The custom was for a poet to produce three tragedies and a satyric drama, which closed the day's entertainment much in the way that modern theatres relieve serious drama with a farce at the end of the evening[2].

CHAP. IV

by influence of the Satyric Drama

---

[1] The young reader is warned that 'Satyric' and 'Satiric' are totally distinct words.

[2] One of these satyric dramas has been preserved: the *Cyclops* of Euripides : it is here subjoined in outline.—

> *Scene* : Sicily, before the Cave of the Cyclops, Polyphemus.
> *Prologue* by Silenus, the rural demi-god, who recounts his faithful service to Bacchus : yet the ungrateful god has allowed himself and his children to fall into this slavery to the horrid Cyclops, in which—worst of their many woes—they are debarred from the wine they worship.

Now tradition has preserved the important circumstance that Euripides composed his *Alcestis* as a substitute for

Parode: The Chorus of Satyrs, driving their goats, and lamenting how different their state is from the merry service of Bacchus.

Episode 1 : Silenus hurries back, announcing that a ship is approaching to water in the island : fresh victims for the monster. *Enter Ulysses and crew*: Mutual explanations, all couched in burlesque tone. The mariners have had no food except flesh, and gladly accept the Satyrs' milk and fruits, giving in return to Silenus the long-lost luxury of wine. The scene goes on to paint [with the utmost coarseness] the on-coming of intoxication.

Suddenly *enter Polyphemus*: Ulysses and the crew hide. After some rough bandying between the monster and the Chorus the strangers are discovered : and Silenus, to save himself, turns traitor, and tells Polyphemus they have beaten him because he would not let them steal, also what dire woes they were going to work upon Polyphemus. In spite of protests, Silenus is believed. Ulysses promises, if set free, to erect shrines in Greece for the Cyclops, besides dwelling upon the impiety of attacking innocent strangers. Polyphemus replies that he does not care for shrines, and, as to impiety, he is independent of Zeus : which gives occasion for a eulogium on the life of nature. All are driven into the cave to be fed upon at leisure.

Choral Ode: General disgust at the monster.

Episode 2 : *Ulysses* [*apparently standing at the mouth of the cave*] describes Polyphemus gorging—then details his plan of deliverance by aid of the wine.

Choral Ode: Lyric delight of the Chorus at the prospect of deliverance.

Episode 3 : The Cyclops appears sated with his banquet, and settling down to this new treat of drinking; the effects of on-coming intoxication are again painted in Polyphemus with the usual coarseness—a farcical climax being reached when the monster begins to be affectionate to his cup-bearer, old Silenus, in memory of Zeus and his Ganymede.

Choral Ode: Anticipations of revenge.

Exodus: The plan of revenge is carried out—boring out the Cyclops' one eye while he is overpowered with drink. Various farcical effects by the way : e. g. the Chorus drawing back with excuses and leaving Ulysses to do the deed at the critical moment. The drama ends with the monster's rage and vain attempts to catch the culprits, Ulysses putting him off with his feigned name of 'No Man.' Thus all are delivered.

a satyric drama. It is easy to trace such a purpose in the
play itself. Hercules was a favourite personage alike in
tragic and in satyric plots. In tragedy he represents the
human frame raised to the point of divinity, physical
strength in its perfection toiling and suffering for mankind. The satyrist caught a burlesque side to such
an ideal, and realised pantomimically the huge feeding
necessary to keep up gigantic activity. The Hercules
who was to draw together the dark and bright sides of
Euripides' play must harmonise these two conceptions :
it has been accomplished in one of the most inspiring
creations of ancient poetry—an embodiment of conscious
energy rejoicing in itself, and plunging with equal eager-
ness into duty and relaxation, while each lasts. The
hero's entering cheer strikes like an electric shock upon
the crushed mourners ; his reception is shown in the
ode that follows to have introduced a current of hope
into the play. In the stage episode, Hercules appears
at first in the careless abandon of the reveller, and
preaches to the gloomy Steward the easy ethics of the
banquet ; from this bright tone he passes to the heroic as
the truth gradually breaks upon him, and he is fired to a
task of generous rivalry in which he will try his strength on
Death himself. It will be observed that this introduction
of the non-tragic tone is made at a point where the Chorus,
representatives of the unity, are for the time absent. In the
finale the opposites are brought together, Admetus and
the Chorus knowing only the sad aspect of affairs, Hercules
and the audience holding the happy clue ; and all the
resources of stichomuthic elaboration are exhausted before
the sadness and brightness are allowed to blend in the
tumult of emotions that attend the raising of the veil.
The play has won every age : the dramatic experiment was
ruled unsuccessful, and we have no knowledge that it
was ever repeated. Euripides could do no more than

CHAP. IV point out to modern times the most profitable of all paths
————   for dramatic enterprise [1].

Struggle of   I have shown development in the different elements of
thought
and form Ancient Tragedy, its chorus, its unity, its tone and characterisation.   It will be enough just to allude to one more line
of development exhibited in the *struggle between thought
and form*.   In Aeschylus, dramatic interest is subordinate to
thought—the religious brooding over man and the mysteries
of life, brooding conveyed directly in meditations or con-
cretely in the action.   In Sophocles dramatic interest is
supreme, and the very thought embodied in his plays is,
we have seen, moulded in dramatic shape : exact balance of
matter and form is one of the many perfections that meet
in Sophocles.   But Euripides passes beyond perfection
to progress : with him dramatic form is subordinated to
a wider human interest.   He brings the limitlessness of
realism into a literary form developed to fit ideal treatment ;
he breaks away from simplicity of plot in feeling after complexity of passion.   In part, we have seen, he develops
Ancient Tragedy into newness of form.   In part his treatment remains, within its own species, a disturbing element,
which the historian recognises as the re-starting of evolution
for the universal drama.

----

[1] It may be observed that the invention by Euripides of the plot form,
Complication and Resolution [No. 5, page 141], together with the happy
ending often brought about by the Divine Intervention, are pieces of
development akin to this mixture of tones in *Alcestis*.   Accordingly, it
is not surprising to find in the *Iphigenia among the Tauri* that the
resolution in its progress admits a distinctly comic scene—the ' hoaxing'
of Thoas, whose superstition is worked upon by the finesse of Electra
until he is left waiting solemnly, with a veil over his head, while his
prisoners are escaping from him.   It is noticeable that the sudden
thought of this ruse is marked by a change to accelerated rhythm.

V

THE ROMAN REVIVAL OF TRAGEDY

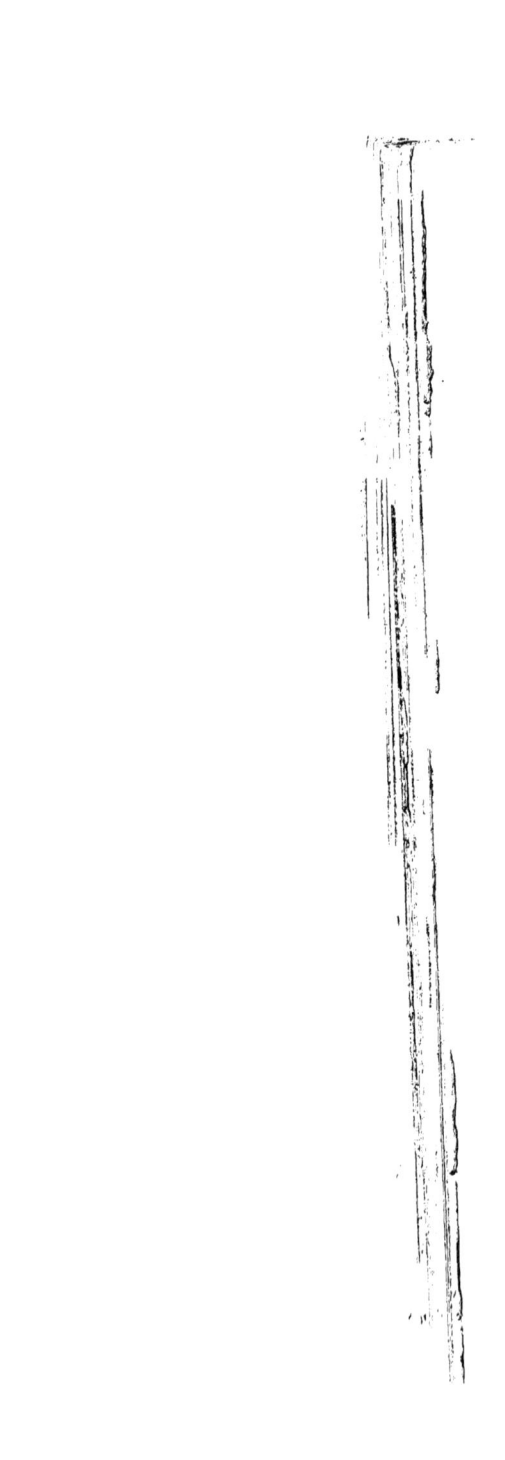

THE Latin tragedies ascribed to Seneca [1] constitute a sort CHAP. V of half-way house in the course of development between an- *Roman* cient and modern drama : Seneca represents Ancient Classi- *Tragedy* cal Tragedy to the Elizabethan age, and the plays which *an imita-* *tion of* stand in his name are rather contributions to Greek Tragedy *Greek,* than a species in themselves. There is the same double form of lyric odes alternating with dramatic scenes. The subjects of the odes are the same : they are mainly odes of situation, with occasional ritual or national hymns, and odes of narrative. The blank verse of the episodes is identical, and there is the same tendency to invade these episodes with lyric monodies and concertos where the emotion of the scene affords an opportunity. And, with one exception, each Roman play is the counterpart of a Greek tragedy, the story of which it at once follows and recasts. Yet a *with dis-* glance below the surface shows a wide gulf between Euripides *sociation* *from the* and Seneca. The Roman plays are clearly not intended *stage as a* for acting, and not arranged for the stage : their motive *disturb-* *ing force*

[1] They are ten in number :—*Hercules Mad, Hippolytus, Daughters of Troy, Women from Phœnicia*, and *Medea*, all following plays of Euripides—*Oedipus* and *Hercules on Oeta* following the *Oedipus the King* and *Maidens of Trachis* of Sophocles—*Agamemnon* following Aeschylus's play—*Thyestes*—and *Octavia*, a Roman subject. The last is by internal evidence determined to a later date than Seneca ; and experts have, for metrical reasons, questioned whether the *Hercules on Oeta* and *Agamemnon* are not separate in authorship from the other seven : it will be seen below (pages 215-7) that the three are bound together by common peculiarities of structure and choral treatment. [I shall ignore altogether the *Women from Phœnicia*, as in too fragmentary a condition to be the basis of any argument.]

CHAP. V is rhetorical or poetic, they are dramatic only in form. Such dissociation from the stage is a disturbing force of the first magnitude; it is as if the opera had passed into the oratorio; the non-dramatic purpose has—perhaps unconsciously to the poet—produced strong divergence even in dramatic form. The object of the present chapter is to describe Roman Tragedy as moulded by these opposing influences:—imitation of Greek models, which acts as a retarding force, and again the revolutionising effect produced by the substitution of literary for dramatic setting.

As in previous chapters, I shall deal with this part of my subject by first describing a single play of Seneca in comparison with its Greek counterpart, and then gather into THE general principles the Roman treatment of Tragedy. The DAUGH-TERS OF *Daughters of Troy* appears to be the point at which the TROY OF Greek stage approaches nearest to Roman conceptions EURIPIDES of dramatic poetry. This is not the place to speak of the pathos and scenic splendour which make this play one of Euripides' greatest masterpieces; we are concerned here with the barest outline of structure and form. Uniqueness of structure characterises the prologue to the Greek version. *Prologue* There is first a formal prologue by Neptune: he is quitting the Troy he has been unable to save, and describes the situation—the town in ruins, and Queen Hecuba with other noble women waiting as captives to be carried away. Athene encounters him, fresh from the sacrilege done to her shrine: she announces her change of mind, and the two deities concert a scheme of vengeance on the Greeks, agreeing to raise a storm which shall destroy them on their homeward voyage. This dialogue constitutes a sort of divine intervention placed at the beginning and not the end of the drama; taken in connexion with the prologue, its effect is to reduce the body of the play to the expansion of a single situation, of which the origin and the issue have been determined extra-dramatically:—the line of action has become a point.

The choral odes are all celebrations of this one situation, Chap. V
and the episodes pourtray different phases of it centering
around the figures of different sufferers, with Hecuba as
a point of unity, since she feels over again all that her
daughters suffer.

The scene is in front of the tent in which the captives are *Scene and*
confined. Hecuba opens the situation in a monody, and *parode*
then calls upon her companions to join her. The Chorus
of Trojan Women enter the orchestra at her call, unite in
a lyric concerto of woe, from which they pass to an ode
inspired by the thought of the various countries to which
they may be carried captive. The first episode is made by *Episode I*
the entrance of the Greek herald Talthybius, who brings
news to the captives of the lots that have settled their fate :
Cassandra has been assigned to Agamemnon, Polyxena is
'to serve at a tomb,' Hecuba herself is the prey of Ulysses,
while the anxious enquiry of the Chorus about their own
fate is passed over in contemptuous silence. Then follows
a splendid scene, drawing out Cassandra's part in the
tragedy. She enters from the tent already dressed in bridal
attire, and—in lyrics and blank verse successively—she
flings her prophetic forecasts of the tragedy in which the
Greek triumph is to end, here (as always) striving vainly to
win credence from friends and enemy. The Chorus have
taken their usual share in this scene : yet they make no
allusion to it in the ode which follows ; they can dwell only *Interlude*
on the one absorbing topic of their city's fall, and brilliantly
picture the sudden capture in the dead of night.

Andromache is the centre of the next episode. She *Episode II*
enters in a chariot, with the infant Astyanax at her breast.
After bringing the news which explains Polyxena's ' service
at the tomb ' of Achilles, she enters into a strange contest in
despair with the aged Hecuba. But there is fresh matter
for despair when the herald re-appears bearing the decree of
the victors that Hector's child must be flung from the towers

Interlude

of Troy; the mother realises her helplessness and has to purchase by quiet submission the right of sepulture for her child. Again the Chorus, though a party to the preceding scene, ignore it in their choral ode, which puts the fall of Troy from a different side, and describes the deified heroes of the land luxuriating with divine selfishness in the joys of heaven while their native city was sinking in ruin.

Episode III Forensic Contest

The third episode gives opportunity for a forensic contest as Helen is dragged from among the captives to her fate, and, seeking to plead her cause, is answered by the Queen and Chorus. The ode which follows starts from the scenery before the eyes of the Chorus, and proceeds to thoughts of ruin and slavery, with a passing curse upon Helen author

Exodus

of it all. There remains an elaborate exodus. The mangled corpse of the child is borne in upon the shield of Hector, and Hecuba pours over it a piteous lament, while the ceremonies of Troy's last funeral are carried through. Then the last step is taken, and Troy is set on fire: by a novel stage-contrivance the scenery changes into a tableau of Troy burning, and amidst the crash of its fall and wild lamentations the Chorus and the nobler captives are dragged to the ships.

THE DAUGHTERS OF TROY OF SENECA

No prologue

The version of Seneca pourtrays in dramatic form the same situation. But there is a total absence of any provision, such as the prologue of Euripides' version, for presenting this situation as part of a story. Another difference catches the eye as we turn over the pages of the Latin version : it is not a continuous poem, but is broken up into five 'acts,' the first four concluding with choral interludes. With the transition from the stage to written literature, Tragedy has lost the unbroken presence of the Chorus from their entry to their exit: and with the loss of this has been also lost its binding effect upon dramatic

No continuous scene

unity. To this may be added that we cannot infer from the words of the Latin tragedy any definite locality or scenery,

but on the contrary the local suggestions in different parts CHAP. V
of the play are inconsistent with one another.

The opening of Seneca's version follows closely that *Act I*
of Euripides: Hecuba laments, with rhetorical fulness, *Monody and Con-*
the woes which she had long foreseen, and at her call the *certo*
Chorus join in a regular wail—tearing their hair, beating
their breasts, and mourning their lost heroes. This, as the
equivalent of a choral interlude, concludes act first.

The second act centres around the incident of Polyxena, *Act II*
but the form in which this is brought out presents great
innovations. The act opens thus : *Chorus purely mechanical*

> *Talthybius.* How long in port the Greeks still wind-bound are,
>   When war they seek, or for their homes prepare !
> *Chorus.* Declare the cause which thus their fleet detains,
>   What god it is that their return restrains.
> *Talthybius.* Amazement strikes my soul—

He goes on to relate, in high-wrought strain, the portent
which he was one to witness: how, amid thunder and
earthquake and bowing woods, the earth opened to the
depths of night, and the spirit of Achilles emerging reproached the Greeks with their want of faith to him, and
demanded the slaughter of the Trojan princess upon his
tomb ; how, thereupon, the hero shrouded himself in night,
and all things returned to their stillness :—

> the quiet main
> Becalmèd lies, the winds their rage restrain,
> The smooth seas move with gentle murmurings,
> And Triton thence the hymeneal sings.

There is nothing to show what errand brings the Greek
herald into the presence of the Chorus [1] or how he leaves

---

[1] I follow the Latin text in treating this as a 'Chorus Troadum.' But
if we might (on the analogy of *Hercules on Oeta* and *Agamemnon*) make
the Chorus in this act a Secondary Chorus of Greeks, consistency would
be secured for the whole act. In the *Octavia* the term 'Chorus
Romanorum' clearly covers two distinct choruses, one the Roman Mob
which sympathises with Octavia, the other the Palace Guard sympathising
with Poppæa.

the scene, nor does he distinctly address any one; the Chorus put to him the formal enquiry, but make no comment on the startling news when it has been given.

Chorus absent   What immediately follows constitutes a scene by itself, in which the Chorus do not take any part, and which obviously belongs to a locality different from that of the Trojan *Forensic contest and* captives. It is a forensic contest between Pyrrhus and Agamemnon. Pyrrhus, in a set speech, presses the demand made by his father's ghost. Agamemnon, in a corresponding rhesis, urges moderation in the hour of success.

> Thou, Priam, make me proud!
> Thou biddest me fear!

The dispute soon becomes an exchange of taunts: Pyrrhus's murder of Priam, and Agamemnon's rash quarrels with Achilles, furnishing ample material. As the pace of the scene accelerates a very characteristic feature of Seneca *use of* emerges—the disputants hurl *gnomes* at one another.

gnomes

> *Pyrrhus.* ''Tis kingly to a king life to afford.'
> *Agamemnon.* Then why a king did you deprive of breath?
> *Pyrrhus.* 'There's mercy sometimes shown in giving death.'
> *Agamemnon.* So you'd in mercy sacrifice a maid?
> *Pyrrhus.* And such a sacrifice can you dissuade
>   Who offer'd your own child?
> *Agamemnon.*   'Their kingdom's good
>   Kings should prefer before their children's blood.'
> *Pyrrhus.* Forbid a captive's death no law e'er did.
> *Agamemnon.* 'What the law does not is by shame forbid.'
> *Pyrrhus.* 'What likes, is lawful by all victors thought.'
> *Agamemnon.* 'The more your licence, to will less you ought.'

Personalities proceed to the extent of calling Pyrrhus a

> girl's bastard, brat
> Got by Achilles when scarce man!
> *Pyrrhus.*   By that
> Achilles, who, to the whole world allied,
> Enjoys the honours of the deified;
> Who can a claim to Sea by Thetis move,
> To Hell by Aeacus, to Heaven by Jove—
> *Agamemnon.* Yes, he who fell by Paris' feeble hand—

Pyrrhus. Whom yet not any of the gods durst stand
 In open fight—
Agamemnon.   Sir, I could rule your tongue—

The ruler of the host saves his dignity by referring the dispute to the seer, and Calchas pronounces the will of heaven to be the slaughter of Polyxena and the death of the infant Astyanax.

This closes the scene. The choral interlude which *Interlude* succeeds illustrates the furthest point to which odes can reach in the direction of irrelevancy. The early part of the act has narrated the apparition of a departed spirit: the theme of this ode is a blank denial that there is anything after death—a theme dissociated equally from the scene and the speakers.

> Is it a truth—or fiction blinds
>   Our fearful minds—
> That when to earth we bodies give
>   Souls yet do live?
> That, when the wife has closed with cries
>   The husband's eyes,
> When the last fatal day of light
>   Has spoiled our sight,
> And when to dust and ashes turned
>   Our bones are urned,
> Souls yet stand in no need at all
>   Of funeral,
> But that a longer life with pain
>   They still retain?
> Or die we quite, nor aught we have
>   Survives the grave,
> When, like to smoke lost in the sky,
>   Our spirits fly,
> And funeral tapers are applied
>   To the naked side?
> What the sun rising doth disclose,
>   Or setting shows,
> Whate'er the sea with flowing waves
>   Or ebbing laves,
> Old Time, that moves with winged pace,
>   Doth soon deface.

With the same swiftness the Signs roll
     Round, round the pole;
With the same course Day's Ruler steers
     The fleeting years;
With the same speed the oblique-paced Moon
     Doth wheeling run:
We are all hurried to our fates,
     Our lives' last dates,
And when we reach the Stygian shore
     Are then no more.
As smoke, which springs from fire, is soon
     Dispersed and gone,
Or clouds, which we but now beheld,
     By winds dispelled:
The Spirit which informs this clay
     So fleets away.
Nothing is after Death: and this,
     Too, nothing is:
The goal or the extremest space
     Of a swift race.
The covetous their hopes forbear,
     The sad their fear: :
Ask'st thou, whene'er thou com'st to die
     Where thou shalt lie?—
Where lie the unborn. Away Time rakes us,
     Then Chaos takes us.
Death, not divided, comes one whole
     To body and soul.
Whate'er of Tænarus they sing,
     And Hell's fierce king,
How Cerberus still guards the port
     O' the Stygian court—
All are but idle rumours found,
     And empty sound,
Like the vain fears of melancholy,
     Dreams, and invented folly.

Act III   The third act is devoted to Andromache and her child.
The Chorus take no part in it until the final interlude, and
Substitu- their absence is the more remarkable as an ' Aged Person '
tion of
Confidant is imported to serve the function proper to a chorus—that
for Chorus of the confidant who draws out a disclosure. To this Aged
Person Andromache relates a dream in which Hector

appeared to warn her of the child's danger. This incident Chap. V
is told with all the conventional setting of classical *Narration*
dreams. *conven-*
tionalised

> Two parts of quiet night were almost spent,
> And now the seven Triones had wheeled round
> Their glittering train, when rest, a stranger found
> To my afflicted thoughts, in a short sleep
> Upon my wearied eyes did gently creep.

There is not the slightest attempt to adapt the incident to
the character of the night just past, which witnessed the
sack of Troy. The dialogue ends by Andromache's se-
lecting Hector's tomb as the hiding place for the boy.
Ulysses then enters, charged with the mission of securing *Dramatic*
Astyanax, and the scene is given up to the ra ati *interest*
interest of dissimulation. Ulysses puts his painful de- *lation*
mand with his proverbial eloquence, against which the
mother is proof. Ulysses changes his tone, and threatens
her with death.

> *Andromache.* No, Ithacus! if me thou'dst terrify
> Threaten me life!

He tries sympathy : he would give way to her woe, but he
has his own son and all the sons of the Greeks to consider,
to whom it may be ruin to let the son of Hector grow up an
avenger. Andromache repays dissimulation with dissimulation, and affects to be so far overcome as to acknowledge to
her foes that the young hope of her nation is—dead ! For
a moment Ulysses is deceived by joy, but soon becomes
suspicious, and says he will sift the news. Feigning a
search, he suddenly cries out that he has discovered the
boy—marking at the moment Andromache's instinctive
glance in the direction of Hector's tomb. With this as
a clue, he announces to Andromache that there . is an
alternative offered by Calchas—that the ashes of Hector
shall be scattered to the winds : and he orders the tomb
to be opened. Distracted by conflicting emotions, Andro-

CHAP. V   mache at length resolves to prevent this sacrilege to her
husband's sepulchre, and submits with lamentations and
taunts to the sacrifice of her child. Ulysses seeks to put
the blame of the sacrifice on Calchas, but Andromache
turns upon him as a 'night soldier,' only stout enough by
day to kill an infant. Then, with mourning long drawn out,
the parting is effected.

Position of Chorus in this act   In the ode that follows, the Chorus give themselves
up to questionings touching the lands into which cap-
tivity may lead them; they make no allusion to the
matter of the act, unless it be an allusion to describe as
their greatest dread the Ithaca in which Ulysses dwells.

Act IV Forensic contest   In the fourth act Helen comes, charged with the mission
of enticing Polyxena, without her knowing it, to her fate:
Helen quiets her conscience with the thought that such
deception will soften the cruel experience. She announces
a project of marriage for Polyxena and Pyrrhus: but this
is received by the Trojan women as an augmentation and
not an alleviation of their calamities, and a bitter forensic
contest ensues. Moreover, the honesty of her message is
doubted:

> For this from our woes' sum may well be spared—
> To be deceived! To die we're all prepared.

Then Helen admits the cruel project, and Polyxena becomes
transformed by the news: heavy at the announcement of
Dumb show or action con-ventionalised   marriage, she triumphs in the prospect of death. But
all these emotions of hers are depicted in dumb show only,
and it is in dumb show that Pyrrhus enters and—amid the
taunts of Hecuba—drags away his victim: so devoted is
the scene to exchange of speeches and not to dramatic
action. Helen also announces the lots which assign the
Chorus in Act IV   captives to their respective masters. Then the Chorus—
who have taken no part in the scene—perform an ode in
which they work out the thought that society in suffering is

a consolation. The conclusion of this ode recalls the closing CHAP. V
portions of Euripides' drama.

> But these sad meetings, these our mutual tears
> Spent to deplore our miserable state,
> The fleet, which ready now to sail appears,
> Will straight dissolve and dissipate.
> Soon as the trumpet's hasty sound shall call
> The mariners a-board, and all
> With favouring gales and oars for sea shall stand,
> When from our sight shall fly our dear loved land:
> What fears will then our wretched thoughts surprise
> To see the land to sink, the sea to rise!
> When Ida's towering height
> Shall vanish from our sight,
> The child shall then unto its mother say,
> The mother to the child, pointing that way
> Which tends unto the Phrygian coast:
> 'Lo, yonder's Ilium, where you spy
> These clouds of smoke to scale the sky'!
> By this sad sign, when all marks else are lost,
> Trojans their country shall descry!

This is the last word of the Chorus: they have no *Act V* place in the fifth act, in which a Messenger relates, with *Messenger's Speech:* elaboration, to Hecuba and Andromache the double mar- *no Chorus* tyrdom of the child and of Polyxena at the tomb. Hecuba speaks her final words of mourning and the Messenger orders all the captives on board the ships. So the play ends.

Turning to review the development of Roman Tragedy as *General* a whole, the first feature which strikes us is the dedramatisa- *Development of* tion of the Chorus. So far as choral odes are concerned, *Roman* it is true, the connexion of these with the story is not less *Tragedy* than in Euripides. But in the episodes the Roman Chorus *Dedrama-tisation of* appears to have lost most of its position as a minor personage *the Chorus:* in the play. Even before the conclusion of Greek drama, *in episode* a tendency was perceptible for the choral function in the scenes to become more mechanical. But mechanical

CHAP. V business—announcing new-comers, questioning messengers
—constitutes the sole activity of the Chorus in Seneca's
episodes. Even their passive presence is no longer assumed. The parode is seldom distinctly provided for in
the Latin plays, and only two contain an exit-song. In the
Hercules Mad the Chorus do not speak once outside the
odes. In the very scenes in which they have mechanical
functions they can be none the less ignored by the personages of the scenes : thus in the final act of the *Oedipus*
the Chorus draw attention to all the entrances of persons or
the other incidents which distinguish the different phases of
this elaborate scene, yet no one addresses them or notices
their words [1]. We have seen in the *Daughters of Troy* how
they can be demonstrably absent from particular scenes.
And at times they appear not only to be ignored, but to be
positively ignorant of what has happened in the course of
the drama, as may be seen in the *Thyestes*, where the Chorus
conclude act second with an ode celebrating the union of
the two brothers, which the scene immediately preceding
has commenced to destroy. Such treatment would suggest
that the Chorus was as much outside the action as the
chorales of a modern oratorio. But this is not the case.

in odes The odes of the Chorus are at times introduced by speakers
in the scenes ; as where Medea hears with anguish the
epithalamium which closes the first act, or Theseus (in
Hercules Mad) prepares for one of the odes by his description of a joyous multitude coming, laurel-crowned, to
sing the triumphs of the hero. Again, the Chorus regularly
retain a characterisation consistent with the plot [2]. Yet
there is a certain unreality in their attitude to the story.
Thus the Chorus in *Hercules on Oeta* address an ode of

---

[1] Similar cases occur all through the *Hippolytus*.

[2] The *Hippolytus* seems to be an exception : the Chorus is described
in the heading as Athenian Citizens, but I have not noted anything in
the text to determine this.

loyalty to their Queen Deianeira, though it is only at the
conclusion of the ode that the Queen enters, and then in a
state of distraction ; similarly an ode in the *Thyestes* appears
to describe as a visible scene the convulsion of all nature,
which was an element in that legend, though the scene
which follows is needed to complete the crime at which
that convulsion of nature expressed horror. All this equivocal position of the Chorus as between recognition and
ignoring would be possible only in a drama not designed
for acting. It is a transition stage of development, in which
the Chorus is fast passing into an interlude external to the
action, but has immanent in it still enough of its old function for this to be recalled at will [1].

In Greek Tragedy the instability of the chorus appeared *Increased*
not only in its dedramatisation, but elsewhere in an opposite *dramatic activity :*
tendency towards increased dramatic activity and the position *the Second-*
of an actor. The counterpart of this in Roman Tragedy *ary Chorus*
may be seen in the rise of the Secondary Choruses which
distinguish one group of plays. The process of change,
however, seems to have been different: it is not that the
regular Chorus have passed into actors, but that a body
of actors has gradually absorbed choral functions. The
Secondary Choruses of the Greek stage—such as those performing the ritual hymn at the close of Aeschylus's trilogy,
or the hunting song in *Hippolytus*—differ from an actor only
in their numbers : in the Latin plays they always serve a
further purpose. The simplest case is that of the *Hercules
on Oeta*, where—in addition to the regular Chorus of Deianeira's subjects, a band of Oechalian captives is brought

---

[1] The extent to which an ode may be merely an interlude is well
shown in the *Hercules Mad.* Amphitryon, at the close of Act II, hears
the rumbling of the earth which proclaims Hercules' return from Hell.
At the commencement of Act III he enters. Between comes an elaborate
ode, in which the hero is celebrated as if still engaged in his terrible
mission.

CHAP. V in by the hero on his triumphant return, and in concerto
with Iole, their princess, they bewail their fate and sing the
irresistibility of Hercules.   These have been called 'protatic
personages,' because they belong only to the 'protasis,' or
that portion of the play preceding the entanglement of the
plot.   But for the single scene in which they are before us
they are a substitute for the other Chorus, and their concerto
serves as the interlude needed to conclude the first act.
Similarly in the third act of the *Agamemnon* there is a band
of Trojan captives, headed by Cassandra, who form a part of
the conqueror's triumph.   But these perform the full functions of a Chorus for the act in which they appear : they sing
an ode of lamentation, they are recalled by Cassandra to
thoughts of present horror, throughout her vision their blank
verse brings out the inspired motions of the prophetess, then
—this concerto having taken the place of an interlude—they
mechanically introduce Agamemnon to open the fourth act,
and appear no more.   Such Secondary Choruses become
important from their bearing on another phase of develop-

The unity ment.   The Chorus, it has been shown in an earlier chapter,
of stand- was the main unity bond, which limited the ancient drama
point im- to single stories and the exhibition of these from single points
paired of view; more stories in a play, or the presentation of one
from more than one side, would (it has been argued) have
involved to a Greek mind more choruses.   This is found in
Roman Tragedy to be actually the case.   In the two plays
just described we are taken into the sympathy of the vanquished only by the aid of special choruses of Oechalians and
of Trojans.   And this comes out still more clearly in
a third play.   In the *Octavia* the two parties to the story are
more nearly on a par : it is not a case of an accomplished
victory, but a court struggle is being fought out between the
empress and the mistress.   Each party has its representative
chorus.   The Roman Mob sympathises with Octavia : in the
first act it laments the degeneracy of the people that suffers

such tyrannical oppression as it describes, in another act it CHAP. V
is being dissuaded by Octavia from showing sympathy with
her, and at the close of the play it attends the fallen queen
on her start for her place of exile, its exit-song being a prayer
for her prosperous voyage[1]. But the Chorus in act fourth is
plainly the Palace Guard, who are on the side of the favourite;
they sing an ode of triumph, then in dialogue with a messenger learn the rising of the mob, and then resume their
ode to prophesy the uselessness of arms in contest with love.
In this case both sides of the story have been separately
developed before us by the full machinery of choruses and
actors proper to each, and in this way the classic unity of
action has been broken down[2].

Roman Tragedy then evaded in its own way the limitations
implied in the unity of action. It may be added that the
encroachments which Greek Tragedy made upon the unities
are also represented in the Latin plays. A Greek drama
could withdraw particular scenes from the cognisance of the
Chorus, regularly in the prologue, by special contrivance
in the stage episode. Seneca's *Daughters of Troy* has
exhibited to us a scene occurring necessarily at a distance
from the Chorus, and there is no suggestion of any attempt
to account for their absence. Such an omission would be
possible only in a drama not intended for acting, and
suggests how, with the loss of a visible chorus, the unity of
place has ceased to be felt as binding. Again, the Euripidean *Impaired*
drama could multiply actions by the mode of agglutination: *unity of*
a second plot being added as a continuation of the main plot, *story:*
and involving the same hero and chorus. A Roman example *tion*
of this is found in the *Hercules on Oeta*. This follows the

---

[1] There is no interlude, or equivalent for an interlude, to Act II: as
no other such omission occurs in Roman Tragedy, I suspect something
has been lost.

[2] In these Secondary Choruses we have the nearest counterpart to the
underplots of Euripides: they are secondary interests, but brought out
chorally, without any rise and fall of plot.

Maidens of Trachis up to the point where explanation is made to the dying hero of the motive which prompted his wife's fatal act. In Sophocles this is the final note in the drama : what follows amounts to an acquiescence by Hercules in his fate. But the Latin play makes this a new turning-point from which the whole action becomes reversed. The reception of the news is preceded by a vision resembling a prologue, in which Hercules beholds the heavenly beings who have so long excluded him from their ranks unbending to attitudes of welcome. In the story told him, he recognises the oracular foundation of his destiny. The train of action then initiated by his directions involves the suffering and triumph of which the interchange is the essence of plot ; a new personage, Philoctetes, is imported to carry out these directions, and successive lyrical and dramatic scenes embody the events that follow. Even while he is being lamented as dead, Hercules appears in glory from heaven, and the exit-song of the Chorus makes it clear that the Roman play has added an apotheosis to the tragedy of the Greek version.

Roman Tragedy favourable to imperfect dramatic unity   But in Greek drama unity could be invaded in a direction the opposite of multiplicity, and a tendency was observable, especially under Euripides, towards imperfect dramatic unity, when the external influences of rhetoric and epic served to withdraw one section after another of the action from dramatic treatment, and produced such effects as the formal prologue, the divine intervention, the forensic contest, and the messenger's speech. Such a tendency would be greatly favoured by the conditions of Latin literature, when the support which a stage would give to the dramatic element had been lost, and rhetoric had become the master passion of the age. Accordingly, in Roman Tragedy extraneous influences have triumphed over dramatic spirit, and the decomposition of dramatic unity has become disintegration ; the component elements of Greek Tragedy—dramatic, lyric, epic, rhetoric—are in Roman Tragedy developed

separately, animating separate scenes, while the movement CHAP. V
of the story is scarcely more than a formal frame which
connects these scenes together.   No play will illustrate this
better than the *Daughters of Troy*.   The sense of story,
exceptionally small in the version of Euripides, has in the
version of Seneca vanished altogether as an interest in
the poem.   What story there is links together scenes, one of
which is devoted to the dramatic interest of dissimulation,
another is a lyric meditation on death untouched by
dramatic surroundings ; one is an epic description, another
is a rhetorical picture of a ghost incident which scarcely
affects to be in dialogue, and others have the interest of
forensic pleadings.

 It is the extraneous interest of rhetoric that is the *Rhetoric*
dominant force in Roman Tragedy : rhetoric leavens every *the domin-*
part of it, and constitutes its main literary strength.   Epic *ant inter-*
narrative lends itself readily to rhetorical ornament, and *est of*
the messenger's speeches in Seneca do not differ materially *Roman*
from those of Euripides.   Rhetoric has a natural place in *Tragedy :*
forensic contests, and if these scenes have any distinctive-*forensic*
ness in the Latin plays it is the greater degree of conven-*contests,*
tionality which they admit.   An example may be taken
from the *Hippolytus*.   The situation is dramatic enough,
where the Nurse seeks to win Hippolytus to her mistress's
corrupt will; and later on the incident becomes the main
dramatic scene of the play.   But the first encounter of the
Nurse and Hippolytus is treated forensically.   The temptation is put in the form of a set speech (of fifty lines),
advocating a life of natural pleasure and family joys,
without which all the beauty of the world would decay.

> No ships will sails on empty seas display,
> Skies will want birds, woods will want game to kill,
> And nought but wind will air's vast region fill.

The temptation is met by a still more elaborate eulogium

Disinte-
gration of
Tragedy
into its
component
elements

(nearly a hundred lines in length) on the higher natural life of the wood-ranging votary of Diana.

> He harmless wandering in the open air
> The solitary country's sweets doth share;
> No cunning subtleties nor craft he knows
> But to entrap wild beasts. And when he grows
> Weary with toil, his tired limbs he laves
> In cool Ilissus' pure refreshing waves;
> Now by the banks of swift Alpheus strays,
> And the thick coverts of the woods surveys
> Where Lerna's streams with chilling waters pass,
> Clear and pellucid as transparent glass.
> His seat oft changes: from their warbling throats
> The querulous birds here strain a thousand notes,
> Whilst through the leaves the whispering zephyr blows,
> And wags the aged beeches' spreading boughs;
> There by the current of some silver spring
> Upon a turf behold him slumbering,
> Whilst the licentious stream through new-sprung flowers
> With pleasing murmurs its sweet water pours.
> Red-sided apples, falling from the trees,
> And strawberries, new gathered, do appease
> His hunger with soon purchased food, who flies
> The abhorred excess of princely luxuries.

dramatic action a veil for rhetorical description, The influence of rhetoric is more decisive in cases where what is nominally a dramatic dialogue is made a medium in which a rhetorical picture is painted. The opening of the *Hippolytus* is in reality an elaborate description of hunting scenes thrown into the imperative mood and vocative case.

> Go—you the shady woods beset,
> You tall Cecropius' summits beat
> With nimble feet; those plains some try
> Which under stony Parnes lie,
> And where the flood borne with swift waves
> Headlong, Thriasian valleys laves.
> Climb you those lofty hills still white
> With cold Rhipæan snows: their flight
> Some others take where stands the grove,
> With spreading alders interwove,

> Where lie the fields which the Spring's sire,
> The fostering Zephyr, doth inspire
> With balmy breath, when to appear
> He calls the vernal flowers, and where,
> Meander-like, 'bove Agra's plains
> Through pebbles calm Ilissus strains
> His course, whose hungry waters eat
> Away his barren banks.

Under the same form of addressing his comrades and praying to his divine patroness, Hippolytus depicts every phase of the hunt, from the hounds held in slack line or straining their necks bare with the leash while the wound-marked boar is yet unroused, to the joyous home-coming—

> whilst the wain's back
> Does with the loaded quarry crack,
> And every hound up to the eyes
> In blood his greedy snout bedyes.

A curious illustration in the *Oedipus* must not be passed over. Sacrifice is offered upon the stage, but the blindness of the seer, Teiresias, obliges him to make use of his attendant's eyes to describe the result : how the flame will neither rise direct to heaven nor fall back indecisive over the altar, but wavers in all the shifting colours of the rainbow, until it finally is cloven in two, while—terrible to relate—the wine becomes mingled with blood, and a dense column of smoke bends off to envelope the head of Oedipus, who stands by. The absorption of drama by rhetoric can go no further than such utilisation of dialogue to translate visible action into rhetorical description.

In this connexion it is proper to notice the prologues as *prologues* a marked feature of Seneca's plays : these exhibit the full power of rhetoric in a situation specially adapted to it. In one tragedy Juno appears as the outraged wife, seeking earth in disgust at heaven, which the bastard Hercules is doomed to enter in spite of her opposition ; reviewing how all her efforts to destroy him have fed his triumphs, she brings out

CHAP. V the past of the story, and then casting about for fresh devices she arrives gradually at the climax of fiendish vengeance which is to be the burden of the play.   In another play the Ghost of Tantalus, first founder of the family of which Thyestes is now chief, is driven on to the scene by the Fury Megæra, and forced by secret pangs to breathe on the household of his descendants fresh pollution—a tangle of violence and suffering enough to disturb heaven itself—until he cries to return to the tortures of hell. In the *Agamemnon* it is the turn of Thyestes to come as a disembodied spirit, fugitive from the powers of hell and seeing mortals fugitives from his ghastly presence: he visits the home he helped to pollute in order to watch the new woe, when his proud successor, king of kings and chief of myriad chiefs, shall return in triumph only that he may offer his throat to the axe of his wife.

Summary   Other aspects of Greek dramatic development, such as the widening of field and characterisation and tone, will hardly be expected in the Roman plays, which are on the face of them imitations.   There is even a going back: the approach made by Euripides to the mixture of serious and comic finds no favour with the severe Roman tragedians.   To sum up our results.   Looked at in the light of the universal drama, the chief interest of Roman Tragedy is the equivocal position given to its chorus by dissociation from acted performance; this prepared the way for that loss of the lyric element which makes the great distinction between ancient and modern drama. Viewed in themselves, the distinguishing feature of Seneca's plays is the degree to which they show extraneous influences triumphing over dramatic, until Tragedy is little more than a dramatic form given to a combination of scenes, epic, lyric and dramatic, all strongly leavened by rhetoric.

VI

SHAKESPEARE'S 'MACBETH' ARRANGED AS AN ANCIENT TRAGEDY

VI

Ancient Tragedy has now been surveyed in the light of the development which connects it with the drama of modern times: it would seem a not inappropriate conclusion to present our results in a concrete shape, and essay the problem of recasting a modern tragedy in the form that would adapt it to the ancient stage. Shakespeare's *Macbeth* naturally suggests itself as the play approaching nearest to the spirit of antiquity; its action rests upon the same oracular mysteries which the Attic tragedians loved, and the same spirit of irony underlies the movement of its story. The purpose then of the present chapter will be to arrange *Macbeth* as a Greek tragedy; my aim will be to introduce as much as possible of what was normal in ancient drama, while exceptional peculiarities or features of advanced development will be avoided.

Problem: to adapt 'Macbeth' to the ancient stage

Broadly viewed there are two fundamental differences of form which distinguish ancient from modern drama. The first is the lyric element. While a Shakespearean play appears throughout as pure drama, an ancient tragedy is on the face of it double: combining drama and lyric, stage and orchestra, actors and chorus, speeches delivered in blank verse and odes executed in dancing. Accordingly our adapted *Macbeth* must take shape as an alternation of scenes and odes, the whole bound together by the Chorus — not, as in oratorio, a band of external performers, but personages taking a slight part in the story, to whose constant presence all the scenes have to be fitted, and whose odes

Lyric matter to be collected from all over Shake-speare's play:

CHAP. VI between the scenes at once break up the tragedy into sections and make it a continuous poem. The amount of adaptation required is, however, not so great as might have been expected. There is in reality as much lyric matter in *Macbeth* as in a Greek tragedy : the difference is that in Shakespeare it is seen in outbursts or isolated phrases spread over a vast number of dramatic speeches ; in a Greek play it would be concentrated in a few odes or concertos. If such an illustration might be allowed, Elizabethan tragedy is moist and undrained land, no part of which is water and no part entirely dry ; an ancient drama would represent the difference made by irrigation, when the same amount of liquid has been brought into fixed channels and reservoirs. A main part then of our task of recasting will be to gather lyric thought and expressions from all over Shakespeare's poem and dispose them in regular odes and stage lyrics.

supple- Such choral matter may be reinforced by allusions to classic *mented by* myths and Scripture stories—natural sources of devout *Classic and* *Scripture* thought to a Scottish Chorus in its wandering meditation *allusions* upon the vicissitudes of human life.

Adapta- A second essential difference of structure between ancient *tion to the* and modern drama is connected with the unities. Here *unities* the Elizabethan and Attic stages are at opposite extremes of dramatic construction : the former loves to crowd into a play multiplicity of matter and interest, the latter sees beauty in rigorously excluding and reducing to singleness. Recasting in this case will mean leaving out. Our new *Macbeth* must fit in with unity of story, interest centering upon only one hero. Shakespeare's play gives us a companion story—a Scottish warrior and statesman, Macbeth's only rival, rising to fame in the same war as Macbeth, exposed to the same temptation, who stood where Macbeth fell : the contrast of the two brings out the character of the principal hero at every turn. In the adapted version however the story of Banquo must disappear, and every trace

of him must be excised. Another contrast adds interest to
the English play—that between Macbeth and his wife.
Even in a Greek tragedy it would be natural to introduce
such a personage, but she would be so treated as never
to appear an interest distinct from her husband. The old
conception of unity, we have seen, went further still. The
single story must be told from a single point of view : opposite confidences being impossible where the whole has
to be seen through the eyes of a chorus attached to the
hero. This affects our treatment of Macduff. He is essential to the story as the heaven-sent adversary of the hero ;
but it will be impracticable to represent him, as Shakespeare
does, in close confidence with his ally Malcolm, and he
must appear only as such an adversary would appear to the
hero's clansmen who will form our chorus. Once more,
ancient unity extended to the scene : only the crisis of the
story was presented on the stage—such an amount of incident as would fit in with a single unbroken scene, all
external to this being made known by other than dramatic
means. The natural scene for our version will be the
courtyard of Macbeth's castle, and the portion of the story
selected for acting will correspond roughly with Shakespeare's fifth act. Previous incidents of importance—such
as the meeting with the Witches, the murder of Duncan, the
massacre of Macduff's family—must be told in the choral
odes, or otherwise indirectly introduced.

The permanent scene will, as already suggested, stand for *Prologue*
Dunsinane castle : the arrangement of stage and orchestra
has been sufficiently indicated in previous chapters. Our
prologue we find ready made : the speech of Hecate in the
third act has only to be changed into a soliloquy and
makes a perfect Euripidean prologue. She would begin :
I am Hecate, and I rule over the Witches of Hell. She
would tell how she is angry with her servants who have
been trading with Macbeth in riddles and affairs of death—

> While I, the mistress of their charms,
> The close contriver of all harms,
> Was never called to bear my part,
> Or show the glory of our art.

Enlarging, after the fashion of Euripides, on this topic, she would be recalling to the audience earlier parts of the story. Then she would proceed to hint the future in declaring that amends must now be made. She has summoned the Witches to meet her this day at the pit of Acheron, whither Macbeth is coming to learn his destiny; there they are to provide vessels and charms, while she herself is for the air :

> Upon the corner of the moon
> There hangs a vaporous drop profound;
> I'll catch it ere it come to ground :
> And that, distilled by magic sleights,
> Shall raise such artificial sprites
> As by the strength of their illusion
> Shall draw him on to his confusion :
> He shall spurn fate, scorn death, and bear
> His hopes 'bove wisdom, grace and fear:
> For, know all men, *security*
> *Is mortals' chiefest enemy.*

The whole speech breathes the spirit of the formal prologue, and concludes with the inevitable gnomic verse; while the effect of this glance into past and future is to tinge all that follows with the irony so strongly affected by Greek poets, who loved to let their audiences watch a story in the light of its divinely determined issues.

Parode The Chorus appear in the orchestra—aged Clansmen of Macbeth. They enter in marching rhythm, and their first words are inspired by the scene before them : the pleasant seat of the castle [1] where heaven's breath smells wooingly, nimbly and sweetly recommending itself unto the gentle ʹsenses, approved by summer's guest, the temple-haunting

---

[1] The distinction in the original between different castles of Macbeth may be ignored for purposes of the present problem.

martlet, whose loved mansionry proclaims from every CHAP. VI
jutty, frieze, buttress, and coign of vantage that the air
is delicate. They indicate how they are come to pay their
duty to the king, the hero of their clan, Bellona's bridegroom, who carves out like valour's minion a passage to
victory where Scotland's rebels swarm on either side. They
are come also to learn tidings of their Queen, now smitten
with affliction—and what may that affliction be !

> Foul whisperings are abroad : unnatural deeds
> Do breed unnatural troubles: infected minds
> To their deaf pillows will discharge their secrets.

At this point their march is transformed into an ode, *strophe*
with its regular strophic alternations. It starts with the
favourite Greek theme —many are the woes of our life, but
none is like the woe of a passion-driven woman, or of a man
on whom frenzy has been sent from heaven for dark deeds
done. Such keep alone, of sorriest fancies their companions making : their mind is full of scorpions : their deed
is as a snake scotched, not killed, ever ready to close and
be herself again: they eat their meal in fear, and sleep in
affliction of terrible dreams that visit them nightly : longing
to be as the dead—whom they, to gain their peace, have
sent to peace—they lie instead on the torture of the mind
in restless ecstasy.

Such was Ajax, who sinned against Athena, and was *antistrophe*
visited by her with a deception of the eyes, in which he took
simple sheep for his insolent foes, and revelled in inglorious
slaughter. Such again was Hercules, who, inflamed by the
goddess he had offended, shot down his own children with
his irresistible arrows. And beneath the wrath of a greater
Power than the gods of Ajax and Hercules was the ruler of
Babylon driven from his throne, and made his dwelling with
the beasts of the field, eating grass like the ox, his body wet
with the dews of heaven, until he had learned of Him before
whom all the inhabitants of the earth are as grasshoppers :

CHAP. VI none can stay His hand or say unto Him, What doest
Thou?[1]

Episode I   The ode gives place to an episode as a Physician is seen
upon the stage, coming through the entrance of neighbourhood. He enquires of the Chorus for the Queen's Lady
Attendant, adding that he has watched with her for two
nights yet seen nothing of the strange symptoms said to
accompany the Queen's malady : now he will try the effect
of a third visit. The Chorus bid him enquire no further, for
here the Attendant herself comes from the castle. The two
discuss the patient's condition, how she walks in her sleep,
receiving the benefits of repose while she does the effects of
watching. As Lady Macbeth at this juncture enters from the
palace the change of feeling is reflected in the parallel verse
of the speakers.

> *Attendant.* Lo, here she comes: this is her very guise.
> *Doctor.*   Observe her: fast asleep indeed she is.
> *Chorus.*   How came she by that light ?
> *Attendant.*   She keeps it by her.
> *Chorus.*   Her eyes are open.
> *Attendant.*   But their sense is shut.
> *Doctor.*·   What does she now ? look how she rubs her hands.
> *Attendant.* So have I seen her by the hour together.

The Queen's delirious visions then find expression in
words. It is precisely for such agitated passion as this that the
ancient tragedy reserved its stage lyrics : the scene ceases for
a time to be in blank verse, and alike the utterances of the
dreamer and the comments upon them of the Chorus fall
into irregular metres bound together by the play of strophe
Concerto   and antistrophe. If the disjointed sayings of Lady Macbeth
in Shakespeare's scene be examined there will be found to
be three trains of thought running through them ; in the
adapted version it will be well for that which belongs to each

[1] Compare for the whole parode, *Macbeth*, I. vi. 1–10; v. i. 79; III.
ii. 7–26 ; &c.

train of thought to be collected together by itself, and each C<small>HAP.</small> VI
will stir its own kind of reflections in the Chorus.

First, Lady Macbeth's mind runs upon the thought *strophe*
of blood.—Out, damned spot!—Who would have thought
the old man to have had so much blood in him ?—Here's the
smell of blood still !—Ah ! all the perfumes of Arabia will
not sweeten this little hand ! The Chorus (carrying on the
rhythm) seem to recognise the bloody story that has stained
the fame of their chieftain : the morning of horror inconceiv-
able, confusion's masterpiece, when sacrilegious murder was
found to have broken open the Lord's anointed temple, and
stolen thence the life of the building : and they who looked
felt their sight destroyed by a new Gorgon, as before them
lay Duncan, his silver skin laced with his golden blood, while
gashed stabs upon his corpse looked like a breach in nature
for ruin's wasteful entrance.

The rhythm reverses for antistrophe as Lady Macbeth *antistrophe*
speaks a second time, and now she is taunting her husband
with cowardice.—Fie, my lord, fie ! a soldier, and afeard?
What need we fear who knows it, when none can call our
power to account? . . . No more o' that, my lord, no more
o' that : you mar all with this starting.—To bed, to bed !
there's knocking at the gate ! The Chorus remember the
old suspicions of Macbeth as the chiefs of Scotland stood in
his castle on the fatal morning : fears and scruples shook
them as they sought to fight against the undivulged pretence
of treasonous malice. And one spake a bitter word : He
hath borne all things well !—How did the grieved Macbeth in
pious rage tear the delinquent slaves of drink and thralls of
sleep—a noble deed, and wise : for who could have borne to
hear the men deny it?—So he hath borne all things well !

The Queen speaks yet a third time : The thane of Fife had *epode*
a wife : where is she now ? The Chorus respond in amazement : the thane of Fife, the valiant Macduff?—this passes
our comprehension.—Is some new deed impending ?

CHAP. VI   As Lady Macbeth passes again within the palace the sense
of relief is reflected in the return to blank verse. The
Physician bids the Lady Attendant watch well her patient ;
no other remedy is possible, for this is a disease beyond his
practice.   Here would be an opportunity for one of those
rhetorical discourses in which Greek Tragedy abounds, and
Rhesis   in this case it would be a rhesis of the Euripidean order,
consisting in the expansion of a theme.   Indeed both the
theme and the speech are at hand in Shakespeare, except
that the dramatic conditions of an Elizabethan tragedy reduce
all speeches in length to an amount inconsistent with the
present purpose.   But it will be easy to piece out our rhesis
with fragments on kindred themes drawn from other parts
of the play.   The Physician would open with the thought
of mental disease.

> What leech can minister to a mind diseased,
> Pluck from the memory a rooted sorrow,
> Raze out the written troubles of the brain,
> And with some sweet oblivious antidote
> Cleanse the stuffed bosom of that perilous stuff
> Which weighs upon the heart? therein the patient
> Must minister to himself.

He might naturally enlarge by passing on to the idea of
the distracted land, longing that his skill could avail his
country—

> Find her disease,
> And purge it to a sound and pristine health :
> That rhubarb, cyme, or some purgative drug,
> Could scour the foe away.

With all this it would be easy to link on thoughts belonging
to the crisis of Duncan's murder.   Medical art (the rhesis
would continue) is for the disordered body, not for the impious soul.   He who does a deed of murder has murdered
his own sleep—

> The innocent sleep,
> Sleep that knits up the ravelled sleave of care,

The death of each day's life, sore labour's bath,   CHAP. VI
Balm of hurt minds, great nature's second course,   ————
Chief nourisher in life's feast :—who this destroy
More need they the divine than the physician [1].

The personages on the stage retire, and the Chorus have
the orchestra to themselves for the purposes of a full ode.
The scene has carried their thoughts to the night of
Duncan's murder—one of the main incidents for the introduction of which we have to rely upon lyric celebration.

The ode might start in the form of a hymn to Night, *Choral*
mother of Crime : seeling night, that scarfs up the tender *Interlude*
eye of pitiful day, with bloody and invisible hand cancels *strophe*
and tears to pieces the great bond which keeps the criminal
pale. Light thickens, the crow makes wing to the rooky
wood, the bat flies his cloistered flight, the shardborne beetle
with drowsy hum rings night's yawning peal, the owl shrieks
—that fatal bellman who gives the sternest good-night :
then good things of day begin to droop, and night's black
agents rouse them to their preys. O'er the one half world
nature seems dead ; wicked dreams abuse the curtained
sleep, and witchcraft celebrates pale Hecate's rites, and
withered Murder, alarumed by his sentinel the wolf, whose
howl is his watch, with stealthy pace, with Tarquin's ravish-
ing strides, moves towards his design like a ghost.

But when Duncan was murdered the night was unruly : *antistrophe*
chimneys were blown down, lamentings were heard in the
air, strange screams of death, and prophesyings with accents
terrible of dire combustion and confused events new hatched
to the woeful time. Some say the earth was feverous and
did shake. There was husbandry in heaven : their candles
were all out, and the ministers of murder, waiting in sight-
less substances on nature's mischief, palled the night in the

[1] The whole episode is parallel with v. i. of the original. For the concerto compare further II. iii. 71–8, 117–22, 135–8 ; III. vi. For the rhesis :
v. iii. 40–56, II. ii. 35–43.

CHAP. VI dunnest smoke of hell, a blanket of thick darkness through which heaven might not peep to cry to the murderer, Hold. And night's predominance was extended to the morrow's day, and darkness yet entombed the face of the earth when living light should be kissing it : a sore night, trifling all former knowings.

epode   Unnatural omens had gone before, like the unnatural deed they foreshadowed. A falcon towering in pride was hawked at by a mousing owl ; Duncan's horses, beauteous and swift, minions of their race, turned wild in nature, flung out and made war with mankind. Verily the heavens were troubled with man's act and threatened his bloody stage. And now some new crime has been darkly hinted : what this dread deed may be nought but time can reveal.

> Come what come may,
> Time and the hour runs through the roughest day[1].

Episode II   The lyric ritual breaks up as Macbeth enters by the distance-entrance, newly returned from his visit to the Witches at the pit of Acheron. The first meeting between the Clansmen and their chief would give occasion for those elaborate interchanges of courtesy for which Greek blank verse is so suitable, and matter for which abounds in the intercourse between Duncan and his lords. Macbeth would acknowledge his clansmen's devotion to his house.

> Kind gentlemen, your pains
> Are registered where every day I turn
> The leaf to read them.

The Chorus might respond :

> The labour we delight in physics pain :
> The service and the loyalty we owe
> In doing pays itself. Your servants ever
> Have theirs, themselves and what is theirs, in compt,
> To make their audit at your highness' pleasure.

---

[1] For the whole ode compare *Macbeth*, III. ii. 40-53 ; II. i. 4, 49-60 ; II. iii. 59-68 ; I. v. 51-55 ; II. iv. 1-20 ; I. iii. 146.

Macbeth unfolds to the Chorus—as accepted confidants CHAP. VI
on the Greek stage—the nature of the expedition from
which he is just returned, and how the oracles had given
him sure ground of confidence against the foes who so
sorely threaten him.   He would describe with some minute-
ness the incantations and apparitions; where the actual
point of the oracular disclosure was approached it would no
doubt be drawn out in parallel verse.

> *Chorus.* And wilt thou tell the vision, or conceal?
> *Macbeth.* An infant, crowned, bore in his hand a tree.
> *Chorus.* And spake he bodements? or how goes the tale?
> *Macbeth.* That I should careless live who chafes or frets —
> *Chorus.* Meant he for ever, or some season fix'd?
> *Macbeth.* Till Birnam wood should come to Dunsinane.
> *Chorus.* Who can impress the forest, bid the tree
>   Unfix his earth-bound root?
> *Macbeth.*   So long a time
>   High-placed Macbeth shall sleep in spite of thunder.
> *Chorus.* Saw'st thou aught else, or ends the vision here?
> *Macbeth.* A bloody child bade me be bold and bloody—
> *Chorus.* Dread things thou tell'st: my heart throbs to know
>   more—
> *Macbeth.* For none of woman born should harm Macbeth.
> *Chorus.* Then mayst thou laugh to scorn the pow'r of man.

Macbeth continues that there was one drawback in the
promises of the oracle: he was bidden to beware of Macduff.   But this caution he has already observed, making
assurance doubly sure and taking a bond of fate : an expedition has already been sent against his enemy, to slay him
and his wife, and extirpate the whole stock.   The Chorus
tremblingly recognise the meaning of the dark sayings in
Lady Macbeth's delirium.   With the cautious reticence
proper to a Chorus they tell their king they cannot praise
this deed of his, yet they can wish him joy in its success.
Macbeth, in surprise, asks how the matter can be known
already.   They explain the supernatural illumination of the
sick Queen's fancy.   This reminds Macbeth of the con-

CHAP. VI   dition of his wife, and he passes within the palace, leaving
the Chorus to another interlude[1].

*Choral
Interlude*
This ode, starting from the thought of the strange
clairvoyance of Lady Macbeth, works gradually towards the
second main incident that has to be introduced indirectly—
the meeting with the Witches on the heath of Forres.

strophe
How is it, they cry, that the eyes of some are mysteriously
opened to the invisible, the distant, the future? To the
brain disordered by sickness the illumination comes in
delirium, as our Queen has seen the deed done in the far
distance. So the vision of the seer can pierce the future,
and reads time as a book. So the murderer, plotting his
impious crime, sees an air-drawn dagger, the painting of his
fear, proceeding from his heat-oppressed brain—palpable
in form, the handle towards his hand, and on the blade and
dudgeon gouts of blood—not to be clutched, yet ever before
him, and marshalling him the way that he was going. And
so to the same murderer, when the deed is done, comes the
opening of the eyes as haunting Ate: though the brains be
out the victims will not die: they rise before him with twenty
mortal murders on their crowns, until he is unmanned with
flaws and starts, though bold to look on that which might
appal the devil.

antistrophe
Most dread of all are those beings who to gain such unholy knowledge will do a deed without a name, and give
their eternal jewel to the common Enemy of man! They
will look into the seeds of time though to compass their end
they untie the winds, and bid the yesty waves swallow
navigation up, though palaces and pyramids must slope their
heads to their foundations, even till Destruction sicken.
Such were the secret black and midnight hags that met our
Chieftain on the blasted heath, hovering through the fog
and filthy air, bubbles of earth melting as breath into wind.

---

[1] Episode II follows in the main the matter of IV. i: compare also
I. iii. 150; I. vi. 10–28, I. iv. 22; II. iii. 54.

The ode follows out the triple prediction of Glamis, Cawdor, CHAP. VI
King : and how when two truths had been told as happy ——
prologues to the swelling theme dark deeds did the rest.
Strange web of true and false woven by the Erinnyes, who
to win us to our harm bait for us the trap with honest trifles
to betray us in deepest consequence [1].

Cries heard from the direction of the women's quarters *Episode*
bring Macbeth again upon the stage. *III*

> *Chorus.* It is the cry of women, good my lord.
> *Macbeth.* I have almost forgot the taste of fears :
> Direness, familiar to my slaughterous thoughts,
> Cannot once move me.

The Attendant enters and announces the Queen's death.
After a brief exclamation of woe from the Chorus, Macbeth
speaks, and his words fall into the lyric strains of a monody. *Monody*
Alas! for his beauteous Queen! yet why mourn her death?
if not now she must have died hereafter [2]. Inevitably as
morrow after morrow goes creeping on, history spelling itself
out syllable by syllable—inevitably would have come the
time for that word death : even as all our yesterdays have
succeeded one another only to form a long train of servants
lighting fools the way to dusty death. What is life to mourn
over? a brief candle—out with it! a walking shadow! a
poor player strutting and fretting his hour upon a stage,
then silent for ever! Man spends his years as a tale told
by an idiot, full of sound and fury, signifying nothing [3]!

---

[1] The ode puts I. iii : add II. i. 33–49 ; III. iv. 50–106 ; IV. i. 48–60.
[2] In this difficult and much disputed passage I understand *should* in
its sense of *must* [number 2 of Schmidt's lexicon: the *should* of inevitable futurity—compare : This day my sister should the cloister enter
(*M. for M.* I. ii. 182), Your grace shall understand that I am very sick
(*Merch.* IV. i. 150.)]. The words succeed the speech in which Macbeth
has said that he is grown callous to fear : in this speech a similar callous-
ness appears in his thought that death is too inevitable to be worth
mourning : all life is but a bundle of opportunities for death.
[3] *Macbeth*, V. v. 8-28.

CHAP. VI   Blank verse is resumed, as a Herald from England enters

Forensic contest   by the distance-entrance. It is essential that one episode should be reserved for the forensic contest, in which the case of Macbeth and his fate-appointed adversary Macduff should be brought into formal opposition. There are ample materials for such a debate in Shakespeare's play, particularly in two scenes [1], one in which Macduff is censured by his own family for his strange step in fleeing alone to England, the other in which Macduff seeks to win Malcolm by his account of the wretched state of Scotland under the tyrant. The Herald advancing declares he is come from the Scottish exiles in England, from the pious Edward, Northumberland and warlike Siward: these are so exasperated with the reports of Macbeth's tyrannies that they are preparing war, with the help of Him above. Macbeth answers with defiance :

> Our castle's strength
> Will laugh a siege to scorn : here let them lie
> Till famine and the ague eat them up.

But the Herald continues : he has further a special message from the thane of Fife. The story is told of Macduff receiving the news that his wife and children were slaughtered : on the point of quitting his country for ever he was brought back to the task of revenge, praying heaven to cut short all intermission. He now challenges the tyrant to mortal combat :

> Within my sword's length set thee : if thou scape,
> Heaven forgive thee too !

So Macbeth learns that his rapid precaution has come too late : the man of fate has escaped alone from the massacre. In bitterness of heart he begins to taunt Macduff, thus furnishing the rhesis on one side. He taunts him as a coward, who could rawly leave wife and child, those precious

----

[1] IV. ii. and iii.

motives, those strong bonds of love, without leave-taking.
Macduff lacks the natural touch : the very wren, the most
diminutive of birds, will fight, her young ones in the nest,
against the owl. The Chorus endorse this reflection on
Macduff :

> His flight was madness : when our actions do not
> Our fears do make us traitors.

Before the answering rhesis, there might be interposed some
of the usual parallel verse, as the Herald makes defence for
the thane he represents.

> *Herald.*   You know not
>   Whether it was his wisdom or his fear.
> *Macbeth.* Little the wisdom when the flight
>   So runs against all reason.
> *Herald.* Love lacked he not, yet knew the fits o' the season.
> *Macbeth.* All was the fear, and nothing was the love.
> *Herald.* That which has been has been : hear what remains.
> *Macbeth.* Speak to a heart that cannot taint with fear.

The Herald then, in one elaborate outpouring, gathers
up the denunciations of Macbeth by those for whom he
speaks. He addresses him as a tyrant whose sole name
blisters the tongue :

>   Not in the legions
>   Of horrid hell can come a devil more damned
>   In evils to top Macbeth.

He stigmatises him as bloody, luxurious, avaricious, false,
deceitful, sudden, malicious, smacking of every sin that
has a name. He paints the afflicted country sunk beneath
his yoke :

>   Each new morn
>   New widows howl, new orphans cry, new sorrows
>   Strike heaven on the face.

But at last hands have been uplifted in her right, and from
England goodly thousands are coming. Now shall the
usurper feel the hollowness of his power :

                                    Now shalt thou feel
Thy secret murders sticking on thy hands;
Now minutely revolts upbraid thy faith-breach;
Those thou commandest move but in command,
Nothing in love: now shalt thou feel thy title
Hang loose about thee, like a giant's robe
Upon a dwarfish thief. Thy way of life
Is fall'n into the sear, the yellow leaf :
And that which should accompany old age,
As honour, love, obedience, troops of friends,
Thou must not look to have; but in their stead
Curses, not loud but deep, mouth-honour, breath,
Which the poor heart would fain deny, and dare not.

The comment of the Chorus on this is the conventional distinction between threatening and doing.

Thoughts speculative their unsure hopes relate,
But certain issues strokes must arbitrate.

Macbeth bids the Herald go and hasten on the war he
threatens :

The mind I sway by and the heart I bear
Shall never sag with doubt nor shake with fear.

*Choral
Interlude
strophe*

The ode which follows indicates the shadow of turning
which has come over the action. Dark oracles bade our
chief 'beware Macduff,' and in seeking to destroy the man
he was to fear he has turned him into a fierce avenger.
Verily our evil deeds have still their judgment here : and
the ode works in the thought of Macbeth's famous soliloquy[1],
that the evildoer cannot feel sure his blow will be the be-all

antistrophe

and end-all even here, on this bank and shoal of time : else
might he jump the life to come. But his crime becomes
a bloody instruction whose teaching returns to plague the
inventor, evenhanded justice commending the ingredients
of his poisoned chalice to his own lips. The outlook is
evil, yet the Chorus will hope: things at the worst will
cease or else climb upward.

[1] I. vii.

The next episode will contain the Messenger's Speech. CHAP. VI
No matter could be more suitable for this than the incident
of Birnam wood: but the incident needs adaptation to change *Episode IV*
it from dramatic to epic form. The first announcement may
appropriately be made, as in Shakespeare, by the Watchman
who has that moment beheld the spectacle[1], but he must be *Messen-*
followed by a Spy[2] who has been with the English army, and *ger's*
Speech
can thus relate the strange event in all its fullness. As soon
as he has got his breath, he would settle down to a formal
description of the English forces arriving at Birnam wood on
their march, and halting for rest and refreshment. He would
tell how the chieftains held a council of war. One advised
that it would be safer to wait for night, and make the
advance in the darkness that would hide inferiority of numbers. But another leader denied that the invaders were the
lesser host, and bade advance at once. Thereupon was
much discussion whether the tyrant or themselves had the
advantage in numbers, and when they could not agree, Malcolm
rose up and made a notable proposal. He counselled that
they should cut down every man a bough of a tree, and
holding these before them shadow the number of their host
and bewilder the foe. Then the speech would describe the
bustle and movement in the camp as this novel device was
being carried out: how the army disposed themselves to the
task in regular order, each division choosing a separate
tree :—here on the march groves of beeches rode on horse-
back, there fir branches concealed the main body of the foot,
while tasselled larches shook under the light movements of
the skirmishers. In conclusion, the Spy says they will be
here anon, and throwing down their leafy screens show
themselves as they are in the assault :

> War ne'er beheld such warrior host of woods.

The shock which Macbeth feels at this strange fulfilment of

[1] v. v. 29–48.   [2] Compare iv. iv. 200.

R

CHAP. VI the oracle lasts only for a moment : then the soldier's spirit
kindles in him as he rapidly orders his defence.   Such sudden animation a Greek tragedy would convey by a burst of
accelerated rhythm, into which it is easy to fit the many
phrases of valour and defiance scattered through Shakespeare's fifth act [1].

> Ho, mine armour—ring the alarum—give the clamorous trumpets
>   breath :
> Bid them speak to every quarter, harbingers of blood and death !
> Hang our banners from the ramparts : to our kingdom's utmost bound
> Horsemen ride, and yet more horsemen, let them skirr the country
>   round ;
> Hither sweep our Scottish forces, thane and kerne assemble here ;
> Hang each recreant, lily-livered, whey-faced counsellor of fear.
> What though England's thousands round us, though the cry be still,
>   They come,
> Thousand Scots shall meet them dareful, beard to beard, and drive
>   them home.
> Who am I to play the Roman, fall on my undeeded sword,
> While before me better gashes English foemen's lives afford ?
> Foemen that must lose their labour, such a charmed life I bear,
> Spirits that know mortal issues so have freed my life from fear :
> What Macduff, what stripling Malcolm, meets me, not of woman born ?
> His sole weapon may I yield to, other swords I laugh to scorn.
> Lo, I throw before my body warlike shield : blow wind, come wrack,
> One push cheers me ever—or I die with harness on my back !

Choral   Macbeth has gone to the battle : the Chorus left behind
Interlude feel another stroke of fate overwhelming them, cabin'd,
strophe   cribb'd, confined to saucy doubts and fears.   They sing how
oracles of heaven have ever misled men : how Crœsus
trusted in the assurance that he was to overthrow a kingdom,
antistrophe and knew not that it was his own kingdom he should destroy ;
how the wise Oedipus obeying the divine mandate used all
his wisdom to discover the slayer of Laius, and wist not that
he was discovering his own shame.   There is no safety but
in the path of righteousness.

---

[1] E. g. scenes iii. 3–5, 15–17, 33–35 ; v. 1, 2, 5–7, 51, 52 ; vi. 9, 10 ;
vii. 12, 13, 17, 20, 26 ; viii. 1–3, 12, 32.

The final denouement of this play is part of a battle, and CHAP. VI
therefore cannot in the most fragmentary way appear on a
Greek stage. Accordingly, the explanation as to Macduff's *Exodus*
birth has to be made indirectly. An English prisoner, we
may imagine, is brought in : as he crosses the stage the
Chorus ask who he is, and how he comes to be fighting
against Scotland's king. The prisoner might reply, in words
of the play,

> I am one
> So weary with disasters, tugged with fortune,
> That I would set my life on any chance
> To mend it, or be rid on't.

The Chorus say, in conventional phrase, that he is involved
in the net of destruction. In the same strain he replies that
it is the fortune of war : our turn to-day, yours to-morrow.
Nay, reply the Chorus, we have no fear for our king in this
contest. The prisoner enquires the ground of such confidence. Fate, answer the Chorus, has spoken goodly truths
out of the dark.

> *Prisoner.* What truth can fend a mortal man from death !
> *Chorus.* That none of woman born can harm Macbeth.

The prisoner laughs the Chorus to scorn ; he has served under
Macduff and knows the secret story of his birth. As he is
borne away, the Chorus in a burst of lyrics express their consternation. Their charm is despaired ! the cursed tongue that
has told this news has cowed the better part of man in them !
they are weary of the sun, and wish the estate of the world
undone ! they curse the juggling fiends that can lie like truth,
keeping the word of promise to the ear, and breaking it to the
hope. As a climax, the Chorus break into two bands : one
semichorus would fain seek out some desolate shade and there
weep their sad bosoms empty : the rest cry out to make
medicines of revenge, and holding fast the mortal sword like
good men bestride their downfallen kingdom [1]. While the

[1] Compare *Macbeth*, v. viii. 13–22 ; v. v. 49, 50 ; IV. iii. 1–4.

R 2

CHAP. VI Chorus are still irresolute, tidings of the English victory and the death of Macbeth are brought. The semichoruses unite to wail the news in a lyric outburst : had they but died an hour before this chance they had lived a blessed time ; for from this instant there's nothing serious in mortality ! Renown and grace is dead : the wine of life is drawn and the mere lees is left this vault to brag of[1] ! At this juncture, amid flare of trumpets, Malcolm appears as conqueror, his victorious troops pouring upon the stage, all waving boughs of Birnam woods, which they have picked up again as tokens of triumph. Malcolm reassures the Chorus : he has warred not against the land, but only against the tyrant, whose death will

> Give to their tables meat, sleep to their nights,
> Free from their feasts and banquets bloody knives.

The Chorus cannot forbear a strain of lamentation for their lost chief, but they recognise that the will of heaven has triumphed over wrong. An earlier couplet in the play will supply the Chorus with an appropriate word of dismissal :

> God's benison go with you, and with those
> That would make good of bad, and friends of foes.

[1] *Macbeth*, II. iii. 96-101.

VII

Origin of Comedy

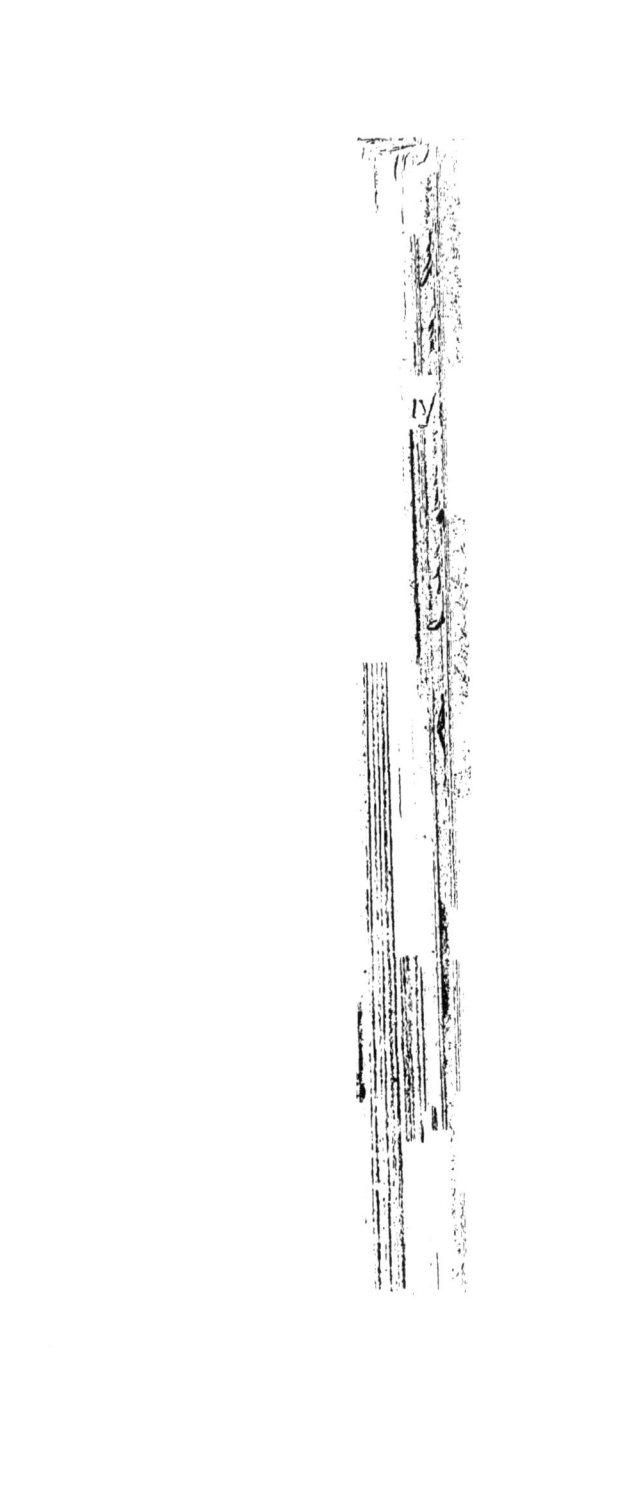

VII

CHAP. VII

A parallel
origin for
Tragedy
and
Comedy

THE origin of Comedy in antiquity goes for the first part of
its course step by step with the origin of Tragedy. However
widely contrasted the two things were destined to become,
they drew a common inspiration from the nature-worship of
Dionysiac orgies, in which there was enthusiasm to generate
dramatic passion, connexion with nature-changes to found
the conception of plot, while the carnival-like disguisings of
the revellers were already a form of dramatic characterisation.
But even to a Bacchic orgy there was a higher and a lower
side. The Dithyramb was the direct address to the jolly
god of nature : the Phallic Procession gave vent in yet
wilder abandon to the loosest of nature joys [1]. Aristotle has
preserved the tradition, which agrees with the nature of
things, that the Dithyramb was the starting-point of Tragedy,
the Phallic Procession of Comedy.

Such a Phallic Procession was, like the Dithyramb, a
'Comus,' or wandering dance : not confined to an orchestra,
but leading the revellers in a sort of sacred romp through
the whole of a village or country-side. It would be specially
appropriate to the Rural Dionysia—the harvest-home of
the vintage, or the Greater Dionysia which celebrated the
return of Spring. To an English reader, such a ritual is best
brought home by the fossil comus which is still to be seen
among the traditional customs of a remote country district.

[1] Thus in the Phallic Procession introduced into the *Acharnians* the
farmer addresses Phales as Comus-fellow of Dionysus, and connects him
with the pleasures that belong to night (264-6).

*The
Cornish
Furry
as a fossil
comus*

I refer to the Cornish Flower-Dance, or Furry[1], which is kept up at Helstone on the 8th of May. From an early hour the place is alive with drums and fifes, and townsmen hoarsely chaunting a ballad, the burden of which conveys the spirit of the festival :

> With Hal-an-tow,
> Jolly rumble O,
> And we were up as soon as any day O,
> And for to fetch the Summer home,
> The Summer and the May O ;
> For the Summer is a-come O,
> And Winter is a-go O !

The verses of the ballad seem to convey topical allusions that have become traditional. One speaks of Robin Hood and Little John as gone to the fair, and the revellers will go too ; another triumphs in the Spaniards eating the grey goose feather while the singers will be eating the roast. Another runs thus quaintly :

> God bless Aunt Mary Moses
>   With all her power and might O ;
> And send us peace in merry England
>   Both day and night O.
>   With Hal-an-tow,
>   Jolly rumble O,
> And we were up as soon as any day O,
> And for to fetch the Summer home,
>   The Summer and the May O ;
> For the Summer is a-come O,
> And Winter is a-go O !

Thus singing they troop through the town ; if they find any-one at work, they hale him to the river and make him leap across ; arrived at the Grammar School they demand a holi-day ; at noon they go 'fadding' into the country, and come back with oak-branches and flowers in their hats and caps ; then until dusk they dance hand-in-hand down the streets,

---

[1] The word is variously derived from the Cornish word *fer*, a fair or jubilee, and *fray*, a sudden excursion, and the Latin Floralia, a flower-festival celebrated about the same date.

and through any house, in at one door, out at another ; when CHAP. VII
night falls they keep up the dancing in-doors. The character ——
of the dancing is exactly that of the ancient Comus ; and the
whole spirit of the Cornish Furry is a fair representation
of primitive nature festivals, except, of course, that modern
devoutness has banished from the flower-dance all traces of
a religious festival :—unless a trace is to be found in the fact
that the dancers at one point make a collection.

So far the line of development for Tragedy and Comedy *Differen-*
has been the same : the divergence begins where the common *tiation of*
Comedy
ancestor, the Comus, becomes united with other forms of
the ballad-dance. An earlier chapter has shown how, under
Arion, the Comus amalgamated with the Chorus and originated Tragedy. It united also with 'Satire,' and from the
union sprang Comedy.

This 'Satire' is one of the four main varieties of the ballad- *Satire as*
dance, and its development proceeded side by side with that *an early*
literary
of epic poetry and the lyric Comus and Chorus. In subject- *form*
matter the name Satire suggests something like the modern
lampoon. Its distinction of form was due to the rapidity with
which it shook off the music and gesture it had inherited from
the ballad-dance, and led the way in those metrical changes
which bring verse to a point nearly approaching the speech
of ordinary life. There are traces of the Satire among the
' Homeric ' poems, which are our nearest representative of
Greek primitive ballad poetry ; and three lines, in Homeric
metre, have survived of the *Margites*, which appears to have
been a lampoon on some learned fool of the primitive world.

Many the crafts of the craftsmen he knew, and all of them badly.
Him nor of earth a digger the gods had made, nor a ploughman:
Wise was he in no art: but at failing in all of them skilful.

But a great master of Satire soon arose, whose name became *Archi-*
as great a power as the name of Homer ; and as legends of *lochus*
the blind minstrel gathered around Homer, so to Archilochus were attributed the traditional stories of the lam-

CHAP. VII pooner, such as that which represents him in the light of a
rejected suitor taking such a bitter satiric revenge against
the women of Lycambes' house that they hanged themselves.
The great work of Archilochus was to lay the foundation of
a metrical revolution, substituting for the stately dactylic
metre the tripping *iambic* system, which was destined to
become, alike for ancient and modern literatures, the basis
of 'blank verse': so clearly is Satire the origin of this
metrical system that in Greek to *iambise* means to lampoon[1].
The actual compositions of Archilochus have come down to
us only in disjointed fragments ; but an idea of the Satire
as a literary form may be gathered from Archilochus's
avowed imitator, Horace, and I give one of his 'epodes' in
a form retaining the iambic metre. It attacks another
satirist.

> Why play the cur that snarls at harmless stranger's step
>   But stirs not when the wolf is come?
> Why not your empty threats on me turn, if you dare,
>   And when you will be bitten bite?
> For like Molossian hound, or tawny Spartan breed,
>   The shepherd's bulwark and his love,
> Will I through wintry drifts of snow, mine ears erect,
>   Drive headlong all the forest kind:
> You, while the woodland echoes still your threatening barks,
>   Already smell the offered sop.
> Take heed, take heed: horns ready for the toss I hold,
>   Bitterest of bitter 'gainst the bad:
> Such as Lycambes found the suitor he deceived,
>   Or who the sculptor railed to death.
> What, am I likely, singled out by vicious tooth,
>   To whimper, harmless, as a child?

Satire and   It was this Satire, then, that combined with the Comus to
the Comus
the element's create Comedy. The union of the two was not, as in the
of Comedy case of Tragedy, the work of a distinct revolution by which
the characteristics of the two rituals were joined in one.

[1] It appears that the versions of the *Margites* known to the Alex·
andrian critics contained iambic lines mingling with the hexameters.

Before anything like amalgamation took place the two
elements were for a long time maintained side by side.
The Comus-procession, besides chaunting the praises of
Bacchus, would exchange extempore 'chaff' with the passers-
by, and halt at intervals for regular bouts of satire before
resuming the dance : alike the song and the interruptions
constituted the vent for high spirits which the ancients
regarded as worship. This preparatory stage in the development of Comedy we can enter into with considerable clearness, for we have an example of it in a glorified form in the
Comus of the Initiated which Aristophanes has introduced into his *Frogs*. The scene of the play is the world of
the dead : even here the Initiated—the inner circle of the
religious world—have reserved for them regions devoted to
their mysteries, and to these they are on their way in torchlight procession when they encounter the personages of the
drama. Bacchus, its hero, and his servant Xanthias, are
in broad farce undergoing the inconveniences incident to
travellers in a new country, when their ears are caught by
the sound of flutes, and after some moments of terrified
suspense the troop of the Initiated come pouring into the
orchestra, hymning the god and waving torches 'with each
invocation. With Bacchus and Xanthias on one side of
these revellers, and the audience in the theatre on the
other side, to serve as spectators or passers-by, the requisites
of a Dionysiac procession are complete.

The two combine by alternation in the Comus-procession

Comus of the Initiate in the 'Frogs' of Aristophanes

Full Comus

Come from thy holy seats,   *comus*
Come from thy deep retreats,
   Come, come, Iäcchus.
Dancing along the mead,
Come, thy own troop to lead,
   Come, come, Iäcchus.
Let the fresh myrtle bough,
   Studded with flowers,
Wave o'er thy crownèd brow
   Free mirth is ours.

So let thy foot advance,
Bold in the graceful dance.
This holy company,
Gathered for revelry,
Wistfully waits for thee :
    Come, come, Iäcchus.

interruption [But the by-standers on the stage interrupt : the slave being
of by-
standers more attracted by food than music.

Xanthias. Much-honoured Proserpine ! this smell of pork is nice !
Bacchus. Pray you be still, and you may chance to get a slice.]

comus   *Comus.*   Kindle the flaming brands,
resumed   Uplift them in thy hands,
                                Light! light! Iäcchus.
                            All the field shines afar ;
                            Thou art our Evening Star,
                                Bright, bright, Iäcchus.
                            Elders, by thee inspired,
                                Cast away pain,
                            Cast away years, and, fired,
                                Dance in thy train.
                            Be thy bright torch on high
                            Polestar to every eye ;
                            While o'er the dewy lea,
                            Dancing in company,
                            Fleetly we follow thee,
                        ·   Blessed Iäcchus.

anapæstic· Here the dance stops, and spreading themselves about the
interlogue :
general   orchestra the revellers change to satire ; at this point the
satire   satire is of a more general character than that of individual
              lampooning, and the metre is therefore not iambic but ana-
              pæstic—a mock proclamation for the uninitiated to depart
              from the mysteries.

            A reverent silence fits this place ;
                    and from our chorus let him depart
            Who is yet untaught in the Mysteries ;
                    who has stain of guile on his heart ;
            Who has not won from the Muses' secrets
                    freedom of thought and bodily grace ;
            Who has not learnt from Cratinus the bull-fed
                    what is befitting the time and the place ;

Who takes pleasure in scurrilous jesting,
    not regarding the 'whom' and the 'when';
Who stays not a strife in the city, but
    is a churl to his own townsmen;
Who, for a private object, fans their
    factious fury and mutual hate;
Who, for a gift or favour, ministers
    wrong for right as their magistrate;
Sells his ship, or deserts his post, or
    under colour of trafficking, sends,
Like a Thorycio, thongs, or hemp, or
    pitch, to serve the enemy's ends;
He who, at the feast of Bacchus
    having been smartly lashed in a play,
Goes to the courts and, bringing his action,
    nibbles a hole in the poet's pay:
These, one and all, I forewarn, I forbid, I pro-
    hibit from hearing our Mystical song!
And summon, all others to lend us their voices
    and keep this feast the merry night long.

Then the Initiated fall loosely into two bands, as if to follow *comus resumed* separately the two sides of nature-worship, the mysteries of Ceres and of Bacchus.

Worshippers of Bacchus

Where the turf invites our feet,
Where the flowers are rank and sweet,
    Brave hearts, advance, advance !
Stirring foot and merry lip,
Flinging wanton dance and quip,
    Befit the Mystics' dance.

Worshippers of Ceres

Nay, enough of frolic wit;
Wear the palm who wins in it.
    Praise ye the Holy Maid :
Lady, Saviour, unto thee
Rise our strains ; for thou wilt be
    Our never-failing aid !

Full Comus

And now, with holy hymns adorn
Queen Ceres of the golden corn.

Worshippers of Ceres

Ceres, let thine eye be o'er us,
    Lady of the Mysteries!
Look benignly on thy Chorus;
    Shield us from our enemies.
So in mirth and dance and song
We may while the whole day long.

Worshippers of Bacchus

Much to please the laughter-loving,
    Much to please the wiser head,
May I speak: that, all approving,
    Everywhere it may be said,
Worthily our part was done,
Worthily the garland won.

Full Comus

Invoke ye now the lusty god
Who oft with us the dance has trod.

Come, master of the sweetest strain,
Iäcchus come, to guide our train
    Forth to the goddess' dwelling;
    And show how, toil-dispelling,
Thy guidance in our festal sport
Beguiles the way, and makes it short.

Come, lover of the dance and song,
Iäcchus come: to thee belong
    The skirt in frolic tatters,
    And sandal rent. What matters?
Protected by thy festal sway,
Unchided we may dance and play.

Come, lover of the song and dance,
Iäcchus come: looking askance,
I saw two eyes that twinkled,
A cheek with laughter wrinkled,
For she looked merrily on me.
Iäcchus, join our company.

interruption [The last words provoke another interruption from the
by-standers on the stage:

    Xanthias. Where is that lass? for I am much disposed to try
        To break a jest and dance with her.
    Bacchus.   And so am I.]

Again the revellers break up and spread over the orchestra, CHAP. VII
facing the audience in the theatre ; the metre becomes
iambic
iambic as they extemporise lampoons on individuals pre- *interlogue :*
individual
sent.   *satire*

> Now shall we, fellow-mockers,
> Make game of Archidemus?
> Who at the election brought forth nought but black-balls:
> But now has a large following
> In the tomb's upper circles,
> And sets the fashion in hell's rascalry.
> And Cleisthenes, it's rumoured,
> Amid the musty tombstones,
> Tears his fair hair, and wounds his dainty cheek,
> Upon the bare earth flings him,
> To whine and wail and weep for
> Sebinus, late of Rogue-and-Rascal street.
> And Callias, they tell me,
> The son of Lady Slattern,
> Fought at the sea-fight, bravely clad in—wench-skin.

[The travellers on the stage here break in upon the ritual *interruption*
to ask directions for their journey, and the Comus answer
without any sense of interruption. Then they fall once
more into two bands.]

> ### Worshippers of Bacchus   *comus*
> *concluded*
> Ye who have the holy sign,
> Ye who share the feast divine,
> Through the flowery grove advance,
> Form the circle, lead the dance.

> ### Worshippers of Ceres
> I must to the deeper shade,
> Where holy women, wife and maid,
> Worshipping shall spend the night:
> For them I must lift the light.

> ### Full Comus
> To our meadows sprent with flowers,
>   With our measured step and sound,
>   Gracefully tread ye the ground,
> Ever as the blessed hours
>   Bring the festal season round,

> Onward to our rosy bowers.
> Unto us, and us alone,
>   Who, at the divine behest
>   Duteously have shared our best
> In service to our own
>   And to the stranger-coming guest,
> Is this cheerful sun-light shown.

The Mystics are thus withdrawing in two bands when their attention is arrested by what takes place on the stage, and the play resumes.

The two elements essential to Comedy

Such is the character, idealised by the artistic power of Greek poetry at its climax, of that Bacchic ritual in which the Comus-song and Satire existed side by side and interchanged.   It is Comedy, but not yet drama.   Both parts of it were essential to the product that was to be : from the iambic Satire came the satiric purpose that was supreme to the end of Greek Comedy, while the Dithyramb has been shown by the history of Tragedy to have contained dramatic power in embryo.   But at present the dancing and satire were like elements of a chemical substance, mixed and charged with a mutual attraction, but waiting the shock that should combine them into a single new form : Comedy could become drama only when the dancing should absorb the satire and convert it into satiric acting.   For there are obviously two modes of satirising that may be distinguished as abstract and concrete ; the one declares a thing ridiculous, the other exhibits it in a ridiculous disguise.   Reducing the two to their lowest terms, in the one you call a man a fool, in the other you disguise yourself in his likeness and then play the fool.   Abstract and concrete satire might be represented in modern journalism by the *Saturday Review* and *Punch* : the first alleges folly, the latter presents it ; the *Review* would declare that a statesman's over-vaunting of his policy descended to the level of a cheapjack's advertisement, while *Punch* would simply represent the familiar features in cheapjack costume and

attitudes, with the bill, done up in shape as a bottle, CHAP. VII
peeping out of his pocket. If then the question be asked,
At what stage in its development were the two elements of *The two elements*
Comedy so far fused that the whole became drama? the *fused and*
answer is: *When the body of performers, the Comus, exchanged* *Comedy becomes*
their Bacchic characterisation for a rôle in the story they *Drama*
acted. They began by appearing in the guise of Bacchanals,
and in that guise indulging the taste for satiric attack; they
ended by impersonating that which they attacked: at the
point where the one impersonation gave place to the other
Comedy became a branch of drama.

No historic materials remain to throw light on this *Illustra-*
critical point in dramatic development: it passed without *tion of such fusion from*
observation, and was over before men began to take notice *English*
of social changes. But development in folk-lore is much *folk-lore*
the same all the world over, and if we turn to our own
popular customs we can find an illustration of the literary
revolution in question—an illustration giving us that which
is a prize to the student of development, an institution
caught in the act and article of transforming. A sword-
dance is still (I believe) kept up in Northumberland in the
course of which there is a transition from lyric to dramatic.
At the opening it is all skill and martial spirit: the ballad
rings of combat and the gestures are feats of sword-play.
But gradually the dance works into a plot: as it increases
in passion the Rector rushes in to part the combatants,
receives a thrust and falls. Then all say 'Not I' and 'O
for a doctor!' A doctor enters, painting himself in accordance with popular conceptions: his is a ten-pound fee,
but for a favour he will make it nine pound, nineteen and
elevenpence; he has a pill that will cure

> The plague, the palsy, and the gout,
> The devil within, the devil without,
> Everything but a love-sick maid
> And the consumption in the pocket.

S

CHAP. VII Examining the patient he comes to a favourable conclusion, whereupon all cry

> Parson, rise up and fight again,
> The doctor says you are not slain.

The Rector comes to, and all ends with rejoicings. The performance which began as pure dancing concludes as pure acting.

Primitive Comedy: various names,   Similar in principle must have been the transformation which in Greece led the Comus to create dramatic Comedy by simply making their dance imitate that which they wished to attack, instead of breaking off the dance when the time came to satirise. Such Primitive Comedy we find in all parts of Greece, and appearing under a variety of names. Such are the Exhibitions (*Deicelictæ*) at Sparta and elsewhere : dances parodying—in what proportion of words and dumb show we cannot tell—social types obnoxious to popular ridicule, more especially the fruit-stealer and the foreign quack, whose ways would readily lend themselves both to mimicry and to rude poetic justice. Other names are ' Dances ' (*Orchestæ*), and the untranslatable *Bryalictæ* —a word formed from the battle-shout, and which suggests *summed up* a resemblance to the sword-dance. The generic term for *in 'Lyrical* them is ' Lyrical Comedy,' a term bringing out parallelism *Comedy' or* *'Iambic* with the ' Lyrical Tragedy ' of Arion : the one is a performance of the Comus, the other of Tragi or Satyrs. A more descriptive term was the ' Iambic Dance,' a phrase which conveyed to Greek ears just what ' Lyric Satire ' would suggest to us. All the terms indicate a fusion of lyric and dramatic poetry : without ceasing to be lyric Comedy has become drama by the simple circumstance of the lyric performers borrowing their characterisation from their plot ; dancing has turned into acting for purposes of satire.

Survival of Primitive Comedy in   How from such Primitive Comedy as a common stock other literary forms were derived has now to be shown. I

may first however mention—anticipating—that even in the CHAP VII
times of literary Comedy the primitive form still survived as ——
a popular amusement; under such names as Spectacles *historic*
times
(*Theamata*), Marvels (*Thaumata*), or simply Mimes, the
imitative dance was cultivated in private entertainments,
while the literary drama was consecrated to the theatre.
One such Spectacle has been preserved for us by Xenophon,
and may serve to illustrate what Primitive Comedy had
become in historic times. In his *Symposium* Xenophon
gives what appears rather as a reporter's notes than an
idealised sketch of a banquet in which Socrates was the
chief guest. Through the different stages of the entertainment the company had been amused by a Syracusan with
his pupils in dancing, a girl and a boy. For the most part
the amusement consisted simply in dancing, or feats with
hoops and swords; at the close it became a dramatic
performance as the Syracusan announced, 'My friends,
Ariadne will now enter into her bridal chamber, and
Bacchus, who has been drinking a little with the other gods,
will afterwards join her.' Accordingly Ariadne entered in
bridal costume, and reclined on an elevated couch that had
been placed in the centre of the room. Bacchus not yet
appearing, a bacchic measure was struck up by the flute:
great admiration was aroused as Ariadne, at the sound of
the music, expressed by attitude and motion her pleasure,
not rising to meet Bacchus, yet showing with what difficulty
she could keep quiet. Bacchus, when he entered and
caught sight of his bride, fell dancing with delight; he
embraced and kissed her, she with modesty and coyness
as a bride, yet lovingly, returned his embrace, while the
company clapped and cried, Encore. But the climax of
acting was when Bacchus rose and raised Ariadne and they
embraced again. There was the utmost admiration for the
beautiful Bacchus and the blooming Ariadne, and the way
they embraced in earnest and not in pretence; when

S 2

CHAP. VII Bacchus asked if she loved him, and Ariadne vowed she did, all the spectators were ready to declare that the boy and girl were in love with one another, and not actors taught their part. As a piece of lyric acting this survival of Primitive Comedy appears complete: it is, however, only an entertainment, and there is nothing corresponding to the original satiric purpose, which had by now become sufficiently served by the literary comedy of the theatre [1].

Comedy Aristocratic and Democratic So soon as Comedy rises one step beyond primitive form it begins to show that line of cleavage which ran through all Greek institutions, and which had a racial basis in the Doric and Ionic stocks of which the Greek peoples were for the most part composed. In Tragedy, as we have already seen, the difference of dialect between the odes and episodes reflects the fact that it was from the Doric peoples that Tragedy received its chorus, while the dramatic element was developed in Attica. In Comedy, however, the distinction mainly affects subject-matter. For the Doric race leaned to aristocratic institutions; where, on the contrary, the stock was Ionic there was always a tendency to pass early from an aristocratic to a democratic form of government. Now it is not surprising to find that Comedy, as a branch of literature depending mainly on satire, followed a different course in aristocratic and in popular surroundings: where the government was popular in its basis there would be encouragement to personalities and the handling of public questions in the drama, while aristocratic influence would confine the satiric attack to human nature in general, or to those external distinctions of social types that belong to the spectacle of life. Accordingly we find in Greece Aristocratic and Democratic Comedy running two separate courses of development, and to a large extent prevailing in separate localities.

---

[1] The description is given with naive simplicity by Xenophon, in his *Symposium*, cap. ix.

Universal tradition ascribes to Megara the invention of
Comedy, that is, of the first changes beyond the primitive
comedy that was universal. The tradition is interesting *First known*
from the relation of this state to the line of cleavage just *species of*
mentioned. The territory of Megara was situated on the *Comedy: the*
isthmus which separated Doric Peloponnesus, the mainland, *Megarian*
from the Ionic peninsula of Attica; in the state itself *Farce*
happened very early the revolution which converted it from
an aristocracy into a democracy; while in its aristocratic
phase it had contributed a colony (also styled Megara) to
the west—that Greater Greece of Italy and Sicily which
was destined to be the stronghold of aristocratic government and the aristocratic comedy; again, when Megara
turned to the other side of politics, it found itself favourably
situated for infecting with a taste for comic literature the
great leaders of democratic peoples, the Athenians. The
first species ·then of Comedy appearing in history is the
Megarian Farce. Little is known of it beyond the name;
and we may safely assume that this, as other early species,
consisted in little more than regulating what before was
extemporaneous: prepared plots, and sometimes prepared
speeches, took the place of improvisation. As to the form
of the Megarian Farce—how far, for example, it remained
a dance—no tradition has survived. Its subject-matter
seems to have been confined to class-caricature, cooks and
scullions being the favourite types. Very indirectly we may
form some idea of its general character from the parody of
its treatment which Aristophanes introduces into a scene
of his *Acharnians*. Old Honesty is enjoying the benefits of
peace and an open market, while his countrymen are still at
war. A Megarian is represented as coming to this market:
the war has left him nothing but his two little daughters
to dispose of, and, as he enters, he is soliloquising, in broad
provincial dialect, on the hopelessness of procuring a buyer
for such a commodity.

                                          Wha's sae doylt
As to buy *you*, wha'd bring mair scaith nor gain?
But, hoolie! I've a douce Megarian plan.
I'se dress ye up as pigs, and say 'tis pigs
I bring to sell. Pit on your nieves thae cloots,
An' seem the bairntime o' a buirdly sow!
For by the meikle deil, an ye gang hame,
Fient haet a bit o' bread ye'se hae to eat.
An' pit upon your gruntles too thae snouts;
Syne gang into the sack, like cannie weans.
An' tak guid heed ye grumph and say 'koï'
An' raise sic noises as the haly pigs
Bred to be kill't i' the Muckle Mysteries.

The rest of the scene is the attempt to palm off this
commodity upon Old Honesty, and all the joking and
chaffering that such a transaction gives rise to, the Megarian
calmly meeting with positive assurances any objections
about the human character of the pigs.   His great reliance
is on the squeaking.

Megarian. Hae ye a min' to hear their voices?
Old Honesty.   Yes,
              For god's sake, yes.
Megarian.   Quick, pig, and make a noise!
              Deil tak ye baith, ye mauna haud your tongues;
              Haith, an ye do, I'se tak ye hame again.

At this threat the girls respond with a feeble *koï, koï*, and
more doubts and calm assertions follow, until the amused
buyer starts the experiment of food.

Old Honesty. What do they eat?
Megarian.   Whate'er ye gie them. Speir
              Your ainsell at them.
Old Honesty.   Pig!
First Girl.   Koï, koï!
Old Honesty. Can you eat tares?
First Girl.   Koï, koï, koï!
Old Honesty. What, and dried figs?
First Girl.   Koï, koï, koï!
Old Honesty. What, and can *you* eat figs?
Second Girl.   Koï, koï!
Old Honesty. How loud you call out, when I talk of figs!

He calls for figs, and attendants, bringing from behind CHAP. VII
the scenes great stores of them, scramble them among the
audience in the theatre, according to a common stage trick
in Athenian dramatic performances. At last the bargain is
concluded, and the children sold for a rope of garlic and
a pint of salt :

> *Megarian.* Thou Mercury o' merchants, may I sell
> My wife this gate, and my ain mither too!

From this Megarian Farce as a common starting-point ·
Comedy spread to the aristocratic west, and eastwards to the
home of Democracy in Attica. The aristocratic form was
the first to reach maturity, and the second known species of
Comedy is the Sicilian Comedy of Epicharmus and Sophron, *Sicilian*
which had its flourishing period during the lifetime—nearly *(Aristo-*
cratic)
a century long—of its earlier master. Unquestionably this *Comedy :*
Sicilian species of drama was developed by the marriage of
Comedy with Philosophy, and it is a characteristic circumstance that Epicharmus spent the larger half of his life as
a Pythagorean philosopher at Megara (in Sicily), and only
the latter part as a comedian at Syracuse. So in general
character this Sicilian Comedy was the primitive satiric
dance reduced to regular form, with less of the extempore
and more of the literary element, together with a strong
infusion of moralising, both in the form of gnomes freely
introduced and of individuality in the dramatis personæ.
Its subject-matter was social satire and class-caricature :
'The Rustic' and 'The Ambassadors to the Festival' are
amongst the titles that have come down to us of Epicharmus's plays, and he is credited with the invention of two
most familiar social types—the drunkard and the parasite.
Each of its two masters left a distinctive mark on Sicilian
Comedy. To Epicharmus is attributed the introduction of *Epi-*
mythology as a mode of satire. As remarked in an earlier *charmus*
and mytho-
chapter, the Greeks were apt to look upon deity as humanity *logic satire,*
writ large : to such thinkers mythological plots afforded a

CHAP. VII ready means of hyperbolically parodying human ways and
foibles. So the *Busiris* of Epicharmus paints gluttony on
the divine scale of Hercules, and his *Hephæstus* is simply
a family squabble in Olympus, the blacksmith deity going off
in a huff with his mother, and brought back, drunk, by the
Sophron and his Mimes arts of Bacchus. Again, it was the work of Sophron to give
specific form to the Mime, hitherto one of the many names
for the primitive comic dance. Besides other characteristics
of Sicilian Comedy the Mimes of Sophron possessed a very
marked metrical form, a rhythm midway between prose and
verse. The fertility of this branch of drama was such that
we read of several varieties of mime, serious and comic[1]:
the *hypotheses*, distinguished by a regular subject or plot and
by considerable scenic contrivance, and the mere *pægnia* or
trifles. The productions both of Epicharmus and Sophron
reached a literary rank that attracted the strong admiration
of Plato; to us, except in isolated quotations, they are
entirely lost.

Democratic Comedy: the improvements of Susarion Turning to the other section of Greece, we can easily
understand how the Megarian Farce would find its way
into so closely neighbouring a territory as Attica. Once
imported, the first signs of democratic handling we find
impressed upon it are the 'improvements' of Susarion:
what these improvements were we have no clear information, but there is nothing to suggest that they were such as
to constitute a new species, and they probably consisted in
the substitution of prepared plots for improvisation, and the
adoption of some distinct metrical form. Such elementary
comedy satisfied the wants of Attica during the eclipse of
the democratic spirit in Athens under the tyranny of the
Pisistratid family, a period followed by the concentration of
all interest in the life and death struggle of Greece against
the Persian invaders. In that struggle the Athenians, alike
by their statesmanship and their sufferings, took the leading

---

[1] *Spudæi* and *gelæi*.

position, and at its close there came, with the suddenness of
a revolution, a golden age for democracy with Athens at
the head of the Greek world. Between the repulse of the *Demo-*
cratic Re-
Persians and the close of the Peloponnesian war, which *naissance*
decided the material supremacy of the aristocratic over the *at Athens,*
and Old
democratic states, we have, crowded into little more than a *Attic*
long lifetime, the whole of that Renaissance in political life, *Comedy*
in thought, literature and art, which made Greece a leading
factor in the world's history. With other democratic institutions Comedy felt the general impulse, and the period
is marked by the 'Old Attic Comedy'—the first species
that has become a part of permanent literature, laying the
foundations of Comedy for the universal drama through
its own vigour and the genius of its great master Aristophanes.

The new species has two distinguishing features, both *Its imi-*
derived directly from the democratic influences which *tation of*
tragic
surrounded it. The first is that Old Attic Comedy came *form*
to imitate the form of Tragedy. The key to this important
literary revolution is given in the pregnant words of Aristotle,
that 'it was late before Comedy obtained a chorus from
the archon.' The reader will recognise a technical term
connected with the mode of bringing tragedies on to the
stage : how wealthy citizens placed so many 'choruses' at
the disposal of the government which, through one of its
magistrates, allotted these to the poets competing. Under
the new state of things Comedy also, as a political weapon
under a democratic system of government, is important
enough to claim dignity as a state ceremonial. But there
is more in the words of Aristotle than this. It will be noted
that it was a *chorus* which Comedy obtained, not a comus.
The chorus is a thing belonging to Tragedy, with which
Comedy has no connexion. But Tragedy was a generation
ahead, and had become a public function with a prescribed
machinery of initiation ; the composers of Comedy in their

CHAP. VII sudden accession of importance thought it better, it would seem, to adapt themselves to existing machinery rather than suffer the delay of devising other machinery more appropriate for the work of giving publicity and dignity to their branch. Accordingly they applied in due form for a 'chorus,' and, when they obtained it, naturalised it as well as they could in its uncongenial surroundings. Thus Comedy adopted bodily the form of Tragedy, the union (in brief) of lyric odes by a chorus in the orchestra with dramatic scenes by actors upon the stage. Development had for a time been superseded by imitation, as distinctly as when a savage people, visited by missionaries, adopt wholesale a western civilisation instead of developing it—as the western race itself had done—through many ages of time. But the chorus was felt to be a foreign element in the Comedy that had admitted it, and such Choral Comedy was largely a disturbing influence in the dramatic history of Greece.

Its licence The second main feature of Old Attic Comedy is the wild licence that made it a fit reflection for the spirit of its age. The licence extended to both matter and form. The subject-matter of Comedy in this stage was political satire, a term which in this connexion must be understood to include social and religious questions, all of these being traversed by the same dividing line of conservative and popular. Of the eleven comedies which Aristophanes contributed to this species four are direct manifestos of the peace party; five deal with such social and religious topics as rationalism (*The . Clouds*), political enterprise (*The Birds*), the forensic furore (*The Wasps*), and socialism (*The Women in Parliament* and *Plutus*); and the remaining two are satires upon the man who may be called the poet laureate of the popular party [1]. Again, the licence of Aristophanes' comedies is

---

[1] Similar interference with public life may be inferred from the titles of lost plays by an earlier poet, Cratinus—the Aeschylus of Comedy: such are *The Laws*, *The Boroughs*, *The Allied Cities*, *The Baptists*.

equally seen in their style : the broadest farce occupies the
main plot, and direct attacks are made throughout both on
public characters and private individuals, the history of this
species being marked by a continual passing and repealing
of the decree 'against introducing persons by name into
Comedy.' But all these points will be expounded in detail
in subsequent chapters : it is necessary first to illustrate
Choral Comedy by describing one of its masterpieces [1].

[1] It may be well to warn the English reader that the different manners
and customs of the Greeks from those of our time make *literal* translations of Aristophanes very gross reading to modern taste. See below,
page 323.

VIII

CHORAL (OR OLD ATTIC) COMEDY

The ' Birds' of Aristophanes

VIII

The Birds of Aristophanes is a brilliant and entirely
goodhumoured satire on speculative enterprise. It was
composed in an age when enterprise and speculation were
among the most powerful motives of mankind; when
Athens, raised for a few years to a dizzy height of glory,
was in touch through her unrivalled fleet with commercial
and colonial enterprise all the world over, and a war on
the largest scale was being managed by a debating society
of the whole city, with every voter for a strategist. In this
play a project far surpassing in wildness the wildest ideas
of human speculators is transferred to bird life : and the
working out of this scheme in detail constitutes the plot
of the piece. The hero is the speculative man of genius
Talkover[1], and he is appropriately accompanied by one
Sanguine[2]. Hoopoe king of the Birds, his valet, and a
Chorus of his subjects are the representatives of the bird
world.

Speaking generally, we may say that Comedy in adopting
the form of Tragedy also adopted its stage arrangements;
though, as we might expect, these are in Comedy treated
with more elasticity than in the graver branch of drama[3].
There is the same orchestra and stage, and the scene, if no
longer the conventional façade of a palace, yet regularly
represents some exterior. In the present play, which was

---

[1] Peisthetærus.   [2] Euelpides.

[3] The English reader will bring his mind into the right focus for
appreciating Old Attic Comedy if he imagines a modern Pantomime
into which is infused a strong element of the highest literary power.

mounted with the most costly magnificence, the scene exhibits open country, rocky, with a grove in the centre. Talkover and Sanguine are discovered wandering about as if they had lost their way, one holding a jackdaw, the other a raven, to which they seem to be looking for directions. Their conversation brings out how they are on their way to the realm of birds, and in search of king Hoopoe, who, as once the human king Tereus, but now transformed (in one of Sophocles' tragedies) into a king of birds, is fitted to introduce them in this new realm. It is naturally to Philocrates (the fashionable poulterer of Athens) that they have applied for guides, and these two birds he has assigned them as conductors are now betraying their trust by giving hopelessly contradictory directions.—Suddenly turning to the spectators in the theatre, Sanguine begins directly to explain the plot: how he and his companion are emigrating to a new country,—not that Athens is not the most glorious city in the world (in which to lose your fortune by lawsuits), but they prefer comfort to glory. Talkover interrupts, perceiving that the birds now agree to point in one direction. In this direction they advance, and knock at the bare rock: the valet to the king of birds appears to open the door. There is much mutual embarrassment; gradually the valet explains how when Tereus was metamorphosed into a hoopoe he made a special condition that his faithful servant should be converted into a bird-page. After some hesitation king Hoopoe is summoned from the siesta which he is taking after a meal of myrtle-berries and ants. The two men are terribly alarmed at his enormous beak and crest: Hoopoe seems to feel this as a slight, and lays the blame on Sophocles who so dramatised him. When he has heard his visitors' story, he enquires why they have come to him for information. Because (they respond) he was a man, and so are they; he used to run in debt, and so do they; he used to chuckle when he evaded

paying, and so do they ! Moreover in all their flying about CH. VIII
the birds must have discovered a city of ease, if there
be one in the world :—a city where there will be no strife,
save when a host angrily bids you come earlier to a feast, or
a father reproaches you for not courting his pretty daughter.
The conversation is running on, garnished with the usual
topical hits and personalities, when Talkover is suddenly
struck with a profound thought—what the birds might do if
they only realised their position. At the risk of screwing
Hoopoe's neck off he makes him look up, down, all round,
and tells him he may become the practical ruler of all
he sees. For the birds hold a strategic position that
commands the universe—the line of passage between heaven
and earth. If they found a city and fortify their atmosphere
they will be able to bring both gods and men to their own
terms : from men they can hide heaven like a locust cloud,
while if the gods prove stubborn, the birds can starve them
out by intercepting the smoke of human sacrifices on which
they feed. Hoopoe swears 'by snares, meshes, and nets' it
is the best idea he ever heard, and prepares to summon his
subjects in order that they may learn the scheme from the
projector's own lips.

The prologue has served its usual purpose of leading *Invocation*
up dramatically to the extravagant idea which is to be the *of the Chorus*
basis of the whole plot. The next section of the play is the
Invocation of the Chorus [1]. The proper musical accompaniment of the comic drama was the flute ; one of the attrac-
tions of this particular performance was a flutist prima
donna, long absent from Athens and to be heard for the
first time in her re-appearance this day. She was easily
linked to the plot : in place of a human flourish of trumpets
her call was to summon king Hoopoe's subjects. Accordingly he goes to a part of the scene supposed to represent

[1] Not distinguished in ancient technical nomenclature from the rest
of the prologue, though the lyrical passages were *asmata* or songs.

the nightingale's abode and calls upon her to exert her art.

> Up from thy slumbers, mate of mine :
> Let forth the flood of strains divine,
> As when, the wonder of thy throat,
> Thou trillest Sorrow's bubbling note,
> For Itys wailed with many a tear
> By thee and me. The warbling clear
> Forth of the yew-tree's close-leaved tresses
> Issues, and mounting upward presses
> To Jove's own seats ; when golden-haired
> Apollo hears. To answer dared,
> His ivory-fashioned lyre he takes,
> And such soul-touching chords awakes,
> That, as the melody advances,
> The gods move forward to their dances ;
> And lips immortal deign to borrow
>   And sing with thee
>   In harmony
> A marvellous sweet song of sorrow.

From behind the scenes is heard the nightingale's call in the form of an elaborate flute-performance.   Then crossing the stage Hoopoe turns to another part of the scene, and himself in lyrical invocation summons his subjects.

> Epo po po po po po po po po po po po poi,
> Holloa ! holloa ! what ho ! what ho !
> Hither haste, my plume-partakers ;
> Come many, come any
> That pasture on the farmers' well-sown acres,
> Tribes countless that on barley feed,
> And clans that gather out the seed ;
> Come, alert upon the wing,
> Dulcet music uttering :
> Ye that o'er the furrowed sod
> Twitter upon every clod,
> Making all the air rejoice
> With your soft and slender voice :
> Tio, tio, tio, tio, tio, tio, tio, tio,
> Ye that feast on garden fruits,
> Nestling 'midst the ivy shoots :

Ye that all the mountains throng,   CH. VIII
Olive-croppers, arbute-loppers,
Haste and fly to greet my song.
Trioto, trioto, totobrix!
Ye that o'er the marshy flats
Swallow down the shrill-mouthed gnats;
Ye that haunt the deep-dew'd ground,
Marathon's sweet meads around,
Ouzel, and thou of the speckled wing,
Hazelhen, hazelhen, speed while I sing.
Come many, come any,
With the halcyon brood that sweep
Surges of the watery deep,
Come and list to novel words,
Which to hear, from far and near
We gather all the tribes of neck-extending birds.
Here is arrived a sharp old man
Of revolutionary mind,
To revolutionary deeds inclined;
Come all, and listen to his plan.

Strange cries of birds are heard in the distance, and *Parode or* *Chorus-* gradually we get a grand pantomimic tour-de-force which *Entry* constitutes the parode[1] or chorus-entry. Single figures appear on the stage, and later the twenty-four members of the Chorus enter the orchestra, all as birds got up in splendid array, and on a colossal scale. The scene is conveyed to a reader in the free movement of accelerated verse, as the entries made singly or in groups give scope to the human on-lookers for comments, which include the usual bad puns and personal applications to individuals present in the audience. A flamingo is identified by his flame colour ; another figure is a ludicrous reproduction of Hoopoe himself, but 'Hoopoe Junior' has had all his feathers stripped off by the lady-birds (like Callias) ; a

[1] The structural divisions of Ancient Drama as recognised by critics of antiquity are not always mutually exclusive. Strictly speaking the parode should not begin until the great body of the chorus appear in the orchestra : but the diamatic scene of the chorus-entry really commences at this point.

pompous-treading crested cock is pronounced a turbaned
Mede ; and a party-coloured Gobbler is a double of Cleonymus.　But at last the Chorus appear in a whole cloud that
hides the entrance.

> *Hoopoe.*　　Hither is a partridge coming, there a hazelhen is shown ;
> 　　　　　Upon this side is a widgeon : upon that a halcyon.
> *Talkover.*　What's the one we see behind her?
> 　　　　　　　　　　　　*Hoopoe.* That one? Razorbill's the name.
> *Talkover.* Razorbill's a bird then?
> 　　　　　　　　　　*Sanguine.* Call it Sporgilus, 'twill be the same.
> *Hoopoe.*　　Here's an owl.
> 　　　　　　*Talkover.* What's this you tell me? Who to Athens
> 　　　　　　　　brought an owl?
> *Hoopoe.*　　Pye and turtle, lark and pigeon, goat-sucker and guinea-fowl.
> 　　　　　Hawk and falcon, cushat, cuckoo, redshank, redpole, come in
> 　　　　　　view,
> 　　　　　Gannet, kestrel, diver, osprey, flycatcher and woodchat too.
> *Sanguine.* Merrily, merrily come the birds, merrily come the blackbirds
> 　　　　　　all :
> 　　　　　What a twittering! what a fluttering! what a variety of squall!

But the scene appears less merry to Sanguine when he
realises that the huge-beaked creatures are behaving in
a threatening fashion to their visitors : for the birds do not
fall in with their monarch's views, but outbursts of lyric
excitement convey their consternation at being betrayed to
their natural enemies mankind.

> 　　　Upon them! at them in a ring
> 　　　　Encircle them with bloody force :
> 　　　Make onslaught with embattled wing!
> 　　　　For these two men must die of course,
> 　　　　　And glut my beak with prey.
> 　　　No gloomy glen is there, nor airy cloud,
> 　　　Nor hoary sea, that can their persons shroud,
> 　　　　　And let them get away.
> 　　　Pluck them, tear them ; bite them, scare them :
> 　　　　　do not let us be afraid.
> 　　　Where is he who should command us?
> 　　　　　let him lead the light brigade.

Talkover and Sanguine have the presence of mind to arm

themselves with a spit for spear, and vinegar-cruet and bowl CH. VIII
for shields. But before the hostile forces meet, Hoopoe
manages to calm down his comrades' suspicions; they
gradually assume a more peaceful attitude, and prepare
to listen to Talkover's proposal—the metre reflecting the
change of mind by settling down into blank verse.

An attentive audience before him, Talkover plunges into *Episode I*
anapæsts.

> I'm filled with the subject and long to proceed ;
> My rhetorical leaven is ready to knead.

He puts his project with all possible formality : Sanguine
relieving the effect by persistent interruptions and farcical
comments. Talkover begins with the ancient dignity of the
birds. As evidence of their antiquity he quotes Aesop's
fable of the lark that buried his father in his head—clearly
because there was as yet no earth in which to make the
grave. [Sanguine adds that Bury Head[1] was named after
this circumstance.] Then the authority of the birds is seen
in the way the working classes all obey the cock's call
to labour in the morning. [Sanguine tells how he once
got up at cock-crow and was robbed for his pains.] Then
Talkover dwells upon the wrongs done by men to the
birds : they snare and trap them, and take them in heaps ;
they buy and sell them, and feel them all over ; they
not only roast them, but, adding insult to injury, pour over
them scalding sauce ! This final touch brings a burst of
lyric indignation from the chorus, which gives a break
in the long anapæstic scene before the orator proceeds
to his proposed remedy.

> Then I move, that the birds shall in common repair
> To a centrical point, and encamp in the air ;
> And entrench and enclose it, and fortify there :

---

[1] Professor Kennedy's ingenious modernisation for *Kephalæ* = Heads,
the name of an Attic borough.

And build up a rampart, impregnably strong,
Enormous in thickness, enormously long;
Bigger than Babylon, solid and tall,
With bricks and bitumen, a wonderful wall.

Then they must send heralds to the gods and dictate terms. Men shall hereafter sacrifice to birds at the same time as to gods: a sacrifice to Venus shall be accompanied with an offering of wheat to the coot, or if a ram is offered to Jove a male ant must be presented to king Wren. If the gods resist, declare a Sacred War, and blockade them when they wish to make their love visits to earth. If mankind resist, swallows can pick up all their seed, crows peck out the eyes of cattle, and locusts eat up the vines; on the other hand, if they are obedient, the birds can offer men good 'auguries,' pointing out treasures, and favourable seasons for sailing, besides granting a century or two of long life out of their own endless years. The metre quickens as Talkover perorates on the economy of having birds for deities: there will be no expensive temples to rear, but the new gods will live cheaply,

Lodging, without shame or scorn,
In a maple, or a thorn;
The most exalted and divine
Will have an olive for his shrine.

The Chorus accept with lyric enthusiasm: then blank verse expresses the preparations for carrying the scheme out. But first the two human friends of the birds are taken inside to be feasted and furnished with wings. The Chorus have requested that the nightingale might be sent out to entertain them in the interval of waiting. The flute-girl then makes her appearance on the stage, in bird costume complete to the beaked mask: but, as a mask presented difficulties to a performer on a wind instrument, it is contrived that Sanguine breaks the mask under pretence of kissing, and the audience thus see the face of their favourite.

Parabasis   The play has reached its parabasis. This parabasis was

a singular institution of Ancient Comedy, a counterpart to
the point in the primitive comus-procession where the revellers broke off their chaunting in order to extemporise
satire. So the parabasis is essentially a digression, covering
an interval in the action : the word 'parabasis' conveys both
this, and also the way in which the Chorus—as would be
natural in such a digression—'stepped from' their proper
position in the orchestra during the dramatic action, and
faced the audience while addressing them directly. This
portion of Comedy is complete in itself, with a regular
structure of its own, being divided between short choral
hymns, more or less infected with comic spirit, and long
addresses in special metres, handling political or social
topics without regard to the characterisation in which the
Chorus appear, or humorously utilising this characterisation.
The present example is, however, exceptional in treatment.
It is complete in structure, but its subject-matter is strictly
relevant to the plot : the poet forgets to digress, so absorbed
is he in the brilliant idea of his bird scheme, and the subtil-
ties of fancy and ingenuity by which he is to make it seem
probable.

The first part of the parabasis—the Lyric Introduction— *lyric intro-*
is a summons to the flutist to perform. *duction (or commation)*

> O my ownie, O my brownie,
>   Bird of birds the dearest,
> Voice that mingling with my lays
>   Ever was the clearest;
> Playmate of my early days,
>   Still to me the nearest,
> Nightingale, thus again
>   Do I meet thee, do I greet thee,
> Bringing to me thy sweet strain!
>   Skilfullest of artists thou
> To soft trillings of the flute
>   Vernal melodies to suit,
>   Our homily demands thy prelude now.

Accordingly an elaborate flute solo, the second in the play,

succeeds.   Then (forming the Parabasis Proper) we have a
long address in anapæstic measure, setting forth the claim
of the Chorus for supremacy over mankind.

> Ho! ye men, dim-lived by nature, closest to the leaves in feature,
> Feeble beings, clay-create, shadowy tribes inanimate,
> Wingless mortals, in a day, doleful, dream-like, swept away:
> Note the lessons that we give, we the immortals formed to live,
> We the ethereal, the unaged, with undying plans engaged.

Utilising the theory of a reigning philosopher, which evolved
the universe out of wind (air and motion) as the embryo of
all things, the Chorus substitute 'egg' for embryo, and so
make out a bird-origin for the world.

> Chaos was and Night of yore, in the time all times before,
> And black Erebus beside Tartarus extending wide.
> Earth, Air, Heaven were yet unknown; in huge Erebus alone
> First, our oldest legend says, black-winged Night a wind-egg lays;
> Which, as circling seasons move, brings to birth the charmer
>   Love,
> Bright with golden wings behind, semblant to the whirling wind.
> In the vast Tartarean shade him the dull dark Chaos made
> Sire of us: we nestled there till we saw the light of air.
> Race immortal was there none till Love's sorcery was begun:
> But, when all things mixed in motion, rose the sky, the earth, the
>   ocean,
> And the blessed gods were made, everlasting, undecay'd.

Again, playing upon the idea of 'augury,' the Chorus represent birds as the source of all material comfort.

> Mortal men for their convenience
>   owe to us wellnigh everything.
> First we announce to them the Seasons,
>   such as Autumn, Winter and Spring.
> When the crane departs for Lybia
>   then the sowing they know is to do;
> Then the seaman, hanging his rudder,
>   settles to sleep for the whole night through.
> Then should they weave a coat for Orestes,
>   lest in the cold he be driven to steal.
> Afterwards comes the kite, another
>   change in the time of year to reveal;

Then from the sheep you take its spring-fleece;
    after that comes the swallow to say
Sell your great-coat, and provide some
    dress that is fit for midsummer-day.
Ammon, Delphi, and Dodona,
    Phœbus Apollo are we to you.
'What do the birds say?' is the question
    first to be answered whatever you do.
Whether it be to buy or sell, or
    earn your living or take to a wife,
Everything is a 'bird' to you that
    betrays the shadow of coming life;
A phrase, a sneeze, two people meeting,
    a sound, a slave, an ass is a 'bird.'
So, that we are your prophet Apollo,
    is too clear for another word.

    Take us as gods, and for your uses
    You will have in us Prophets, Muses,
    Winter, Summer, wind and weather,
    To your liking altogether.
    We shall not retire for state
    Up to the clouds like Jove the Great:
    But residing handily by you
    We shall hear and not deny you
    All that you may wish to possess;
    Health and wealth and happiness,
    Length of days, a state of peace,
    Laughter that shall never cease,
    Constant feasting, dances, youth,
    With milk of birds: so that in truth
        You and your heirs
        Shall have no cares
        But how to live
    On the very abundance of wealth we give.

The long address which formed the bulk of a parabasis is broken by short lyrics, two such interruptions making a strophe with its antistrophe. The strophe comes at this *strophe* point, invoking a Muse, and having point given to it by reproducing the lofty rhythms of the old poet Phrynichus, amid an accompaniment of bird-twittering (which the reader must imagine).

Muse, that in the deep recesses
　Of the forest's dreary shade,
Vocal with our wild addresses,
　Or in the lonely lowly glade,
Attending near, art pleased to hear
　Our humble bill, tuneful and shrill,
When to the name of Omnipotent Pan
　Our notes we raise, or sing in praise
Of mighty Cybele, from whom we began,
　Mother of Nature, and every creature,
Winged or unwinged, of birds or man:
　Aid and attend, and chant with me
The music of Phrynichus, open and plain,
The first that attempted a loftier strain,
　Ever busy like the bee ╵
　With the sweets of harmony.

after-speech (or epir- rhema) Then the address to the audience is resumed[1] (in what is called the After-Speech), and in pure farcical style are put the conveniences of birds' ways. People with whom the law interferes in this world might be free among the birds.

Here by law 'tis very bad if a youngster beats his dad:
There with us 'tis usual rather, even grand, to cuff a father,
Strutting up, and crying, 'Sir, if you'll fight me, lift your spur.'

antistrophe Then the antistrophe[2], taking up from the strophe, finds a bird analogy for Phrynichus in the swan-song.

Thus the swans in chorus follow,
　On the mighty Thracian stream,
　Hymning their eternal theme,
Praise to Bacchus and Apollo:
　The welkin rings with sounding wings,
　With songs and cries and melodies,
Up to the thunderous æther ascending:
　Whilst all that breathe on earth beneath,
　The beasts of the wood, the plain and the flood,
In panic amazement are crouching and bending
　With the awful qualm of a sudden calm
Ocean and air in silence blending,

[1] For variety of metre anapæsts have changed to trochaics.
[2] In the original the metres of the two passages are antistrophic.

> The ridge of Olympus is sounding on high,
> Appalling with wonder the lords of the sky,
> And the Muses and Graces enthroned in their places
> Join in the solemn symphony.

The After-Response continues the After-Speech, with further *after-re-*
conveniences of birds' ways. A spectator who is tired of the *sponse (or antepir-*
play might, if he had wings, just fly home, get a bit and snack, *rhema)*
and come back fresh.

> Flying oft with good success crowns a lover's happiness.
> If he spies his rival here, in the senatorial tier,
> He can spread his wings and fly, love-directed through the sky,
> Keep his happy tryst, and then fly into his seat again.

The play resumes as Talkover and Sanguine reappear in *Episode II*
bird costume, and discuss with the Chorus the founding of
the new city. First its name is after deliberation settled—
Cuckoo-borough-on-Cloud [1]. Preparation is made for the
solemn initiatory sacrifices : but these are perpetually interrupted by fresh arrivals of persons anxious to have a hand
in or to oppose the new project. A Priest comes first, with
a scraggy goat : he is allowed to officiate. He has scarcely
commenced when a Poet follows, reciting fragments of lyrics
he has begun to compose on the new city. As with Pindar's,
his sublime strains contain hints that gifts would not be un-
acceptable, and Talkover manages to gratify him econom-
ically by making the Priest strip and give up his garments
to the Poet. Then follow, one after another, a Prophet with
a bag of oracles, an Astronomer with instruments for street-
mensuration, a Commissioner from the mother-state to the
new colony, a Hawker of Decrees—all of whom are made to
furnish 'knock-about business,' being first 'chaffed' and then
thrashed by Talkover off the stage. But finally the latter has
to give up and finish his sacrifice indoors.

His retirement makes a second interval, filled by a second *Second*
Parabasis only partially complete. Without any Introduction *Parabasis*

---

[1] Nephelococcuguia.

CH. VIII   or Parabasis Proper, it commences with a Strophe, which puts
strophe   the rights of birds, in queer metre supposed to represent
birds' attempts at human verse.

> Henceforth—our worth,
> Our right—our might,
> Shall be shown,
> Acknowleged, known;
> Mankind shall raise
> Prayers, vows, praise,
> To the birds alone.
> Our employ is to destroy
> The vermin train,
> Ravaging amain
> Your fruits and grain:
> We're the wardens
> Of your gardens,
> To watch and chase
> The wicked race,
> And cut them shorter,
> In hasty slaughter.

after-   In the After-Speech the Chorus attack (in accelerated rhythm)
speech (or   their mortal enemy—the fashionable poulterer Philocrates:
epirrhema)   a reward is promised if he is brought in alive or dead,—

> He, that ortolans and quails to market has presumed to bring,
> And the sparrows, six a penny, tied together in a string,
> With a wicked art retaining sundry doves in his employ,
> Fastened, with their feet in fetters, forced to serve for a decoy.

Also, all spectators keeping birds in cages are bidden to let
antistrophe   them free.   The Antistrophe pictures the allurements of
bird life.

> Blest are they,
> The birds, alway:
> With perfect clothing,
> Fearing nothing,
> Cold or sleet
> Or summer heat.
> As it chances,
> As he fancies,
> Each his own vagary follows,
> Dwelling in the dells or hollows;

> When with eager, weary strain
> The shrilly grasshoppers complain,
> Parched upon the sultry plain,
> Maddened with the raging heat,
> We secure a cool retreat
> In the shady nooks and coves,
> Recesses of the sacred groves ;
> Many a herb, and many a berry,
> Serves to feast and make us merry.

The After-Response promises bird-gifts, and threatens bird- *after-response (or antepirrhema)* penalties, to the judges, according as the play shall win or lose the prize.

The next episode is made by the entrance of Talkover to *Episode III* announce the sacrifices as propitious. He is joined by a messenger, who arrives breathless with tidings of the marvellous rapidity with which the new city had been built. Thirty thousand cranes (it might be more) travelled from the African desert with stones in their gizzards ; these were worked into shape by stone-curlews and stone-chatterers ; sand-martins and mud-larks presided over the department of the mortar, moor-fowl and river-hens bringing water to temper it, while ten thousand storks with their beaks upheaved clay for bricks.—But who could serve the mortar and carry it ? Obviously carrion-crows and carrier-pigeons.—How were the hods loaded ? Geese with their webbed feet trampled the mortar, and then laid it in the hods quite handy. [Quite footy, ejaculates Talkover.] Ducks clambered up the ladders like duck-legged bricklayers' apprentices : the carpentry was done by yellowhammers and wood-peckers, their hatchet-beaks keeping up a din like that of a ship-yard. The whole is complete : gates up, beats paced, the bell borne, and the beacons set.

The strength of these fortifications has scarcely been described when a second messenger enters with news that the blockade has already been broken by Iris, messenger-maiden of the gods : thirty thousand light-armed hawks have

CH. VIII been sent in pursuit of her.   After a brief strophe of defiance
———   by the Chorus, Iris is seen flying across the stage in a
grotesque costume that suggests a ship in full sail.   Talkover
hails her and bids her stop, while a guard of birds enforces
his command.   A dialogue follows, contemptuous on both
sides.   Iris is on her father Jupiter's business, and scouts
the idea of asking passports from any one.   Talkover says
that if he did his duty he would have her put to death.

> *Iris.*   But I'm immortal.
> *Talkover.*   That would make no difference.

Finally, as he cannot stop the intruder, Talkover shoo's her
off like a trespassing bird, to her great indignation.—Then
enters the Herald who had been sent to mankind, and reports
their complete and joyful submission : birds have become
all the rage, he says ; and Athenian family names are
punned upon to show this.   The metre breaks into lyrics as
Talkover and the Chorus prepare bundles of wings for the
mortals who will presently come to claim the rights of
citizenship : the detail is no doubt introduced for the sake of
a great colour effect in the heaps of feathers strewn over the
long stage.—There is one more incident in this long episode,
when there arrive, successively, a would-be Parricide, a
dithyrambic Poet, and an Informer, all claiming wings and
the bird-franchise.   To keep up the idea of reversing all
things the first is fairly received and given a military command, while the other two, after some badgering, are horse-
whipped back again.

Choral   The breaks between the episodes are for the remainder
Interlude of the play filled by Choral Interludes, as in Tragedy.
The interludes are irrelevant to the plot ; their subject-
matter consists of what was a favourite form of wit in ancient
comedy—the surprise, by which a speaker setting out to
describe some marvel in heroic terms suddenly converts the
marvel into something highly familiar.   For the first interlude

the stock taunt of the comic poets against the politician CH. VIII
Cleonymus—in whose history there was an unfortunate
incident of a flight from battle without a shield—does duty *strophe*
once more in the new form of a botanical wonder.

> We have flown, and we have run,
> Viewing marvels, many a one,
> In every land beneath the sun.
>   But the strangest sight to see
>   Was a huge exotic tree
> Growing without heart or pith,
> Weak and sappy like a withe,
> But, with leaves and boughs withal,
> Comely, flourishing, and tall.
>   This the learned all ascribe
>   To the sycophantic tribe;
> But the natives there, like us,
>   Call it a Cleonymus.
> In the spring's delightful hours
> It blossoms with rhetoric flowers.
> I saw it standing in the field,
> With leaves in figure like a shield:
> On the first tempestuous day
> I saw it—cast those leaves away!

The antistrophe makes a similar stroke at the famous foot- *antistrophe*
pad of the neighbourhood.

> There lies a region out of sight,
> Far within the realm of night,
> Far from torch and candle light.
> There in feasts of meal and wine
> Men and demigods may join,
> There they banquet, and they dine,
> Whilst the light of day prevails.
> At sunset their assurance fails;
> If any mortal then presumes,
> Orestes, sallying from the tombs,
> Like a fierce heroic sprite,
> Assaults and strips the lonely wight.

Then follows an episode illustrating the mythological form *Episode IV*
of burlesque that has already been noticed as a characteristic
of Sicilian Comedy. Prometheus enters, disguised with

mufflers, and carrying an umbrella. He appears in great
terror lest Zeus should see him, and does not feel comfortable
till he has put up his umbrella between himself and heaven.
He is acting his traditional part as the friend of mortals, and
comes to give them secret information, that the gods are
dreadfully distressed by the blockade, and, if the birds hold
out, must yield to their terms. But they must be sure to insist upon one condition—that Jupiter gives up Queenship [1]
the damsel who keeps his thunder-closet and looks after his
whole government: she will make a nice wife for Talkover.

Amongst other things Prometheus has announced that an
embassy from the gods to the bird-city is on its way. The
Choral In- interval of waiting for its arrival is filled by a half ode—a
terlude :
strophe strophe, of which the antistrophe comes at the conclusion
of the visit. The strophe is another case of surprise wit, this
time attacking Socrates and his friends.

> Beyond the navigable seas,
> Amongst the fierce Antipodes,
> There lies a lake, obscure and holy,
> Lazy, deep, melancholy,
> Solitary, secret, hidden,
> Where baths and washing are forbidden.
> Socrates, beside the brink,
> Summons from the murky sink
> Many a disembodied ghost;
> And Pisander, reached the coast,
> To raise the spirit that he lost;
> With a victim, strange and new,
> A gawky camel, which he slew,
> Like Ulysses,—whereupon
> The grizzly sprite of Chærephon
> Flitted round him, and appeared,
> With his eyebrows and his beard,
> Like a strange infernal fowl,
> Half a vampire, half an owl.

Episode V The Ambassadors from Heaven now arrive—Neptune,
Hercules, and the Triballian Deity. The last is treated as

---

[1] Basileia.

a barbarian ally of the gods, a comrade of whom the other
two are ashamed. He speaks unintelligibly, and will not
keep his robes straight. Neptune, of course, is of the
highest divine family, while Hercules is one who becomes
ambassador for the sake of the feasting he will get. Talkover understands the respective positions of the ambassadors,
and affects not to notice their approach, while he is giving
orders about cooking, the steam of which is making Hercules
anxious for a speedy settlement. Under such circumstances
they quickly agree to terms and form an alliance: the barbarian assenting in gibberish which is interpreted as approval.
At the last moment Talkover recollects the condition about
Queenship: the very mention of this makes Neptune break
off the negotiations. Talkover calmly goes on with his
cooking, while hungry Hercules protests. But Neptune
rallies him upon risking his own reversion in Jupiter's
sovereignty for the sake of a meal. Talkover hears this
and, taking Hercules aside, warns him that his uncle is
making a tool of him : that he will get nothing in the way
of inheritance from Jupiter since he is illegitimate—the
'son of a foreign woman.' He appeals to him as to whether
his father has ever shown him to the wardmen, or taken
the other legal steps for making him his heir. Hercules
admits that nothing of the kind has ever been done, and
indignantly makes common cause with the birds. Thus two
of the embassy are disagreed : the casting-vote lies with the
barbarian, who is appealed to for his opinion.

Triballian. Me tell you, pretty girl, grand, beautiful queen,
 Give him to birds.
Hercules. Ay, give her up, you mean.
Neptune. Mean! he knows nothing about it. He means nothing
 But chattering like a magpie.
Talkover.   Well, 'the magpies.'
 He means, the magpies or the birds in general.

Neptune is forced to be content with this : the treaty is
made, and the ambassadors go in to the feast.

U

CH. VIII   The remainder of the interlude follows, another treat-
―――   ment of familiar things under the guise of foreign wonders.
Choral In-
terlude :   Along the Sycophantic shore,
anti-   And where the savage tribes adore
strophe   The waters of the Clepsydra [1],
                     There dwells a nation, stern and strong,
                     Armed with an enormous tongue,
                         Wherewith they smite and slay.
                     With their tongues they reap and sow,
                     And gather all the fruits that grow,
                         The vintage and the grain;
                     Gorgias is their chief of pride,
                     And many more there be beside,
                         Of mickle might and main.
                     Good they never teach, nor show
                     But how to work men harm and woe,
                         Unrighteousness and wrong;
                     And hence the custom doth arise,
                     When beasts are slain in sacrifice,
                         We sever out the tongue.

Exodus   All is now ready for the finale, which is a grand spectacular tour-de-force, representing the union of Talkover and
Queenship, and elaborated with all the gorgeous display of
the highest tragedies.   Talkover is seen descending from
heaven, with Queenship by his side, and the thunderbolt of
Zeus in his hand, amid subtle odours rising from the
wreathed smoke that curls in the tranquil air.   The Chorus
raise the Marriage Anthem, Hymen's songs of glee, the
bridal carols sung before when the fates allied Hera to the
king of Olympus:
                     Golden-wing'd the blooming Love
                     His chariot lightly reining drove,

and all sang Hymen Hymenæus! Talkover bows his thanks,
and adds his quota to the triumph strains in the hurled bolt of
Zeus with its peals of thunder and rush of rain. Finally the
Chorus are invited to join the procession, and with fresh
triumph-shouts they unite in escorting the hero up to heaven.

[1] The water-clock of the law-courts, naturally associated with rhetoric.

IX

Choral (or Old Attic) Comedy as a Dramatic Species

1 *Structure of Choral Comedy*

2 *The Comic Chorus*

3 *The subject-matter of Aristophanes*

4 *The Dramatic Element in Old Attic Comedy*

IX

1 Structure of Choral Comedy

THE Old Attic play, of which *The Birds* has been given
as a type, may be best designated, when viewed as a species
of the universal drama, by the name 'Choral Comedy.'
Its distinction consisted·in the combination, under exceptional circumstances, of what was in the highest degree
comic matter with a chorus and details of choral form
which were borrowed from Tragedy, and which for a long
time existed as a disturbing force in the development of
Comedy.

From the nature of its origin this Choral Comedy might
be expected to present a highly complex structure.   The
primitive Comedy was already double in its component
elements—that is to say, satiric *plus* dramatic.   It developed
the new species by a fresh adaptation to the form of Tragedy.
Again, tragic poetry was composed in a variety of metres :
in the combination with Comedy not only were these metres
absorbed, but there was further a tendency to create modi-
fications of them fitted to the new surroundings.   Such
various tendencies are sure to be reflected in variations of
outward form, and the first step in the exposition of Old
Attic Comedy must be to review its dramatic and its
metrical structure.

The dramatic analysis of Aristophanes' plays reveals the
structural elements that belong to Tragedy, with such
variations as are readily understood.   The Prologue is the
name for all that precedes the appearance of the Chorus.
It includes one, and sometimes more than one, dramatic
scene.   A change of scene may occur in the course of the

CHAP. IX prologue, as in that to the *Acharnians*, which opens in the
parliament place of Athens, and closes in the country near
The Parode Old Honesty's farm. The Parode, or Chorus-Entry, may be
or Chorus- no more than a joyous procession, or a hostile demonstra-
Entry tion like that of the colliers from Acharnæ village, who run
in to stone the man that has sought to make peace. It is
however usually seized upon as an opportunity for special
masque or pantomime effects : great scenic strokes are evidently intended by the first appearance of the Clouds with
their flimsy upper garments and black trains for shadows,
the Birds with their terrible beaks, the enormous stings and
impossibly thin waists of the Wasp-Jury, while a similar
appeal is made to the ear by the croaking of the unseen
Frogs over whose waters Bacchus rows.

Attach- By strict definition the parode ought immediately to fol-
ment of the low the prologue : in reality, however, we find an intermediate
Chorus : section of the play worth distinguishing from the prologue,
and the function of this is the attachment of the chorus to
the rest of the play. As the chorus was an element foreign
to Comedy it is not surprising that we should find, in the
course of the prologue, some distinct device preparing the
way for the introduction of this novelty. The Attachment
of the Chorus is never omitted [1]. Sometimes it consists in
nothing more than a call for help : as where the Sausage-
seller flies at the appearance of Cleon, and the slaves call the
knights to the rescue, or where Trygæus learns in heaven
where Peace is to be found, and cries out to the Country
Party for assistance in recovering her [2]. Other cases
show more contrivance. In the *Acharnians* Amphitheus

---

[1] The only case at all analogous in Tragedy is the *Oedipus at
Colonus* (36–116), and perhaps the *Children of Hercules* (from 69)
where there is a call for help. Such summons to join in rejoicing or
lamenting as is found in the *Bacchanals*, *Iphigenia among the Tauri*,
and *Daughters of Troy* is rather a commencement of the Chorus-Entry
than a preparation for it.

[2] *Knights*, 242 ; *Peace*, 296.

tells breathlessly the escape he has had from the angry colliers as he journeyed, laden with truces : at the conclusion
of the incident these colliers appear in the orchestra. In
the *Wasps* Hate-Cleon warns the slaves who are watching
his father that his fellow-jurors will be coming at daybreak
to fetch him. In the *Mysteries* not only is the whole prologue a preparation for the festival, but further the signal is
seen on the temple of Ceres some lines before the Chorus
of Mystics enter. Similarly in the *Lysistrata,* near the
close of the prologue, a shout behind the scenes is understood as a signal that the Acropolis has been seized, and the
conspirators discuss the probable rush of men to fire and
force the door, which (after a change of scene) takes place.
In the long introductory scenes to the *Frogs,* the hero has,
at an early point, enquired from Hercules directions for his
journey, and heard, with other information, about a joyous
company with torches and flutes who will point out the way :
these appear later on, and, as the Band of the Initiated,
constitute the Chorus to the play. The *Women in Parliament* brings the individuals who are to form the Chorus
upon the stage first as conspirators ; we watch the course of
their conspiracy, and then see them descend to the orchestra
and commence their choral function. The hero of the
Plutus, as soon as the god shows signs of accepting his invitation, sends his slave to fetch his neighbours to do the
visitor due honour, and these neighbours appear presently
as the Chorus[1]. In all these cases the contrivance for introducing the Chorus amounts to no more than a detail ; *or Invoca-*
in two plays it is enlarged into an elaborate Invocation. In *tion*
the *Birds* attention has already been directed to the important section of the play made up of the appeal to the
nightingale, the music supposed to represent her response,

---

[1] *Acharnians,* 177 and 204; *Wasps,* 214, 230; *Mysteries,* 277, 312 ;
Lysistrata, 240, 254; *Frogs,* 154, 324; *Plutus,* 222, 257. For the
Women in Parliament, compare 282, 289, and 478.

CHAP. IX and the subsequent summons of the epops to his subjects ;
this and the similar Invocation of the Clouds by Socrates
contain some of the loftiest lyric poetry that even Aristophanes has composed [1].

Odes, Epi-   From the entry of the Chorus a comedy consists in the
sodes, and alternation of Episodes and Choral Odes to any number of
Exodus each. The Episodes, as in Tragedy, include forensic contests, rheses, and messengers' speeches, and stage-episodes
transacted in the temporary absence of the chorus. The
final episode is called an Exodus : it is itself full of choral
effects, and usually works up to a spectacular finale. As in
Tragedy, the choral element in Comedy not only consists of
lyric interludes, but further invades the episodes in the form
of monodies and concertos. It is not surprising to find in.
Comedy, as compared with Tragedy, a tendency to diminish
the length of choral odes, and further, to substitute for these
shorter lyric pieces, not so much separating episodes as
breaking up a long episode into sections and so relieving
its tediousness. Accordingly among the structural parts of
Nexus of Comedy we ought to reckon the Nexus of episodes and lyric
dramatic breaks woven into a single prolonged scene. One such
scenes and nexus represents the women's Mysteries and covers five
lyrics hundred lines ; another example is the contest between
Aeschylus and Euripides in the *Frogs*, and is longer still by
a hundred and fifty lines.

The Para-   One more structural element of Comedy has yet to be
basis or mentioned, both remarkable in itself and peculiar to the
Dramatic Old Attic stage. This is the Parabasis, already illustrated
Digression in the preceding chapter—one of the lyric interludes in
which the Chorus turned round, severing in part their
connexion with the play, and directly addressed the audience : the word 'parabasis' may be literally translated
as 'digression.' The Parabasis is one of the curiosities
of literary evolution : alike its regular structure and its

[1] *Birds*, 209-262 ; *Clouds*, 263-274.

irregularities reflect the play of forces which developed CHAP. IX
ancient comedy. In the main, the digression is to the
form of Primitive Comedy: like it the Parabasis consists *It reflects*
essentially of two parts—a long satiric tirade, broken by *the develop-*
lyric invocations of deities. It also reflects the revolution *Comedy*
which raised Comedy to the dignity of a national festival
by the new importance of satire as a political weapon:
hence the satire of the Parabasis is not the iambic lampoon
on individuals, but the handling of public questions in
somewhat more elevated metres. But Comedy, before
reaching its Old Attic form, had passed through, as we have
seen, an intervening stage, in which the satirisers adopted
a particular characterisation. This period in the history
of Comedy is also reflected in the Parabasis, at different
parts of which the Chorus either drop their character,
or resume it in order to utilise it for their satiric purpose.

As already remarked, the Parabasis consists fundamentally *Structural*
of two elements, the satire and the lyric invocation. The *parts of the*
latter is regarded as an interruption, dividing the satire *Parabasis*
in two parts : the law of comic variety would soon differen-
tiate these two satiric sections as the Parabasis Proper and
the After-Speech, the first in an anapæstic metre modified
from the marching rhythm of Tragedy, the latter in the
accelerated (or trochaic) rhythm which even in Tragedy was
the metre of bustle and movement. Further, as the lyrics
would be antiphonal, it would be a natural step to separate
the antistrophe from the strophe, thus breaking up the later
section of satire into an After-Speech and After-Response.
These five parts make up the structure of a Parabasis : the
Parabasis Proper, the Strophe of Invocation, the After-
Speech, the Antistrophe, and the After-Response—not to
mention a brief Introduction that dismisses the previous
scene or bespeaks attention [1].

[1] The Greek names are *Epirrhema* for After-Speech, *Ant-epirrhema*
for After-Response, *Commation* for Introduction.

It is only in the Parabasis Proper—and, where this is lacking, in the After-Speech which supplies its place—that the Chorus rise to the degree of seriousness implied in their dropping all characterisation [1], and speaking directly in the author's name. This section is so entirely identified with anapæstic metre that the Introduction several times speaks of preparing for anapæsts. The subject-matter of the Parabasis Proper is literary satire. Here we find Aristophanes, as in a modern preface, giving information about previous works of his, and remonstrating with the public for unfavourable reception of them, while he regularly contrasts his merits with those of his rivals. In the *Peace* the Chorus formally enumerate their poet's services to Comedy.

> But if ever, O daughter of Zeus, it were fit with honour and praise to adorn
> A Chorus-Instructor, the ablest of men, the noblest that ever was born,
> Our Poet is free to acknowledge that he is deserving of high commendation :
> It was he that advancing, unaided, alone, compelled the immediate cessation
> Of the jokes that his rivals were cutting at rags, and the battles they waged with the lice.
> It was he that indignantly swept from the stage the paltry, ignoble, device
> Of a Hercules needy and seedy and greedy, a vagabond sturdy and stout,
> Now baking his bread, now swindling instead, now beaten and battered about.
> And freedom he gave to the lachrymose slave who was wont with a howl to rush in,
> And all for the sake of a joke which they make on the wounds that disfigure his skin :
> ' *Why, how now, my poor knave !* ' so they bawl to the slave, ' *has the whipcord invaded your back,*
> *Spreading havoc around, hacking trees to the ground, with a savage resistless attack ?* '

---

[1] This is practically the case in all the five earlier plays: the Knights retain their characterisation, but this characterisation is itself political.

Such vulgar contemptible lumber at once he bade from the drama CHAP. IX
depart,
And then, like an edifice stately and grand, he raised and ennobled
the Art.
High thoughts and high language he brought on the stage, a
genius exalted and rare,
Nor stooped with a scurrilous jest to assail some small-man-and-
woman affair.

Humorous exaggeration often relieves these serious literary
prefaces, as where the Acharnian Chorus represent that the
recent demand of the enemy for the island of Aegina was
made with a view to gain a hold over the formidable satirist
through his estate there, and that the Persian king backs the
nation most abused by Aristophanes to win in the war,
because his strictures can do nothing but improve their
character [1].

In the five earlier plays of Aristophanes the Parabasis *The Para-*
Proper is confined to this function of literary satire. But *basis some-*
times
when we come to the *Birds* and the *Women at the Mysteries* *attracted*
we find a difference. The steady advance of Comedy as *into the*
plot
drama, together with its decay as an instrument of politics,
are beginning to tell, and we find the Parabasis drawn within
the dramatic plot, and assisting to work out its ideas.
Illustrations have been given of the way the Birds devote
their anapæsts to mock-serious celebration of their mythic
antiquity and religious supremacy over men. And in the
other play the antipathy of the sexes is treated in the same
spirit. Woman, say the Chorus of women, is universally
classed amongst misfortunes of life. But it is a misfortune
the men are uncommonly fond of, seeking to unite themselves with it in the closest ties ; when they have got the
misfortune into their houses they look sharply after its
preservation, and go wild if it has escaped them ; if a pretty
misfortune looks out of a window every eye strains to

[1] For references and further illustrations, see Tabular Analysis of
Parabases, below, pp. 447-8.

CHAP. IX catch sight of it, and if her modesty takes alarm and she
retires they are all set longing to get their misfortune back
again [1].

The The Strophe of Invocation separates the Parabasis Proper
Strophe of from the After-Speech, and its main function is thus to give
Invocation variety, and break the strain of continuous satire. Comic
spirit is infused into it in two ways. In some plays there is
a humorous connexion between the deities selected for
invocation and the characterisation of the Chorus. The
knights call upon the equestrian deity, Neptune ; the Clouds
invoke Zeus, Aether, and the Sea-god ; the miserable old
men who form the Chorus to the *Wasps* make a god of their
lost youth. Perhaps the boldest flight is that of the Acharnian colliers, who find an object of adoration in their own
charcoal braziers.

> O, for a muse of fire,
> Of true Acharnian breed ;
> A muse that might some strain inspire,
> Brightness, tone and voice supplying,
> Like sparks which, when our fish are frying,
> The windy breath of bellows raise
> From forth the sturdy holm-oak's blaze:
> What time, our cravings to supply,
> Some sift the meal and some the Thasian mixture try.
> O fly to my lips, strong Acharnian muse—
> And grant such a strain—'tis your wardman that sues.

In other cases the humour of the Strophe is found in the
familiar device of the parody, what the audience would
recognise as high lyrics being suddenly converted into
lampoons, or in some other way made comic [2].

and Anti- The Antistrophe follows the subject of the Strophe, either
strophe adding more parodies, or invoking other—chiefly patriotic
—deities. In the *Acharnians* and *Wasps*, however, the
Antistrophe is attracted to the subject of the After-Speech

---

[1] *Mysteries*, 786.

[2] The parabases of the *Birds*, described in the previous chapter, seem
to illustrate both modes of treatment. See in the Table, page 448.

and After-Response between which it stands, all three forming, in matter, a continuous whole.

For the After-Speech, the trochaic metre, called in this
work accelerated rhythm, is as essential a feature as the
anapæstic system is necessary to the Parabasis Proper.
The Speech is spoken in character, and its subject is, not
literary satire, but public questions and patriotic emotions.
The Response follows the subject of the Speech, but with a
difference of treatment : except for the characterisation the
former may make its attack serious, the Response must
invent some grotesque form in which to present its argument, or at least include some effect of comic ingenuity.
Thus the Acharnian veterans complain in the Speech that
Athenian law-courts give the young an unfair advantage
over the old : the Response humorously suggests a division
of proceedings by which old and toothless judges should
deal with old prisoners, and the youthful chatterboxes
banish and fine one another. So the knights, having in the
former section told their ancestral greatness as conservators
of public morals, proceed in the Response to present their
naval prowess under the guise of horses who took kindly to
the transport boats, laid well to their oars, and disembarked in
perfect order. Another Response in the same play attacks
naval administration by describing an indignation meeting
of ships held to denounce their officers. In the *Frogs* the
Speech is an earnest and direct plea for a political amnesty :
the Response follows this up by comparing the present state
of the public service to the new coinage. The old coinage
was sound through and through :

> Fairly struck from perfect die, and ringing with a cheery sound,
> Equally with Greek and stranger current all the country round :

while the new

> Is of yesterday's production, faulty die and metal base.

So the good and well-known citizens are excluded from office
and those substituted for them—

Are a trash of brass, and strangers ; 'slave' is written on each face ;
Rogue-born sons of rogue the father; latest comers to the place.

If such humorous presentation invades the Speech, the
Response maintains its difference by being a degree more
extravagant or fanciful. An ingenious example may be
seen in the *Clouds*. In their After-Speech the Cloud deities
take advantage of the ancient superstition by which foul
weather was an ill omen for a public meeting, in order
to represent a recent election in the light of an offence
against themselves.

> And remember, very lately, how we knit our brows together,
> 'Thunders crashing, lightnings flashing,' never was such awful
> weather,
> And the moon in haste eclipsed her, and the Sun in anger swore
> He would curl his wick within him, and give light to you no more,
> Should you choose that cursed reptile, Cleon, whom the gods abhor,
> Tanner, slave, and Paphlagonian, to lead forth your hosts to war.
> Yet you chose him ! Yet you chose him!

But even this is surpassed in indirectness by the Response,
which, wishing to reprove the general laxity in religious
ceremonials, makes this a grievance of the Moon, the natural
guardian of the calendar.

> We, when we had finished packing, and prepared our journey down,
> Met the Lady Moon, who charged us with a message for your
> town.

She saves the city a drachma a month in torchlight, and
yet they neglect the days which it is her special function to
mark :

> And, she says, the gods in chorus shower reproaches on her head,
> When in bitter disappointment they go supperless to bed.

The *Peace* utilises this distinction between After-Speech and
After-Response for another purpose : the first presents the
husbandman at peace, getting a friend in to feast while a
gracious rain is swelling the seeds, and there is nothing to
fear but that the cat may have stolen the hare ; the Response

puts the contrast in time of war, the hateful sight of the CHAP. IX
triple-crested, scarlet-coated captain writing down the con-
scripts' names at random[1].

So far we have been reviewing the dramatic structure   II
of Comedy. But considered as a composition in verse, *Metrical structure of*
its metrical elements are not less important. Six different *Ancient*
metrical styles figure in an Old Attic drama. There are the *Comedy*
Blank Verse and Lyric measures which Comedy received
from Tragedy as the staple medium of its episodes and
interludes. Next there is the anapæstic system, so closely *Anapæstic*
associated with Aristophanes that one variety of it is called *Rhythm*
after his name. Anapæsts were the basis of what in Tragedy
I have called marching rhythm. But the anapæstic lines of
a tragedy are for the most part short and measured : to
make a comic metre, the feet are multiplied into a long
sweeping verse of rushing syllables.

> *Strepsiades.* O Socrates, pray, by all the Gods say, for I earnestly
>   long to be told,
>   Who are these that recite with such grandeur and might?
>   Are they glorified mortals of old ?
> *Socrates.* No mortals are there, but Clouds of the air, great Gods
>   who the indolent fill.
>   These grant us discourse, and logical force, and the art of
>   persuasion instil,

[1] The After-Speech, when like the Parabasis Proper it is absorbed into
the plot, still keeps up the air of treating public topics. The first
Speech of the Birds applies bird ideas to the relation of parents and
children, and its Response carries these on to minor conveniences of life ;
so the second Speech proclaims a poulterer as a public enemy, its sequel
gives a surprise in applying bird promises and threats to the judges
actually adjudicating upon the chorus's own performance. In the
companion play, the *Mysteries*, the loss of Antistrophe makes the
Speech and Response an unbroken whole. Its theme is the Rights of
Women presented as a public question : the mother who has given birth
to a worthy son ought to take precedence in the festivals of the sex,
while she whose son has manœuvred badly or steered his ship on to a
rock should be forced to take a back seat, and have her hair cropped
basin-wise, like a Scythian fright. See the Table, below, pp. 447–8.

And periphrasis strange, and a power to arrange, and a marvellous judgment and skill.

Strepsiades. So then, when I heard their omnipotent word, my
spirit felt all of a flutter,

And it yearns to begin subtle cobwebs to spin and about
metaphysics to stutter,

And together to glue an idea or two, and battle away in
replies:

So, if it's not wrong, I earnestly long to behold them myself
with my eyes.

Where a considerable scene is composed in such lengthy
lines it is not uncommon to use shorter lines for a climax;
an example occurs where Strepsiades, satisfied with the
claims of the cloud deities, surrenders himself in the fullest
legal form as their worshipper.

> So now, at your word, I give and afford
> My body to these, to treat as they please,
> To have and hold, in squalor, in cold,
> In hunger and thirst, yea by Zeus, at the worst,
> To be flayed out of shape from my heels to my nape
> So along with my hide from my duns I escape,
> And to men may appear without conscience or fear,
> Bold, hasty, and wise, a concocter of lies,
> A rattler to speak, a dodger, a sneak,
> A regular claw of the tables of law,
> A shuffler complete, well worn in deceit,
> A supple, unprincipled, troublesome cheat;
> A hang-dog accurst, a bore with the worst,
> In the tricks of the jury-courts thoroughly versed.
> If all that I meet this praise shall repeat,
> Work away as you choose, I will nothing refuse,
> Without any reserve, from my head to my shoes.
> You shan't see me wince, though my gutlets you mince,
> And these entrails of mine for a sausage combine,
> Served up for the gentlemen students to dine [1].

Accelerated Rhythm The trochaic system, called in this work accelerated rhythm,
is taken intact from Tragedy. But the trochaic is often

---

[1] *Clouds*, 314, 439.

varied, for effect, by being united with a kindred metre, the CHAP. IX
cretic rhythm ; this is founded on a foot which consists of a
double trochee shorn of its final syllable, and thus giving two
accents separated by a light syllable :

> *double trochee* fŏllŏw făstĕr
> *cretic foot*   hē's ĕscāped.

The combination of these allied rhythms is excellently
illustrated in Hookham Frere's spirited rendering of the
parode to the *Acharnians.*

Chorus. Follow faster! all together! search, enquire of every one. − ᴗ − ᴗ
Speak, inform us, have you seen him ?   Whither is the rascal run ?
'Tis a point of public service that the traitor should be caught
In the fact, seized and arrested with the treaties that he brought.

First Semichorus. He's escaped, he's escaped—
　　　　　　　　Out upon it ! Out upon it !
　　　　　　　　Out of sight, out of search.
　　　　　　　　O the sad wearisome
　　　　　　　　Load of years !
Well do I remember such a burden as I bore
Running with Phaÿllus with a hamper at my back,
　　　　　　　　Out alack,
　　　　　　　　Years ago.
But, alas, my sixty winters and my sad rheumatic pain
Break my speed, and spoil my running, and that old unlucky sprain. − ᴗ − ᴗ
He's escaped—

Second Semichorus. But we'll pursue him. Whether we be fast or
　　　slow,
He shall learn to dread the peril of an old Acharnian foe.
　　　　　　　　O Supreme Powers above,
　　　　　　　　Merciful Father Jove,
　　　　　　　　Oh, the vile miscreant wretch ;
　　　　　　　　How did he dare,
How did he presume in his unutterable villainy to make a peace, − ᴗ − ᴗ
Peace with the detestable abominable Spartan race.
　　　　　　　　No, the war must not end,
　　　　　　　　Never end—till the whole Spartan tribe
　　　　　　　　Are reduced, trampled down,
　　　　　　　　Tied and bound, hand and foot.

x

Chorus. Now must we renew the search, pursuing at a steady pace.
Soon or late we shall secure him, hunted down from place
    to place.
Look about like eager marksmen, ready with your slings and
    stones.
How I long to fall upon him, the villain, and to smash his
    bones !

*Long
Iambics*

A metre peculiar to Comedy may be called Long Iambics ;
it is related to its root, the iamb, as accelerated rhythm is
related to the trochee.

You doat, old man.—But, modest youth, I'd have you think at
    starting
How many pleasant things in life you never can have part in ;
Wife, children, Cottabus, good wine, fish dinners, fun and
    laughter !
And if all these are gone away, is life worth living after ?
Well, be it so. Be virtuous ; at least intend to be it ;
But under some temptation slip, and let a tattler see it :
You're ruined quite. You cannot speak. You have no word to
    offer.
Take part with me, and be yourself a wag, a scamp, a scoffer.
You are detected in the act ; ' detected '—but what matter ?
Your words are stout, you face it out :—it all goes off in
    chatter.
Or, at the worst, some God has done the like : and you cut
    short all
Reflections on your virtue by alleging—you are mortal [1].

*Hexame-
ters*

For completeness it is necessary just to mention the familiar
hexameter, the metre of epic poetry, which occasionally finds
its way into Comedy.

Tribeless, lawless and heartless is he that delighteth in blood-
    shed,
Bloodshed of kith and kin, heart-sickening, horrible, hateful [2] !

*Literary
effect of
metrical
variations*

Questions of prosody and the metrical analysis of particular passages belong to the study of language. But in the
literary effect of Comedy a large element is the choice and
interchange of the six metrical styles just enumerated—a

---

[1] *Clouds*, 1071.   [2] *Peace*, 1097.

variety that should be maintained by every translator, CHAP. IX
though the exact reproduction of the original rhythms is a ———
very secondary matter. Such transitions between one metre
and another are analogous to the less multiform, but more
intense, interchange of verse and prose with which the
Shakespearean drama reflects the play of tone and movement.
The next question, then, is to ascertain the significance of
the different metrical styles ; though if any usage be claimed
for particular rhythms this must be understood as subordinate to the higher law that *change* from one metre
to another is a mode of expressing change in the spirit or
working out of the scene.

It has been already remarked how anapæsts are associated *Anapæstic*
with the Parabasis Proper, in which comic characterisation *an elevated*
is dropped and the discussion becomes entirely serious. *Rhythm*
This suggests the conception of the anapæstic system as
the most elevated of the rhythms that are intermediate
between blank verse and full lyrics. This relation of the
anapæstic to other metres is well illustrated in the parode
to the *Frogs*, already cited in a previous chapter : here,
when the satire in imitation of the old Comus-procession
is personal, it is conveyed in the old iambics ; when it
rises to the public topics that had given a new dignity
to Comedy, anapæsts are used. It would seem, indeed, *Used for*
that this rhythm might be considered the normal me- *the Para-*
dium for the political digression in Old Attic drama, and *Proper,*
that it was chiefly the law of comic variety that made the
After-Speech change to a different measure. With the
employment of anapæstic rhythm for the Parabasis other
usages are allied. A great feature in Old Attic Comedy, *for the*
which rested its plot upon some bold and extravagant *Paradox-*
idea, was a tour-de-force of elaborate explanation by which *planation,*
this idea was made good : the mock-serious character of
such sustained explanation made the anapæstic system a
fit vehicle in which to convey it. This metre, then, is the

CHAP. IX medium for the long discussion in the *Clouds* by which the claims of the new deities are vindicated, and for the similar dispute where Poverty, in the *Plutus*, bursting in upon the men who have secured the god of riches, is sustaining her paradox that in banishing poverty they are destroying luxury. Quotations in the preceding chapter illustrated the speech in which Talkover, at great length, expounds to the Birds his airy project ; and it is in similar anapæstic rhythm that the heroines of the *Lysistrata* and the *Women in Parliament*

for invoca- unfold their socialist revolutions[1]. Again, the elevation of
tions, the anapæst makes it the natural metre for invocations— such as Socrates's invocation to the Clouds, or the Hoopoe's call to the nightingale—and for the hymns of religious

religious celebrations : the marriage song at the end of the *Birds*,
celebration, the triumphal processions concluding the *Frogs* and the *Plutus* are anapæstic, and so to a large extent is the worship of Peace through the later scenes in the play of that name[2].

proclama- Proclamations are in this metre, such as the warning by the
tions, servant of Agathon not to disturb his master while he is composing[3] ; so are the short bursts of feeling that usher in a new-comer, or dismiss an incident, or prepare for some-

and scenic thing that is to follow[4]. So imposing a rhythm is naturally
marvels allowed a place in the boldest of all Aristophanes' scenic wonders—the rise of a beetle to heaven at the opening of the *Peace*[5]. There is one more usage of the anapæstic metre

---

[1] *Clouds,* 314-477; *Plutus,* 487-618 ; *Lysistrata,* 484-607; *Women in Parliament,* 582-709.

[2] *Clouds,* 263-74; *Birds,* 209-22, 1726-54; *Frogs,* 1500-27; *Plutus,* 1208-9; *Peace,* 974, 1316, &c.

[3] *Mysteries,* 39.

[4] *Knights,* 1316 ; *Lysistrata,* 1072 ; *Acharnians,* 1143-9; *Birds,* 658. The long anapæstic explanations are usually led off by those to whom they are addressed : e.g. *Birds,* 460 ; *Women in Parliament,* 514. Similarly speeches in other metres are led off by the Chorus: *Clouds,* 1034, 1397 ; *Mysteries,* 531.

[5] *Peace,* 96-101, 154-172.

which it is not difficult to understand. It is natural that CHAP. IX
Comedy, in those passages which are the counterpart of the
forensic contests that belong to Tragedy, should avoid the *It has the*
blank verse which in such association would only lend itself *honour in*
to rhetorical effect. Accordingly, the law of such comic *forensic*
contests
contests seems to be a change of rhythm in the middle, with
a sort of preference or place of honour given to the anapæst.
Great part of the *Knights* is made up of a contest in political
blackguardism between the two rival demagogues, the
leather-seller and the sausage-seller : in the formal dispute
before Democracy anapæsts appear up to the point where
Democracy begins to be impressed and turns away from his
old favourite Cleon, then the scene changes to long iambics.
Similarly in the *Clouds* the forensic contest is in anapæsts as
long as Right Argument leads the discussion, after which it
changes to iambics. In the competition between the poets
which is the main part of the *Frogs* the order is reversed :
iambics convey the case of Euripides, while the scene rises
to the dignity of anapæsts when Aeschylus condescends to
reply [1].

Accelerated rhythm shares the Parabasis with the ana- *Accelerated*
pæstic system : as the latter belongs to the earlier part, so *Rhythm*
proper to
the trochaic rhythm is the fixed medium of the After- *the After-*
Speech. Partly, I think, this change is for variety ; pos- *Speech*
sibly also the return to comic characterisation in the After-
Speech assisted a descent in the metrical scale. Accelerated *Metrical*
rhythm has also a considerable place in the chorus-entries *usage in*
the Chorus-
of Comedy. But the whole treatment of the chorus-entry *entry*
clearly illustrates Greek metrical conceptions. Associated
in Tragedy with sudden movement and moments of excitement, accelerated rhythm would seem peculiarly suited to
the entry of a comic Chorus. As a fact, it may be called
the normal metre of the parode—the term being used to

[1] *Knights*, 761, 836, and compare Demus's tone in 821 ;—*Clouds*,
961-1023 and 1036-1104 ; *Frogs*, 907-91, and 1006-98.

CHAP. IX include the whole scene following the entrance of the Chorus : and in this metre are the elaborate parodes of the *Acharnians*, the *Knights*, the *Birds*, and the *Peace*. But there are cases in which the character of the Chorus, or some part of their function, passes outside the range of comic effect, and then other metres are used. The Cloud deities as conceived by Aristophanes are amongst the most delicate products of poetic fancy in all literature : it is natural to find the parode to the play they inspire composed in lofty anapæsts, with antiphonal lyrics to mark the actual entry. So in the *Mysteries*, whatever may be the character of the women who form the chorus, their first utterances are hymns of the sacred mysteries, and these make the parode lyrical ; for a similar reason the Comus of the Initiated in the *Frogs* is in lyrics broken by the metres of satire. But on the other hand, there are cases in which the Chorus of a comedy sinks below the normal level, and then accelerated rhythm gives place to long iambics. It is in this last metre that we get our first impressions of the Wasps as they enter, in a play where the poet has made his Chorus out of the very jurymen his satire is to attack. The same contemptuous rhythm is allotted to the parode in the *Plutus*, a mere arrival of decrepit old neighbours, who need the news of Plutus's capture, and the thought of being able to fleece him, to make them dance at all. The unnatural revolt which is the subject of the *Women in Parliament* explains how it is that no higher metre than long iambics is used for their parode (so far as it is not antiphonal), and the same rhythm takes the place of anapæsts for the triumph at the end of the play. And long iambics are appropriate to the parode of the *Lysistrata*, since it displays the bitterest hostility between the parties which the action of the play is to be engaged in reconciling.

Use of Accelerated   The case of the *Peace* is particularly worthy of attention, as it illustrates a tendency of the comic poet to treat

a particular metre much in the way that a *leit-motif* is
employed by a modern musician. The Chorus to this
play consists of jolly husbandmen, who are presented as
the honest party in politics and the friends of peace.
Accelerated rhythm is naturally chosen to harmonise with the
noisy joy of their entrance, and this trochaic metre is in a
marked degree connected with these husbandmen in the
scenes that follow. The introductory incidents have been
mainly in blank verse, until the point at which the hero,
conceiving the hope of recovering Peace, calls upon the
country party to help him: this appeal breaks into accelerated
rhythm, and in similar strains the Chorus enter rejoicing,
a climax being (as in the case of anapæsts) made by shorter
lines of kindred metre[1].

> I'm so happy, glad, delighted, getting rid of arms at last,
> More than if, my youth renewing, I the slough of age had cast.
> *Trygæus.* Well, but don't exult at present, for we're all uncertain still,
> But, when once we come to hold her, then be merry if you will;
> > Then will be the time for laughing,
> > Shouting out in jovial glee,
> > Sailing, sleeping, feasting, quaffing,
> > All the public sights to see.
> > Then the Cottabus be playing,
> > Then be hip-hip-hip-hurrahing,
> > Pass the day and pass the night
> > Like a regular Sybarite.

Blank verse marks the transition to the business of raising
Peace from the pit[2]. But this is at the outset interrupted
by the appearance of Hermes to forbid it : the scene of the
god's intervention is as a whole cast in blank verse, but
where he orders the Chorus to abstain his words fall into
trochaics; and again where the hero, vainly interceding,
calls on the Chorus to second him, his summons and their
response are trochaic; and finally when Hermes gives way

---

[1] *Peace*, 299, 301, 339.   [2] *Peace*, 361.

CHAP. IX he addresses his permission to the Chorus in the same rhythm [1]. The scene of raising the image is in blank verse, with variations of lyrics to convey the actual strain of hauling, and again, where the half-hearted workers are ordered to drop the rope, of the rhythm of contempt [2] to express how much better the work goes without them. When the operation is successful the rejoicings continue in blank verse while they are confined [3] to Hermes and Trygæus : as soon as success is brought home to the Chorus accelerated rhythm rules [4]. In trochaic metre the Chorus enquire of Hermes the reason for the long absence of the goddess, and receive his account of the matter ; as soon however as Trygæus turns from the Chorus to put the same enquiry to Peace herself the metre changes to blank verse [5]. So through this, the main business of the play, the accelerated rhythm that first introduced the Chorus of husbandmen is consistently associated with their share in the action.

Long Iam-bics as a leit-motif of evil

The treatment of long iambics has been anticipated in the remarks on the metres that contrast with it. It stands lowest in the scale of rhythmic dignity: it is a sort of *leit-motif* of evil, appearing in the parode of a degraded Chorus or the inferior stage of an action or a forensic contest [6]. It is in accordance with the spirit of such usage that long iambics should be the metre in which Pheidippides (in the

---

[1] Compare lines 362, 383-99, 426. Hermes's first words as he bursts in—a solitary trochaic line (362) in the midst of blank verse—I understand as addressed to the whole company before him, Chorus and others, though the singular is used as if he were accosting the man nearest to him. When Trygæus answers, the rest of the dialogue is with him, and is in blank verse.

[2] Long Iambics : 508-11.

[3] 520-49 of Bergk's text which differs greatly from Dindorf's.

[4] From 553: with lyrics interspersed (582-600).

[5] 601-56 ; 657.

[6] I think this may possibly explain its use in the *Mysteries*, 533. The speech of Mnesilochus has been one side of a forensic contest : the answer of the women descends (in iambs) to corporal threatenings.

Clouds) gives his monstrous justification of his action in Chap. IX beating his father[1]. So it is perhaps the effect of contrast that is sought where Trygæus, at the conclusion of the *Peace*, moves himself in anapæstic rhythm to the festal banquet, while in iambics he bids his friends the husband-men stay behind 'to munch and crunch and bite' by themselves[2]. The hexameter, the regular metre of epic *Comic use* poetry, appears in Comedy chiefly for oracles and quoted *of the Hex-ameter* songs. But it finds its way occasionally into the framework of the play as a *leit-motif* of the lofty themes for which epic poetry is supposed to be the proper vehicle. Thus hexameters mingle with anapæstic lines in the scene of the beetle rising to heaven; and again this metre dominates the reception given by the Chorus in the *Frogs* to their supreme poetic hero, Aeschylus[3].

> To the Heavenly Nine we petition :
> Ye that on earth or in air are for ever kindly protecting
> The vagaries of learned ambition,
> And at your ease from above our sense and folly directing,
> Or poetical contests inspecting,
> Deign to behold for a while, as a scene of amusing attention,
> All the struggles of style and invention,
> Aid, and assist, and attend, and afford to the furious authors
> Your refined and enlightened suggestions ;
> Grant them ability, force and agility, quick recollections,
> And address in their answers and questions,
> Pithy replies, with a word to the wise, and pulling and hauling,
> With inordinate uproar and bawling,
> Driving and drawing, like carpenters sawing, their dramas asunder.
> > With suspended sense and wonder
> > All are waiting and attending
> > On the conflict now depending !

I have yet to speak of the treatment in Comedy applied *Comic* to lyrics and blank verse, so far as it differs from their *treatment of Lyrics* treatment in Tragedy. It has been remarked above that, as might be expected, the odes serving as interludes in

---

[1] *Clouds*, 1399.   [2] *Peace*, 1305, 1316.
[3] *Peace*, 118–23 ; *Frogs*, from 814.

Comedy are shorter and less elaborate than in Tragedy, and further that short lyrics are often substituted which rather break the course of a scene than separate between *dichotomy,* one scene and another. A kindred phenomenon is the wide use in Comedy of the dichotomous treatment, by which a strophe is separated from its antistrophe, often at a considerable interval. Thus the narrative speech in which the Sausage-seller relates the scene at the council, is preceded by a strophe of expectation from the Chorus and followed by an antistrophe of satisfaction. There are many similar examples of incidents—the anapæstic contest in the same play before Demus, the first appeal from the chopping-block in the *Acharnians,* the rhesis of Right Argument in the *Clouds,* Talkover's delineation of the wrongs of birds—which are marked off by being enclosed between the antiphonal halves of a complete lyric [1]. Such a tendency to respond later on to a rhythm started at an earlier point is akin in spirit to the unwritten law of the modern stage by which accomplished actors will, in a scene that runs to any length, contrive by natural movements to cross the stage in the course of the action, so that a speaker who has begun a long dialogue on the right side of the *and other* theatre will conclude it on the left. Even the more *devices* elaborate devices of lyric symmetry are not entirely outside comic effect. A neat example occurs in connexion with the incident of hauling up Peace out of the pit. Here we have two pair of stanzas: they are interwoven (that is, the second strophe is added before the first is matched with its antistrophe), and reversed (that is, the pair commenced first is completed last), and this antiphonal elaboration is in both respects significant, as the following table will suggest.

[1] *Knights,* 616–23 and 683–90 ; 756–60 and 836–40 ; *Acharnians,* 358–65 and 385–92 ; *Clouds,* 949–58 and 1024–33 ; *Birds,* 451–9 and 539–47.

Strophe A : The Chorus express their longings and vows for the recovery of Peace
  Strophe B : They engage later on in an
  unsuccessful bout of hauling
  Antistrophe B : Later still they engage in
  another unsuccessful attempt
Antistrophe A: At last when they have succeeded
they give themselves up to rejoicings [1].

One more instance of antiphonal treatment utilised for
comic effect is too good to be passed over. In the reversal
of all things which constitutes the plot of the *Women in
Parliament* free love is a part: the principle of equality is
carried so far that the old and ugly are granted a legal
preference to compensate for their inferior natural attrac-
tiveness. In one scene a fair youth, false to the spirit of
the new constitution, steals softly to the house of his fair
and youthful love, and beneath her windows sings a strophe
by way of serenade.

   Youth with youth should sweetly blend :   *strophe*
  Not, by law, to some cursed creature,
  Bowed with years, cross-grained in feature,
   Forced false preference to extend :
    This is the liberty
    Due, blest Freedom, from thee !

Up goes a window on the other side of the street, and
a hideous old hag putting her head out answers *sotto voce*
his strophe rhythm for rhythm with an antistrophe, in which
she marks him out for her prey.

   Just you try, by Zeus above,   *antistrophe*
  Your old-fashioned trick of mixing
  Youth with youth, instead of fixing
   On our rightful age your love,
    Slighting our gift from thee,
    Blessed Democracy [2] !

[1] *Peace* : lines 346–60 are antistrophic with 582–600 ; between these
come strophe 459–72, and antistrophe 486–99.
[2] *Women in Parliament*, 938–41 and 942–5.

CHAP. IX Irregular lyrics, in which the antistrophic treatment is
――― wanting, abound in Comedy. They include brief inter-
Irregular ludes, bursts of rejoicing or expectation, fragments of songs
Lyrics in or quotations, and especially hymns or the words of a ritual :
Comedy the ambiguous comments of the Chorus in the *Clouds* while
Strepsiades fetches his son, the coarse hilarity of the colliers
from Acharnæ when they see a market in operation again
after five years of war, the Mystery Hymns, Epops's call to
the birds, are examples [1]. Sometimes they seem to be used
for contrast with antiphonal lyrics : thus the two failures to
drag up Peace having been conveyed in a strophe and
antistrophe, the successful hauling is done in irregular
lines.

> Pull again, pull, my men,
>   Now we're gaining fast.
> Never slacken, put your back in,
>   Here she comes at last.
> Pull, pull, pull, pull, every man, all he can ;
>   Pull, pull, pull, pull, pull,
> Pull, pull, pull, pull, all together [2].

Comic use   Finally, blank verse represents the dead level of metrical
of Blank effect, to which the action always returns after special im-
Verse pulses have kept it for a time in other rhythms. But the
point of return to blank verse is often itself a dramatic
effect. When, in an anapæstic scene, the Birds have
thoroughly discussed Talkover's daring proposal, there is
a change to blank verse with the thought, 'We must take
action!' In the *Clouds*, Right Argument is beaten from
anapæsts to long iambics, until she gives up her case and
blank verse ensues. Later in the same play the father
hears in dismay the long iambics of his son's plea for
beating fathers : when he can bear it no longer he turns to

―――――――――

[1] *Clouds*, 805 ; *Acharnians*, 836 ; *Mysteries*, 312, 352 ; *Birds*, 208.
For fragments of songs compare *Birds*, 904, and following incident.
[2] *Peace*, 512–19 irregular ; 459–72 and 486–99 antiphonal.

the Chorus and makes indignant protest in blank verse[1]. CHAP. IX
Such cases might be multiplied indefinitely. It will be
enough to give a single example of a somewhat more
elaborate transition between blank verse and other metres.
When in the *Mysteries* the disguised Mnesilochus has made
his rash attack on the sex, the storm rages about him in the
long iambic measure. There is a sudden hush to blank
verse at the arrival of Cleisthenes with news that a man is
said to have penetrated in disguise into the secret rites.
Search is made for the interloper and Mnesilochus is at
once discovered. Then in a wild confusion of anapæsts,
iambics, and trochees further search is made for other
possible intruders: this terminates in a brief spell of blank
verse as Mnesilochus creates a diversion by seizing a baby
from one of the women, and holds his enemies at bay: in
the hesitation of the women the confusion of rhythms
breaks out again, until the cry to bring fire and burn the
wretch restores confidence, and the scene settles again to
blank verse[2].

These examples are intended merely to illustrate the *Metrical*
significance of particular metres and of transitions from one *flexibility a branch of*
metre to another: to bring out the degree to which Greek *poetic effect*
poets rely on this source of effect it would be necessary to
traverse in detail whole plays[3]. But enough has been said
to distinguish the literary from the linguistic use of metres:
quite apart from the interest attaching to the analysis of
particular rhythms, the effect of their interchange raises
metre from a mere conventional form of language to a
flexible medium capable of conveying to eye and ear the
most subtle change of poetic spirit.

[1] *Birds*, 639; *Clouds*, 1105, 1452.
[2] *Mysteries*: compare 533, 574. 654–88, 689, 700–27, 728.
[3] See Metrical Analyses below, pages 439–41.

2 The Comic Chorus

The Comic Chorus: the serious naturalised amid the humorous   The term 'Comic Chorus' would sound to a Greek ear like a contradiction in terms. The Chorus was a form of art embodying beauty ordered by law; it was created by the Dorians, the race of military discipline, and was sacred to Apollo, whose lordship was over the brightness and subtlety of intellect. The Comus of the merry Dionysus was a ritual of romping, given up to self-abandon and the joy that cannot contain itself; nothing less than a whole countryside would suffice for its evolutions and arbitrary wanderings; it was inspired by a sacred zeal for violating ordinary conditions, accepted costume being exchanged for disguise, the decencies of life for satiric licence, and routine giving place to a festal holiday in which work was a crime, excess a law, and probability or coherence of thinking a mistake. Yet twice in ancient history these opposites were brought together. By the personal force of Arion the Chorus and the Comus were amalgamated into Tragedy, and Dionysiac spirit, locked up in Dorian forms, obtained at last a vent in scenes of action, mingled with interludes in which the Chorus entirely ruled. Again at a later period, when Tragedy was a pompous State ceremony and Comedy a mere satiric parody of life, the newly revived democracy of Athens raised at a bound its favourite sport to the dignity of its rival: Comedy accepting wholesale the form of Tragedy, and setting itself the not uncomic task of naturalising the solemn Chorus amid whimsical surroundings.

Its serious side: a Bacchic and other religious themes   Viewed merely as a literary feat there is interest enough in watching how this naturalisation was accomplished. One element of Comedy needed no adaptation to harmonise it with the Chorus. The performance of every drama was regarded by the ancients as an act of worship to Dionysus: where the course of comic poetry touched the god there was nothing in-

congruous in its springing to the height of poetic elevation, CHAP. IX
and from one religious theme it could pass to another. The ‾‾‾
Mystery Hymns seem quite natural as interludes in one of
Aristophanes' plays. The worshippers lift their hearts to
those exalted sympathies and sentiments which to them
were deities. Their brains all a-whirl with the dance they
hail the race of Olympian gods—Apollo with his lyre of
beauty, the Archery-Queen, mistress of maidens, and Juno
who holds the keys of wedlock. They add the joys of open-
air nature : Hermes of the sheep-folds, the huntsman Pan,
and our loves the Nymphs, calling them to inspire the dance
with their smile. Chief of all they invoke Bacchus himself,
wreathed with ivy-leaves that burst out with fresh tendrils as
they clasp his brows, centre of the sacred dance in the secret
heights of Cithæron, amid hymning Nymphs, and circle
beyond circle of dancing echoes from rock or thick-shaded
bank.

All this was special to Greek life. But in universal *Fancy*
thought there is a point at which the serious and comic meet,
and their spheres overlap : this is 'fancy.' Fancy, as distinguished from 'imagination,' is a form of beauty that rests
upon surprise, upon distance from the rational and probable,
upon brilliant modes of presenting and linking ideas which
will no more bear examination than the hoar-frost will bear
the sunlight, but which none the less appeal to our sense of
truth, and are bound to our affection by a tie as elementary
as the attraction which draws the strong man to the fragile
child. No one will question that fancy can inspire the most
elevated poetry : and for fancy what could give greater scope
than the serious Chorus transplanted into the soil of
Comedy ? The exuberant wealth of ideas that gather round
the conception of the Bird-City produce sustained amusement and at times roaring fun : but through the whole there
is an undercurrent of genuine sympathy with bird life. But
in another play Aristophanes has a theme in which he can

revel as a storehouse of delicate fancies: nowhere in all literature has this faculty been more glorified than in the *Clouds*. Here the lyrics can celebrate our king and master, Air, in whose infinite the mighty earth may freely balance itself; Aether burning to a glow; and above all the lady embodiments of the Air, the ever-virgin Clouds. Or, these Clouds are the curls of the hundred-headed Tempest, or the birds of the sky; the zigzag lightnings are their weapons, and their trumpet-strains the angry blasts; they are the sap of the atmosphere, children of dews, mothers of showers. Cloud life passes before us, in touches of suggestion: how these creatures of softness and motion take their rest on the snow of some sacred mountain peak; now over the mirror of ocean they sport with their nymph-like reflections; now they are engaged in drawing up vapour from the glorious Nile stream, as it were in mist-pitchers which the sun paints golden; now they roam free over some wintry landscape. Our conception is strained to take in all that the Clouds can behold, high poised in the heavens. They look up and behold the Eye of Aether, never for them wearied into shade; they look down and see far below the loftiest watch-tower of earth's solitary peaks; broad beneath are spread golden harvests, streaming rivers and thundering sea: all nature flashing in the joy of freedom, and human life one Springtide of sacred revel in garlanded shrines to ringing strains of the flute.

Purely comic treatment of the Chorus   But the scale of thought at its opposite end is equally touched by the comic Chorus: all that is grotesque and ugly can inspire it, and all that is coarse, if, like the matter of the two women's dramas, it is coarse enough. Perhaps the lowest point is reached where Aristophanes introduces his favourite butt, the jurymen of Athens, as a Chorus of Wasps—useless creatures, but with a sting in their tail. They enter in pantomimic disguise, keeping step, drawn by the smell of honey in the form of some rich prisoner, preceded by link-boys who turn their lights from side to side in imitation of

the restless heads of insects. When they meet opposition, CHAP. IX
the old men's bilious anger suggests a hornet's nest disturbed : ———
they draw stings, and fly at their foes like good bitter-hearted
wasps, and when they are beaten off they cry that the days
of tyranny are come again. The plot they inspire settles
down to a realisation of the ideal that every man's house
should be his jury-box, where he can exercise his forensic
functions at his ease, by his fire-side, snatching a snack when
he likes, with a brazier to keep his gruel warm, and a cock
to crow him awake when he nods. The bar at which his
suitors stand is the pigsty-gate ; the suit tried is an action
brought by Sicilian Cheese against Dog Seizer for assault,
and the defendant exhibits puppies to melt the hearts of
the jury; Dish, Pot, Pestle, Cheesegrater are amongst the
witnesses; and, for climax, the hero-juryman faints at discovering that he has, by accident, for the first time in his
life voted acquittal.

All this range of tone, from the elevated to the grotesque, *The Comic*
the comic Chorus, as an embodied contradiction, can cover. *Chorus a*
It strikingly illustrates the peculiar religious sentiment *reflection of*
of the Greek mind which could sanctify and present as *Greek reli-*
worship all emotions, even some which modern morality *gion :*
considers licentious. In the development of art it laid a *and a foun-*
foundation in Comedy for the mixture of tones, the goal to *dation for*
which dramatic art steadily moved, until it culminated in the *the mix-*
Shakespearean Drama, where sorrow and joy, real and ideal, *ture of*
mingle on equal terms in a diapason of creative force. *tones*

3 The subject-matter of Aristophanes

All drama must be the expression of thinking : the question *The matter*
arises, what was the field of thought to which Greek Comedy *of Aristo-*
was applied? what was the subject-matter which inspired it ? *phanes'*
plays :
We have seen that it was the application of Comedy to

Y

*conserva-
tism with-
out any
rational
basis*

politics which created the Old Attic species. Aristophanes was a party politician in the strictest sense of the term, no worse and no better. His was conservatism for the sake of conservatism. When all his writings are put together it is difficult to trace beneath the surface any principles or any political system. He had adopted the easier rôle of believing blindly in the past, and jeering at the dominant sentiment of his time in whatever forms it manifested itself: for him whatever is is wrong. It is convenient to divide the matter of Greek Comedy into the three classes political, social, literary, and the three are identified with three prominent individualities of the Athenian world: but the poet's own attitude in all is the same antagonism to what is new.

*Antagon-
ism to de-
mocracy
and Cleon:*

The general politics of Aristophanes amount to the stock denunciations of democracy, which is summed up to him in the personality of Cleon. There is the usual representation of the 'masses' as gullible to flatteries, oracles, and cries of tyranny; the agitators bid against one another with promises of cheap food and material comforts; the 'classes' are re-

*no alter-
native
ideal*

presented by the knights. But there is no positive to match this negative, no non-popular system of government nor even any definite reform is shadowed: when Demus is boiled down he appears simply restored to youth, with all subsequent to the age of Marathon blotted out like a bad dream.

*Attitude
to special
topics:*

peace,

The most definite political topic in Aristophanes is naturally that which touches the life and death struggle of his age between the Athenian and Spartan leagues. He is the spokes-man of the peace party, and four of his plays are passionate and eloquent pleas for peace. No one can doubt their sincerity. But here again we look in vain for any high politics, however disguised in mode of presentation; there is no trace of the poet's having felt the issues at stake in this war, nor does he betray sympathies or antipathies as regards the different types of Greek peoples drawn into this mortal conflict. The speech in the *Acharnians*, where he

makes claim for Comedy to give serious political advice, CHAP. IX
minimises the cause of the war to a quarrel over three harlots;
but here he takes care to add that he hates Lacedæmon, and
longs for an earthquake to level its proud city with the
ground. It is significant that when Peace is drawn up from
the pit she is accompanied by Sport and Plenty; all the
glories of peace, as painted by Aristophanes, amount to
creature comforts and joys, with freedom from the trouble-
some burdens of war. Elsewhere this advocate of peace is
for ever identifying all that is good and true with a life of
martial training and naval prowess : but it is the training and
prowess of the last generation [1].

Intermediate between political and social satire may be *the forensic*
noted a topic of constant recurrence in Aristophanes—the *mania*
furore for forensic proceedings, which transformed Athens
into a city of jurymen. This is treated as a part of democracy,
and Cleon is the rallying-point of the wasp-jurors; it is also
presented as a modern intellectual interest in subtleties,
contrasting with the out-door life of the last generation.
But social morality enters largely into the matter of Greek *Treatment*
Comedy. If it were necessary to approve or condemn the *of social*
morals,
moral teachings of Aristophanes, it must be confessed it would
be very difficult to disentangle the poet's actual ideas from
the comic medium in which they are conveyed, and from the
paradoxical wildness of the Dionysiac festival. But it is a
great tribute to the genius of Aristophanes that this poet—
who disputes with Rabelais the palm of coarseness for the
whole world's literature, whose highest appeals are to our
animal nature, who reforms his repentant juryman into a life of
utter dissoluteness—has impressed half his readers, from the
days of St. Chrysostom downwards, as a sublime moralist.
Some of those who admire him in this capacity are troubled *and anta-*
by the circumstance that Aristophanes should have attacked *gonism to*
Socrates
Socrates. But this is intelligible enough when we recognise

[1] E. g. Right Argument in the *Clouds*.

that in morals, as in every other department, Aristophanes was the antagonist of what was new. The science of his age he presents as so much quackery, all its religious enquiry he regards as atheism, its varying schools of philosophy are comprehended under the idea of substituting grammatical subtleties for open air gymnastics : the whole new thought is lumped together and identified with laxity of morals and presumptuousness of youth, in order to make a contrast for the primitive simplicity which is so easy to imagine as preceding our actual experience of the world. Then so little open to moral impressions is Aristophanes in actual fact, that he selects from the band of prominent philosophers, as a personal embodiment for his caricature, the one personage who by common consent is allowed to have lived, and lived openly, the highest life of goodness that the pre-Christian world ever saw.

Literary Satire and antagonism to Euripides Turning to the department of literature we find all poetry from that of Pindar onwards made food for the comic poet's parody. But here again we find that Aristophanes reserves his main efforts for the representative in poetry of what was new in the age. Euripides appears, to modern readers, far from advanced as a type of democracy ; some of his opinions —such as his distrust of oratory and of the town life, and his idealisation of the country—might have been expected to recommend him to Aristophanes. But Euripides was the idol of his own age, and he was the great innovator in dramatic composition ; accordingly all that is distinctive in his poetry—his pathos, his realism, his stage management and the ingenuity of his plots, down even to the simple flow of his verse—has been bathed by Aristophanes in a flood of brilliant and exhilarating parody that, after a lapse of twenty-two centuries, is still an obstacle to the appreciation of

Aristophanes a reformer in Comedy Euripides. When, however, we pass to another division of literature the case is entirely altered : in his own department of Comedy the conservative appears as a reformer. In his

serious parabases Aristophanes attacks the old-fashioned
works of his rivals, boasts that he has driven from the theatre
the countrified tricks and stage jesting of his predecessors,
and elevated Comedy from its gluttons and weeping slaves
to make it a war upon the Hercules' monsters of public life.
He is amply entitled to all the credit he claims. But to us,
who can view Greek life as a completed story, it is one of the
ironies of history to find Aristophanes resting his claim to
greatness upon the change of Comedy from mere social
to political satire, a change representing the impulse
given to dramatic literature by the sudden revival of that
democracy which Aristophanes of all men most hated.

But the matter of party politics does not exhaust the field *General*
of ancient Comedy. It was equally inspired by satire upon *satire :*
Comedy as
human nature in general : as Tragedy was the idealisation *the bur-*
of life, so Comedy is its burlesque. In the plays of Aris- *lesque of*
life
tophanes, the whole panorama of Greek society passes
before us, each phase touched with the poet's inexhaustible
humour. One play is opened with a meeting of parliament,
and the whole machinery of government is presented in caricature—president, ambassadors with high-sounding titles,
luxurious envoys ; elsewhere a magistrate with his archers of
the guard perform their functions, and the punishment of
the stocks and of scourging is administered on the stage.
The proceedings of the law courts are continually before us,
and we are familiar with the ways of the smooth-tongued
advocates, and the insolence of lawyer-youths. A description is given of a night in the temple of Aesculapius —
prototype of our modern hospital, and one scene presents
the secret mysteries of the women ; while other religious
celebrations—bridal and funeral processions, thank-offerings
and consecrations—are constantly used to fill up the scenes.
Abundant space is devoted to caricaturing the different
classes of society, whose outward guise and varying manners
do so much to make up the spectacle of life. Not to speak

CHAP. IX of Spartans, Megarians, Bœotians, we have priests, sophists, poets, astronomers, public commissioners, news-vendors, leather-sellers, sausagemen ; the opposing trades of sicklemen to represent the arts of peace, makers of crests, helmets, spears, trumpets, with soldiers, to represent war ; slaves, informers, flute-girls ; artisans in general rising at cock-crow, and inn-keepers fleeced by travellers and making their successors suffer.   The merry war of the sexes is a constant topic with Aristophanes, and no direct attacks on women are so sharp as the innocent self-exposure he puts into the mouths of the sex when they are supposed to be free from the presence of men.   All this is the social satire of the older comedy broadened by the added machinery of the Attic type.   It reaches a climax in the *Birds* and the two latest plays of Aristophanes, in which, avoiding party questions, he rests the idea of his whole plot upon general satire, exaggerating for us the spirit of speculation in enterprise and in social science to a degree that passes outside practical politics, and the whole becomes a genial mockery of human nature itself.

4 The Dramatic Element in Old Attic Comedy

Greek Com-edy : an ex-travagant fancy worked out   Old Attic Comedy is unique in its conception of dramatic plot.   This has no relation, as in Tragedy or the burlesque Satyric Drama, to legendary stories, or the elaboration of striking situations.   It makes no attempt to trace poetic justice or any other principle of order in human affairs.   It is wholly divorced from the probability that conditions modern story, and indeed fetches its interest from an opposite source. The Old Attic plot consists always in the starting and working out of an extravagant fancy as a medium for satire, and the extravagance of the fancy is the main ingredient in the

comic flavour of the whole. Aristophanes is an advocate
for peace : the plot of one play is to present the honest
country farmer making peace for himself while all the rest
of the nation continues in the miseries of war ; in another
Peace is hauled up bodily out of the pit in which she has
been buried ; a third play supposes a strike of the women
all over Greece to maintain celibacy until the war is concluded. The *Knights* is a match in political shamelessness
between two champion demagogues, maintained breathlessly
until the Sausage-seller outbids the Leather-seller and the
state is saved. In the *Clouds* the question so often asked in
regard to educational systems—what will be the good of
them for actual life ?—is raised in the case of the cloud-
inspired subtleties supposed to distinguish the new system of
the Sophists, and these are tested by practical application to
the business of paying debts. A similar practical test is
in another play brought to bear upon the dramatic art of
Euripides, and it is seen whether in the awkward situations
of real life his pathos will be found to have a moving
efficacy. The other play of Aristophanes devoted to
criticism of the same poet makes its attack in the form of a
contest between Euripides and Aeschylus for the laureateship
of Hades. In the *Wasps* the forensic tastes of the Athenians are presented as a sort of madness, which is medically
treated on the stage and cured. The previous chapter
showed how another play starts a strategic project of
fortifying the atmosphere in the interests of the birds, and
thus giving them control over gods and men. There remain
the two comedies that satirise socialist ideals : in one
communism is brought about by the agency of petticoat
government, the other sets up a socialist millennium [1] by
opening the eyes of the blind Money-god.

[1] I purposely use a vague term, because there is a genuine confusion
in the original between two conflicting socialist ideals : (1) equality of
wealth for all, (2) equitable distribution of wealth. The latter is

CHAP. IX

Four essen-tial ele-ments in its structure

The Gene-rating Action

Comedy of this type has a perfectly regular structure, its plot consisting of four essential parts[1]. The whimsical fancy which is to be the soul of the play must be introduced with due emphasis, and accordingly we have what may be called the Generating Action, leading up to the point at which the foundation idea of the plot is disclosed. Sometimes this is a single scene, such as the meeting of parliament in the course of which the hero of the *Acharnians* hits upon his idea of a separate peace. Or it may be an elaborate journey: Trygæus in the *Peace* has to rise to heaven on a beetle in order to learn about the pit in which the object of his worship is hidden; again Bacchus has descended to Hades with a view of carrying off Euripides, when he is utilised to preside—as the guardian deity of the Drama—over the contest between Euripides and Aeschylus which has been standing still for want of a fit umpire. In some plays the Generating Action almost vanishes, the scheme of the plot having been laid outside the action and only needing to be announced; in other cases there is a tendency to prolong this element of plot, until in the *Frogs* the adventures of Bacchus in Hades, before the poetic contest is mentioned, cover nearly half the play.

Disclosure of the Plot

Then comes the Disclosure of the Plot. Usually this takes the form of a sudden thought, like that which bursts upon Talkover in the midst of his conversation with Hoopoe. In the *Acharnians* it is the ejecting of the advocate for peace that suddenly suggests to the country-man the idea of making peace for himself; in the *Clouds* the inspiration comes after a whole night's cogitation. Where

explicitly stated as the purpose of opening Pluto's eyes in 489–97, and this is supported by several other passages (e.g. 90, 386, 751, 779). Equally explicit in favour of equality is 510, supported by 463, 1178. The confusion seems to be noted in the course of the play, and the Informer accuses Plutus of having altered his intention (864–7).

[1] For details and references see Tabular Analysis of Old Attic Plots, below, pages 445–6.

the idea of the plot has been started before the commencement of the action this Disclosure takes the form only of
announcement. In the two plays of the women this announcement is made after much ceremony and preparation
by the heroine to her fellow-conspirators ; in the *Frogs* we
learn the news by the gossip of Bacchus's slave fraternising
with the slaves of Hades. In the *Wasps* the poet drops
for a time dramatic make-believe, and in a digression lets
one of the personages directly explain the plot to the
audience.

The Development of the Plot follows, in a succession of *Develop-*
incidents or scenes which carry out the idea thus opened. *ment of the Plot*
When the hero of the *Acharnians* has, in the Generating
Action, despatched his envoy to make peace, the scene
changes from the place of assembly to the country ; and we
have the return of the envoy with his samples of truces, the
opposition of the warlike colliers and the appeal by which
they are gradually brought round ; then follow a series of
contrasts between rural festivals and market bustle on the
one hand, and on the other hand the miseries of those
yet under military service. The essence of the plot being
an extravagant idea, a leading element in its development
is some tour-de-force of ingenuity by which this idea is
justified and made to appear feasible. This Paradoxical
Justification is usually marked by anapæstic rhythm; it
may be illustrated by Talkover's long disquisition to the
Birds on their wrongs, and his unanswerable argument on
the commanding situation of the atmosphere in which they
live. Other cases are the anapæstic dialogue in which the
divinity of the Clouds is vindicated to Strepsiades, and he is
made to accept them as the origin of all physical and human
phenomena ; or again the argument in the *Wasps* by which
the unwilling jurymen are convinced that they are the
defrauded dupes and not the masters of the state. In
the *Plutus* the revolutionists who are about to open the

CHAP. IX eyes of the Money-god are forced to defend their paradoxical project against the still more paradoxical claim of
Poverty to be the source of all luxury in life.

Climax or   The Development of the Plot culminates in a Climax,
Reaction usually of the nature of a procession, with spectacular or lyric
effects. The contrasts of war and peace in the *Acharnians*
end in a scene in which the hero wins a drinking match
—the only conflict known to peace—while the military
hero is brought home wounded. This drinking hero is
escorted by two fair girls, and a noticeable feature of
Aristophanes' treatment is his fondness for introducing a
beautiful damsel into the close of his plays, either directly
as a bride, or for sport and flirting, or under some allegorical
guise, as Peace or Reconciliation. The Climax to several
plays is a wedding festivity, the *Birds* furnishing a gorgeous
example with its ascent of Talkover and the Queen of
Heaven; elsewhere some other excuse is found for a torchlight procession, such as that which in the *Frogs* escorts
Aeschylus on his journey to upper air. Sometimes the final
spectacular effect is grotesque in character, like the crab-
dance which concludes the *Wasps*. Where the nature of
the plot allows, the Climax may become a Reaction, the
scheme of the plot being overturned; such is the conclusion
of the *Clouds*, in which Strepsiades having tasted the fruits
of the new education, suddenly turns round and fetches his
neighbours and the crowd to pull down the thinking-shop
about the ears of its sophistic owners.

These are the four natural and necessary elements of comic
plot in Greek Drama. It belongs to the whole spirit of the
Old Attic stage, its wealth of ingenuity and sheer intellectual
force, that a species of plot resting entirely upon extravagance in conception should, in execution, exhibit perfect
regularity of treatment [1].

But if the working out of the plot was regular, an ample

[1] Compare throughout the Table of Plots, below, pages 445-6.

field for the opposite treatment was afforded by the Inci- CHAP. IX
dental Effects.   These Incidental Effects are a specific *Interest of*
feature of Old Attic Comedy, and make an aggregate of *Incidental*
interest not inferior to that of the plot itself; Aristophanic *effects,*
treatment is equally divided between drawing upon ingenuity
to sustain its main idea, and breaking away at every turn for
some independent stroke of wit or humour, which may be
altogether a digression, or a detail of the plot endowed with
an interest of its own.   Technically this is irregularity : but *or Irregu-*
the term must not be misunderstood.   The words ' regular ' *larity*
and 'irregular' as used in dramatic criticism are not meant
to suggest merit or defect; they are simply distinguishing
terms of different treatments.   The irregularity of surface
that would spoil a cricket-field is an essential of beauty
in a landscape : so in the present case, irregularity is a
law of Old Attic Comedy.   It is an outcome of the same
democratic licence which founded the species, and inspires
its main plot; the irregular Incidental Effects combine
with the formally developed extravagance of the main
action to crowd into every play all possible varieties of
comic effect.

Among these varieties of comic effect there is Direct *Varieties*
Satire, regularly in the parabasis, frequently elsewhere. *of Comic Effect*
Lampoons or personal attacks abound ; as where Nicarchus, *Direct*
the informer, is recognised approaching Old Honesty's *Satire*
market.

> *The Bœotian.* He is small in stature.
> *Old Honesty.* But all there is of him is bad[1].

Aristophanes has no fear in attacking whole classes, or even
the public generally : the Sausage-seller has a moment's
twinge of fear when he hears that the contest before Demus
is to come off in the Parliament Place, for, he says, Demus
though sensible enough elsewhere always loses his head
when he gets to that spot[2].   Or the satire may be made *Indirect*
Satire :

---

[1] *Acharnians,* 909.   [2] *Knights,* 752.

CHAP. IX more dramatic by being indirect. A whole character is satirically painted where, as various gods are being invoked, Euripides is made to address his prayer to Air (his food), to his own well-balanced Tongue, his 'Cuteness and his Sharp Scent. Similarly in the *Clouds* the poet, instead of attacking the forensic spirit, paints it enthusiastically as an ideal object of desire—the rattling, dodging, sneaking, shuffling versatility in jury devices—but puts the passage into the mouth of the fool Strepsiades. The women in their Mysteries, protesting against direct attacks of Euripides upon them, make a far worse indirect hit at themselves in the addition that because of these attacks they are no longer able to do their former deeds; and with similar indirectness Mnesilochus, under guise of defending Euripides, carries on his attack, asking the women if it is really worth while to be severe upon the poet for exposing some two or three frailties while there are innumerable enormities (which he proceeds to illustrate) left untold [1]. One important

especially Dramatic Cartooning form of this indirect presentation consists in materialising what is abstract. The envoy sent by Old Honesty to make peace with Sparta brings back samples of truces, as it were in wine-jars; these are regularly tasted,—the five years truce has a twang of pitch and naval fittings about it, the ten years truce smells sharply of embassies and negotiations with allies, but the thirty years sample hangs delightfully about the tongue, and has a smell of ambrosia and nectar and go-where-you-please [2]. When Euripides and his father-in-law go to call upon Agathon, this poet's house is made to appear as a regular manufactory of verse. The servant announces:

> He is laying the stocks for a brand new play,
> He is shaping the wheels of original verse;
> There is turning of lathes, and glueing of airs,

[1] *Frogs*, 892 ; *Clouds*, 444–56 ; *Mysteries*, 398, 473.
[2] *Acharnians*, 178–202.

And coining of gnomes, and metaphor-forging;
Wax models of thoughts are being polished and rounded,
There is casting in moulds, and—[*Interruption.*

The poet will, it is added, come out of his house presently, for in winter time

Strophes are hard to bend except in sunshine[1].

A name for such treatment might be Dramatic Cartooning: it simply realises, in the medium of drama, what *Punch* would effect with the pencil; the knights priming their champion with oil and garlic as if for a cock-fight, Peace being hauled from the pit, the scales standing ready to weigh the verses of Aeschylus and Euripides, can easily be imagined as cartoons for some Athenian weekly periodical[2].

It has already been stated that Burlesque of Life is *Burlesque* a leading purpose of Ancient Comedy; the classes that make up society and the functions of social life are alike presented in caricature. All kinds of Comedy must afford scope for depicting that purely outward aspect of human nature which is called by the name 'manners,' to distinguish it from the 'character' which shows actions and habits only in the light of the inner motives that explain them. Perhaps no bit of manners-painting in Aristophanes is bolder than the passage in which the business man's instinct of bargain-driving is suggested as extending beyond death. In the journey of Bacchus to the world of spirits his slave at one point becomes too lazy to carry the baggage. It suddenly occurs to the travellers to utilise as carrier some corpse bound to the same destination. At that moment a funeral crosses the stage[3].

Bacchus. Hulloh!—you there—you Deadman, can't you hear?
Would ye take my bundles to hell with ye, my good fellow?

---

[1] *Mysteries*, from 39.   [2] *Knights*, 490; *Frogs*, 1378.
[3] *Frogs*, 170.

Deadman. What are they?

Bacchus.   These.

Deadman.   Then I must have two drachmas.

Bacchus. I can't—you must take less.

Deadman (*peremptorily*).   Bearer, move on.

Bacchus. No, stop! we shall settle between us—you're so hasty.

Deadman. It's no use arguing; I must have two drachmas.

Bacchus (*emphatically and significantly*).   Ninepence!

Deadman. I'd best be alive again at this rate.   [*Exit.*

*Literary
Burlesque
or Parody*

But it is in Literary Burlesque that Aristophanes seems to feel the keenest relish. There is nothing in literature high or low which this poet is not ready to parody. The lyrics of Pindar and Phrynichus find themselves suddenly transformed into lampoons [1]; at the other end of the scale the Chorus in the *Peace* burlesque their own comic dancing, when, having solemnly obtained permission from the hero, who is restraining their wild joy, to just kick the right foot once more, they abuse the indulgence by proceeding further to kick the left foot also [2]. Philosophy and science have to suffer the same treatment. Attention has been drawn to the theory of evolution which is adopted, with variations, by the Chorus of Birds in their parabasis. In the conflict between Right and Wrong Argument the latter, in place of the usual set speech, puts her plea in the form of a detailed confutation plainly intended to parody the Socratic dialogue [3]. To the burlesque of current science whole scenes in the *Clouds* are devoted. One of the best hits is the discussion of the thunderbolt, in which Socrates' well-known taste for illustrations from every-day life is transferred to Strepsiades.

[1] E. g. *Knights*, 1263; *Birds*, 750. There is a parody of an Aesopic fable in *Birds*, 471: compare *Peace*, 129.   [2] *Peace*, 322-34.

[3] *Clouds* from 1036. Of course a feature in such treatment will be to make the dialogue as feeble as possible; and it is in this spirit that Right Argument, after having cited warm baths as one item in the luxury that she alleges is enervating modern youth, is driven to admit that the principal warm baths in Athens are the Baths of Hercules, and that Hercules was the least enervated of all heroes.

Socrates. When a wind that is dry, being lifted on high, is suddenly pent into these,
It swells up their skin, like a bladder, within, by Necessity's
 changeless decrees :
Till, compressed very tight, it bursts them outright, and
 away with an impulse·so strong,
That at last by the force and the swing of its course, it takes
 fire as it whizzes along.
Strepsiades. That's exactly the thing that I suffered one Spring, at
 the great feast of Zeus, I admit :
I'd a paunch in the pot, but I wholly forgot about making
 the safety-valve slit.
So it spluttered and swelled while the saucepan I held, till at
 last with a vengeance it flew :
Took me quite by surprise, dung-bespattered my eyes, and
 scalded my face black and blue [1].

Tragedy is naturally the department of literature which *Especially*
serves as butt in ordinary for comic parody; and this *Burlesque of Tragedy*
natural antagonism was enhanced by the party feuds which
pitted Aristophanes against Euripides. Besides the play
which is devoted to a systematic satire upon the poetry
of Euripides by exhibiting it in whimsical comparison with
the poetry of Aeschylus, the same topic affords a basis
of plot to the *Mysteries*, and a digression of considerable
length to the *Acharnians* [2]. This last· commences by
parodying tragic situations. Old Honesty, having to face the
angry colliers, agrees to speak his plea of defence with head
on chopping-block, if only they will grant him a hearing.
He has just got into position when he suddenly bethinks
him of a mode by which he may become yet more tragic ; he
rises, and proceeds to a point in the stage supposed to
represent the house where the great master of pathos lives.
A long scene ensues, in which the Chorus are ignored.
After some difficulty Old Honesty obtains an interview with
Euripides ; by a burlesque of stage machinery the roller-stage
is set in motion and displays the upper storey of the house,

---

[1] *Clouds,* 404–11.   [2] 383–480.

where the poet is engaged in composition, with his legs in the air to indicate how he is wandering in cloud-land. Bundles of dirty rags, and other theatrical properties suggestive of pathos, are scattered about: Honesty begs the loan of these to assist his piteous defence before the colliers of Acharnæ. It appears that each bundle represents a separate play: and after some discussion the rags of Philoctetes and Bellerophon are rejected, but the old coat of Telephus fits the countryman's figure. When he has further petitioned for a beggar's stick, a pipkin mended with sponge, a burnt basket, and a cup with the rim off, Euripides cries out that his dramatic repertoire is exhausted! In the *Mysteries* the parody is applied to the ingenious devices with which Euripides meets critical situations. The disguised Mnesilochus has just been discovered by the infuriated women, when he suddenly effects a diversion by seizing from one of them a baby, which he threatens with his sword and so holds his enemies at bay; the surprise becomes a double one when the women, after some moments of hesitation, advance upon him, and he strips the baby to slay it, finding however no baby at all, but a skin of wine which the good woman had smuggled in under the shape of a child, intending to refresh herself during the long and solemn festival [1]. The rest of this play ridicules the poetry of Euripides by a comic application of it to the unhappy situation in which Mnesilochus now finds himself. His first difficulty is how to inform the poet of his peril. He recollects a play of Euripides in which the secret of a crime is inscribed on oars, and these are sent floating in hopes that some of them may reach the proper quarter: Mnesilochus has no oars, but he writes his message on the statues and busts of the deities which adorn the temple in which he is confined, and then pitches these out in all directions [2].

[1] *Mysteries*, 689–762.   [2] 765–84.

He now realises his situation as that of Helen waiting
in Egypt for Menelaus to rescue her, and utters his com-
plaint with the proper Egyptian colouring. After a time
Euripides comes, and—at a safe distance outside—carries
on the scene: the women guarding their prisoner listen
mystified, yet with patience, until the tragic verse talks
plainly of rescue, when they interfere, and announce the
approach of the magistrate. That, says Euripides, is unlucky, and his ingenuity is devoted to stealing off, with
vows on his lips that he will never desert the sufferer till
all ingenuity has been exhausted[1]. In the next scene
Mnesilochus, now nailed to the pillory, endeavours to
console himself with the tragic situation of Andromeda
chained to the rock. In Euripides' treatment of the subject, before Perseus appears, the wailings of Andromeda
are answered only by the echo. Euripides creeps up behind
the scene to play his part as echo: all goes smoothly for
a time, until the interruptions of echo become somewhat
more rapid than suits the taste of the declaimer on the
pillory; he remonstrates, and his remonstrances come back
as echoes, he loses his temper and the explosion increases
the echo, and the scene crescendoes till it wakes the con-
stable on guard, and when his enquiries and ejaculations
with their echoes are added to the conflicting sounds the
whole scene is plunged in inextricable confusion[2].

Farce is distinguished from other comic effect by the *Farce*
greater prominence of wildness and self-abandon. There
is plenty of it in the *Knights*, especially where a contest
takes place for the favour of Demus, in which the rivals
offer gifts of shoes, coat, cushion, pomatum, eye-wiper, and
finally struggle for the privilege of blowing Demus's nose.
The term will include horse-play and 'knock-about business.'
But the leading type for this species of effect is the *Wasps.*
There is farce in the very description of the disease from

[1] 850-927. [2] 1010-97.

CHAP. IX which the hero is supposed to be suffering. To such
a height has the forensic madness of Love-Cleon proceeded
that his fingers are crooked with holding the vote-pebble;
he keeps a shingle beach in his garden lest pebbles should
run short; he is awake half the night in anxiety to be
punctual at court in the morning, and suspects the household cock of being corrupted and waking him late. The
speaker goes on to tell how they tried hydropathy, but
could not wash his passion out of him; then the Coryban-
tic cure, but the old man simply danced his way to court;
they took him for a night to the temple of Aesculapius
across the water, but he was back in chancery by dawn[1].
As the story is being told to the audience there is a cry
that the patient is escaping by the kitchen boiler: soon
his head is seen above the chimney, and when caught he
persists that he is only smoke. A heavy chimney board
with a log on top of it blocks up this mode of escape, and
Love-Cleon has to try persuasion. He threatens he will
gnaw through the net they have thrown round the house;
' but you have no teeth,' is the triumphant rejoinder. He
pleads the absolute necessity of selling his ass that day.
His son undertakes the task himself, and cautiously opens
the door to let the ass out: struck with the heavy gait
of the beast Hate-Cleon wonders whether the ass is mourn-
ful at the prospect of being sold, when he suddenly perceives
his father under the creature's belly, emulating the exploit
of Odysseus[2]. And this farcical treatment of a novel
disease is continued by other scenes already described,
which present the attempted rescue by the Chorus of
Wasps, and the solution of all difficulties in the establishment of jury proceedings at home.

Masque,   In analysing various forms of comic humour, Masque,
Allegory, Personification and Myth form an independent

---

[1] *Wasps*, 67-135.   [2] *Wasps*, 136-210.

group. In Masque, fancy or allegory mingles with an appeal CHAP. IX
to the eye. Very delicate masque effects might be drawn
from the Chorus of Clouds. More usually in Greek Comedy *Panto-*
we get the rougher spectacular treatment denoted by the *mime*
term Pantomime : the parode of knights with hobby-horses,
the ascent on beetle-back to heaven—at one point of which
Trygæus appeals to the machinery man to be very careful—
and the crab-dance which concludes the *Wasps* are good
examples [1]. There is a notable scene of Allegoric Personi- *Allegory*
fication in the *Peace*. The terrific figure of War appears, *and Per-*
sonifica-
attended by his boy Tumult ; he has a huge mortar, into *tion*
which he throws garlic (emblematic of Megara), cheese
(for Sicily), and Attic honey. But he has no pestle : and
Tumult is sent first to the Athenians and then to the Lacedæmonians only to bring back news that their pestles are
both lost. This is an allusion to the leading advocates
of war in the two nations, Brasidas and Cleon, who had
both been recently killed. War then goes in to make
a pestle for himself, whereupon the hero of the play adroitly
seizes the moment for an attempt to recover Peace [2].
The use of Mythology as a weapon of satire was the form of *Myth*
humour common to Attic Comedy and the Sicilian or aristocratic branch. It may be pointed out that there are two
modes of employing the satiric myth. It is a guise under
which humanity may be satirised ; the previous chapter described the typical example in the *Birds*—the embassy of
gods, in which the peculiarities and frailties of earthly
ambassadors are transferred to the larger canvas of heaven.
On the other hand, mythological personages may be so
treated as to humanise deity. Hermes—herald of the gods—
appears in the *Peace* as the footman of the divine household,
left in charge when the rest of the gods have gone out
of town, chatty and communicative, forbidding the attempt

---

[1] *Peace*, 173; *Wasps* from 1498.　　　[2] *Peace*, 232–88.

CHAP. IX to rescue the buried goddess until a 'tip' restores him to his affable demeanour[1]. Comic exaltation and comic belittling equally fit in with the myth.

The Sustained paradox　A very marked feature of Aristophanes' Comedy is the Sustained Paradox. The idea of the birds' castle in the air is with infinite ingenuity kept up throughout a whole play. Only second in extent to this is the elaboration bestowed on the paradox of the Clouds, and their appearance as maidens and deities. The summons to these deities to take visible form in answer to the prayer of their worshipper is turned into a beautiful fancy picture of the clouds rising from the bed of ocean; their entrance movements are connected with the idea of drifting, and their long trains with cloud shadows. If they look, when fully visible, like women, this is explained by the power of the cloud to assume any shape. Clouds can readily be accepted as the muse of poetry in consideration of the constant use the poets make of cloud imagery; they are vindicated as the originators of all natural phenomena by examples which show their essential connexion with the rain and the thunderbolt. It is not difficult to make the same deities supreme over politics in view of the belief in weather omens; and a claim on their part to be connected with the Moon links them with the calendar of sacred festivals. If one use of a god is to swear by, the oath 'By Air and Respiration' fits in with an atmospheric divinity. Finally, the Clouds establish their authority over the dramatic festival itself by threatening weather penalties in case the judges give the prize away from them[2].

Varieties of Wit　Finally, to all these varieties of comic humour must be added Wit, itself a thing taking innumerable forms. There

Simple Surprise　are several forms of wit that depend upon surprise. Simple Surprises are very common: one example is the explanation

---

[1] *Peace*, 180–235, 362–427, etc.

[2] *Clouds*, 314–436, 576–94, 627, 1114.

given to the open-mouthed Strepsiades of the way in CHAP. IX
which the master found geometry useful when there was
no dinner for the college.

> He sprinkled on the table—some fine sand—
> He bent a spit—he raised some compasses—
> And—bagged a mantle from the Wrestling School [1].

The Reverse-Surprise is a kind of wit specially patronised *Reverse-*
in the *Lysistrata*, where it is used as a vent for the high *Surprise*
spirits of the Chorus when the men and women are united.
Thus, all who want money are invited, on this day of joy,
to come with purses, large and many of them, and borrow
freely all they want, only promising that when peace comes
they will *not* repay. Again, a feast is described as preparing,
to which all are freely invited :

> Come along, like men of mettle;
> Come, as though 'twere all for you:
> Come—you'll find my only entrance
> Locked and bolted too [2].

In the large amount of matter devoted to burlesquing other
poetry Surprise Perversions are of frequent occurrence. *Surprise*
The typical case is the conclusion of the *Frogs*, where the *Perver-*
verdict is given in quotations from the defeated candidate, *sions*
slightly adapted. Just before he makes his decision
Euripides reminds Bacchus that he had sworn to carry
him to earth.

> *Bacchus.* ' My tongue did swear: but'—I choose Aeschylus.
> *Euripides.* After this crime dare'st look me in the face ?
> *Bacchus.* ' Where is the crime, when they who hear approve ? '
> *Euripides.* Villain ! and wilt thou leave me mongst the dead ?
> *Bacchus.* ' Who knows but life may be a kind of death,'
>   Drinking be thirsting, and our sleep but bedclothes ? [3]

Surprise Iteration is another mode of giving sparkle to *Surprise*
comic dialogue. To illustrate from the *Women in Parlia-* *Iterations*

---

[1] *Clouds*, 175–9.   [2] *Lysistrata*, 1043–72 ; compare 1188–1215.
                    [3] *Frogs*, 1469–78.

CHAP. IX *ment*: Simple and Smart are discussing the question of transferring private property to the state under the new constitution that establishes community of goods.

> *Simple.* And what else are people doing but taking steps for handing over their property?
> *Smart.* I'll believe it when I see it.
> *Simple.* Why, they are talking about it in the streets.
> *Smart.* Talk—that's just what they will do.
> *Simple.* They say they will take and deliver.
> *Smart.* Say—that's just what they will do.
> *Simple.* You'll be the death of me, disbelieving everything a fellow says.
> *Smart.* Disbelieve—that's just what they will do.
> *Simple.* Bother you!
> *Smart.* Bother—that's just what they will do.

Later in the same conversation the effect is renewed:

> *Simple.* Oh, they'll deliver up.
> *Smart.* But *suppose* they do not pay in, what then?
> *Simple.* We'll force them.
> *Smart.* *Suppose* they are the stronger, what then?
> *Simple.* You let me be.
> *Smart.* *Suppose* they should sell your goods, what then?
> *Simple.* Be hanged to you!
> *Smart.* *Suppose* I am hanged, what then?
> *Simple.* Why, serve you right[1].

Mock Heroics
Comic Enumeration

Other forms of wit are comic counterparts to serious effects. Mock Heroics have been illustrated from the choral odes in the *Birds*, which sing of familiar topics under the guise of travellers' marvels. Comic Enumeration may be illustrated from a passage in the Plutus, in which an attempt is being made to convince the blind god of his omnipotence.

> *Chremylus.* Your power is infinite: a man may have too much
>   Of everything besides that's reckoned pleasant; such
>   ˙As love.
> *Slave.*   Bread.

[1] *Women in Parliament*, 773-6, 799-804.

Chremylus.	Music.	CHAP. IX
Slave.	Sweetmeats.	
Chremylus.	Honour.	
Slave.	Toasted cheese.	
Chremylus.	Prize-winning.	
Slave.	Figs.	
Chremylus.	Ambition.	
Slave.	Dough-nuts.	
Chremylus.	Office.	
Slave.	Peas.	

Chremylus. But man was never known to have too much of you!
 Give him a round thiee thousand down,—what will he do?
 Wish that it was but four! Well, give him that,—and then?
 Forsooth he'd rather die than live with less than ten![1]

From the same play may be taken an illustration of Comic Persistence, which is however something more than *Comic Per-* a form of expression, and belongs to the borderland *sistence* between wit and humour. The incident is part of the surprise felt by the neighbours at the hero's sudden accession of wealth : one friend in particular has his doubts about the honesty of the business.

Friend. Have you really become as rich as they say?
Chremylus. Well, I hope to be, if heaven please :—there are risks—
Friend. Heaven please? Risks? This looks bad. Suddenly rich and afraid is suggestive of somebody who has done—something not quite right.
Chremylus. How, not quite right?
Friend. If, for example, you should have stolen some gold or silver from the oracle, no doubt intending to repent?
Chremylus. Apollo, averter of evil, not I, indeed!
Friend. Don't talk nonsense, my good Sir, I am certain of it.
Chremylus. You need not think anything of the kind.
Friend. What a thing it is that there should be no good in anybody : all slaves of gain!
Chremylus. By Ceres, you have lost your senses.
Friend (aside). What a fall from his former good name!
Chremylus. I say you are mad, man!
Friend (aside). His very glance has a strange wavering, that tells of a man who has made a villain of himself.

[1] *Plutus*, 188-97.

Chremylus. I understand your croaking. You want to go shares.

Friend. Shares in what?

Chremylus. In what is at all events different from what you think.

Friend. You mean that you did not steal it, you carried it off?

Chremylus. You are an idiot.

Friend. You mean to say that you have not even committed fraud?

Chremylus. Certainly not!

Friend. Hercules! What am I to do? The man won't tell the truth.

Chremylus. You accuse before you know.

Friend. My good friend, let me settle it for you; I'll do it at the smallest possible cost. I'll stop the orators' mouths before the town gets an inkling of it.

Chremylus. You'll lay out three halfpence in a friendly way, and send in a bill for a shilling.

Friend. I fancy I see a certain person sitting at the bar, with suppliant staff in his hand, and wife and children weeping round him: for all the world like Pamphilus's painting, the Children of Hercules.

Chremylus. On the contrary, I have wherewith to bring it about that none but the good and the wise shall be rich.

Friend. What do you say? Have you stolen as much as that?[1]

Wit and humour combined: Raillery of the sexes

Dramatic pretence dropped

It will be enough to name two more kinds of fun which, like the last, seem to combine both wit and humour. One is the mutual 'chaff' of the sexes, which is a constant source of incidental effect, besides being a main motive to two plays. The other is a comical confusion between the dramatic representation and reality. There were constant references to the audience in ancient comedies, and no doubt many extemporised personalities. It is a regular thing for a personage in some early scene to turn round and begin to tell the plot to the audience; in the *Wasps* the explanation is complete, more usually it is interrupted after enough has been said to stir curiosity[2]. More dramatic effect is got out of such confusion between make-believe and earnest in an early scene of the *Frogs*, where

---

[1] *Plutus*, 346–89.   [2] *Wasps* from 54; compare *Birds*, 30–49.

the effeminate Bacchus, overpowered by the terrors of the
under-world, rushes to the front of the stage to claim the
protection of his priest, who, in a Dionysiac festival, would
naturally have the presidential seat among the spectators [1].

Such are the principal varieties of comic effect on which
the poet of Greece could draw for his double work of
maintaining the extravagant conception of his plot, and
relieving this plot with constant flashes of incidental effect.
No analysis however can convey the inexhaustible wealth of
humour and elastic play of mind which marks the poetry
of Aristophanes, and which, conveyed in the most flexible
of metrical mediums, makes it one of the world's literary
marvels. Old Attic Comedy was the product of a very
special age, a single generation of time that was the blos-
soming period for a great people. It was moreover the
comedy of the world's youth ; and its spontaneous fun was
needed, not as a stimulus to jaded spirits, but as a relief for
exuberant energy.

[1] *Frogs*, 297.

X

ANCIENT COMEDY IN TRANSITION

X

1 Nature and Range of the Transition

THERE is a remarkable hiatus in the history of Greek
drama. Old Attic Comedy came to an end, so far as we
know it, with Aristophanes. The next comic species that
has found representation in literature is the 'New Attic,'
which we possess not in its original Greek form, but in its
Roman imitation. Between the old and the new came
what has been called by historians the 'Middle Attic
Comedy,' the whole of which has been lost. It appears to
have been a highly fertile department of literature: a single
historian speaks of eight hundred plays, the work of thirty-
nine poets, which he himself had seen. And the loss of all
these dramas is the more unfortunate as they represent
a stage in the history of Greek literature during which most
important problems of dramatic development were in
course of solution. For our idea of this Middle Attic
Comedy we are confined to a few scattered notices of
historians, and to inferences from comparison between the
character of Comedy when it comes to an end in Greek
literature, and again where we recover it in the literature of
Rome. The evolution of Comedy resembles a river that
runs during part of its course underground: by examining
the direction of the stream where it disappears, and again
the mode of its re-emerging from the earth, some notion
may be formed of the course taken by the river where this
has been invisible.

From what we can learn by such means of the Middle
Attic Comedy there seems no reason for supposing that it in
any sense constituted a distinct species of drama ; the term

*Middle
Attic
Comedy :*

*not a sepa-
rate species
but*

CHAP. X

*a transi-
tion stage*

rather covers a continuous and gradual transition between two species, each of which had a marked individuality of its own. The transition had begun in the days of Aristophanes. Old Attic Comedy was created by a political revolution, which both gave it its specific form, and also furnished the social surroundings favourable to its spirit of licence; this chapter of political history is considered to have closed with the end of the Peloponnesian War in 401 B. C., after which the leadership of the Greek peoples passed away for ever from the Athenians. But alike in political and literary history great movements do not punctuate themselves by exact chronological dates. The democratic impulse was weakened at Athens before it was destroyed, and ten years before the conclusion of the Peloponnesian War an oligarchic revolution had set up the government of the Four Hundred. So Comedy, before it leaves the hands of Aristophanes, shows unmistakable signs of change in the direction in which the Middle Attic dramas were to carry it. The work then of the present chapter is to trace a transition, commencing in the later plays of Aristophanes, proceeding through something like a century[1] of great literary activity, and culminating in the new species which will be the subject of the following chapter.

2   Instability of the Chorus

*Natural
instability
of the comic
Chorus*

In looking for evidence of the transitional stage in Greek Comedy we turn first to the Chorus. It was as Choral Comedy that the Old Attic drama became a separate literary species, and the decay of its specific distinctiveness

---

[1] It seems reasonable to date Middle Attic Comedy, considered as a transition, from 411 B. C., the year of the oligarchic revolution. In 311 B. C. Menander, great master of the New Attic Comedy, would be thirty-one years old.

will be most apparent as the Chorus is touched by change. CHAP. X
Again, this Chorus was a foreign element in Comedy, and
for that reason a disturbing force. Even in Tragedy we
have seen how the Chorus was a source of instability,
wavering as it did between dramatic and lyric functions.
In Comedy, then, it is not surprising to find that the Chorus
existed in a state of highly unstable equilibrium, and was
a source of rapid developmental changes.

Six distinct tendencies are traceable in the comic Chorus. *Reversion*
Two of them are in the direction of Primitive Comedy, to *to Prim-*
itive Com-
which the whole parabasis is in a measure a reversion. *edy: in its*
earliest
The parabasis proper suggests a tendency to revert to the
original body of Bacchic satirisers, who broke off their
·procession to indulge in jeering : so the anapæstic digression
severed connexion altogether with the play, and the Chorus
spoke directly as an author to the public. In the after- *and its*
final stage
speech, on the other hand, the Chorus resumed their comic
characterisation ; they selected such aspects of political
questions as would appeal, in the *Acharnians* to old men,
in the *Peace* to representatives of the agricultural interest.
This recalls the final stage of Primitive Comedy, when the
satirisers had adopted a dramatic rôle in which to bring out
their attack. In neither case does the change amount to
more than a tendency, for the whole of the parabasis
handles matter of public moment in loftier rhythms than the
iambics consecrated to personal satire.

Again, the Chorus of Comedy shows attraction to the *Attraction*
to the tragic
tragic Chorus in its two normal functions, which have *Chorus: as*
been described in an earlier chapter by the terms 'spec- *spectators*
of the
tators of the drama' and 'spectators in the drama.' The *drama,*
Chorus of Tragedy were spectators of the drama in
the way they were made to lead the thoughts of the
audience through the mental impressions which the poet
wished his play to produce. A comic counterpart is
found to this in the practice of Aristophanes to connect his

CHAP. X choruses with the right side in politics. The Chorus in the
Knights and the Peace are completely described by this
phrase.   In the Mysteries and the Frogs the Chorus represent the right side in the sense that they are bitterly
hostile to the personage attacked in these plays.   The case
of the Clouds is peculiar.   Here the Chorus appear at the
summons of Socrates, and seem to identify themselves with
his system.   But at a later stage they hint a coming change
in the action, bidding the arch-sophist make all he can of
his victim speedily :

> For cases such as these, my friend, are very prone to change and bend.

At the end of the play, when the outraged Strepsiades
seeks to upbraid the Clouds with having led him to his
ruin, the Chorus promptly vindicate their position :

> Such is our plan. We find a man
>   On evil thoughts intent,
> Guide him along to shame and wrong,
>   Then leave him to repent.

These words seem to set the Chorus right with the audience,
suggesting that they have only made pretence of support-
ing evil [1].   Two more plays exhibit the principle in a varied
form : the colliers of Acharnæ and the wasp-jurors are vio-
lently on the wrong side at the commencement, but are by
the course of the action brought round to political sound-
ness.   And we have another interesting variation of the law
in the Lysistrata, where there are two choruses, presenting
the right and the wrong side with bitter opposition, but
gradually reconciled by becoming unanimous in favour of
peace.   In the remaining three plays of Aristophanes the
subjects hardly admit of a right and a wrong side.

*and as
spectators
in the
drama*   The function of spectators in the drama is illustrated by
the casual way in which the Chorus of a comedy are often
brought into the action.   In the Acharnians the bearer of
truces has to pass through a certain colliery village on his

----

[1] Clouds, 810, 1458.

way to Honesty's farm, and the colliers, who are strong for CHAP. X
war, detect and pursue him, thus becoming the Chorus of
the play. So in the *Frogs* the Band of the Initiated are
connected with the action as passers-by of whom the hero
is to ask directions for his route. Even where the Chorus
represents a particular party—the knights, or husbandmen
in the *Peace*—they can still be brought together in a casual
manner, the hero, in a sudden emergency, calling all who
are on his side to his assistance [1].

But if the comic Chorus thus imitated the Chorus of *Opposing
tendencies*
Tragedy in its normal functions, it shared also the insta- *(as in*
bility as between dramatic and lyric which led the tragic *Tragedy):*
Chorus to develop in two opposite directions, towards what
was purely lyric or purely dramatic. On the one hand *towards
dedram-*
there was a tendency for the Chorus in Comedy to lose its *atisation,*
dramatic character, its odes approaching more and more
nearly to the position of mere lyric interludes, irrelevant
to the plot. Not to speak of the parabasis, which was
avowedly a digression, we have lyrics in Aristophanes made
up of miscellaneous personalities, or in the *Mysteries* of
serious festival hymns. It is not uncommon for the Chorus
to speak in their own interests as professional performers,
appealing to the judges to give them the prize, or (in the
Acharnians) making exposure of a choregus who had on a
previous occasion disappointed them of their complimentary
supper [2]. In the two latest plays of Aristophanes this change
has proceeded to much greater length, and in places we
have not only the loss of relevancy in the words of an ode,
but the loss of words altogether, the ode sinking into a mere
performance of music and dancing. The law for the choral
element in these two plays would seem to be that the Chorus
show activity in the parode scene, and are then ignored till
the exode, except that they interpose once in the forensic

[1] *Frogs*, 154; *Knights*, 242; *Peace*, 296.
[2] *Clouds*, 1115; *Birds*, 1101; *Acharnians*, 1150.

CHAP. X   contest to urge on to the argument the champion they
favour.   In each play there is a section of more than five
hundred lines, during which the Chorus do not speak a word,
nor is their presence recognised, which however includes
several scenes that are clearly distinct : the break must have
been made by dances in connexion with which no words
have been written [1].   This is a not inconsiderable advance
in the transition by which, as we learn from historians,
the Middle Attic Comedy lost the Chorus altogether, and
Roman Comedy was brought into the form of acts or scenes
separated by performances of music.

and to-
wards in-
creased
dramatic
activity
The opposite tendency for the Chorus to rise in dramatic
function and pass into actors would seem particularly natural
in Comedy.   In the *Birds* the Chorus are the motive force
for the plot; in the *Wasps* they join in a free fight with
personages on the stage [2].   But the great illustration for
this line of development is the *Lysistrata*.   This play is
unique.   It rests its plot mainly upon choral action ; a sure
Multipli-
cation of
Choruses
sign of breach with the normal function by which the Chorus
represented the audience is given in the multiplication of

[1] In the *Women in Parliament* the Chorus complete their parode
action at line 516 ; they do not speak again [according to Bergk's text]
until line 1127, except the speech, 571–83, in which they urge the
heroine to speak boldly in their cause against the husband.   Bergk's
text indicates the position for the dancing interludes by the word
Chorou: this occurs after lines 729, 876, 1111.—In the *Plutus* the
parode is completed at line 331, the interposition in the forensic contest
is at line 487, and the concluding interposition of the Chorus is at line
1208.   They do however speak during the interval : once (631, 637, 640)
to welcome the god on his return from the temple with his eyes opened
(which may be regarded as a part of the parode scene separated from the
rest, the purpose of their entry being to rejoice at the opening of Plutus's
eyes), again (962) to mechanically direct a newcomer to the house.   The
dances are placed by Bergk after lines 321, 626, 770, 801, 958, 1096, 1170.

[2] Two plays, the *Women in Parliament* and the *Mysteries*, reflect
both the opposite tendencies: in the generating action the Chorus
have an active share, while in the main plot they are irrelevant or
ignored.

choruses [1], which is carried so far that five distinct speaking CHAP. X
choruses are introduced on the stage or in the orchestra, and ———
are massed together in the choral climax.   In modern terms
the *Lysistrata* might be described as the triumph of opera *Lysistrata*
over drama [2].

The prologue of the play is occupied with a conspiracy of *prologue*
the women, led by Lysistrata, to refuse all intercourse with
men until peace shall be made.   At the close a shout
within the Acropolis—in front of which the scene is laid—
shows that the first step in the revolution has been accomplished, and the band of women to whom the task had been
committed have seized the citadel.   All separate to carry out
their respective parts in the plot.   Then on one side of the *double pa-*
orchestra enter a Chorus of Men, carrying logs of wood and *rode leading*
to
pans of smoking charcoal.   The degraded iambic rhythm rules
this parode, with lyrics interspersed : the old men grumble at
their toilsome task of clambering heavy-laden up the ascent
to the Acropolis in order to burn out the shameless women:—

> Dear, how these two great fire-logs make my wearied shoulders toil
> and ache.
> But still right onwards we needs must go,
> And still the cinders we needs must blow,
> Else, we'll find the fire extinguished ere we reach our journey's end.
> Puff! puff! puff!
> O the smoke! the smoke!

[1] I use the term 'Secondary Chorus' in this work for *bands* of persons
(other than the regular Chorus) for whom words are written.   Examples
are the Eumenidean procession in Aeschylus's trilogy, and the Huntsmen
in *Hippolytus*.   The term may include cases like the Frogs and the
Chorus trained by Agathon, which do not appear, but are heard singing
behind the scenes.   The Greek term *parachoregema* would include
further the children of Trygæus in the *Peace*, whose characterisation is
individual not collective.   This word is sometimes translated *by-chorus*,
but this is misleading, its connexion being not with *chorus*, but with
choregus : a fair rendering would be *chorus-provider's extras*.

[2] The play is ineffably coarse in the original : in the version of
Mr. Rogers it is made readable without any loss of force.—For references,
see Table on page 441.

CHAP. X As they are spreading their logs and preparing to fire them,
—— enter on the other side of the orchestra a Chorus of Women
bearing pitchers of water.   They are hastening to the defence
of the citadel, and fear they may be too late.

> Yea, for hither, they state,
> Dotards are dragging, to burn ·us,
> Logs of enormous weight,
> Fit for a bath-room furnace,
> Vowing to roast and slay
> Sternly the reprobate women.   O Lady, Goddess, I pray,
> Ne'er may I see them in flames !   I hope to behold them, with gladness,
> Hellas and Athens redeeming from battle and murder and madness.

Suddenly the two Choruses face one another, and exchange
of defiance begins, ending in volleys of water from the
women's·buckets, with which the Chorus of Men are drenched,
and·their charcoal pans extinguished.   At the height of the
episode tumult enter a Magistrate with his officers to assert the
majesty of the law against both parties ; the diversion
brings the scene to blank verse.   It may be noted that the
choral spirit so permeates this play that the action even of
individual personages makes an approach to the evolutions
of a dance.   Thus when the Magistrate is in a lordly way
dealing out censure on all sides, Lysistrata enters from the
citadel and confronts him.   He orders an officer to arrest
her.   But another woman comes out to tackle the officer,
and when a second officer attempts to take her into custody,
yet another woman appears to confront him : and so on,
until a crowd of women fill the stage, and a scrimmage with
the·police takes place, Lysistrata cheering on her companions.

> Forth to the fray, dear sisters, bold allies !
> O egg-and-seed-and-potherb·market-girls,
> O garlic-selling-barmaid-baking-girls,
> Charge to the rescue, smack and ·whack and thwack them.

The women holding their own, a parley takes place, which
becomes the anapæstic vindication of the plot by Lysistrata.

Even this is relieved by evolutionary effects. As Lysistrata
makes her attack on the old theory that war is man's
business, the testy Magistrate becomes indignant in his
interruptions: whereupon some of the girls begin dancing
round him—the dialogue going on unbroken—and, before
he knows what is being done, have thrown their wraps
about him and put a spindle into his hand, until he looks
a model spinning woman by way of accompaniment to
Lysistrata's

> War shall be women's business now!

So in the latter half of the discussion, where the case for
women's rule is being put with great skill, the Magistrate's
impatience becomes greater than ever, until his girl tor-
mentors dance round him once more without interrupting
the scene, throw over him this time a shroud, and then
drive him away telling him he is keeping Charon waiting.
The officers are driven off with buckets of water and the
stage is vacant.

We now have the unique interest of an interlude by *interlude*
a Double Chorus. The Choruses of Men and of Women
stand facing one another in the orchestra, and exchange
fierce defiance; the play passes into its trochaic stage,
strophes of accelerated rhythm being answered by antistrophes, each ending with a blow, or missile, with which
words have been unexpectedly translated into action. Thus
the first strophe of the Men ends ·

> And I'll dress my sword in myrtle, and with firm and dauntless
> hand, .
> Here beside Aristogeiton (*creeping up to a statue in the orchestra*)
> resolutely take my stand,
> Marketing in arms beside him. This this the time and this the place
> When my patriot arm must deal a—BLOW upon that woman's face !
> [*One of the Chorus has darted out and suddenly struck
> one of the women.*]

There is a similar ending to the antistrophe ·of the
Women :—

Murmuring are ye? Let me hear you, only let me hear you speak,
And from this unpolished slipper comes a—SLAP upon your cheek!
    [*One of the women shies her slipper and hits the leader of
            the Men's Chorus.*]

So the second strophe of the Men ends by the evolutions
of the dance bringing them close up to the Women, whereupon several of the Men unexpectedly seize several women
of the Chorus, and shake them before they can get free.
But in the antistrophe the Women dance nearer and
nearer to the Men, and, while the latter are watching
against a repetition of their own manœuvre, the leader of
the Women suddenly seizes the foot of the Men's leader,
and upsets him against his unthinking companions, till
the whole Chorus of them are floundering on the floor
together.

And you'll never stop from making these absurd decrees, I know,
Till I catch your foot and toss you—Zeus-ha'-mercy, there you go!

*episodes and
interludes*   Next we have two scenes of ordinary verse separated by
another Double Chorus. In the first is seen the inconstancy
of the women conspirators, one after another being caught
deserting, and offering absurd excuses. In this women's
scene the Chorus of Women have a share of the dialogue;
the Chorus of Men are ignored. The second scene exhibits
a husband teased by his wife in his attempts to bring her back
to domestic intercourse: here the Chorus of Men share in
the dialogue with the husband, and the Chorus of Women
are silent. The interlude shows that the Choruses of Men
and of Women have not been facing one another for so
long in the orchestra without a mutual attraction making
itself felt. Thus, though they still exchange defiance, there
are suggestions of relenting, such as an offer of a kiss made
in a tone of threatening, and a threat of a blow accepted as
an amatory challenge.

    After a mechanical scene, in which an offer of peace
comes from Sparta, we reach the crisis of the plot, and this

is entirely confined to the Chorus and the orchestra. The
Men and Women continue to exchange defiances, which
show in each line signs of softening, till at last the men give
way with the reflection :

> That was quite a true opinion which a wise man gave about you :
> We can't live with such tormentors, no, by Zeus, nor yet without
> you !

They make peace, and the Double Chorus resolves into *choral ex-*
a Joint Chorus of Men and Women combined—a thing *odus*
entirely strange to Greek ideas of dancing. The words of
the Joint Ode express general abandonment to rejoicings
and indulgence in nonsense verses, which last over two
interludes, before and after a scene in which representatives
of Sparta and Athens meet, and, by aid of Lysistrata and
her beautiful maid Reconciliation, all differences are
harmonised.

Lyric metres rule the play from the point at which the
Choruses of Men and Women unite, and the conclusion is
an elaborate choral climax[1]. The preceding scene closed
with an invitation of the Spartan envoys to a banquet in the
Acropolis. The exodus commences with the return of the
banqueters. First, the Athenian hosts appear, speaking in
praise of their guests, and carrying torches to escort them :
these form a line on the stage and become a Chorus of
Torchbearers. Amid this torchlight the Spartan embassy
pours out of the Acropolis, and extemporises a Laconian
choral ode on the stage, with full Doric ritual and in Doric
dialect. Then Lysistrata bids them take as partners the
Garrison of Women holding the Acropolis, who have not
appeared until this moment : these descend with the Spartans
into the orchestra, and face the Chorus already there.
Thus was reached the unprecedented climax of a Quadruple
Chorus, that is, a Double Joint Chorus, the one of Athenian

---

[1] I follow throughout Bergk's text and arrangement of the speakers,
without which all the latter part of the play is very difficult to understand.

CHAP. X Men and Women reconciled in the course of the play,
the other of Lacedæmonian Men with their partners the
Athenian women guard. Each performs an ode, in the
manner of the two main rituals of Greece, Ionic and
Doric. The Athenian ode is the dithyramb of wild self-
abandonment.

> Now for the Chorus, the Graces, the minstrelsy,
> Call upon Artemis, queen of the glade;
> Call on her brother, the lord of festivity,
> Holy and gentle one, mighty to aid.
> Call upon Bacchus, afire with his Mænades;
> Call upon Zeus in the lightning arrayed;
> Call on his Queen, ever blessed, adorable;
> Call on the holy infallible Witnesses,
> Call them to witness the peace and the harmony,
> This which divine Aphrodite has made.
> Allala! Lallala! Lallala! Lallala!
> Whoop for victory, Lallalalæ!
> Evoi, Evoi, Lallala, Lallala!
> Evæ, Evæ, Lallalalæ.

The Lacedæmonian ode maintains the measured self-restraint
of the Doric mode, and is in the dialect which the translator
represents by Scotch ·

> Sae we' se join our blithesome voices,
>   Praisin' Sparta, loud an' lang,
> Sparta wha of auld rejoices
>   In the choral dance an' sang.
> O to watch her bonnie dochters
>   Sport alang Eurotas' waters!
> Winsome feet for ever plyin',
>   Fleet as fillies, wild an' gay,
> Winsome tresses, tossin', flyin',
>   As o' Bacchanals at play.

With such contrasted choral effects, prolonged ad libitum
by torchlight, this operatic play ends.

3 Other Lines of Development illustrated from Aristophanes

Apart from the Chorus, the distinctiveness of Old Attic *Special* Comedy as a branch of drama may be described as two-fold : *lines of de-velopment* its spirit of licence, and its application to public questions. The loss of both these specific peculiarities, by the force of natural development and other influences, gives certain lines of change by which to trace the transition from Old Attic to Roman Comedy. And the commencement of these changes can be illustrated from the plays of Aristophanes, especially the later plays : of which the *Mysteries* is assigned to the year of the oligarchic revolution, the *Frogs* is later by six years, while twenty years from that landmark in time have elapsed before we get the *Women in Parliament* and the *Plutus*.

The wild licence, extravagance, improbability, which dis- *Irregu-* tinguished the Old Attic play, needs special external *larity (by natural de-* surroundings if it is to be maintained ; unsupported from *velopment)* without, the force of natural development will lead steadily *working towards* in the direction of probability and strictness of form. In a *strictness of* general way such development of regularity must have been *form* at work through the lost Middle Attic dramas, since the Roman Comedy in which they merge is entirely regular. But under this head there is a very definite line of tran-sition to be noted, which can be traced within the plays of Aristophanes : this is the rise of the Underplot out of the Incidental Effects.

I have remarked above on the power of Greek Comedy to *Rise of the* break away at any moment from its plot for every variety of *Underplot out of the* comic diversion. The advance from such incidental effects *Incidental* in the direction of the regular underplot may be clearly seen *Effects* by putting together three plays. It will be recollected how in the *Acharnians* the hero suddenly raises his head from the chopping-block from which he is to speak his defence, how he is supposed to go to the house of Euripides, has him wheeled out by the machinery, and in a long scene appeals for the loan of various tragic properties, with the aid of which Old Honesty makes his speech sufficiently pathetic for his critical situation.   This is not so much an incidental effect as an incident complete in itself; it is wholly foreign to the subject of the play, being a piece of literary parody let into a plot of political satire; its disconnectedness is further brought out by the curious way in which the presence of the Chorus is ignored.   In the *Mysteries* there is a similar digression where Euripides and Mnesilochus make a call upon Agathon, in the hopes of securing him to represent their interests at the festival of the women, to which his effeminate figure will, they think, readily gain him admission. They find Agathon in the act of composing, dressed in female attire as realistic stimulus to invention for a play in which the chief personage is a woman.   They hear the Chorus practising behind the scenes, and singing invocations to Artemis and Latona and the Phrygian Graces that kindle light in the worshippers' eyes, until as connoisseurs they are tickled all over with æsthetic thrills.   But it is all in vain that the visitors put to Agathon the object of their call : he bluntly refuses to undertake the dangerous mission.   As compared with the other case this is an incident expanded on a much larger scale ; it is moreover linked in its subject-matter to the rest of the play, the attack upon Euripides the arch-innovator being supported by a briefer fling at a less distinguished poet of the future.   When we come to the

The Frogs *Frogs* we find the important advance from a single incident to that combination of many incidents in one unity which is the definition of a dramatic action.   The relation moreover which binds this series of details to the main part of the play is precisely that subordination which belongs to the under-plot : the main story is of Bacchus undertaking a journey to

Hades, the underplot is made by the farcical behaviour of
the slave Xanthias who accompanies him [1].
The opening scene of the *Frogs* is laid before the temple
of Hercules. Bacchus and Xanthias enter, the former with
the lion's skin of Hercules thrown over his dandy's dress, the
latter riding an ass and carrying his master's baggage on
a pole. Bacchus is making a call on his divine cousin
Hercules. Euripides is just dead, and Bacchus (as head of
the dramatic interest) complains that there are no poets left :
he is resolved to emulate Hercules' great feat of a descent
to Hades, from which he will carry off his poet, as Hercules
carried off Cerberus. Hercules is greatly amused at the
effeminate Wine-god's attempts to mimic his brave appearance, but gives him the advice he asks as to the journey—
the harbours, confectioners, lodging-houses, restaurants,
springs, rooms, cities, hostesses and clean beds : further
directions he may ask from the Band of the Initiated whom
he will meet. Throughout this opening of the main plot
the underplot has been presenting and satirising what was
destined to become one of the stock interests in later
Comedy—the 'cheeky' slave. Xanthias complains of having
all the heavy carrying to do, and not being allowed to relieve
his task by making the regular jokes of the stage, at which
everybody always laughs : he may not say, 'Oh my bundle,'
nor even 'How my back aches.' Old-fashioned quirks are
made, about his not carrying because he is carried (by the
ass), and all through the conversation between Bacchus and
Hercules, Xanthias cries at intervals : 'Nobody notices me !'
The scene changes to the banks of the Styx, and Charon
from the ferry of the dead hails the travellers :

Any passengers for Cease-from-Troubling, or Land of Forgetfulness,
or Nowhere ?
Anybody to visit the Hellhoundians, or the Dogs, or the Bot-
tomless Pit ?

[1] *Acharnians*, 383–480 ; *Mysteries*, 1–265 ; *Frogs*, 1–813.

Bacchus embarks : Xanthias being sent round the land route
(apparently to get rid of the ass). Bacchus is to row, and
after some comic business made out of his floundering
attempts, the boat at last starts to an accompaniment of
a Frog Chorus, chaunting indignation at the disturbance
from the thick waters of the marsh. To a hoarse burden of
Brek-ke-ke-kex-koax-koax, they tell how they too are dear to
Pan and the Muses, and they too have their choral songs —

> As oft on sunny days
>   Into the sedge we spring
>   And reappear to sing
> Our many-diving lays :
> Or flying sudden thunder
>   And darkening skies, we go
>   To weave our dance below
> With sinking, rising, over, under,
> Timed in many whirls and doubles
> To the bursting of the bubbles.

After a good deal of furious striking at these musical frogs
with his oar, Bacchus at last silences them, and, arrived at
the other side, is rejoined by Xanthias. The next phase of
the journey is mainly occupied by the slave playing upon his
effeminate master's terror, amid the darkness and horrors of
the world below. Then, with the sound of flutes, we have
the entrance of the Chorus to the play, the Comus-procession
of the Initiated to which I have so often had to refer. By
directions from these the travellers reach the house of Pluto,
and knock at the gate.

But Bacchus in his project of going Hercules' journey
over again had entirely lost sight of the reputation his precursor might have left behind him in Hades. Accordingly
when Aeacus answers the knock and sees the familiar lion's
skin, he instantly falls foul of the visitor who stole the hound
of hell. While Aeacus has gone to get help, Bacchus makes
his slave exchange clothes with him in order to bear the
punishment in his place. This is scarcely accomplished

when a servant of Proserpine runs in to say how delighted
her mistress is to hear of Hercules' return, and how dainties
are being got ready and girls are to be among the guests.
Then Bacchus protests to Xanthias that he did not mean
seriously the exchange of personalities, and Xanthias has
sulkily to resume the slave. Suddenly they are encountered
by two Innkeepers of Hades, who recognise the villain that
devoured such a big meal and went off without paying the bill.
They go to Cleon, Mayor of Hell; Bacchus has to wheedle
his slave again into assuming the culprit's part. When
Aeacus and the constables come and bind Xanthias, Bacchus laughs at him; whereupon the ready slave takes a new
line, denies the charge of theft, and offers (according to the
legal usage of the time) his slave to be tortured for evidence.
Aeacus, an authority on matters of justice, says this is fair.
To get out of this scrape, Bacchus has to declare his
divinity.

> *Aeacus.* What do you say to that?
> *Xanthias.* Whip him all the harder: if he's a god he won't feel it.

The incident ends in a farcical scourging of both, to see
which cries first, and so proves himself an impostor.

The Chorus of the Initiated have been looking on and
commenting upon these scenes. They proceed to their
parabasis as the master and slave are carried into Pluto's
house, that the divinity may judge which of the two is divine.
At the close of this parabasis Aeacus and Xanthias reappear
on friendly terms: the matter in dispute has been settled,
and as slaves of Pluto and Bacchus the two fraternise. In
the talk between them the subject of the contest between
Euripides and Aeschylus is brought forward, and the play
passes to its main business.

From this sketch it will be clear how Xanthias in the *Frogs* *The Under-*
is the centre of an independent interest, and how, during *plot even in*
the Frogs
this first half of the plot, the interest centering round Xan- *incomplete*
thias is developed on equal terms with that belonging to the

CHAP. X hero of the play. It fails in completeness as an underplot only in the fact that it is entirely dropped at this point, nothing further being heard of the slave, and no provision being made for terminating his connexion with the story. An underplot carried to completeness we do not find before we reach Roman Comedy.

Other multiplication of actions This same play of the *Frogs* is also the best illustration for another line of development. A natural law of literary progress is the expansion of matter and passage from simple to complex ; this applied to Greek drama, with its unity of plot, tends towards the general multiplication of actions, in which the combination of plot and underplot is only one variety. In Tragedy, where the Chorus acted as a force favourable to unity, the tendency towards this multiplication of actions appeared chiefly in the modified form of agglutination, the union of two actions centering around the same personages, the first concluded before the second begins. Something like this agglutination belonged to Comedy from the first, where, as we have seen, there was a generating action leading up to the main plot. Development is seen in the expansion of this generating action : in the *Mysteries* it takes one half of the whole play to get Mnesilochus into the peril from which the main plot schemes to deliver him, and a similar proportion of the *Frogs* is devoted to initiating the grand contest [1]. What is more important than mechanical length is the dramatic completeness with which the generating action in this latter play is treated. In some plays the subordinate element of the drama loses itself in the plot which it initiates : the two slaves who, in the *Knights*, discover the mighty oracle, gradually disappear, and in the climax of the play the Sausage-Seller is the sole hero. But in the *Frogs* the journey which occupies our attention in the first half of the play is brought to as regular a conclusion as

---

[1] *Mysteries*, 1–764 ; *Frogs*, 1–813.

the contest which fills up the latter half. Bacchus descends CHAP. X
to Hades to carry off Euripides: in the final catastrophe he
changes his mind and brings away Aeschylus. Euripides
has challenged Aeschylus to a competition for the place
of poetic honour in Hades: Aeschylus defeats him, and
nominates Sophocles to fill the place during his own absence
with Bacchus on earth. Two distinct actions, completely
worked out, unite in a common climax.

I pass to the second distinguishing peculiarity of Old Attic *Subject-*
Comedy, its application to public questions of political and *matter of Comedy*
literary warfare. This feature was impressed upon Comedy *narrowed*
as a result of a democratic revival, and with the decline of *with the decline of*
democracy it gradually was lost. The Middle Attic dramas *democracy*
—so the historians tell us—divided themselves between
literary and social satire; when Roman Comedy is reached
the literary satire has entirely dropped out, and the matter of
that dramatic species is confined to the social satire which
belongs to Comedy in all ages. The earlier phase of the
transition may be illustrated from the *Mysteries*, which unites
in about equal proportions literary and social satire: its
generating action is dramatised raillery at woman, the main
plot is a parody on Euripides. Development has proceeded
a stage further in the *Women in Parliament*, which is entirely *The Wo-*
devoted to burlesquing socialist theories of communism. *men in Parlia-*
The women, by means of a conspiracy, have obtained the *ment*
rule of their city: they announce a revolution, which their
leader explains in detail to her objecting husband[1]. All
things are henceforth to be in common: land, property,
even women and children.—But, it is asked, how will people
be induced to give their property in to the common stock?
—The answer is, that there will be no object in keeping it
back, when they can get everything for nothing.—But, if there
is no money, how will a defeated suitor pay his damages?—

---

[1] *Women in Parliament*, 584-729.

There will be no law-suits.   But if he has committed some criminal offence?—Deprive him, is the answer, of his share in the Common Meal.   Though, why should he want to steal, when everything is his without stealing?—Subsequent scenes display the working of this social system.   Community of goods is illustrated in its application to two contrasting types of character.   Simple is seen bringing out of his house all the articles of his moveable property, arranging them in processional order: he is preparing to transfer them, as in duty bound, to the common stock.   Smart comes upon him, and is wholly unable to understand his neighbour's zeal in the duties of citizenship.

> Do you think any man with a head on his shoulders will give up his property?   It is unconstitutional.   Man's whole duty is summed up in receiving what is given.   And the same with the gods: the statues before which we pray, have they not the hollow of the hand turned upward as if to accept, not downward as if they meant to bestow?

After a long discussion Simple still refuses to be moved from his purpose.   Just as he is starting with his goods for the town hall, a proclamation is heard summoning the citizens to the Common Meal.   The zeal now passes from Simple to Smart: the latter is active in fulfilling this part of citizenship, while Simple has scruples because he has not yet taken the preliminary step of handing over his property. Smart of course is in the same position.

> *Simple.* And you mean to go to the Meal all the same?
> *Smart.* What is one to do?   An honest man must do all that in him lies to serve his country.

Another scene exhibits in operation the principle of community in women.   Everybody may love everybody else, and the old and ugly are to have the prior right.   The scene represents a young and an old woman contending for a handsome young man: two more old women come as allies to their comrade, carry off the young man, and then fight over him with one another.   The conclusion is a pro-

cession to the Common Meal in which the audience are CHAP. X
invited to join [1].

The spirit of licence and application to politics came into *Aristo-*
Old Attic Comedy, not naturally, but as a result of a *cratic*
Comedy as
distinct disturbing influence; it is necessary to point out *a new dis-*
that when this passed away a new disturbing influence ap- *turbing in-*
fluence :
peared in its place. Democracy yielded at Athens to
aristocracy, and aristocracy, we have seen, had its own type
of comedy. Accordingly from the time of Aristophanes the
Sicilian model—which even under the democratic régime
had been represented by one Athenian poet, Crates—came
to the front; and one particular feature of Sicilian Comedy,
the use of mythology as a means of satire, was, historians *especially*
say, a distinction of the lost Middle Attic comedies. This *Mythologi-*
cal Satire
phase of the transition is illustrated in the last play of
Aristophanes, which is a social satire conveyed in a mythic
story.

The *Plutus* is a dramatised allegory of money viewed *The Plutus*
from various [2] standpoints, and it is made to centre round
Plutus, mythical god of wealth. The hero, accompanied by
his slave, follows a blind old man whom, by advice of an
oracle, they seek to secure. After some enquiries the old
man admits himself to be no other than the god of wealth.
After they have got over the sensation produced by the
announcement the master and slave pursue their enquiries.
They remark on the squalor of the god, and he explains
this as due to a certain miser's house in which he has
resided. His blindness, Plutus says, was the act of Jupiter,
who feared he might confine his favours to the good, as
a result of which the gods would lose the uncertainty of
fortune which leads mankind to prayers and offerings. The
hero proposes to open the god's eyes : Plutus is terrified at
the thought of Jupiter's anger, and is reassured only with

---

[1] *Women in Parl.*, 730-876, 877-1111.
[2] See above, page 327, note.

CHAP. X   a difficulty that suggests the timidity of capital.   When at
last he is convinced that he himself, and not the gods, is
the real source of all power, Plutus gives himself up to his
human captors.

When the Chorus of Neighbours has been summoned to
rejoice, and another neighbour of the hero has—in a scene
already quoted—illustrated the suspicions which a sudden
accession of wealth will arouse in a man's friends and
gossips, a diversion is effected which brings out one of the
most important phases in the allegory.   A hideous hag
bursts in, and reproaches the hero with doing a hasty and
unholy deed in seeking to open the blind god's eyes.   This
is Poverty, and she wages a long contest with the hero.
His case is that Plutus, when once his eyes are opened,
must reverse the inequalities of society, and bestow fortune
on the good.

> Here is a rogue, who is rolling in riches
>   robbed from his fellows to feather his nest ;
> There are the honest, who never knew fortune,
>   never from hunger or scantiness free,
> All through a life of toil unending,
>   desperate Poverty, stable with thee.

Poverty calls the hero a dotard for not perceiving that with
the loss of such inequalities will cease the motive of all
enterprise.

> Plutus will see and divide himself equally ;
>   Science and Art will fall into decay.
> Who will be smith ? or shipwright ? or shoemaker ?
>   who will tan leather ? or puddle in clay ?
> Who will look after the ploughing and reaping !
>   washing of linen ! or setting a stitch ?
> Who is to care for laborious arts, when
>   all may be idle, as all will be rich ?
>
> *Hero.*   Truce to your list, and the nonsense you're talking !
>   all that we want our slaves will supply.
> *Poverty.* Aye,—but who will supply you the article, slaves ?
> *Hero.*   Slaves !—have we not money to buy ?

Poverty. Who is to sell them, when money's an article
    not in demand?
Hero.   Some lucre-led hound,
Merchant in man-flesh from Thessaly coming;
    where, as we know, man-stealers abound.
Poverty. Softly! but, as you order the world, there
    never will be a man-stealer at all:
Who that is rich will encounter the risks that
    must to the share of a kidnapper fall?

Poverty presses her claim to be the origin of all luxuries :

    I, like a sharp tyrannical mistress,
        ever sit by the artificer's side
    Threatening death, or making him work for a
        call from within that will not be denied.

The contest is kept up with spirit on both sides, until, neither party convincing the other, Poverty is driven off.

After scenes devoted to the opening of Plutus's eyes in the temple of Aesculapius, and the rejoicings at this event, we get to the effects upon society of the new distribution of wealth. In one scene a Just Man arrives for the purpose of offering thanksgiving to Plutus at his deliverance from life-long poverty, the result of helping ungrateful friends. He brings his thread-bare cloak and clouted shoes to dedicate them before the god. To him then enters an Informer, in distress that his trade no longer pays, and he is being ruined. The usual badgering of this unpopular occupation follows. The Informer tries to represent himself as a pillar of the state, whose sole object is to uphold the laws and hinder wrong-doing.

Hero. Has not the constitution appointed magistrates for this express purpose?
Informer. But who is to act as accuser?
Hero. The constitution provides—whoever pleases.
Informer. That means me. The burden of the constitution rests on my shoulders.
Hero. Alas, poor constitution!

In the end the Informer is compelled to change clothes

with the Just Man and then driven off. In another scene an Old Woman complains of a youth, poor but wondrous fair, who but a little while ago loved her, and loaded her with caresses: but now for some reason has suddenly deserted her. The reason is apparent as the youth enters, crowned with chaplets and accompanied by a band of torchlight revellers, manifestly one who has prospered by the new dispensation.

The far-reaching effect of the social revolution is brought out when Hermes appears, complaining that his office of usher to heaven is fast becoming worthless, since men no longer look to the gods for their prosperity. He proposes to take service with Plutus : and goes through the list of his divine offices. He will be their Turnkey.—But they never lock their doors.—Then their Chief Merchant.—But with their fill of riches they have no need to drive bargains.— Then let him be made Trickster-General.—But men are going in for innocence.—At least he can be Marshal of the Way.—No : the god with his opened eyes can see to walk alone.—So Hermes has to enlist as Pudding-washer. A climax is reached when last of all comes the Priest of Jupiter himself: the temples are deserted, and his occupation is gone. He too enlists in the service of Plutus, and a farcical procession of triumph closes the play.

Struggle between comic form and satiric application   These are the lines of development which may be traced as commencing in the plays of Aristophanes, and proceeding through the lost Middle Attic Comedy to culminate in the drama of Rome. There is one more phase of Transitional Comedy, from a modern stand-point the most important of all, which hardly admits of illustration from Aristophanes. This depends upon the varying balance between dramatic form and satiric application. In all Greek Comedy, as we know it, the comedy is the means, and satire is the end. But in proportion as the satire became more general it was necessarily weakened ; satire implies hostility, and when the foibles attacked are those common to human nature in general they cease to excite hostility.   Accordingly in time the comic effect became the end, and satire sank into one amongst many modes of comedy.   But to see with any clearness this emergence of pure Comedy out of satire we must wait for the drama of Rome.

XI

ROMAN COMEDY

XI

1 Roman Comedy as a Dramatic Species

THE next and final stage of the Ancient Ďrama has come
down to us in the form of Roman Comedy. It has already
been pointed out that this was wholly founded on the lost
New Attic Comedy, of which the great master was Menander [1]. Upon the relation between Roman Comedy and its
Greek original considerable light is thrown by the prologues
to the Latin plays, especially in the case of Terence, who has
continually to defend himself against the malicious criticism
of a rival. The prologues generally give the name, and often
the author, of the Greek play, adding the new name under
which the Roman poet has ' made his barbarian rendering ' [2];
this is done with a regularity which suggests that the audience
expected such use of foreign material, and indeed in one
play the Greek author's name is omitted on the ground that
most of the spectators will be aware of it [3]. The scene of
the story is laid in Greece, usually at Athens.

> 'Tis the way
> With poets in their comedies to feign
> The business passed at Athens, so that you
> May think it the more Grecian.—For our play
> I'll not pretend the incidents to happen
> Where they do not: the argument is Grecian,
> And yet it is not Attic, but Sicilian [4].

So little attempt is there to give a Roman colouring to the
incidents that the spectators are sometimes referred to as

[1] Other names are Philemon, Apollodorus, Diphilus, Demophilus.
[2] *Vortit barbare* : it must not be assumed that this means to translate.
[3] The *Self-Tormentor* of Terence.
[4] Prologue to the *Menæchmei* of Plautus.

CHAP. XI 'barbarians.' Occasionally apology is made for some exceptional peculiarity of Greek manners, as where the slave Stichus, granted a wine-cask with which to celebrate his master's return, bids the spectators feel no surprise at slaves having their parties and sweethearts and bottle, for such *Not trans-* customs are allowable at Athens [1]. Yet it must not be *lation :* supposed that the Roman poets merely translated individual Greek plays. Too literal adaptation is made by Terence a charge against his adversary, who is described as giving the close rendering that is loose writing, and turns good Greek into bad Latin : yet even this cannot have been continuous translation, since Lucius Lavinius is further charged with a fault of arrangement—the clumsiness of making a defendant *but adapta-* plead before the charge has been stated [2]. It is clear that *tion* the Latin authors exercised a certain amount of selection in their use of Greek materials. We hear of omissions : the *Brothers* of Terence is described as being from a Greek original which had also been translated by Plautus ;—

> In the beginning of the Grecian play
> There is a youth, who rends a girl perforce
> From a slave-merchant : and this incident,
> Untouched by Plautus, rendered word for word,
> Has our bard interwoven with his *Brothers*.

A more important matter is the weaving together of two Greek plays for the purpose of getting a more complex Latin plot.

> Menander wrote the Andrian and Perinthian :
> Know one, and you know both ; in argument
> Less different than in sentiment and style.
> What suited with the Andrian he confesses
> From the Perinthian he transferred, and used
> For his : and this it is these slanderers blame,
> Proving by deep and learned disputation,
> That fables should not be compounded thus.
> Troth ! all their knowledge is they nothing know :
> Who, blaming him, blame Naevius, Plautus, Ennius,

---

[1] *Stichus*, 446.   [2] Prologue to the *Eunuch* of Terence.

> Whose great example is his precedent, CHAP. XI
> Whose negligence he'd wish to emulate
> Rather than their dark diligence[1].

All this tends to show that Roman Comedy stood to the New Attic Comedy in the same general relation in which Latin literature as a whole stood to the literature of Greece. Just as in philosophy Cicero shows no ambition to be an independent thinker, but declares it his purpose to demonstrate that the Latin language is capable of expressing Greek dialectics, so the comic poets of Rome merely endeavoured to give their countrymen, in their own language, what was the acted drama of the educated classes throughout Greece. What differences there were between *The two* Roman and New Attic Comedy were differences affecting *form one dramatic* authorship and the credit of individual poets: in literary *species* development the two form one dramatic species.

The same principle applies to the course of Roman Comedy viewed by itself. The names of eleven dramatists[2] have been preserved: the works of only two amongst them have come down to us. The earliest comic poet of Rome followed Menander by about half a century: in another half century we come to Plautus, and Terence is a quarter of a century later still. But the close following of the Greek original gives a unity to Latin drama, irrespective of the period over which its history may be spread. It is easy to

---

[1] Prologue to the *Andria* of Terence. It would seem that such combination of Greek plays was rather the rule than the exception, since the prologue to the *Self-Tormentor* makes a point of its being 'an entire play from an entire Greek source.' [Parry's explanation of *integra* as *fresh* (the meaning being that the Greek play had never before been translated) seems to me very difficult to accept : such a sense could not apply to both the uses of the word—*ex integra Graeca integram comoediam*. Moreover *novam* is used for a fresh play in *Phormio*, 25.]

[2] Livius Andronicus, Naevius, Ennius, Plautus, Pacuvius, Caecilius, Porcius Licinius, Terence and his adversary Lucius Lavinius, Accius, Afranius.

point out characteristic differences between Plautus and Terence; but these amount to no more than may safely be assigned to the genius of the individual poet, and offer nothing that suggests any distinct process of literary development.

2 The Trinummus of Plautus

Stage arrange-ments

The Roman stage, though not a permanent erection but only a temporary platform, was even more limited in its conventionalities than the stage of the Athenian theatre. It was not furnished with machinery or movable scenery, but represented a fixed exterior—some street into which houses or other public buildings opened: and to this limited scene all the business of every play had to be adapted. One characteristic the Roman stage shared with the Greek—that of size, a frontage of as much as 180 feet being claimed for it. This accounts for the frequency with which the scenes present long wanderings, slaves running about, and keep persons who enter or make exit a considerable time in view [1].

Scene and Personages

Plautus's play *The Fee of Three Pieces (Trinummus)* has its scene laid at Athens in the street adjoining the house of Charmides, one of its leading personages. This Charmides is absent on a mercantile expedition during the greater part of the play: his family includes a daughter and a spendthrift son Lesbonicus, and in close connexion with them is a friend, Callicles, whom the merchant, before departing, had begged to exercise a general superintendence over his heedless son's affairs. This family is by the plot of the play to

---

[1] It may be well to explain that the doors of these houses opened outwards, persons coming into the street from within being supposed to give a warning knock; often in comic scenes a personage thus entering holds a long colloquy first with those inside the house.

be brought into connexion with another, consisting of an
old gentleman, Philto, and his son Lysiteles.

The Roman comedies have no chorus, and are cast in the familiar modern form of five separate acts ; there is no dramatic provision made for filling up the intervals between these acts, though, as a fact, performances of music were used for this purpose. The prologue to the *Trinummus* is *Prologue* allegorical : it is spoken by Luxury, who appears conducting her daughter Poverty to the house of Charmides. She explains to the audience :

> There is a certain youth dwells in this house,
> Who by my aid has squandered his estate.
> Since then for my support there's nothing left,
> My daughter I'm here giving him to live with.

After the usual explanation as to the Greek source of the play, Luxury disappears with her daughter into the house, and leaves the scene free for the opening of the play.

The friend who is supposed to watch over the merchant's *Act I* interests in his absence has himself a confidential friend, Megaronides. The latter is the first personage to appear before us ; he is on his way to make a call upon Callicles, and soliloquises upon the painful duty he feels of reproaching his comrade with declension from his old uprightness. Callicles meets him, and in the small talk with which their conversation opens we have a stock topic of Roman wit— abuse of wives.

> *Meg.*　　　　　　　Save you, Callicles:
> 　　How do you do? how have you done?
> *Cal.*　　　　　　　　　　　So, so.
> *Meg.* Your wife how fares she?
> *Cal.*　　　　　　　　　Better than I wish.
> *Meg.* Troth, I am glad to hear she's pure and hearty.
> *Cal.* You're glad to hear what sorrows me.
> *Meg.*　　　　　　　　　　　I wish
> 　　The same to all my friends as to myself.
> *Cal.* But hark ye,—how is your good dame?

Meg.   Immortal:
　　Lives and is like to live.
Cal.   A happy hearing!
　　Pray heav'n, that she may last to outlive you.
Meg. If she were yours, faith, I should wish the same.
Cal. Say, shall we make a swop? I take your wife,
　　You mine? I warrant you, you would not get
　　The better in the bargain.
Meg.   Nor would you
　　Surprise me unawares.
Cal.   Nay, but in troth
　　You would not even know what you're about.
Meg. Keep what you've got. The evil that we know
　　Is best. To venture on an untried ill,
　　Would puzzle all my knowledge how to act.

Megaronides suddenly dismisses jesting, and begins to talk
severely about the change in his friend's character. He would
fain have him free from blame and even suspicion.

Cal. Both cannot be.
Meg.   For why?
Cal.   Is that a question?
　　Myself of my own bosom keep the key,
　　To shut out misdemeanour; but suspicion
　　Is harboured in another.

Conjured by Callicles as a close friend to say what is the drift
of these suspicions, Megaronides details the opinion which
the town is beginning to have of him—how he is nick-named
Gripe-all, Vulture, and the like : and particularly how people
talk about his behaviour to his absent friend Charmides.
This Charmides is understood to have committed the general
welfare of his family and affairs to Callicles, his own son
being a fast youth, not to be trusted with money : now,
instead of seeking to restrain the young man, people say
Callicles is abetting his extravagances, and has actually, when
the scapegrace sought to raise money by selling his father's
house, aided his plans by himself becoming the buyer. To
the astonishment of Megaronides, Callicles admits that this
rumour is perfectly true; he then, with great caution and

secrecy, lets out the whole story. Charmides, on leaving Chap. XI
Athens, committed to him a family secret, that a huge
treasure was buried in the house, of which the father dared
not let the son have any knowledge lest in his absence he
should appropriate it. Now Callicles learned all of a sudden
that Lesbonicus was going to sell the house : alarmed lest the
treasure should pass out of their hands altogether, he saw
no better device than for himself to purchase the house, and
keep it in trust for the father's return, or for the daughter's
marriage portion. Megaronides is confounded at the mistake
he has made, and, when the two friends have amicably parted,
inveighs against the gossip of busybodies who had led him
astray :

> Everything
> They will pretend to know, yet nothing know.
> They'll dive into your breast, and learn your thoughts,
> Present and future : nay, they can discover
> What the king whispered in her highness's ear,
> And tell what passed in Juno's chat with Jove.

With the exit of Megaronides the first act concludes. The *Act II*
second introduces us to the family of Philto. Both father
and son in this family are distinguished by a strongly marked
characteristic—the strain of moralising which they carry
through all the scenes in which they appear. This tendency
to indulge in moral reflections, especially in lengthened
soliloquies, is a great note of Roman Comedy. It is in part
a survival from the Chorus, which had by now passed out
of the comic drama. The highly conventional tone which
distinguished the musings of the tragic Chorus appears also
in these moral declamations of Comedy. And often, as in the
present case, such reflections are expressed in highly lyric *Lyric*
style—lyric, both in the choice of metres [1] far removed from *scenes*
blank verse, and in the continual variation of the metres
within the compass of a few lines.

---

[1] Especially those founded on the *Cretic* foot [a short between two
longs : – ◡ –] and the *bacchiac* foot [a short followed by two longs : ◡ – –].

CHAP. XI   Lysiteles is presented soliloquising on life with its per-
——   plexing alternatives.

> Unnumbered the cares that my heart is revolving,
> Unmeasured the trouble I bear while I ponder;
> Myself with myself is afflicted and wasted,
> My thoughts are a master that cruelly drives me:
> Yet still comes no answer, no end to my query—
> To which life of two shall my years be devoted,
> To love, or to business? to which cause give verdict
>   And firmly pursue it?

ᴜ –   The matter never will conclude: unless—the thought just strikes
>   me—
> I bring the parties face to face, myself both bar and jury.
– ᴜ –   So I'll do. So be it. First in order
ᴜ –   I'll speak for the pursuit of love, and see what recommends it.
– ᴜ   Love has none but willing subjects: in his nets none other snares
> But the loving: these he aims at, these pursues, their substance
>   wastes.
> Smooth-spoken, sharp-finger'd, a liar, a sweet-tooth,
> A robber, a bane to the life of seclusion,
>   A hunter of secrets.

– ᴜ   Let a lover but be stricken with the kiss of her he loves,
> In a trice all he has creeps away, melts away.
> 'Give me this, honey dear, by our love, do not fail':—
> And the goose must reply, 'Heart of mine, be it so:
> Also that, also more, what you wish shall be given.'
>   Thus a victim bound she strikes:
>   Begs for more, unsatisfied.

Lysiteles details the endless waste of money that such a life
of pleasure involves, and how moments of bitterness and
loss of higher joys counterbalance its sweet carousings.
The case goes against love.

> Begone, Love, the word of divorcement is spoken:
> Love to me never more be a lover;
> Seek the sad wights who still must obey thee,
> Made thy slaves by too willing obedience.
> It is fixed: I am all for what profits,
> Never mind what the toil be of seeking.
> This the prize is of good men's endeavour—
> Solid gain, credit high, posts of honour:
> This the grace, this the glory of living.
> Be it mine: other life is but hollow.

Philto enters looking for his son : his opening words seem
attracted to the general rhythm of what has preceded.

Philto. Where on earth has the man found his way from the   _ .. _
    house ?
Lysit. I'm here, sir : command me : I'll not be found backward :   ᴗ _ _
    In me is no skulking, no fear of your presence.
Philto. That will be like the rest of your dutiful life,
    If the son to the sire never fails in respect.

The father, without further preface, plunges into lyric denunciation of modern degeneracy :

Upsetting all the good old ways, an evil, grasping, greedy crew,   ᴗ _
They hold the sacred as profane ; public or private, all is one.

Night and day Philto is tormented with thinking on the
age of villainy into which his years have been prolonged,
from which he beseeches his son to hold himself aloof :

I am weary of all these new fashions,
All that goodness adorns overthrowing.
If but these my injunctions you follow,
Words of wisdom will sink in your bosom.

The son gives in his adhesion to his father's views : it will
be noticed that, having a purpose to lead the conversation
in a particular direction, Lysiteles abandons lyrics for a set
rhythm which is maintained to the end of the scene.

Lysit. From my earliest youth, my father, to this present age have I   _ ᴗ
    Bound myself a duteous bondsman laws by you laid down to
    heed :
    Free I ranked myself in spirit, but, where your command
    came in,
    Duty have I ever deemed it will of mine to yours to bind.

The father continues his lecture, and depicts youth fighting
its own desires :

Routed by desire, he's done for : slave to lust, no freeman he,
If desire he routs, then lives he, conqueror of conquerors.

The son repeats his claim to have lived an obedient and
innocent life.   The father seems to resent such a claim : if

his son has done well, the gain is his, not his father's for whom life is wellnigh over.

> Cover o'er just deeds with just deeds, tile-like, till no rain come through.
> Only he is good whose goodness ever keeps him penitent.

For this very reason, the son replies, he wishes to ask his father's assistance in doing a kindness to a friend in trouble. But the mention of trouble sets the father off on a fresh train of moralising, and he shows the danger of so helping the bad as to feed their distemper. Gnomic verses garnish the dialogue. When Lysiteles speaks of being ashamed to desert a comrade in his adversity, Philto replies :

> He that shames to sin has gained o'er sinner shamed by all that shame.

But, urges the son, they are rich enough and to spare.

> *Philto.* From however much however little take : is't more or less?

Gnome answers gnome : Lysiteles quotes the saying to the churlish citizen :

> All you have may you be lacking : what you now are free from, have :
> You who neither give to others, nor for your own profit save.

When Philto hears who the friend is that his son wishes to relieve—the spendthrift Lesbonicus—the father becomes severe again, and will not listen to the plea that Lesbonicus has been unfortunate,

> For, by heaven, the wise man's fortune only by himself is shaped.

Lysiteles urges that time is required to mature such wisdom.

> *Philto.* Length of years is but the relish : wisdom is the food of life.

At last Lysiteles is allowed to explain that he wishes, not to give his friend anything, but to receive from him his sister in

marriage without a dowry. After further discussion, Philto
is brought not only to give his consent, but also himself to
undertake the task of making overtures to Lesbonicus.
When his son has left him (and the scene has dropped to
blank verse), Philto indulges in one more reflection, that—
unless in a matter particularly affecting himself—a father is
a fool who thwarts a son's wishes :

> Plagues his own soul, nor is the better for it;
> And stirring up a storm that's out of season,
> Makes the hoar winter of old age more sharp.

It is a convention of the Roman stage—a result of its
inability to present the interior of houses—that when a
personage in a play goes to make a call upon another, this
other is usually brought to meet him accidentally in the
street on his way. So in the present case Philto's soliloquy
is interrupted by the approach of the very man to whom he
has undertaken a mission. Lesbonicus is seen coming
up the street, attended by his slave Stasimus. The master
is angry at hearing that all the money so lately received for
the sale of the house is already gone ; he demands what
has been done with it.

> *Stas.* Eaten and drunk, and washed away in baths;
> Cooks, butchers, poulterers, fishmongers, confectioners,
> Perfumers, have devoured it;—gone as soon
> As a grain of corn thrown to an ant.

With the permitted pertness which ancient Comedy loved
to introduce into its pictures of slave life Stasimus adds
that his master must not forget to allow for his own pilfer-
ings, and Lesbonicus admits that that will be a heavy item.
Philto discovers himself, and after general courtesies makes
his proposal. While the slave can hardly keep himself
quiet at the idea of so grand a match, Lesbonicus treats it
as a mockery : he is no longer on a footing of social equality
with Philto's family.

C C 2

Philto.   What of that?
> If you were present at a public feast,
> And haply some great man were placed beside you,
> Of the choice cates served up in heaps before him
> Would you not taste, but at the table rather
> Sit dinnerless, because he neighboured you?

Lesb. Sure I should eat, if he forbade me not.

Stas. And I, even if he did;—so cram myself
> I'd stuff out both my cheeks: I'd seize upon
> The daintiest bits before him, nor give way to him
> In matters that concerned my very being.
> At table no one should be shy or mannerly,
> Where all things are at stake, divine and human.

Philto. Faith, what you say is right.

Stas.   I'll tell you fairly.
> Your great man if I meet, I make way for him,
> Give him the wall, show him respect, but where
> The belly is concern'd, I will not yield
> An inch,—unless he box me into breeding.

The opportunity for moralising is not lost by Philto. He urges that where perfection is unattainable the policy yet remains of nearness to perfection.

>   What are riches?—
> The gods alone are rich: to them alone
> Is wealth and pow'r: but we poor mortal men,
> When that the soul, which is the salt of life
> Keeping our bodies from corruption, leaves us,
> At Acheron shall be counted all alike,
> The beggar and the wealthiest.

Lesbonicus, moved by this persistent kindness, at last bethinks him of a little farm he has, the only bit of his ancestral estate now left to him : he insists upon making this his sister's dowry. In the utmost alarm the slave protests against parting with this land—their nurse that supports and feeds them. Chidden by Lesbonicus for interfering, Stasimus sees nothing but ruin before him unless he can manage to make an impression upon Philto. He takes him aside, with the air of confiding to him an important secret.

By gods and men
I do conjure you, let not this same farm
Come into your possession, or your son's,
The reason will I tell.

Philto.   I fain would hear it.

Stas. First, then, whene'er the land is ploughed, the oxen
Ev'ry fifth furrow drop down dead.

Philto.   Fye on it !

Stas. A passage down to Acheron's in our field ;
The grapes grow mouldy as they hang, before
They can be gathered.

Lesbonicus is surprised at the length of this whispered
colloquy, but supposes his faithful rogue is taking the task
of persuading Philto off his shoulders.

Stas.   Hear what follows.
When that the harvest promises most fair,
They gather in thrice less than what was sown.

Philto. Nay !—then methinks it were a proper place
For men to sow their wild oats, where they would not
Spring up.

Stas.   There never was a person yet,
That ever owned this farm, but his affairs
Did turn to bad :—some ran away, some died,
Some hang'd themselves. Why, there's my master, now,
To what sad straits is he reduced !

Philto.   O keep me
Far from this farm !

Stas.   You'd have more cause to say so,
Were you to hear the whole. There's not a tree,
But has been blasted with the lightning ; more—
The hogs are eat up with the mange ; the sheep
Pine with the rot, all scabby as this hand :
And no man can live there six months together,
No, not a Syrian, though they are most hardy,
The influenza is to all so fatal.

Philto. I do believe it true : but the Campanians
The Syrians far outgo in hardiness.—
This farm is a fit spot, as you've described it,
Wherein to place bad men, and, as they tell us
That in those islands still ' The Fortunate '
Assemble the upright and the virtuous livers,
So should the wicked here be thrust together

Philto has been as ready to be deceived as Stasimus to deceive him, and so, when the slave adds that his master is seeking some one simple enough to take the dangerous possession off his hands, declares he will have none of it. Returning to Lesbonicus, Philto makes the betrothal a formal agreement, adding that this business of the farm must be settled between Lesbonicus and the bridegroom. The scene ends with the slave pressing his master to follow up such a chance instantly.

Act III Stasimus has been sent to announce the betrothal to the lady concerned. On his way he meets her guardian Callicles, and at the opening of the third act he is telling Callicles the news : the dialogue is in the same rhythm in which the first idea of the marriage was opened to Philto. Callicles goes off wondering how the girl can have secured so good a match without dower.—Then the slave sees his master and Lysiteles disputing warmly, evidently about this vexed question of the farm, in which Stasimus feels so keen a personal interest that he stands aside and listens. This dispute is long and earnest, bringing out the contrast of character between the two friends. Lesbonicus is presented as a spendthrift who is notwithstanding stubborn in his notions of family honour, though the assertion of it be at the cost of his own ruin. Lysiteles, with his tendency to moralising, reads lectures to his companion upon his dissipated life, pressing upon him not to throw away this last chance of making a fresh start. Lesbonicus admits everything: how he has dissipated his inheritance and tarnished the family name, and has no excuse but that he has been subdued by love and idleness. Lysiteles will not give up the cause, though grieved that his friend has so little shame :

> Once for all, unless you heed me, this occasion unimproved,
> You will lie in your own shadow, hid from light of honour's sun.

He knows the better nature of Lesbonicus; and he has CHAP. XI
himself experienced the power of love :

> Like a stone from warlike engine, swiftest speed has passion's
> flight :
> Passion's ways are ever wayward, passion is all frowardness :
> Disinclined to what is offered, coveting what is withheld,
> Made by scarcity desirous, careless when abundance comes.

Lesbonicus lightly turns off his friend's warnings, but sticks
to his point, that he cannot, after wasting the family property
for his own enjoyments, let his sister go without her natural
dowry, a mistress rather than a wife :

> Let me not by loss of honour seek relief from loss of wealth.

Lysiteles sees what all this means. His friend will insist on
giving up this the last bit of property left him and the only
hope for recovering his losses, and then, as soon as the
marriage is over, he will fly from his native land, a needy
adventurer in the wars. At this—the very fear that has
been troubling him all along—the concealed Stasimus can
restrain himself no longer. ' Bravo ! ' he cries to Lysiteles,
' encore ! you've won the prize '—and follows up the attack
upon Lesbonicus, who promptly snubs him.

> *Lesb.* What brings here your meddling chatter ?
> *Stas.*   What—shall take it back again.

Stasimus retires into the background, and the conversation
at last ends by Lysiteles insisting that there shall be no
marriage portion, and that Lesbonicus shall use his purse as
his own, or there must be an end of their friendship. They
part, and the slave gives himself up to despair, with no
prospect before him but the arduous life of a soldier's
attendant, as his master attaches himself to the army of
some prince or other.

> Verily to highest standard will he rise—of swift retreat !
> Glorious spoils will there be taken—where a foe my master fronts !
> So shall I myself, once furnished with my quiver and my bow,
> Helmet on my head, be snatching—sweetest slumber in my tent.

Exit Stasimus. Enter Megaronides and Callicles. They are consulting (in blank verse) upon the entirely new turn given to the affairs of the family in which they are interested by this matter of the betrothal. Callicles cannot let his friend's daughter be married like a pauper : he could easily get money enough for the dowry out of the buried treasure, but under what pretext can he present it to the girl, without exciting suspicion ? At last Megaronides hits upon a brilliant idea. Let them get one of the professional Sharpers that are ready to be hired for any purpose of conspiracy ; and let him—for a consideration—pretend that he has come from Charmides who remains abroad, bringing to Callicles money with which to dower his daughter should she marry. Difficulties of detail, such as forging the letter, and accounting for the absence of the signet-ring which would naturally accompany it, they rapidly arrange, and proceed to the execution of the scheme.

Act IV   This concludes the third act : the fourth opens with the arrival of the person whose absence was the foundation of the whole intrigue. Charmides has just landed from his voyage, and is heard offering thanks to the gods for his safety. He speaks in a rhythm which is an elongated variation of that in which the more important scenes of the play have been cast.

> Him who rules with mighty ruling briny ocean, Jove's own brother,
> Nereus too, and thee Portumnus, glad I praise : I thank the salt
> waves,
> You that had me in your power, me and mine, my life and riches,
> That from out your dread dominions thus far safe have brought me
> homeward.
> And to thee before all others, Neptune, is my spirit grateful,
> For, while men have called thee cruel, stern of mood, unsatiated,
> Measureless in might and foulness, I thy kindly aid have tasted.
> Merciful and calm I found thee, all that heart could wish of ocean.
> This fair word of thee hath uttered human voice in human hearing,
> How thou lov'st to spare the poor man, mulct the rich, and break
> their spirit ;

Fare thee well: I praise thy justice worthy gods, that men so rankest,
To the poor thy hand restraining, letting it on pride fall heavy.
Faithful thou, whom men call faithless. Surely, but for thy pro-
    tection
Foully had thy underworkers torn in pieces, widely scattering,
Wretched me and my belongings, broadcast o'er the sky-blue
    meadows:
Lo, like hungry hounds the whirlwinds round about the ship were
    circling,
Floods above us, waves beneath us, howling gales on mainmast
    swooping,
Toppling yards and canvas splitting: then a gracious calm was
    sent us.
Here we part: henceforth to leisure am I given: enough is
    gathered;
Cares enough have I encountered, seeking for my son a fortune.

His meditation are interrupted by the approach of the
hired Sharper, who enters peering up and down the street,
dressed in a queer imitation of foreign costume, especially a
broad hat, which makes Charmides refer the stranger to the
mushroom genus.   The Sharper is heard naming the day as
the Feast of the Three Pieces, the price of his art.

    Here am I, from Seleucia just arrived[1],
    Arabia, Asia, Macedon,—which I never
    Saw with my eyes, nor ever once set foot on.
    Behold, what troubles will not poverty
    Bring on a needy wretch!

Charmides does not like the man's face, and, when he perceives him looking hard at his own house door, thinks it time
to make enquiry.   He finds that the man is actually seeking
his son Lesbonicus, and pours out a flood of questions as to
his name and business, which the Sharper coolly proposes to
take in regular order.

    Sharper. Should you set out before the day began
        With the first part and foremost of my name,
        The night would go to bed ere you had reach'd
        The hindmost of it.

  [1] These quotations are from Bonnell Thornton's blank verse translation:
the scene in the original is trochaic.

Charm.   He had need of torches
    And of provisions, whoso undertakes
    To journey through it.
Sharper.   I've another name, though,
    A tiny one, no bigger than a hogshead.
Charm.   This is a rogue in grain!

As to his business, the Sharper tells Charmides, much to his
astonishment, that he is the bearer of letters from the father
of Lesbonicus to his son and Callicles.   Charmides thinks
he has caught a cheat in the very act of cheating, and prepares to have rare fun with him in pushing his enquiries as
to the person from whom the letters come.

Charm. What sort of man?
Sharper.   He's taller than yourself
    By half a foot.
Charm. (*aside*).   Faith, he has gravell'd me,
    To find that I was taller when away
    Than now I'm here.

Of course the Sharper knows the man in question, and was
his messmate; but, asked his name, finds to his dismay
that his memory has played him a trick, and the name is
clean forgotten.   In vain he evades the question: he is
pressed with a string of queries and tantalising suggestions,
before the name 'Charmides' is tried.—

Sharper.   That's it.   The gods confound him!
Charm. 'Tis fitter you should bless a friend than curse him.
Sharper. A worthless fellow, to have lain perdue thus
    Within my lips and teeth.
Charm.   You should not speak
    Ill of an absent friend.
Sharper.   Why did the rogue
    Then hide him from me?
Charm.   He had answer'd, had you
    But called him by his name.

In the course of further questionings the Sharper, whose rôle
is boldness, volunteers an account of his wonderful travels:
how they came first to Araby in Pontus.—

Charm. Is Araby in Pontus?
Sharper.   Yes, it is;
  But not that Araby, where frankincense
  Is grown, but where sweet-marjoram and wormwood.
Charm. (aside). 'Tis the completest knave!

When the story begins to tell of sailing in a small cock-boat
up the river that rises out from heaven itself, and of finding
Jove out of town, it becomes too much for Charmides'
patience. The Sharper coolly returns to his first enquiry—
where Lesbonicus lives. The father thinks it will be the
cream of the joke if he can get from this Sharper the three
thousand Philippeans with which, as well as the letters, he
claims to have been trusted.

Charm.   You received them, did you,
  Of Charmides himself?
Sharper.   It had been wondrous
  Had I received them of his grandsire, truly,
  Or his great-grandsire, who are dead.
Charm.   Young man,
  Prithee give me the gold.
Sharper.   Give you what gold?
Charm. That which you own'd you did receive of me.
Sharper. Received of you?
Charm.   I say it.
Sharper.   Who are you?
Charm. Who gave to you the thousand pieces:—I
  Am Charmides.

But the Sharper can now turn the balance of suspicious
appearances against his interrogator:

  When I said I had brought gold
  You then were Charmides; before you were not,
  Till I made mention of the gold. 'Twont do.
  So prithee, as you've taken up the name
  Of Charmides, e'en lay it down again.

Besides, he has brought only bills, not coin. On hearing this,
Charmides bids him begone under pain of a thrashing.
Before moving off, the Sharper puts the question once more.

  I pray you, are you he?
Charm.   .   Yes, I am he.

Sharper. What say you! are you he?
Charm.   I am, I say.
Sharper. Himself?
Charm.   .I say, I'm Charmides himself.
Sharper. And are you he himself?
Charm.   His very self.

Then the Sharper confounds him by all the gods for his inopportune arrival, just spoiling a job. Fortunately he has pocketed his fee: he will go to those who hired him, and let them know their money is thrown away.

When he is at last alone, Charmides wonders what the meaning of all this business can be: the bell does not clink without being handled. The first explanation he gets comes in the form of a scene peculiarly popular with Roman dramatists, who had many different tastes to satisfy:—the conventional incident of a slave running to and fro and talking to himself. Stasimus has lost a ring at the tippling-shop, and hesitates whether it is worth while to go back and seek it from amongst a host of whipped knaves, one of whom stole a shoe from a runner's foot at the top of his speed. He at last decides not to go, and finds a vent for his ill-humour at the loss in a tirade against the degenerate morals of the day. Charmides recognises his own slave, and, after some trouble in stopping him, gives Stasimus an opportunity of recognising 'the best of masters,' but cuts his raptures short to make enquiries. From Stasimus Charmides hears the worst insinuations as to the action taken by Callicles in his absence: but the appearance of Callicles at this point soon removes the misunderstanding: the slave characteristically maintains his unfavourable opinion to the last.

Act V   The final act is occupied with the meeting between Charmides and the other personages of the story, together with the clearing up of all that is obscure. The merchant confirms the betrothal of his daughter to Lysiteles, and provides an ample dowry for her, notwithstanding her lover's protest:

if he likes the girl, Charmides insists, he must like the CHAP. XI
portion too. Lesbonicus has to bear only gentle reproaches
from his father : to assist his reform the daughter of Callicles
is offered him for a wife. Lesbonicus declares he will take
her, and, he adds, any one else his father wishes.

> *Charm.*   Angry though I be with you,
>   One man one woe, is the quota.
> *Callicles.*   Nay, too little in this case :
>   Since for such a hardened sinner twenty wives were not too much.

Lesbonicus promises amendment, and all ends happily.

3 Traces of the Chorus in Roman Comedy

When we survey Roman Comedy in comparison with what *Loss of*
Chorus and
we have previously seen of the ancient drama, the feature that *transition*
most prominently strikes us is the total loss of the Chorus [1] *to modern*
structure
—that which gave to the ancient drama its chief distinctiveness. Under Aristophanes the use of the Chorus had
already begun to decline, and we saw examples of plays
in which it was neglected for hundreds of lines together. In
the period of transition we are told that the difficulty of
finding volunteers to undertake the great expense attaching
to choral performances favoured their disuse. Moreover the
Chorus was a foreign element in drama, and doubly foreign
in Comedy, and it could maintain itself only by struggling
against the full force of natural development. By the loss
of the Chorus, Comedy ceased to be a double form of art in
which lyric was combined with dramatic. But even on the
dramatic side the effect of the change was considerable.
The Chorus had been the unity bond of the ancient drama,
and the foundation of its structure as an alternation of odes
and episodes : Roman Comedy, instead of being a continuous

---

[1] Once in Plautus we have (in the *Rudens*, Act II) 'Piscatores,'
which may be translated 'A Chorus of Fishermen' : but this is what
would have been called in Greek Drama a Secondary Chorus.

CHAP. XI whole, falls structurally into the form familiar to modern literature—a series of separate scenes (or acts) succeeding one another, with the intervals between them filled up, if necessary, by music. And—though the further stage was not reached by Roman Comedy—such multiplication of scenes was the preliminary step towards free change of scene, carrying with it unlimited assumption of intervals in time between the scenes, which is so essential an element of Shakespearean dramatic art. The transition from Old Attic to Roman Comedy is by far the most distinctive phase of the transition from ancient to modern literature.

The Chorus leaves traces in moral reflections: But the lyric element, which had played so important a part in ancient drama, had impressed upon Comedy certain features which survived when the Chorus itself had passed away. It has already been pointed out how moral reflections, of precisely the same type as those proper to a Greek Chorus, abound in Roman Comedy; what before was concentrated in set odes is now scattered through the whole of a play, or gathers round particular individuals of a moralising turn, like Philto and Lysiteles in the *Trinummus*; the approach to a Chorus is nearer still when these reflections are, as in the

in the soliloquy: *Trinummus*, expressed in lyric metres. The soliloquy too— a thing hardly less conventional in an acted drama than a choral ode—becomes in the Latin plays a prominent dramatic device: great part of the action in Terence's *Hecyra* is

and in the prologue and epilogue brought out in soliloquies. Besides these representatives of the old Chorus, its general function has been partly absorbed by the prologue and epilogue.

Various sources of the Latin prologue The term 'prologue' has in Roman Comedy its modern sense: it is no longer the opening scene, but a speech entirely outside the action. This prologue is manysided in its origin and developmental connexions. In part it associates itself with the direct explanation addressed to the audience so often by personages in plays of Aristophanes: in the Greek an occasional diversion, such explanations become,

by the general tendency towards regularity, a fixed function
for the prologue of Roman Comedy. Aristophanes usually
employed such an explanatory digression to make clear the
opening situation of his plays, and this is a leading purpose
of the Latin prologue. An example is the *Captives* of
Plautus ; and here—the situation being particularly intricate
—the speaker of the prologue, after putting it once, finds
a comic excuse for putting it a second time.

> Thus far d'ye understand me ?—It is well—
> Yet I see one at distance, who in troth
> Seems as he heard not.—Prithee, friend, come nearer ;
> If not to sit, there's room at least to walk.
> What ! would you make the player strain his voice,
> As if he were a beggar asking alms ?

And such direct relations between performers and audience
are sometimes resumed at the close of the play, in a manner
foreshadowing the modern epilogue. In the *Cistellaria*
the last scene ends with the principal personage entering the
house to acknowledge his newly discovered daughter : the
whole 'caterva' of actors advance to the front and speak
a conclusion.

> Spectators, wait not for their coming out.
> None will return.—They'll finish all within.
> That done, they will undress.—He that's in fault,
> Will suffer for't,—he that is not, will drink
> Your healths.—Now, as to what remains for you,
> Spectators, this our Comedy, thus ended,
> Follow your ancient custom and applaud.

Where such explanation extends to a forecast of events yet
to come, we may see a suggestion of the Euripidean prologue
in Tragedy. This is especially the case in the allegorical or *Allegorical*
mythic prologues of Plautus. One beautiful example is that *prologues*
to the *Rudens* : the story turns on a shipwreck, and the
prologue is put into the mouth of Arcturus.

> By night I shine in heaven among the gods,
> And in the day-time mix with mortal men,
> Passing with other stars from heaven to earth.

> Jove, supreme sovereign of gods and men,
> Spreads us throughout all nations, several ways,
> To mark the people's actions, learn their manners,
> Their piety and faith, that so each man
> May find reward according to his virtues.

Then follows a statement of the story—an attempt to carry away a slave-girl from the lover to whom she was pledged—and how he who speaks the prologue was going to defeat the wicked purpose, and by a storm bring the fugitives into a situation which should issue in discoveries they little expected :—

> For I Arcturus am, of all the signs
> Most turbulent.

Connexion of the prologue with the Chorus But in addition to all these other originating influences for the Roman prologue, it has clearly taken over one important function of the Greek comic Chorus—that by which, in the parabasis, the Chorus spoke in the author's name to the public, after the fashion of a modern preface. It has been observed above how the Latin prologues regularly put the authorship and origin of the play, and how those of Terence carry on a literary war with another poet. Sometimes, as in the *Captives*, the poet contends for the purity of his play, as Aristophanes had done. The prologue has a further point of connexion with the Chorus in the fact that it is not always at the commencement of the poem. In Plautus's *Mighty Man of Valour* the first act is given up to displaying Pyrgopolinices vapouring amongst his followers : at the beginning of the second act comes the ordinary prologue. In the *Amphitryo*, Mercury, who at the beginning makes a normal prefatory explanation, speaks again to the spectators in the second scene, while the third act opens with a regular Euripi-

Its approach to the moder prologue dean prologue spoken by Jupiter. In these various ways the prologue of Roman Comedy associates itself with the Chorus or other elements of the ancient drama. But it passes beyond these, and makes advance towards the modern prologue, in the circumstance that it is often not assigned to any per-

sonage, but is an abstract speech not connected with any CHAP. XI
characterisation of the speaker : the prologue is not a portion ——
of, but an external comment upon, the drama.

There is one literary usage, the product originally of *Metrical*
lyric influence, which survived the loss of the Chorus, and *variation a*
survival
became a permanent element of poetic art : this was the *from the*
dramatic utilisation of variety in metrical style. The *Chorus*
peculiarities of pronunciation which make the prosody
and scansion of Latin dramatic verses so intricate are
outside the scope of this work : from the standpoint of
literature we have to do only with whole passages in
single or varying metres [1]. The Roman comedians are
scarcely less remarkable than Aristophanes for their metrical
elasticity. The metres employed are much the same in both *Latin me-*
languages. Latin and Greek blank verse are for the present *tres :*
blank verse,
purpose identical. The lyrics of Roman drama differ in one *lyrics,*
important respect from Greek lyrics : the strophic treatment
almost entirely disappears, and the lyric effect in Latin is
made (as remarked before) by the use of metres peculiarly
distinct from blank verse, and by rapid variations of metre
in successive lines. There is a Latin accelerated rhythm *two tro-*
identical with the Greek metre I have called by that name, *chaic and*
two iambic
and a still longer variety of trochaic style [2] : the two may be *metres*
illustrated by lines already quoted—

[1] I attach great importance to this principle. In Latin Comedy we
find that, while metres like trochaics or blank verse will be maintained
for scores or hundreds of lines together, there are passages in which
metrical changes follow one another rapidly, often in successive lines. It
seems clear to me that it is a mistake to seek literary significance in the
analysis of individual lines : a passage over which these rapid changes
extend should be treated as a whole, bound into a unity by the principle
of variation in metre. I have treated such passages as 'lyrics.' [E. g.
Trinummus, commencement of Act II, lines 223–300.]

[2] The technical names are *trochaici septenarii* and *octonarii* (or *trochaic sevens* and *trochaic eights*) ; or, with grammarians who measure
by metres, *trochaic tetrameter catalectic* and *acatalectic*. [*Catalectic*
implies that the final syllable is lacking.]

D d

Length of years is but the relish : wisdom is the food of life.
Merciful and calm I found thee, all that heart could wish of ocean.

Precisely corresponding to these there are on the iambic
side the counterpart of long iambics in Greek, and a yet
longer line[1] :

I'll speak for the pursuit of love, and see what recommends it.
Upsetting all the good old ways : an evil grasping greedy crew.

These are the metrical elements of Latin drama : in describing the employment of these different metres I shall

Metrical practice of Plautus

deal separately with Plautus, who as the older poet seems
nearer to the Greek usage, and Terence whose metrical
usage is somewhat different, and approaches nearer to the
dramatic practice of Shakespeare.

The prelude usage of lyrics

Commencing with what is most nearly choral, I will
mention first what may be called the 'prelude use' of lyrics.
It is a marked feature of Plautus's verse that he regularly
uses the wild and rapidly flexible metres which I comprehend
under the name of lyrics for the commencement of a long
and important scene[2], the rest of which is to be in accelerated rhythm : the change from the one metre to the
other harmonises with some distinct change in the general
tone of the dialogue. An example has already been noted
in the *Trinummus* : the moralising soliloquy of Lysiteles
followed by the moral lecture of his father are cast in lyrics,
until the son, where he claims to have observed all these
principles from his youth up, breaks into the accelerated
rhythm in which he gradually leads up to the proposal which
starts the main business of the play. The same usage may
be traced all through the *Captives*[3]. This play turns upon

[1] *Iambici septenarii* and *octonarii* (*iambic sevens* and *iambic eights*), or
iambic tetrameter catalectic and *acatalectic*.

[2] I use the term 'scene' for a dramatic division in a general sense :
not necessarily agreeing with the numbering of scenes.

[3] For exact references to this and the preceding play see the Metrical
Analysis, below, pages 442–3.

an exchange of identities between two captives, a master and CHAP. XI
a slave, the purpose of which is that the real master may,
under the supposition that he is the slave, be set at liberty
to negotiate the other's ransom. The second act opens in
lyrics, where the captives are receiving expressions of sympathy and speaking generally to one another of their secret
purpose : with the first solemn appeal for mutual fidelity
comes the change to accelerated rhythm, which is maintained
during the execution of the intrigue. In the third act, after
the master has escaped, the plot is discovered by the introduction of Aristophantes, who knows both the captives :
while Tyndarus watches him approaching and vainly seeks
to evade the necessity of meeting him the scene is lyrical,
but the change takes place exactly where Aristophantes
advances and addresses him by name. The fourth act
brings the Parasite with the news that is to constitute the
resolution of the action : the Parasite is overheard indulging
in lyric rapture, but tells his news in accelerated rhythm.
Then in the fifth act, when the course of events has restored
a son to his father, the first gratitude is in lyrics, which
change to the other metre with the thought 'let us proceed
to business [1].'

[1] This prelude usage is again well illustrated in the *Pseudolus* (a
play which cannot be recommended for indiscriminate reading). The
opening act (from line 133 of Fleckeisen's edition) displays a slave-
merchant at home, and the hero endeavouring to soften his hard heart :
the merchant resists, and the whole is in lyrics, until the suggestion is
made that there is a chance of profit, whereupon (265) Ballio changes
his mood—with a corresponding change of metre—for, he says, profit
is a thing he never neglects. The play, it may be explained, is one of
the large class which exhibit clever slaves outwitting their masters, with
the special feature in this case that Pseudolus has been dared by his
master to deceive him in the affair under consideration. At the opening
of the second act (574) the slave, who had admitted in the previous
scene (567) that he had no idea what plan of deception he should
pursue, appears transported with delight at a brilliant thought which
has struck him. What this thought is we never hear, for accident at
the moment throws in his way the very messenger he is scheming to

CHAP. XI   I have dwelt at length on this prelude use of lyrics in
―――   Roman Comedy because it seems to be an important link
Its import-
ance as a in the development from the choral to the modern variety of
link in   drama.   In the earlier form a choral ode would have separ-
dramatic
develop-   ated the scenes.   When this is lost the taste for choral effects
ment   tends to throw the commencement of the following scene
             into lyric metres.   After these lyrics have been maintained
             for—speaking roughly—the usual duration of an ode, the
             scene changes into a more dramatic rhythm.   But the
             transition from one metre to another is not thrown away :
             it is made to harmonise with some break, however slight, in
             the spirit of the scene, thus bequeathing to modern drama
             its important art of reflecting in metrical changes minute
             variations of tone and movement [1].

Use of   The other use of lyric metres in Roman Comedy needs
lyrics for
agitation, only to be stated : they constitute an appropriate form
             in which to clothe agitated emotion of any kind.   The
             Pseudolus, a play of amatory intrigue, ends with a long lyric
             scene presenting the intriguer as triumphant and drunk.   So
             the girls who, in the *Rudens*, escape from the shipwreck,
             express lyrically their sensations upon reaching dry land ;
             and in a later scene a burst of lyrics marks the point where
             they take refuge from their persecutor at the altar of Venus [2].

intercept :—the preliminary soliloquy is lyric, the change of plan and its
execution are in accelerated rhythm (604–766).   Pseudolus's scheme is
of course to find some one to personate the messenger.   At the opening
of the fourth act he is (in lyrics) congratulating himself upon the
perfection in villainous arts of the tool he has secured for his purpose
(905–51) ; the scene of the actual personation is trochaic (952–997).
And there is an exactly parallel variation of metres in a later scene,
between the lyrical soliloquy of the real messenger (1103–36), and the
dialogue in accelerated rhythm in which he does the business only to find
himself anticipated (1137–1245).

     [1] It is a circumstance favouring this theory of lyric usage that such
lyric metres usually begin at the commencement of the second act : they
seldom appear in the first act.

     [2] *Pseudolus* from 1246 ; *Rudens*, 185–289, 664–80.

It is natural again that a sudden rise in the action of a CHAP. XI
scene should for a time give a lyric turn to the metre. In ———
the long opening scene of the *Amphitryo*, Sosia is over- *and for climaxes*
heard by Mercury making up a pompous account of his own
position and adventures: wherever he comes to a thrilling
point in the narrative he breaks into irregular rhythms, subsiding afterwards into very ordinary metrical tone. So in
the last act, the servant-maid tells the events within the
house in the same ordinary metre, but rises to lyrics for the
miraculous signs attending the birth of Hercules[1].

Lyrics then are in Roman Comedy the medium for the *Normal*
exceptional: the normal metres are (in Plautus) accelerated *metres in Plautus*
rhythm and blank verse. The place of honour is assigned *Inter-*
to accelerated rhythm, both in regard to quantity and to the *change of*
character of the scenes it expresses. Blank verse, on the *accelerated and blank*
other hand, marks the position of rest in the action: *verse*
besides prologues and opening situations it is used for
sudden soliloquies, or diversions and scenes interposed; it
is also used for relief scenes, especially where a play of
intrigue is relieved by the display of life and social manners.
All this is part of the wider law of variety and contrast, *Law of va-*
which is the root purpose of variations in metre. *riety, and contrast*

In the *Trinummus* two interests enter into the plot: one
is the marriage intended to unite the two families of Philto
and Charmides, with all the complications arising out of its
negotiation, the other is the equivocal position in which
circumstances have placed the character of the guardian
Callicles, and which is brought out in the play by the
agency of his friend Megaronides. The working out of
these separate interests is distinguished by variation between
accelerated rhythm and blank verse. The proposal of the
match to Philto, the dispute between the young men over

---

[1] *Amphitryo* 153–262 is the soliloquy scene of Sosia (in iambic
eights), the lyric passages being 159–79 and 219–47. In the same metre
is Bromia's soliloquy 1053–75, broken by lyrics 1062–72.

CHAP. XI the dowry, the main business of the pretended dowry and
meeting. between the actual Charmides and his supposed
messenger, are all in the trochaic rhythm.   On the other
hand, the scene in which Callicles clears his character to his
friend is in blank verse, and the same metre obtains where
these lay their plan for providing a dowry without revealing
the secret entrusted to Callicles, and again where the final
explanation takes place between Callicles and Charmides on
his return.   There is one exception to this principle, which
is itself significant.   The proposal of the marriage, which
had been opened to Philto in a trochaic scene, is formally

Law of
persistence
put to the brother of the lady in blank verse.   The explanation. of this brings out another law, which may be
called the law of persistence, and modifies the wider law of
variety : this expresses the tendency by. which, where a
scene has, for good reason, changed into a particular
rhythm, an attraction to that rhythm obtains for a while as
against more definite rhythmic laws.   When Philto has
parted from his son, his reflection on the scene that has
preceded changes normally from accelerated rhythm to
blank verse ; the action passes without break from the
soliloquy into the incident of the proposal to Lesbonicus,
who meets Philto at the moment he turns to seek him :
accordingly the metre of the soliloquy persists through the
scene of the proposal [1].

The main intrigue of the *Captives*, it has already been
pointed out, is conveyed in accelerated rhythm.   The blank
verse of the play is used, in the first place, for an incident
interposed in the course of the intrigue, and constituting a
special phase of it.   The scheme for exchanging identities
is carried on by the two prisoners in the presence of their
captor, and with his admiring sympathy.   At one point this
captor feels it incumbent upon him to make his contribution

---

[1] For details and references see Metrical Analysis, below, page 443.

to the intrigue by which he is being deceived, and, by deep CHAP. XI
irony, he formally transfers the supposed slave to his supposed master with free authorisation for sending him out
of the country. It is this transaction that is conveyed in
blank verse : when the two captives resume the thread of
the scheme the scene returns to trochaics. Later on, when,
after the exciting contest with Aristophantes, the plot breaks
down, just where slaves enter to bind Tyndarus, blank verse
naturally appears, and in this metre of rest after action
Tyndarus calmly faces Hegio and justifies his fidelity to his
former master. Again, there is an underplot in this play,
embodying interest of manners—the caricature of a Parasite.
Blank verse is the medium for it so long as it is no more
than caricature, but—as in other plays [1]—where the underplot is drawn into the main action it is attracted into the
rhythm of the latter, and the Parasite brings his critical
news in lyrics and accelerated verse. In this connexion
the law of persistence is again exemplified. The Parasite
makes another appearance intermediate between the other
two, and, as his purpose is only to grumble about his failure
to find any entertainer, it might have been expected that
the scene would be in blank verse : as a fact it follows one
of the main scenes in the intrigue and is attracted to its
accelerated verse [2].

[1] A good example is the *Stichus*, Act II : where the boy Pinacium in
a highly lyric scene comes full of his important news, and tantalises the
Parasite ; when the mistress hears him (330) and bids him tell the news,
he does so in trochaics.

[2] For details and references see Metrical Analysis, below, page 442.
In the *Pseudolus* the movement of the plot is all in scenes of accelerated
verse : in this is expressed the remonstrance with the slave merchant
which is the occasion for the intrigue (265–393), the particular scheme
suggested by accident (604–766), the execution of this scheme (952–
997), and the corresponding scene which constitutes the denouement
(1137–1245). Blank verse is used for the opening situation of the youth's
despair (3–132), the soliloquy of the slave when he admits he has no
plan (394–414), and (perhaps by persistence) the scene immediately

CHAP. XI

Plautus's use of lengthened iambics

It remains to point out that the iambic metres other than blank verse are employed by Plautus as an additional element of variety, and especially connected with servants. In these rhythms the boy makes his comments upon the Parasite of the *Captives*, the servant-girl in *Amphitryo* relates the story of her mistress's labour, and the slave Sosia of the same play composes his vapouring report of the war. Both these last scenes, it has been already pointed out, are varied with lyric climaxes ; it is also notable that where the scene with Sosia is drawn into the mystification of the main plot by Sosia's stumbling upon Mercury there is a change to accelerated rhythm. Mercury himself in this play appears as the slave of Jupiter : where he condescends to the comic convention of a running slave the scene is in lengthened iambics [1].

Metrical practice of Terence

Terence is less lyrical than Plautus, and his treatment of lyrics rests much less on the employment of rare metres than on the rapid variation between metres in ordinary use. Unlike Plautus, Terence makes blank verse the main medium for his scenes, and with him accelerated rhythm [2] is (speaking roughly) on a par with the lengthened iambic metres as an element of metrical variety. But the main distinction of Terence is that in his plays the law of variety throws all other usages into the shade ; apart from the obvious selection of lyrics to express occasional agitation [3]

following where he faces the youth's father and tells him to his face he will outwit him. Blank verse also occupies the whole of the third act, which is simply a relief picture of manners in Ballio's establishment, caricaturing cooks and other servants. Note how in a trochaic scene the reading of a letter (998) (which is naturally in blank verse) produces a change of metre that persists for several smaller scenes.

[1] *Captives*, 909 ; *Amphitryo*, 1053, 153, 263, 984.

[2] Not only *trochaic sevens*, but also *trochaic eights*, which Plautus seems to reserve as a lyric measure (see above, page 383) : compare its use in prelude to Act IV of the *Trinummus*.

[3] E. g. the opening of *Phormio*, Act V (1-20), where Sophrona in her trouble is encountered by Chremes.

I can see no principle of significance in Terence's use of CHAP. XI any particular metre. He gives us however constant inter-change of rhythms to reflect transitions, often the most delicate transitions of tone and movement. To illustrate this would require the detailed analysis of a whole play[1]. Meanwhile it may be pointed out that the usages of Plautus and Terence constitute two links in a chain of continuous metrical development from ancient to modern drama. The ancient drama first arose as a literary species by the institu-tion of the Chorus, which showed how lyric poetry could be an instrument of dramatic effect. The influence of the Chorus extended beyond the strictly choral passages, and the interchange of metres it had introduced was found to serve two dramatic purposes : particular significance could be attached to particular metres, and, more widely, metrical variation was made to reflect variations in the action. When in Roman Comedy the Chorus finally disappeared, this trace of choral influence held its ground : both usages descended to Plautus, Terence allowed the less definite principle of variation to predominate. The usage favoured by Terence was the usage destined to survive ; and metrical variation, in the more powerful form of variation between verse and prose, became a distinguishing feature of Eliza-bethan drama[2].

Law of variety supreme

Metrical develop-ment from ancient to Elizabeth-an drama

---

[1] See Metrical Analysis of the *Phormio*, below, page 444.

[2] The *Tempest* is a good play for studying these variations. Every one feels the passage from the rough prose of the opening storm to the stately verse introducing the enchanted island. A delicate transition is in II. ii. 121, where, amid a scene entirely in prose, Caliban breaks into verse with the effects of alcohol, now first tasted by him : the scene be-comes lyrical as the intoxication reaches its height. The contrast of his set purpose with the sailors' drunken inconstancy is conveyed by verse and prose throughout IV. i. 194-255. Examples from other plays could be multiplied indefinitely. The dramatic turning-point (that is, transi-tion from complication to resolution) is in two plays accompanied with a sudden change of the whole scene from verse to prose (*Meas. for Meas.* III. i. 152, and *Winter's Tale*, III. iii. 59).

4 General Dramatic Features of Roman Comedy

A principle accounting for much of what is distinctive in
Roman Comedy is that the general tendencies of the transition period are seen to be by this time fully developed.
One case is particularly clear : by the tendency to pass from
Develop- irregularity to regularity the incidental effects, so prominent
ment of the in Old Attic Comedy, have now unified and developed into
underplot the complete underplot. Where the Greek dramatist would
have given us continual but isolated digressions into farce,
or miscellaneous jokes on human nature, we get in Roman
Comedy a similar amount of caricature or farce worked up
into a single interest, running through the whole play side
by side with the main plot. A favourite subject for such
secondary interest is a Parasite—an exaggerated anticipation
of the modern diner-out. Such a personage forms a centre
to the underplot running through Plautus's play, the
Captives. He opens the first scene by lamenting the war
from his own point of view : people are so busy that they
have no interest left for men of his profession, who are left
to feed like snails in dry weather on their own juices.
Suddenly catching sight of Hegio he recognises him as the
father of a man with whom he has dined ; he accordingly is
at once plunged in distress at the rumoured captivity of this
son, whom he out-does the father in mourning. The thin
veil of a Parasite's grief is quite understood on both sides.

> *Hegio (half aside).* 'Tis this afflicts him, that the army
> Raised to make entertainments is disbanded.
> . . . . You will stand in need
> Of many soldiers, and of various kinds :—
> Bakerians, Pastrycookians, Poultererians,
> Besides whole companies of Fishmongerians.
> *Parasite.* How greatest geniuses oft lie concealed!
> O, what a general, now a private soldier !

But the father cannot do less than invite the sympathising
Parasite to dinner—that is, if he can be content with little.

> *Parasite.* Oh, Sir, very very little:
> I love it: 'tis my constant fare at home.

The joking is carried to the common conventionality of
a mock auction, the Parasite knocking himself down to
Hegio as the only bidder.   None the less he means to get
a better invitation if he can find one.   In the third act he
reappears unsuccessful, and inveighs against the degeneracy
of young men who only ask those now who will ask them
back again.   He suspects a conspiracy, and will have his
action, with damages at ten dinners when provisions are
dear.   Making one more attempt he tries the strangers
arriving at the harbour, where he is fortunate enough to get
the first sight of Hegio's son newly returned.   Full of the
tidings, on which he hopes to found an open invitation to
the father's table, we have the Parasite in the fourth act
delaying the impatient Hegio with a gastronomic rhapsody
as to the price he expects for the news he is going to tell.
When he has at last told it, the father in his delight bids the
Parasite be free of his larder and kitchen : the subsequent
scene paints the scale on which this freedom is used.   This
Parasite is clearly a distinct interest in the play, appealing to
the same tastes which Aristophanes would have satisfied
with his miscellaneous business.   We have seen how in *The Roman*
Greek drama there was an approach to such a secondary *underplot*
interest in the case of the slave who is attached to Bacchus *the main*
during the first part of the *Frogs*.   But whereas this slave *action*
disappears when the main business of the play is reached,
in Roman Comedy the underplot is both completed and
drawn into the main action : the Parasite has his share in
the catastrophe of the action, and in the situations of
distress and triumph which precede and follow it.   Roman
Comedy abounds in examples of such union between main

CHAP. XI interests of action and underplots of manners or of relief
in some other form. The contrast between these diverse

*An ap-
proach to
mixture of
tones*

interests, and the contrast of both with the element of
moral reflections, constitute the nearest approach made in
Latin drama to the mixture of tones.

*Multipli-
cation of
actions*

The underplot is only one variety in the wider multiplication of actions, which Roman Comedy presents fully developed. Three different sources suggest themselves for this
important process in literary evolution. The growth of the
underplot out of incidental effects just mentioned is one.
Again, in the passage from Greek to Latin we know that
different plays were combined in one plot[1]. And a third
consideration is that the idea of double or multiple actions,
once introduced, would be applied more widely than in the
circumstances which had originated it. Very few Latin
Comedies are content with a single plot. I have already
pointed out how in the *Trinummus* the marriage negotiations
form a distinct interest from that centering in the character
of Callicles, which the action obscures and again clears;
the two interests are worked out side by side, and the
distinction is in this case kept particularly clear by the

*The Sti-
chus illus-
trates:*

metrical differences which, as we have seen, reflect it. The
Stichus of Plautus illustrates within the limits of a single
play four of the recognised modes by which actions are
multiplied in drama. The story is particularly scanty.
Two brothers have married two sisters, have run through
their property and been obliged to take to a life of merchan-
dise, and in a mercantile expedition have been absent and
unheard of for more than three years. At the beginning of
the play the father of the two wives is persuading his daughters to marry again: they however remain faithful to their
husbands, and are rewarded by the return of these husbands
safe and prosperous. Yet this slight material is made
to yield multiplicity of plot. First, we have duplication

[1] See above, page 378.

of actions illustrated in the fact that there are two brothers CHAP. XI
and two sisters, though there is nothing in the story necessarily involving more than one wedded pair; such duplica- *duplica-*
tion can be utilised for contrast of character, one sister *tion,*
being seen to waver in resolution not to marry, while the
other keeps her firm [1]. Again, we have the case of a *independ-*
mechanical personage elevated into an independent interest. *ent actions*
The father, whose function in the main action is no more *of mechan-*
than to advise the remarrying which circumstances suggest *ical per-*
to his daughters, is painted as a comfortable and facetious *sonages,*
old gentleman, who has a design of his own throughout the
play, namely, to get a wife for his old age. When his sons-
in-law return as rich men, he takes advantage of the situation to fish for the offer of a slave-girl well endowed, and
conveys his purpose in a transparent story of what some
young men did for an old friend of his; the sons-in-law
however dexterously miss the point of the story, and are
heartily indignant with the hypothetical old man, instead of
being stirred to emulation by the example of the others [2].
A third source for multiplicity of action—difference of tone *actions*
—is illustrated in the *Stichus*, as in the *Captives*, by the *multiplied*
part of the Parasite, which clearly amounts to a separate *ences of*
interest as he fastens upon one after another of the person- *tone,*
ages in the play, and suffers rebuffs on every side. Once *the depend-*
more, we have illustrated that class of underplot to which *ent under-*
the name most strictly applies, and which has been ingeni- *plot*
ously described as going on in the kitchen while the main
plot goes on in the parlour. The slave Stichus, who gives
the name to the play, has been presented with a cask of
wine by his master, one of the brothers, and celebrates with
his sweetheart and fellow-servants the happy return. To
this the fifth act is given up: they feast and dance outside
the house in vulgar emulation of the rejoicings within, and

---

[1] *Stichus*, 1–57.   [2] *Stichus*, 538–78.

CHAP. XI make much of the situation in which two slaves have the
same sweetheart: .

> With me! why, she's with you:
> With you! with me—one envies not the other.

The play ends as they have just danced the wine out. In
all these ways various interests multiply and combine in
a common action, growing steadily into the complete
Shakespearean conception of plot—the weaving of distinct
stories into a common dramatic pattern.

*Plot form
in Roman
Comedy :*   In the form of its dramatic plots Roman Comedy occupies
a curious middle position between ancient and modern.
On the one hand the Old Attic conception of plot—the
sustained development of an extravagance—has completely
*it rests on
complica-
tion and
resolution:* passed away : Roman Comedy, in as high a degree as any
modern form of drama, is dominated by probability, and it
falls into the modern form of complication and resolution.

*limited by
the strictest
scenic
unity*   But another peculiarity ·of dramatic treatment in Greek
literature was more firmly rooted. It is remarkable that
the strict unities of time and place which were such a
limitation to the ancient stage descended intact from Greek
to Latin. Considering the large degree to which the Chorus
was responsible for these conventionalities it might have been
expected that they would not have long survived its loss.
The reverse is the fact : whereas Greek drama, both serious
and comic, has occasional departures from scenic unity,
Roman Comedy is absolute in its fixity ; it even goes beyond
the practice of the Greek stage, and in the Latin comedies
not only are there no changes of scene in the course of
a play, but further, what is practically the same scene—an
exterior to a few houses—is made to serve for all plays
alike[1]. The effect of this on plot form is very important.

---

[1] So the scene of the *Rudens* is a road in front of Daemones' house,
beside which is the Temple of Venus: from some part of it the sea, with
cliffs and shore, is visible. The action of Terence's *Self-Tormentor*
extends over two days, but involves no change of scene.

Where the unities of time and place are strictly maintained
it is clear that only the crisis of a story can be represented
in action on the stage; hence the universal form of dramatic
action for Roman Comedy is this :—An Opening Situation
of Complication is developed to a Resolution.   But again,
regard must be had to the multiplication of actions just
described : all these separate interests with their inter-
working must be presented within the same narrow limits
of time and place.   It is obvious that the plots of Roman
Comedy will be highly intricate ; and the formula for them
may be enlarged to this :—An Opening Situation of Complication between various conflicting interests is developed
to a Resolution in which they are harmonised [1].

The *Phormio* of Terence may be described as a beautiful
network of intrigues involving four persons, whom I will
here call the father, the son, the uncle and the nephew :
there are also, as motive personages, the usual contriving
slave and a Parasite.   Into the action of this play three
distinct intrigues enter.   The son has fallen in love, during
the absence from Athens of his father and uncle, with an
orphan stranger girl he has seen, and has further, by the
contrivance of the slave and the Parasite, allowed himself
to be forced into marrying her by a mock suit brought
under the law concerning the next-of-kin.   The nephew is
in the common predicament of Athenian youth—smitten
with the charms of a slave-girl, whom he is seeking to buy
out of captivity, if by any resource he can raise the funds.
The old men too have their guilty secret: the uncle has
contracted a bigamous marriage in Lemnos, known to his
brother, but which must at all hazards be kept from his
rich Athenian wife.   The play opens after a lengthened
absence of the father and uncle from home.   At this point

[1] According to the scheme suggested above (page I40, note I) the
general formula for Roman plot would be CR: or, to bring out the
multiplication of actions, $\dfrac{C}{CC} = R$.

CHAP. XI all three intrigues have been brought into conflict with one
another. The marriage of the son has disconcerted a scheme
which the old men had always kept in mind as a means for
hushing up the Lemnian marriage, namely, that this son
should marry the daughter of that household, a provision
being thus made for the girl without risk of inconvenient
questions being asked. Two of the three intrigues have
thus run directly counter to one another, and whatever
tends to produce family difficulties also reduces the chance
of the nephew's being able to wheedle out of those about
him the money he so pressingly needs. A few scenes are
devoted to elaborating this opening situation—the youths'
dread of their parents' return, and the father's indignation
when he hears of his son's match; then the action settles
down to a scheme for annulling the marriage. This scheme
is made to increase the mutual entanglement of the different
intrigues; for the old men have recourse to the contriving
slave who is really in the interest of the youths, and he
makes out a necessary step to be the payment of moneys,
which he intends secretly to hand over to the nephew for
the purposes of his amour. Suddenly an accident reveals
to the uncle that the bride in the recent marriage is no
other than his own Lemnian daughter, brought without his
knowledge to Athens, and that he is thus on the point of
upsetting an alliance which it has been his object for years to
effect. The old men hasten to arrest all proceedings, but not
before the money has been secured for the nephew, and the
slave, possessed of the secret, has brought about a disclosure
to the uncle's wife. Thus the son has secured his marriage,
the nephew is furnished with funds for redeeming his sweetheart, the concealment which constituted the third intrigue
is at an end, and the old men are in a moral position that
forbids their resenting severely anything that has been done:
all the different trains of interest, after passing through so
much complication, are at once resolved and harmonised.

The action of this play, it will be observed, commences CHAP. XI
at so late a point in the story that in the opening complica- *Special*
tion the resolution is already latent : the marriage which is *feature of*
to harmonise the whole entanglement has taken place before *Roman*
the play begins, and is mistaken at the outset for the chief *plot : reso-*
item in the conflict of interests. This beautiful piece of *lution la-*
plot handling is characteristically Roman, and the action *tent in com-*
of several comedies in this species may be stated in this *plication*
form : An apparent Final Complication of an Opening
Situation is shown in development to be a Resolution[1].

The situations to which such complication is applied are *Situations:*
various in kind. .There are situations of Intrigue, suffi- *Intrigue,*
ciently illustrated by the *Phormio*. Of high dramatic interest are the situations of Irony, that rest on the spontaneous, *Irony,*
unlooked-for, unconscious clashings in the course of events.
The *Captives* of Plautus is one of the most exquisite studies
of Dramatic Irony in all literature. There is war between
Elis and Aetolia, and prisoners are being taken on both
sides to be sold as slaves. Hegio of Aetolia has lost his
son Philopolemus, supposed to have been taken captive in
the war ; accordingly the wealthy father buys all the distinguished prisoners he can lay his hands on, in the hope
of sometime negotiating an exchange for his son. When
the play opens he has just purchased in this way two
persons, Philocrates, supposed to be a man of some distinction in Elis, and his slave Tyndarus captured with him.
Hegio does not know, what the speaker of the prologue
gives as information to the audience, that this Tyndarus
is another son of Hegio, stolen away in infancy and sold as
a slave in Elis. Thus the opening situation contains the
irony of a son becoming slave to his own father, neither
of the two having any suspicion of the fact: verily, adds

---

[1] Other examples will be found in the plots of the *Rudens, Menaechmei,
Captives*. The formula (above, page 415, note 2) will in these cases
become $\frac{CR}{C} = R$.

CHAP. XI the prologue, the gods use us as their footballs. As the
action proceeds the irony deepens. The two captives have
a little plot of their own : they have agreed ever since being
taken prisoners to exchange names and costumes, Philocrates pretending to be Tyndarus and the slave, and Tyndarus assuming the part of Philocrates the master ; for
of course Hegio will send away the slave to arrange the
terms of exchange, keeping the master as a valuable hostage,
and so by their exchange of identities the real master will
get free, while the faithful slave will gladly suffer in his
place. The plot is skilfully carried out in the presence of
the unconscious Hegio, who zealously bears his part in the
intrigue by which he is being deceived. A climax of irony
is reached where, all substantial matters having been arranged, Tyndarus in his rôle as master gives his supposed
slave a parting message for his father, and, carrying the
plot a step further than had been concerted with Philocrates, makes a stroke for himself.

> Say, I'm well ;
> And tell him, boldly tell him, that our souls
> Were linked in perfect harmony together ;
> That nothing you have ever done amiss,
> Nor have I ever been your enemy ;
> That in our sore affliction you maintained
> Your duty to your master : nor once swerved
> From your fidelity, in no one deed
> Deserted me in time of my distress.
> When that my father is informed of this,
> And learns, how well your heart has been inclined
> Both to his son and to himself, he'll never
> Prove such a niggard, but in gratitude
> He will reward you with your liberty ;
> And I, if I return, with all my power
> Will urge him the more readily to do it.

To the listening Hegio there seems nothing in this beyond
the kindness of a considerate master : Philocrates quite
understands the covert hint, and replies in the same vein—
the ' you ' and ' I ' must be understood as reversed—

True, I have acted as you say : and much
It pleases me, you bear it in remembrance.
What I have done was due to your desert:
For were I in my count to tell the sum
Of all your friendly offices towards me,
Night would bear off the day, ere I had done.
You were obliging, as obsequious to me,
As though you were my servant.

At this point the situation has reached a triple irony. The
prisoners have developed their plot at the expense of their
unconscious captor, who rejoices to assist it. In the last
detail Tyndarus has given an unexpected turn of irony to
the scene, at the expense of Philocrates, who enters into
the humour of it and carries it on. But beneath the whole
there is a deeper irony, perceived only by the audience, who
see the father and his lost son unconsciously facing one
another, the son plotting against his father, the father about,
when this plot shall be discovered, to visit his son with hard
labour and torture.

Briefly to review other situations of Roman Comedy : we *Character*
have complication taking the form of Contrast in the *Brothers* *Contrast and Re-*
of Terence. One of these brothers has brought up his son *versal,*
with great strictness in the country, the other has adopted
a younger nephew to give him a town life of easy morality,
indulging his follies in the hope of winning his affection. The
scenes present the two parents each believing absolutely
in his own system ; an amusing resolution is found in the
sudden reversal of characters when the country father, en-
lightened by the discovery that his own charge is responsible
for certain excesses attributed to the other youth, turns round
and entirely outshines his popular brother by the prodigality
with which he deals indulgence on all sides. A favourite *Error and*
situation in the Latin plays is that which is technically called *Recogni-*
'Error,' that is, mistaken identity. The *Menæchmei* is a *tion,*
good example, interesting as the foundation for Shakespeare's
Comedy of Errors, in which the plot is duplicated, and to

CHAP. XI the two twin brothers two twin slaves are added to increase
——— the mystification. To the same heading, perhaps, may be
referred plays which turn upon personation, like the *Pseudolus* of Plautus; also another situation, not very edifying,
but popular on the Roman stage, in which injury has been
done to an unknown person under cover of darkness, and
recognition is at last brought about by means of a ring

Conceal- or some similar device [1]. Mystification of a similar nature
ment and is the interest attaching to situations of Concealment, for
Discovery, which the natural resolution is Discovery. The *Mostellaria*
of Plautus is a highly amusing play, in which the master
of a house is kept from entering his own dwelling, where
some riotous proceedings are being carried on, by a terrible
story that the house is haunted; the slave responsible for
this story is driven in the course of the action from invention to invention, till the whole breaks down in a comic

Separation catastrophe. Finally, as an example of simplicity in plot,
and Re- complication in the *Stichus* amounts to no more than
union Separation of persons, whose Reunion is the resolution.

Roman These illustrations give only a partial idea of the intricacy
Comedy a and elaborateness with which plot is handled by Plautus and
model for
modern Terence: to do justice to the subject a separate work would
plot be required. Enough has been said to suggest that the intrinsic interest of the Latin comedies makes them well suited
to the position which actual historical circumstances have
assigned to them—that of being models of plot for the
lighter plays of the modern drama.

5 Motives in Roman Comedy

Dramatic It remains briefly to review the matter of which Roman
supersed-
ing satiric Comedy was composed, and the purpose to which it was
purpose applied. We have seen how the purpose of Greek Comedy

[1] An example is the *Hecyra* of Terence.

was satire, and its application was at first to high questions CHAP. XI of politics: gradually the matter became more general, and the satire grew nearer to humour, while the dramatic handling from being a means to an end was rapidly becoming an end in itself. These tendencies of the transition are found to have reached in Roman Comedy a high degree of completeness: dramatic has now so far superseded satiric purpose that the latter gravitates in the form of caricature to the underplot. I have sufficiently illustrated in previous sections the farcical relief of the Latin plays, and how their main action is a probable story made interesting by the working of events, while interest of character and moral reflection have obtained an equal importance with plot.

In the life painted by Roman Comedy an obvious feature *Love as a* is the very great prominence of love as a leading motive: *leading mo-tive* fourteen out of Plautus's twenty plays turn upon amours and their intrigues. The love is either that of loose life, which is by some plays displayed in all its nakedness, or it is dependent upon a state of slavery, and turns upon some free girl sold into slavery and redeemed by her lover[1]. Thus love scenes in the modern sense are not to be expected; the heroines play a very secondary part, and several plays like the *Trinummus*, are occupied with marriage negotiations in which the bride never appears. The institution of slavery, with the attendant practice of kidnapping, is responsible for another interest almost universal in the Latin plays—a child stolen in infancy and by the action of the drama restored to its parents.

[1] The accepted translations seem to me to give an unnecessary air of looseness to some plays by using terms of modern immorality, like 'procurer.' It is obvious that the institution of slavery, involving concubinage as distinct from marriage, makes a great difference at all events to the grossness of such life; and if the term 'slave-merchant' be substituted for 'procurer,' &c., a great deal of Plautus may be read by modern readers without offence. Of course this does not apply to such plays as the *Bacchides*, which are immoral in the modern sense.

In the relief scenes class types are prominent :—an inheritance, it will be recollected, from the very earliest forms
of Comedy. The cook of the Megarian Farce, and the
parasite of Epicharmus, still hold the stage. A whole set
of these class types are furnished by the institution of kidnapping—the lover, the stolen heroine, the schemer who
procures her deliverance, and the hated slave-merchant :—

> An old bald-pated fellow,
> Hook-nosed, pot-bellied, beetle-brow'd, squint-eye'd,
> A sour-faced knave, the scorn of gods and men.

These are all well illustrated in the *Rudens*, in which, by the
agency of Arcturus and a shipwreck, the various personages
involved in such a story are brought together at the door
of the father's house, to whom in the end the daughter is to
be restored. Other types are the sharper of the *Trinummus*,
the military swaggerer, and the jolly bachelor who assists his
young friends in their intrigues. The miser in terrified guard
over his pot of money belongs to the comedy of all ages.
But the actors, and sometimes the composers, of Latin comedies were slaves, and types of slave life appear in all varieties.
The 'cheeky' slave has been illustrated in the *Trinummus*;
the *Captives* gives example of extremes in the faithful Tyndarus, and the hardened villain who originally stole him in
his childhood, and is in the end brought back to meet his
fate with brazen impudence. Scheming slaves are in universal
request as motive personages for the plays. In the *Stichus*
we have seen a whole company exhibiting the merry side of
a captive's life. And the opposite extreme of moroseness
is of common occurrence—well illustrated in Sceparnio, the
churl of the *Rudens*, who snaps at all comers, and makes
his churlishness an instrument of flirtation where he refuses
Ampelisca her modest request for water except at the price
of a kiss.

> *Sceparnio.*   I am proud and lordly:
> Unless you sue to me with low petition,

You will not get a drop. Our well we dug,
At our own hazard, with our proper tools.
Unless you woo me with much blandishment,
You will not get a drop.

Ampelisca.   Why should you grudge
To give me water, which an enemy
Will give an enemy?

Sceparnio.   Why should you grudge
To grant me that same favour, which a friend
Will give a friend?

These few observations seem sufficient to sum up the *Summary* scanty material out of which the Latin comedies were constructed. The famous line of Terence might well serve as motto for the whole literary species to which Terence belongs—

I'm human: all human nature is my business.

Roman Comedy seeks no deeper inspiration than the simple interest that belongs to human nature as seen in the ordinary play of daily life; and for background to its picture it gives us caricature of manners and social oddities as they existed in dissolute and slave-ridden Greece and Rome.

XII

The Ancient Classic and the Modern Romantic Drama

XII

CHAP. XII

———

The Ro-
mantic

Drama as
a union of
Drama
and Story

THE drama of antiquity has now been traced through the whole course of its development: it remains to state somewhat more formally—what has been a guiding consideration in all parts of our review—the relation in which this Ancient Classical Drama stands to its rival in literary prominence, the Modern Romantic Drama, represented to us mainly by Shakespeare. Put briefly, the Romantic Drama is the marriage of Drama and Story; it is produced by the amalgamation on the popular stage of the Ancient Classical Drama with the stories of Mediæval Romance.

The An-
cient Clas-
sical
Drama
viewed as a
whole

The whole drama of Greece and Rome constitutes a single piece of development. Greek Tragedy was created by the fusion of a lyric chorus with dramatic action; from the fixity stamped upon it by this connexion with the chorus Tragedy began to move slowly in the direction of modern complexity and realism; then its progress came to a sudden end with Euripides, after whom—so far as acted drama was concerned—development was superseded by imitation. The form, however, of Tragedy had been, owing to exceptional circumstances, taken over by Comedy, and in this sphere of incongruous matter tragic form was subjected to a continuous development, which extended through the whole of Greek literature, and passed on from Greek Comedy to the Roman adaptation of it. In this final Roman form ancient drama had proceeded so far in its course of evolution that it had reached the leading characteristics of modern dramatic form: the two fundamental

CHAP. XII varieties of plot, action-drama and passion-drama, were
already distinguished, and the combination of many actions
in one had been carried to a high degree of complexity.
On the other hand, strange limitations were maintained to
the end of the Classical drama.   Its matter was limited, in
Tragedy to the heroic myths into which human interest
could with difficulty penetrate, in Comedy to a slight
and superficial range of common life.   The separation
of Tragedy and Comedy into distinct rituals gave but
slight scope in each for the mixture of tones.   More
important still, the rigid adherence of the ancient stage
to scenic unity, while constituting no doubt a special
interest in itself, hampered all other dramatic effects by
admitting only the final crisis of a story into the acted
exhibition.

The Dark
Ages :
Story
supersedes
Drama in
popular in-
terest

Between the Roman and the Romantic Drama lies the
whole tract of the 'Dark Ages.'   For our present purpose
the main literary phenomenon of this period is that drama
ceases to be, what it had been previously and was destined
to be again, the popular literature, that is, the literature of
the non-reading classes : its place for a time is taken by an
allied form of art-story.   The Latin plays passed to the
literary section of society in the monasteries ; meanwhile
a wandering class of men—under such names as jugglers,
minstrels, bards, scalds, troubadours, trouvères—spread themselves through the nations, and catered for the popular taste
as purveyors of fiction in prose or verse.   There were tales of
all kinds, and taken from the stores of all peoples : tales
founded on Scripture, on the lives of saints, or the doings
of giants, or the ordinary ways of human nature, besides
those in which the attraction lay in the naughtiness, or
the 'histories' that were simply true stories.   So thoroughly
had story superseded drama that the terms 'tragedy' and
'comedy' lost their dramatic significance : 'tragedies' became the regular name for such tales of fallen greatness

as those making up the *Mirror for Magistrates*, and the
original application of the word could be so far obscured
that an epic which is perhaps the most serious poem ever
written was styled by its author the ' Divine Comedy.' As
the centuries went on, such fiction became recognised as the
dominant literary interest of Europe; from the fact of its
being expressed in a variety of kindred languages produced
by corruption from the language of Rome, this mass of
European stories came to be summed up under the name
' Romance.'

Drama and Story had prevailed separately : an agency *Popular*
for bringing the two together was found in the Popular *Mediæval*
Drama that arose towards the close of the Dark Ages. Its *acted Story*
immediate origin was in the ceremonies of religious worship :
these, in mediæval Europe as in Greece, were dramatic in
their general spirit, and further, the circumstance that the
ritual was carried on in Latin naturally led to its being
supplemented on particular occasions with sacred scenes or
lessons acted to the ignorant [1]. Thus the *raison d'être* of the
Mysteries and Miracle Plays was to act stories from Scripture
or the lives of Saints, or stories embodying central doctrines,
such as the incarnation, for the benefit of a populace unable
to read for themselves. Like everything healthy and free
this Popular Drama underwent development. It soon broke
away from its liturgical or homiletic purpose, and the acting
became an end in itself. Single scenes grew into the
Collective Miracle Play covering all time; from simple
reproduction of events a step in the direction of plot was
taken by the allegorical scenes or plays styled Moralities.
And further, the fundamental purpose of bringing home
sacred matter to an ignorant populace produced such
advances in realism and secularisation as led the Old English

---

[1] More remotely this sacred drama was inspired by the Roman plays
themselves, which had never been lost, but were read by the learned in
the monasteries.

CHAP. XII Moralities and Interludes to the very verge of the modern
——   Drama.

The Re- Then came the Renaissance : the new birth of intellectual
naissance : activity brought about when the whole wealth of an ancient
literature was suddenly recovered. This ancient literature
became the school in which the mind of young Europe
trained itself, and the education was through the eye
extended to the common people, for whom all public
rise of Ro- pageants took a classical form. The popular drama felt the
mantic out general movement. Already the old interest of mediæval
of Popular story had been made a new interest by realisation on the
Drama, stage : when the works of the ancient stage were added as a
third influence, Old English rose into Elizabethan Drama,
by the appli- and this to Shakespeare. The three influences continued
cation of to work together in moulding the new Drama. The popular
Classical
form to Ro- character of the audience was a constant factor : the dramatic
mance mat- exhibitions typical of the Elizabethan age rose by gradual
ter steps, from the level of the bear-baitings which shared the
same inn-yard, to the intellectual amusement of the theatre ;
they were adapted throughout to the tastes of a populace
trained in the moralities and interludes, and caring nothing
for the literary traditions which some were calling laws.
The Ancient Classical Drama was represented in the
dramatists themselves. If we look at the fathers of our
stage and the great Elizabethan playwrights, we find nearly
all of them public school or university men : Udall was
master of Eton, Bale was a bishop and Fletcher a bishop's
son ; Edwards, Lodge, Peele, Lyly, Marston, Massinger,
Shirley, were Oxford men ; Greene, Marlowe, Ben Jonson,
Beaumont and Heywood were Cambridge men ; Sackville
and Chapman studied at both Oxford and Cambridge, and
the latter was the translator of Homer. For these, and
equally for those whose names are not in the list, Greek and
Latin literature was the sole standard to which criticism
could appeal. Thus popular taste and literary tradition met

in the Elizabethan plays : for a third influence the stories of CHAP. XII
Romance were the sources from which these Elizabethan
plays were taken. As a matter of fact all Shakespeare's
plots have been, with more or less of probability, already
traced to their sources ; the idea of inventing matter for the
stage had not yet come into vogue, and indeed the main
attraction to the audience lay in seeing a favourite story
acted. It was inevitable that the romances from which the
matter of a play was taken should exercise distinct influence
in moulding the action : how considerable that influence
was is suggested by the fact that it is this element which has
contributed to the new literary product its name of ' Romantic Drama.'

This amalgamation of ancient Drama with mediæval *Value to*
the Roman-
Romance was the happiest of unions. Romance broke *tic drama*
down the absolute scenic unity which had so restricted *of the Ro-*
mance ele-
the scope of the ancient Drama while developing its *ment :*
form ; where the story was an interest on a par with
the dramatic action it would be acted as a whole, not left
to be inferred from its final phase. This fulness of matter
carried with it free change of scene, free handling of time,
and unrestricted intermingling of what was serious and
light ;—in short, a general elasticity of treatment by which
an action would be presented from every side, and the
spectator taken into the confidence of all parties in turn.
On the other hand, from the ancient plays modern drama *the Classic*
element :
gained the strict dramatic form, which had been elaborated
in a field where the accidents of convention had limited
matter, and form had been the only thing left to develop.
Modern Drama has added nothing new in form, it has only
diversified classic form with its own wider diversity of
matter ; the Elizabethan stage starts with the multiplication
of actions with which the Roman Comedy ended, and its
conception of unity becomes a harmony of stories proceeding side by side, bound together by parallelism, by contrast,

by interlacing, or in a variety of ways enhancing one another's effect. The Romantic Drama was a union of complementary elements; and the popular stage, on which the union was effected, itself served as a constant force for realism, balancing the special idealism of the Classical Drama in a way that increased the effectiveness of each.

Interests descending from Classic to Romantic Drama: The Chorus,

The Romantic Drama is thus the descendant of the Ancient Classical Drama, with a strong infusion of new blood derived from its other parent. It is further the heir of all that on the ancient stage was other than accidental. The Chorus was originally, so to speak, a scaffold for building up dramatic unity, restricting matter until the sense of form was strong enough to stand by itself. But it was a great deal more than this. There is the intrinsic value of the lyric poetry which it added to Tragedy: this, upon the loss of the Chorus, was, we have seen, dissipated over the details of a modern dramatic poem, furnishing the variety of thought and pregnancy of expression which make up the 'tragical flights' of Shakespeare, so censured by a more prosaic school of critics. The Chorus again gave to the ancient dramas the metrical flexibility, reflecting variation in tone and movement, which Elizabethan dramatists secured by the interchange of prose and verse. In part the ancient Chorus is represented by the confidant of the modern stage, and by collective actors, such as crowds; in part this lyric element has passed into the setting of the modern play—the music which fills up intervals or accompanies the more emotional scenes. And whereas one tendency of Ancient Tragedy was for the lyric to absorb the dramatic element, this has in modern art been realised by a bifurcation, and separation of the play from the lyric opera. Again, Classical Drama was

Epic and Rhetoric,
enriched by an epic and a rhetorical element. Epic influence is felt by modern drama, not in messengers' speeches, but in the story form of its action; while the rhetorical style of the

Greek and Roman poets has not only descended to the CHAP. XII
Elizabethan drama, but further been reinforced by the
modern rhetoric of euphuism, which with its parallelisms
and antitheses expands the set speeches of Shakespeare
and gives brightness to his wit. Interests of matter have *Motives,*
descended from ancient to modern with or without a difference. The idea of destiny has passed into the idea of
providence ; for irony of fate Shakespeare substitutes irony
in circumstances ; the oracular interest he secures with the
aid of witchcraft and other superstition. Interest of horror
still inspires our tragedy, and for the Greek interest of
splendour perhaps a counterpart may be found in the
splendid imagination of the fairy dramas. The idealisation of life which was so prominent a motive of Greek
Tragedy, and the simple human interest which was the
final interest of classical Comedy, are equally important
to the dramatist in whose words the purpose of the stage is
described as the holding up the mirror to nature. Even the *Minor*
lesser characteristics of Greek and Roman drama have in *points*
many cases survived. The special contribution of Aristocratic Comedy in Greece—the painting of manners, or
caricature—is extensively used by Elizabethan dramatists for
their underplots ; the extravagance characterising the rival
species in antiquity has now a representative in the Shakespearean Fool, who mingles his abandon with the probable
matter of the plot ; and the special function of the parabasis
to serve as the author's preface is taken over by the
modern prologue and epilogue. The Romantic Drama
reproduces the whole of the Classical Drama except its
limitations.

The elaboration of this Romantic Drama out of its two *Struggle of*
constituent elements was naturally a gradual process, and *the Roman-*
tic drama
was effected not without conflict. Many forms of drama *against*
were competing for public favour, and the full strength of *Classic*
criticism
criticism was thrown on the side of those who wished to

F f

CHAP. XII revive the ancient stage with all its limitations. Sidney in his *Apologie for Poetrie* denounces the new departure. He says of *Gorboduc*:

> It is faulty both in place and time, the two necessary companions of all corporal actions. For where the stage should alway represent but one place ; and the uttermost time presupposed in it should be, both by Aristotle's precept, and common reason, but one day ; there is both many days and many places inartificially imagined . . . . But they will say, How then shall we set forth a story which contains both many places and many times?   And do they not know that a tragedy is tied to the laws of poesy and not of history?

This—with his further objection to the rising drama as a 'mongrel tragi-comedy, neither right tragedy nor right comedy'—is a simple and clear statement of the points at issue, coming from a mind which could not conceive any 'untying' of poetic laws.   An equally clear summary of the conflict is given in a casual reference thrown out by the artist who was by his practice, in serene indifference to theory, upsetting for ever the laws of Aristotle and Sidney. Shakespeare's Hamlet introduces

> the best actors in the world, either for tragedy, comedy, history, pastoral, pastoral-comical, historical-pastoral, tragical-historical, tragical-comical-historical-pastoral, scene individable or poem un-limited : Seneca cannot be too heavy for them, nor Plautus too light. For the law of writ and the liberty, these are the only men.

In the struggle between the law of writ and the liberty, the liberty gained the day, and when Ben Jonson is reached classical learning itself is won to the Romantic Drama.   In the prologue to his second play he puts the plea for restric-tion into the mouth of the 'mild' critic, and gives the answer to the 'man of a discreet understanding and judg-ment.'

> *Mitis.*   Does he observe all the laws of Comedy in it?
> *Cordatus.*   What laws mean you?
> *Mitis.*   Why, the equal divison of it into acts and scenes, and
> according to the Terentian manner; his true number of actors;

the furnishing of the scene with grex or Chorus, and that the
whole argument fall within the compass of a day's business.

Cordatus. O no, these are too nice observations.

Mitis. They are such as must be received, by your favour, or it cannot be authentic.

Cordatus. Troth, I can discern no such necessity.

Mitis. No?

Cordatus. No, I assure you, Signior. If those laws you speak of had been delivered to us *ab initio*, and in their present virtue and perfection, there had been some reason of obeying their powers; but 'tis extant, that that which we call *Comœdia* was at first nothing but a simple and continued song, sung by one only person, till Susario invented a second; after him Epicharmus a third; Phormus and Chionides devised to have four actors, with a prologue and chorus; to which Cratinus, long afterwards, added a fifth and sixth: Eupolis more; Aristophanes more than they; every man in the dignity of his spirit and judgment supplied something. And, though that in him this kind of poem appeared absolute, and fully perfected, yet how is the face of it changed since, in Menander, Philemon, Cecilius, Plautus, and the rest! who have utterly excluded the chorus, altered the property of the persons, their names and natures, and augmented it with all liberty, according to the elegancy and liberality of those times wherein they wrote. I see not then but we should enjoy the same licence, or free power to illustrate and heighten our invention, as they did; and not be tied to those strict and regular forms which the niceness of a few, who are nothing but form, would thrust upon us.

I cannot conclude the present work better than with this quotation, in which Ben Jonson uses literary evolution as a plea against judicial criticism:—a plea made in the early days of that Romantic Drama which was destined to become the great achievement of popular taste in conflict with critical principles, and the great vindication of liberty in art as a path to higher law.

APPENDIX

438

STRUCTURE

OF PARTICULAR PLAYS

THE ORESTES OF EURIPIDES

[Dramatic Structure]

Formal Prologue.—Soliloquy of Electra, introducing the general situ-   1–70
ation. [Less formal, or more nearly dramatic than most.]
Dramatic Prologue.—Dialogue between Electra and Helen. [First step   71–139
in the action : getting Hermione separated from her mother.]
 Concerto for Parode.—Soft entry of the Chorus as a visit to the sick   140–210
 Orestes.
Episode I.—Waking of Orestes and scene at the sick bedside.   211
 Choral Ode I.—Pacification of the Furies who have troubled Orestes. ·   316–55
Episode II.—Appeal to Menelaus—including **Forensic Contest** between   470–629
Tyndarus and Menelaus—quickening to a climax of **Accelerated Rhythm** from 729
with the entrance of Pylades and news of the plot.
 Choral Ode II.—Ruin of the House of Atreus.   807–43
Episode III.—The **Messenger's Speech:** Account of the Assembly and   852*
condemnation of Orestes.
 Monody for Choral Ode.—Electra : Ruin of the House.   960–1012
Episode IV.—**Blank Verse.** Brother and sister preparing to die together :   1018*–99
Pylades as friend insisting on dying with them.—**Parallel Verse.** Their   1100–1245
councils of despair.—**Blank Verse and Parallel Verse mixed.** Plot
to slay Helen and seize Hermione.
 Concerto for Choral Ode.—Electra and the Chorus watching for Her-   1246–1310
 mione, while the attempt on the life of Helen is being made behind the
 scene.
Episode V.—Capture of Hermione.   1311–52
 Strophe as Interlude : singing to divert attention.   1353–65
Episode VI.—Lyric **Messenger's Speech:** the Phrygian's account of   1369*–1502
the attempted murder and miraculous rescue—climax of **Accelerated**   1506–36
Rhythm as the Phrygian is caught by Orestes.
 Antistrophe as Interlude : Silence ? or raise an alarm ?   1537–48
Exodus.—Spectacular Finale : Menelaus and the crowd below, Orestes and   1554*–1624
his friend on the palace with torches to fire it, and holding Hermione as
hostage.
Divine Intervention.—Apollo.   1625–93

 * Gaps of a few lines not included in this enumeration will be found to be words of
transition spoken by the Chorus to draw attention to the new personage or incident :—
the analogue of our modern stage-directions.

THE WASPS OF ARISTOPHANES
[Metrical Structure]

—•—

Blank Verse. [Prologue.] The slaves watching the father—explanation   1–229
to the audience as to the father's strange disease and the various kinds of
treatment attempted—incident of the attempted escape.

    Long Iambics. Entry of the Chorus on their way to court, gloating   230
over their unworthy occupation—*varied by a concerto with their linkboys*   248–72
—a strophe and antistrophe of wonder at not finding their comrade—   273–89
another strophe and antistrophe of concerto with linkboys.   291–316

        Irregular Lyrics. Love-Cleon speaking from within the house   317
declares the confinement in which he is kept by his son—*in a strophe*   333–45
of angry questionings the Chorus wonder at such daring impiety
—then a sudden change to

    Anapæsts with the thought that escape must be attempted. *The*   346
antistrophe comes when the Chorus, after repeated suggestions for   365–78
escape have been rejected, urge that something must be done for morning
is at hand. The anapæsts resume as the device of gnawing the net is   379
put in action, though unsuccessfully as Love-Cleon is caught.

        Irregular Lyrics : burst of wrath by the Chorus who send for   403
Cleon.

    Trochaics are heard for the first time as Hate-Cleon, the contriver of   415
all this imprisonment, speaks and demands a parley—this is rejected and
a fight takes place.

        Irregular Lyrics as the Chorus getting the worse in the fight   463
raise the regular cry of 'tyranny.'

    Trochaics resume as Hate-Cleon calls for a second parley, leading up   472
to a regular Forensic Contest, Hate-Cleon undertaking to prove that a
juror's life is slavery. not bliss.

        Irregular Lyrics : bustling preparations for the contest.   526

    Anapæstic * Forensic Contest. Love-Cleon puts the case in favour   546–759
of the juror's lot. [Note two **iambic** couplets in the middle of the   634, 642
contest in which each combatant separately plumes himself on the
strength of his case.] Hate-Cleon puts the case against the jurors.
Towards the end a strophe and antistrophe of the Chorus advising the   729–49
old man to give in.

Blank Verse (resumed after more than five hundred lines). Love-Cleon   760
gives way.—Incident of the jury proceedings, conducted in domestic privacy
with strophic and other lyrics interspersed parodying the inauguration   862–90
ceremonies of a court of justice.

                [Parabasis]   1009–1121
Incident of practising the father in the ways of young men.   1122

[Irregular lyrics at intervals for quoted songs or bits of dancing.]

After a *lyric interlude* scene of the converted juryman outdoing the young   1275–91
rakes—after another *lyric interlude*   1450–73
Spectacular Finale : climax of wildness on the part of the old man leading to   1518–27
[**anapæstic** introduction and] *strophic crab-dance*—the Chorus dancing out
in **irregular iambics.**

* Anapæstic, because the thesis which Hate-Cleon undertakes to prove is, from the
Chorus point of view, a monstrous paradox. See above, page 307.

THE FROGS OF ARISTOPHANES

[Metrical Structure]

— ‡ —

Generating Action

Blank Verse. Bacchus accompanied by his slave Xanthias (with an ass) makes a call on his divine cousin Hercules before repeating Hercules' feat of a descent to Hades—thence to the bank of the Styx. 1–207

    Irregular Lyrics. Invisible Chorus of Frogs disturbed by Bacchus in his row over the Styx. [Concerto.] 209–68

Blank Verse. Scene of Bacchus's terrors on the further bank of the Styx. 269–322

    Lyrics. Comus-procession of the Initiated [Parode] in strophic* lyrics with interruptions: (1) of **blank verse** by actors from the stage, (2) **anapæstic interlogue**, a mock proclamation for the uninitiated to withdraw made an attack on social evils, (3) **iambic interlogue**, lampoons on individual persons. 323–459

Blank Verse. Farcical incident : reception of the supposed Hercules by the people of Hades—*broken by comments from the Chorus (in dichotomous lyrics)*. 460–673

[Parabasis] 674–737

Main Plot

Blank Verse. Gossip of the slaves bringing out the projected contest. 738

    Lyrics including **hexameters** : the Chorus anticipating the arrival of the competitors. 814

Blank Verse : the poets take their seats disputing precedence. 830

    Lyrics including **hexameters** : the Chorus invoke the Muses. 875

Blank Verse. The poets offer prayer to their respective deities. 885

    Strophe of expectation from the Chorus merging in 895

Long Iambics (with climax) : Euripides leads the discussion. 905

    Antistrophe : the Chorus look to Aeschylus : merging in 992

Anapæsts (with climax): Aeschylus takes the lead in the discussion. 1004

    Strophe and Antistrophe : Chorus sing the mighty strife. 1099

Blank Verse : discussion of prologues and versification. 1119

    Lyric burst of anticipation from the Chorus leading to 1251

Mixed verse : discussion of lyric composition. 1261

    Short **lyric** burst from the Chorus at the suggestion of a balance. 1370

Blank Verse. Incident of weighing verses in the balance. 1378

    Strophe and Antistrophe of victory by the Chorus. 1482

Anapæsts with **hexameters** for climax : triumphant procession in honour of Aeschylus. 1500

---

* Note the important variation of strophic form by which we find *two* antistrophes to one strophe [viz. 440–4 and 444–7 to 394–7 according to Bergk's arrangement. Another example (also in a late play) is *Mysteries* 959–61, 962–5, 966–8]. This is interesting as a link in the transition to the modern conception of stanzas. [See above, page 9.]

THE LYSISTRATA OF ARISTOPHANES

[Metrical Structure]

—••—

Blank Verse. [Prologue.] Conspiracy of the Women up to the point   1-253
where a shout indicates that the Acropolis has been seized.
Long Iambic section of the play. Hostile Choruses of Men and of Women   254-483
(to attack and defend the Acropolis) enter from opposite sides and exchange
insult and defiance : *strophic passages interspersed.*
   Blank Verse episode : the Magistrate enters to assert the law—con-   387-466
   fronted by the women conspirators—a scrimmage and return to
Long Iambics as the police get the worse—*climaxing in a Strophe from
the Chorus of Men demanding enquiry :* thus the play passes to its

Anapæstic stage: Lysistrata in response to the Magistrate commences   484-613
the 'paradoxical justification': first she exposes the bad government of Man
—*Antistrophe* from the Chorus of Women expressing devotion to their
cause*—then she puts the advantages of women's management as it is to be.
   Blank Verse: The magistrate scornful: the play passes to its   608-13

Trochaic stage. The Choruses of Men and Women face one another   614-1042
and exchange scorn and violence (*largely strophic*)—this interrupted by
   Blank Verse episode : individual women deserting finally brought back   706-80
   by an oracle. [In this Women's scene the Chorus of Women share, the
   Chorus of Men are ignored.]
Trochaic contest of the hostile Choruses resumed (*entirely strophic*)—
another interruption by a
   Blank Verse episode. A man deserter tantalised by his wife. [In   829-953
   this Man scene the Chorus of Women share, the Chorus of Women are
   ignored.**]—Brief **lyric** climax—then another **blank verse** scene :
   reception of Lacedæmonian Herald.
Trochaic contest of the two Choruses resumed with ever decreasing hostility : as they at last make peace the play passes into its

Lyric stage. *Joint Chorus of Men and Women express their delight at*   from 1043
the reconciliation in (*strophic*) *surprise lyrics.*
   Blank Verse. Reception of the Lacedæmonian Ambassadors : Lysis-   1074
   trata introduces them to Reconciliation. [Both parts of the episode
   introduced by **anapæsts.**]
Strophic surprise lyrics continued.   1188
   Blank Verse. Preparations for Finale : the Athenians and their Lace-   1216
   dæmonian guests coming from the banquet.
Lyric Dance by Lacedæmonians on the stage.
   Blank Verse. Preparations : Lysistrata arranging the partners.   1273-8 and 1295
Lyric Finale. Attic and Doric Dances.   1279, 1296

---

* 541-8 [parallel with 476-83]: introduced by a couplet of long iambics as they lay
their pitchers down to dance (that is, retire from their long iambic position, so to speak).

** The solitary line 970 assigned by Bergk to Chorus of Women is surely better given
to Kinesias, as in Dindorf's text.

THE CAPTIVES OF PLAUTUS

[Metrical Structure]

—◆◆—

Blank Verse	Accelerated Rhythm	

I

| Prologue. | | 1-68 |
| [Underplot.] Caricature Scene: the Parasite condoling with Hegio on the captivity of his son as a means of fishing for an invitation. | | 69-194 |

II

	After a lyric prelude [slaves condoling with the Captives—the Captives referring in general terms to their secret intrigue] the scene passes	195-241
	[with the first solemn appeal to maintain the intrigue] to Accelerated Rhythm—in which is conveyed the long business of maintaining the exchanged identities in presence of Hegio—interrupted by	242-360
Blank verse, as Hegio proceeds to himself take part in the intrigue against himself by a formal transfer of supposed slave to supposed master— then the scene returns to		361-84
	Accelerated Rhythm: final steps in the intrigue and affecting farewells.	385-460

III

	[Underplot complicated.] The Parasite in despair: no invitations: desperate councils.	461-97
	After a lyric prelude of agitation as Tyndarus sees approaching, and seeks to evade, the acquaintance whose recognition will betray the intrigue scene becomes trochaic to mark the actual meeting—acute complication as Tyndarus fences with Aristophantes— change to	498-540
		541-658
Blank Verse: intrigue broken down— despair—Tyndarus calmly defiant— remorse of Aristophantes		659-767

IV

	[Underplot drawn into main action.] *After a lyric prelude [rapture of Parasite over his valuable tidings and all it will buy in the way of entertainment]* there is a change to	768-90
	trochaics as the secret of the son's return is gradually let out—Parasite bidden to made himself at home.	791-908
Long Iambics. [Underplot.] Comment of a servant lad on the Parasite's gastronomic performances.		909-21

V

| | *Lyric prelude of rejoicing at the recovery of the captive son*—a change | 922-9 |
| | to trochaics [at the thought 'let us to business']—Explanations and discovery of another son in Tyndarus— general wind up. | 930 to end |

THE TRINUMMUS OF PLAUTUS

[Metrical Structure]

—◆◆—

NOTE:—Here metrical differences are utilised to keep distinct the two interests of the play: (1) the marriage negotiations, (2) the delicate position of trust in which Callicles has been placed by the absent merchant.

Blank Verse	Accelerated Rhythm	
Prologue.		1–22
I		
An explanation clearing Callicles' character to his friend Megaronides.		23–222
	II	
	After a lyric prelude of moralising by both Son and Father the marriage	223–300
	project is opened by Lysiteles, and Philto undertakes to make the proposal—change to	301–91
Blank verse: Soliloquy of Philto as his son leaves him—so (by persistence as Lesbonicus with his Slave* comes up unexpectedly) proposal scene.		392–401
		402–601
	III	
	News of the projected marriage being conveyed by the Slave*.—Discussion	602–26
	of the dowry question between the bridegroom and the bride's brother.	627–728
Callicles and Megaronides: increased difficulty of Callicles' position in view of the projected marriage—they concert an honest intrigue: a Sharper to personate messenger from Charmides to Callicles.		729–819
	IV	
	After lyric prelude: thanksgiving of the newly-returned Charmides for safe voyage, we get the main complication: conflict of Charmides with	820–41
	the supposed bearer of the dowry money—interrupted by	842–997
Soliloquy of Charmides: doubts as to Callicles.		998–1007
	Complication continued: a second encounter with the saucy Slave*.	1008–92
Resolution: chance meeting with Callicles, explanation and Charmides' doubts of him changed into enthusiastic gratitude.		1093–1114
	V	
	After brief prelude [bridegroom's self-congratulation] we get general meetings, explanations, and preparations for the marriage.	1115–9 1120 to end

---

* The slave, Stasimus, belongs to the family of the bride (a sort of dependent under-plot): the scenes in which he figures are in Blank Verse before the marriage is broached, afterwards in Accelerated Rhythm.

THE PHORMIO OF TERENCE

[Metrical Structure]

——✦——

The play is a network of intrigues and cross intrigues which are in the course of being carried out or concealed. The parties are two old men (brothers) and a son of each, with the usual parasite and scheming slave for motive personages.

I

Blank Verse. Prologue.—Then a mechanical scene bringing out [by aid   i and ii
of a 'protatic personage'] in the form of gossip the opening situation—next
     a **lyric** scene presents the two youths in trouble, dreading their fathers'   iii and iv to
     return from abroad. They see their scheming slave in the distance and   line 17
     call to him : when after some difficulty he hears them there is a change to
Accelerated rhythm: in which the slave announces that one of these   iv. 18
fathers has actually arrived.—There is a further change to
     Blank verse as this father is seen at the end of the street.   iv. 38

II

Iambic eights*. Soliloquies are heard on either side as father and son near   i to 21
one another—the metre changing to
     Blank verse as the two meet : this becomes a main scene.   i. 24
[A new phase of the action sets in : the attempt to get rid of the marriage.]
In **trochaics** the Parasite is prepared for the new departure : and in   ii
     Blank verse he proceeds to play his part.   i, iv

III

Lyrics display the young men [at the beginning of a new Act] in their   i, ii, 1-19
separate troubles : there is a change to
     Trochaics when they meet and take counsel with the slave who is their   ii from 20
     adviser.   and iii

IV

Blank Verse. The next act passes over to the old men and their difficulties :   i, ii, iii, iv
they also have recourse to the scheming slave as adviser—but there is a
change to
     Iambic eights as they proceed to act upon the advice this slave has   v
     given.

V

A **lyric** scene opens the fifth Act, introducing a fresh personage [who is to   i to line 20
be the key to the resolution of the plot]—the lyric excitement of this meeting
suddenly changes to
     Iambic sevens, as her explanation is hushed for fear it may be over-   i from 21
     heard. Two scenes carry on [in the same rhythm] the plan adopted by   ii, and iii
     the old men in the last Act—there is the slight variation in a third scene   1-11
     of the same nature to **iambic eights** where one of the parties, wishing   iii from 12
     to oppose, is compelled, owing to the presence of a particular individual,
     to be content with hinting what he wishes—there is a change back to
     iambic sevens for a brief soliloquy—and again to **iambic eights** as   iv, v.
     the intrigue is resumed—then there is a swing round the metrical
     compass to
Trochaics, as the slave enters, overjoyed at having overheard the secret   vi. 1-43
which has given him the command of the whole situation.
In **blank verse** action is taken on this secret, making the denouement   vi from 44,
—but there is a change to   vii and viii. 1-21
Accelerated rhythm as the Wife [who is the person mainly affected by   from viii 22
the denouement] turns upon her Husband to taunt him. This metre continues to the end.

     * Introduced by and concluded with a trochaic couplet.

ANALYSIS OF ARISTOPHANES' PLOTS

Idea of the Plot	Generating Action	Disclosure of the Plot	Development of the Plot	Climax
Acharnians				
The hero making peace for himself while the rest of the state continues at war	Meeting of Parliament and ejection of the peace advocate	As a sudden thought (128–133) in the course of the Generating Action	Samples sent of truces and selection (174) — Opposition of the Chorus and *Justification* * *of Peace* (496–556) — Series of peace scenes contrasting with war preparations	Flourish: drinking contest [girl escort] contrasting with wounded warrior
Knights				
Match in political Shamelessness between two champion demagogues	Suffering slaves of Demus inspire themselves with wine and steal the oracles of their tyrant fellow-slave	As a sudden discovery of an oracle: the Leather-seller to perish at the hands of a yet worse Sausage-seller (123–46)	The Sausage-seller discovered and brought up to fighting-point — *he justifies* ** *the oracle in a contest with the Leather-seller* (280–481) —the out-bidding in the Council—the contest before Demus in the Pnyx	Spectacular finale: Demus boiled down to youth — betrothed to the girl Peace
Clouds				
Subtleties of the new education tested by practical application to debt-paying	Domestic embarrassment — financial troubles through a horsey son	As a sudden thought after a whole night's cogitation (75–130)	The educational system displayed in operation— *Paradoxical Justification (in anapæsts) of its cloud-inspiration* (314–477)—The system applied to the father—to the son	Reaction: spectacular finale of burning down the thinking-shop
Wasps				
The forensic furore as a form of madness treated and cured	[Outside the action]	A prepared scheme directly explained to the audience in a dramatic digression (54–135)	The guarding the mad juror (from line 1)—rescue by the chorus and fight—*Paradoxical Justification (in anapæsts) as a forensic contest* (546–759) — the Treatment: law-procedure at home — Convalescence: initiation into gay life [Flute-girl introduced]	Cure: the juror turned rake — grotesque finale of crab-dance
Peace				
Peace hauled up bodily out of a pit	Ascent on a beetle † to heaven to discover the whereabouts of Peace	As a sudden thought at a sudden moment of opportunity (289–295)	Summons to the friends of peace—the hauling— *Justification* †† *takes the form of explaining the loss of peace* (601–728)—celebration of its recovery—peace and war trades—peace and war songs	Wedding festivities: The hero and Peace's handmaid Sport

* Not in anapæsts, but blank verse, because it is a serious plea for peace.
** A sort of justification in action. (Blank verse.)
† This idea involves a fable of Æsop. The eagle devoured the young of the beetle. The beetle got into the eagle's nest and rolled its eggs out. The eagle appealed to its guardian Jupiter, and was allowed to lay its eggs in Jupiter's own bosom. The beetle flew up to heaven and buzzed about the ears of Jupiter, who starting up to catch it let fall the eagle's egg: so the beetle had his revenge. The beetle is thus the only creature known to have risen to heaven; hence its utilisation here.
†† Attracted into trochaics by connexion with the countrymen, and blank verse where it becomes a privileged dialogue between the hero and Peace. See above, page 311–2.

ANALYSIS OF ARISTOPHANES' PLOTS (*continued*)

Idea of the Plot	Generating Action	Disclosure of the Plot	Development of the Plot	Climax
Birds				
Strategic project of fortifying the atmosphere for the Birds, giving them the control of gods and men	Emigrants seeking information from the human colony in Birdland	As a sudden thought in course of conversation (162–93)	Summons of the Birds— *Paradoxical Justification* (*in anapæsts:* 460–638) — founding of the city — resistance of the gods (Iris) — human submission — the gods brought to terms	Wedding festivities and ascent to heaven of hero and Queen of heaven
Lysistrata				
Celibacy-strike of the women in favour of peace	Assembly of women to hear a secret scheme	Announced as a prepared scheme (119)	Oath of conspiracy— seizure and defence of Acropolis — intervention of magistrate leading to *Anapæstic Justification* (484–607) — hostility of the sexes with parleys —interjected scenes of attempted desertion on both sides — reconciliation of the sexes with one another and of Athens with Sparta [Reconciliation as a girl]	Choral rejoicings as celebration of reconciliation
Women at the Mysteries				
Euripides' dramatic art tested by application to tragic situations in practical life	Mnesilochus(on failure of Agathon) persuaded to defend Euripides (in disguise) at the Mysteries	As a sudden thought (269–276) providing for possible peril	Origin of the tragic situation : the Mysteries— attack on Euripides and injudicious defence — sensation and discovery of disguise Application of dramatic devices and pathos	Reaction: Euripides agrees to abstain from attacking women [Girl to wheedle away the constable]
Frogs				
Contest between Euripides and Aeschylus for the laureateship of Hades	Adventures of Bacchus descending to Hades to carry off Euripides	Announced as news in gossip between slaves (755–813)	Reception of the contending poets The contest	Reaction : Bacchus carries off Aeschylus— torch-procession
Women in Parliament				
Communism by means of petticoat government	Conspiracy to snatch a vote by disguising women as men in the parliament	Announced as a prepared scheme [in the Justification (from 598)—previously a secret : compare 230, 514, 588]	*Anapæstic Justification* (514–709) interrupted by challenge from a husband — community of goods in operation — community of women	Climax : torchlight procession to the Common Meal [at summons of a girl]
Plutus				
Socialist millennium * by the device of opening the eyes of the blind Money-God	Oracular directions by which the Money-God is met	As a sudden thought (94–99)	Securing (from 100) of the Money-God — rejoicings — suspicion of neighbours — *Anapæstic Justification in the form of forensic contest with Poverty* (487–618) — series of scenes presenting the reversed social conditions	Grotesque procession when Jupiter's priest deserts to Plutus

* See note on page 327.

ANALYSIS OF PARABASES

Introduction or Commation	Parabasis Proper	Strophe of Invocation	After-Speech or Epirrhema	Antistrophe	After-Response or Ant-epirrhema
In short lines or attracted to the metre of the Para-basis Proper	*Always in anapæsts (ex-cept a pecu-liar metre in Clouds)*		*Always in ac-celerated (trochaic) rhythm*		*Always in ac-celerated (tro-chaic) rhythm*

Acharnians (626)

	Character dropped	In character	All three continuous and in character		
Dismisses pre-vious scene—'strip for ana-pæsts'	Humorous ex-altation of the poet as a poli-tical plain-speaker	Kindred deity: Muse of char-coal	Unfair advantage of young over old in Athenian law-proceedings: Put generally		Put with hum-orous sugges-tion: old to try old, and young, young

Knights (498)

	In character	In character	In character	In character	In character
Dismisses pre-vious scene—'attend to anapæsts'	Ingratitude of the public to previous comic poets	Kindred deity: Neptune as equestrian king	Ancestral greatness of knights as conservators of public morals	Patriotic deities	Humorous ex-altation of the knights under the guise of their horses

Knights (1263)

		In character	Character dropped or maintained: no evidence		
None	None	Pindaric rhythm paro-died as lam-poon	Immorality on the scale of a public scan-dal	As Strophe	Naval criticism under guise of an indignation meeting of tri-remes

Clouds (510)

	Character dropped	In character	In character	No evidence	In character
Dismisses pre-vious scene	Exaltation of the poet over his predeces-sors	Kindred dei-ties: Zeus, Sea-god, and Aether	A political elec-tion presented as an offence against the Clouds	Patriotic dei-ties	Ceremonial laxity presented as an offence against the Moon

Wasps (1009)

	Character dropped	In character	All three continuous and in character		
Dismisses pre-vious scene—bespeaks at-tention	Remonstrance with the pub-lic as to the reception of previous plays	Their own youth as kin-dred deity	Athenian character presented as waspish: In prowess		Carried into va-rious details

ANALYSIS OF PARABASES (*continued*)

Introduction or Commation	Parabasis Proper	Strophe of Invocation	After-Speech or Epirrhema	Antistrophe	After-Response or Ant-epirrhema
In short lines or attracted to the metre of the Parabasis Proper	*Always in anapæsts (except a peculiar metre in Clouds)*		*Always in accelerated (trochaic) rhythm*		*Always in accelerated (trochaic) rhythm*
Peace (729)					
	Character dropped	*Character dropped*			
Dismisses previous scene—clothes committed to attendants	The poet's services to Comedy	Parody—lampoon on rivals			
Peace (1127)					
			In character		*In character*
		(A few lines of lyrics commence the After-Speech)	The husbandman in time of peace	(As Strophe)	The husbandman in time of war
Birds (676)					
	Parabasis drawn into the plot: character maintained all through				
Call for a prelude from the nightingale	Religious antiquity and supremacy of the Birds	Muse of the swan-song — Phrynicus's rhythm with accompaniment of bird-twittering	Birds' ways applied to public morals	(Continues Strophe)	Minor conveniences of birds' ways
		The Birds themselves as proper subjects for invocation — bird-rhythm	A poulterer denounced as a public enemy	(Continues Strophe)	Bird penalties applied to the adjudication on the play
Women at the Mysteries (776)					
	In character: Parabasis drawn within the plot as before				
[None: but the conclusion of the previous scene falls into the same form]	Mock-serious defence of women	None	Counter-charge against man	None	(Nothing to distinguish from After-Speech)
Frogs (675)					
		Character dropped all through: lyrics attracted to After-Speech			
None	None	Parody-lampoon	Serious plea for political amnesty	(As Strophe)	Continues Speech, with humorous illustration of the coinage

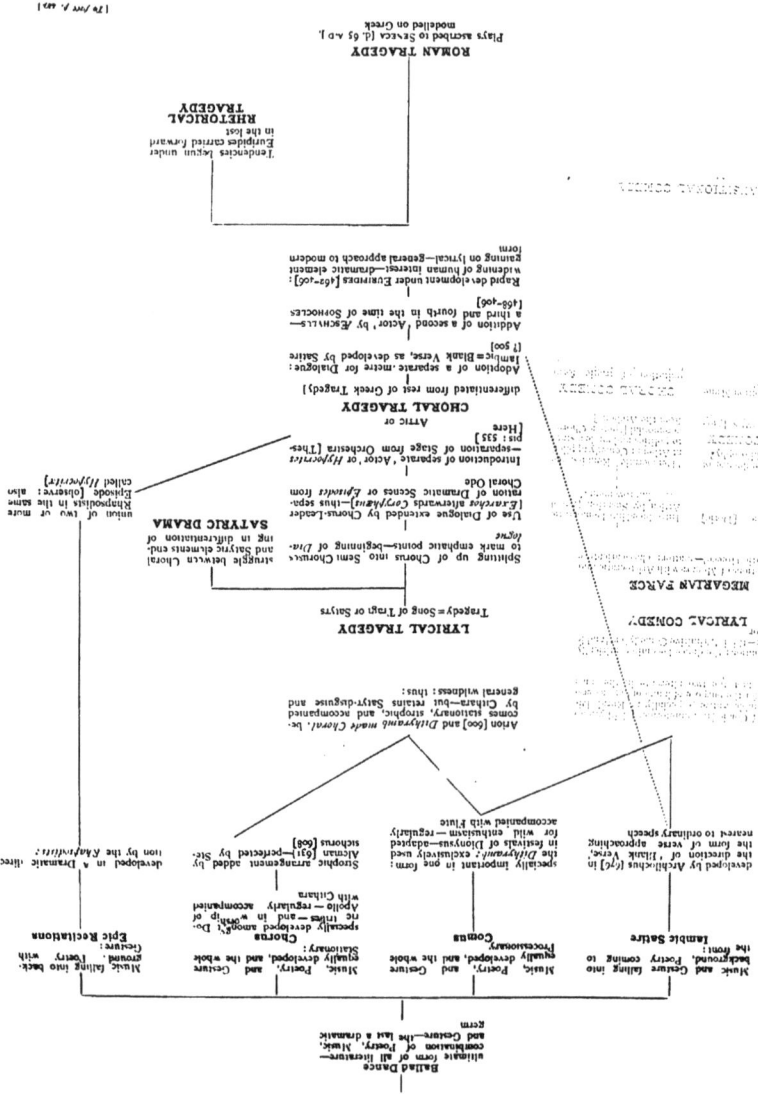

GENEALOGICAL TABLE: ORIGIN OF THE ANCIENT CLASSICAL DRAMA

TABLES

G g

CHRONOLOGICAL TABLES—No. I

N.B.—The dates must be in almost all cases understood as only approximate.

B.C.

700 Archilochus as a Satirist: foundation of the metrical revolution leading to Blank Verse

? Primitive or LYRICAL COMEDY or 'Iambic Dance'

631 Alcman and 668 Stesichorus: authors of the metrical revolution which gave distinctiveness [Strophic form] to Greek Lyric Verse

600 Revolution of Arion and foundation of LYRIC TRAGEDY

600 (and after) MEGARIAN FARCE: first species after Primitive Comedy

580 (and after) Comedy introduced into Attica by Susarion: with 'improvements'

540-443. Earlier period of SICILIAN COMEDY [Aristocratic] under Epicharmus

560-27 Anti-democratic movement (technically 'Tyranny'] of Pisistratus at Athens. During this period the ballad literature known as 'Homer' was worked up into the final form known to us as the 'Iliad' and 'Odyssey.'

535 Revolution of Thespis: addition of 'Actors' to (Attic) Tragedy

[500-400 CHORAL or OLD ATTIC TRAGEDY fully established]

500-478 Persian Wars: rise of a national feeling among the Greek States—Athens gradually taking the lead—the movement culminates in

B.C.

480 Sudden outburst of Athenian influence and general 'Democratic Renaissance.'

460-411 CHORAL or OLD ATTIC COMEDY—Chief names: Chionides, Cratinus, ARISTOPHANES, Eupolis, Phrynichus, Plato. [Crates represents during this period the Middle Attic or transition tendencies.]

460-20 Later period of SICILIAN COMEDY [Aristocratic]: Sophron and the Mime

[460-56 Last years of Aeschylus in CHORAL TRAGEDY]

454-29 Climax of Athenian greatness: Administration of Pericles. Herodotus and Thucydides—earlier life of Socrates.—This passes into

431-400 Peloponnesian War and gradual decline of Athenian Democracy. Socrates and the 'Sophists'.—earlier years of Plato.

[456-406 Sophocles and Euripides reign over CHORAL TRAGEDY.]

425-14 Contributions of Aristophanes to CHORAL COMEDY: Acharnians, Knights, Clouds, Wasps, Peace, Birds

B.C.

411 Fall of Athenian Democracy: Oligarchic Revolution of the Four Hundred (411)—Revolution of the Thirty Tyrants (404)—Execution of Socrates (399).

411 (and after) The lost TRANSITIONAL or MIDDLE ATTIC COMEDY.—Plays of Aristophanes reflecting the transition: *Lysistrata* and *Mysteries* (411)—*Frogs* (405)—*Women in Parliament* (391)—*Plutus* (388)

[411-6 Last years of Sophocles and Euripides in CHORAL TRAGEDY]

406 (and after) Lost RHETORICAL TRAGEDY

342-290 Lost NEW ATTIC COMEDY.—Chief names: Philemon, MENANDER, Diphilus, Apollodorus

240-159 ROMAN COMEDY—Chief names: Livius Andronicus, Nævius, Ennius, besides Plautus and Terence

224-184 Contributions of PLAUTUS to Roman Comedy*

168-59 Contributions of TERENCE to Roman Comedy**

CHRONOLOGICAL TABLES—No. II

N.B.—The dates of plays must be understood as only approximate.

B. C.
525 **Æschylus** born
499 His first competition

484 Æschylus's first prize
480 Æschylus fought at the battle of Salamis
473 *The Persians*
472 *The Seven against Thebes*
? *The Prometheus*
468 Grand dramatic contest, and defeat of Æschylus by Sophocles

461 *The Suppliants*
458 TRILOGY: *Story of Orestes*
456 Death of Æschylus

(70 plays in all)

B.C.
495 **Sophocles** born

480 Sophocles chief dancer at the Triumph for Salamis

[Sophocles aged 39]
440 *Antigone*
? { *Electra*
    Maidens of Trachis

? *Œdipus as King*

? *Ajax*
  Philoctetes

B.C.
480 **Euripides** born

462 Euripides' first play

[Euripides aged 24]
441 Euripides's first prize

439 *Alcestis*
437 *Rhesus*
431 *Medea*
429 *Hippolytus*
425 *Hecuba*
423 *Ion*
421 *The Suppliants*
420 *Andromache*
418 *The Children of Hercules*
415 *The Daughters of Troy*
— *Electra*
413 *Helena*
? *Hercules Mad*
411 *Women from Phœnicia*
408 *Orestes*
407 *Iphigenia among the Tauri*
Posthumous: *Iphigenia in Aulis*
             The Bacchanals
(75 or 92 plays in all)

406 **Death of both Sophocles and Euripides**
Posthumous: *Œdipus at Colonus*
(130 plays in all)

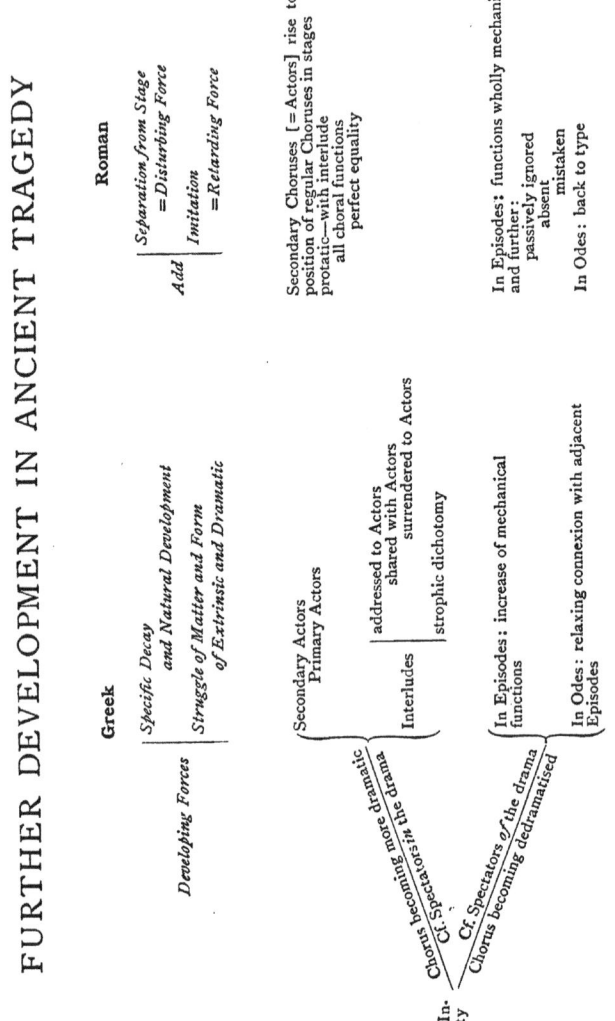

FURTHER DEVELOPMENT IN ANCIENT TRAGEDY

Greek

Developing Forces
- Specific Decay and Natural Development
- Struggle of Matter and Form of Extrinsic and Dramatic

Secondary Actors
Primary Actors
- addressed to Actors
- shared with Actors
- surrendered to Actors

Interludes — strophic dichotomy

In Episodes: increase of mechanical functions

In Odes: relaxing connexion with adjacent Episodes

Choral Instability
- Chorus becoming more dramatic — Cf. Spectators *in* the drama
- Cf. Spectators *of* the drama — Chorus becoming dedramatised

Roman

Add
- Separation from Stage = Disturbing Force
- Imitation = Retarding Force

Secondary Choruses [= Actors] rise to the position of regular Choruses in stages
- protatic—with interlude
- all choral functions
- perfect equality

In Episodes: functions wholly mechanical—and further:
- passively ignored
- absent
- mistaken

In Odes: back to type

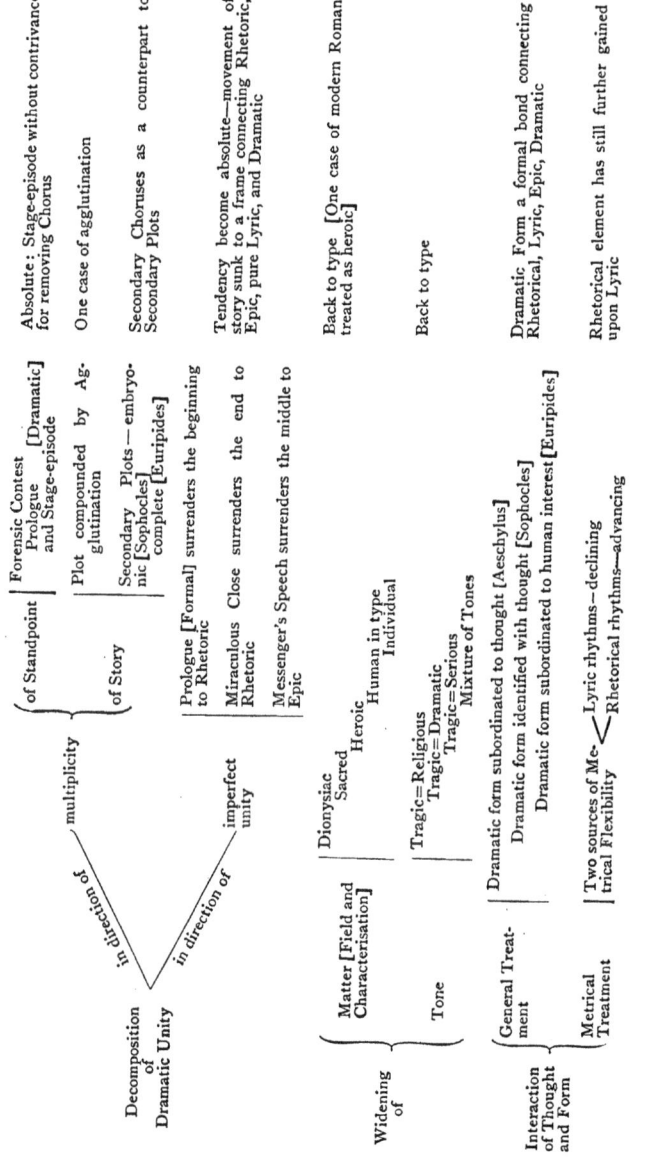

453

Decomposition of Dramatic Unity

in direction of multiplicity
- of Standpoint
  - Forensic Contest [Dramatic]
  - Prologue and Stage-episode — Absolute: Stage-episode without contrivance for removing Chorus
  - Plot compounded by Agglutination — One case of agglutination
- of Story
  - Secondary Plots — embryonic [Sophocles] complete [Euripides] — Secondary Choruses as a counterpart to Secondary Plots

in direction of imperfect unity
- Prologue [Formal] surrenders the beginning to Rhetoric
- Miraculous Close surrenders the end to Rhetoric — Tendency become absolute—movement of story sunk to a frame connecting Rhetoric, Epic, pure Lyric, and Dramatic
- Messenger's Speech surrenders the middle to Epic

Widening of

Matter [Field and Characterisation]
- Dionysiac
- Sacred
- Heroic — Back to type [One case of modern Roman treated as heroic]
- Human in type
- Individual

Tone
- Tragic=Religious
- Tragic=Dramatic
- Tragic=Serious — Back to type
- Mixture of Tones

Interaction of Thought and Form

General Treatment
- Dramatic form subordinated to thought [Aeschylus]
- Dramatic form identified with thought [Sophocles] — Dramatic Form a formal bond connecting Rhetorical, Lyric, Epic, Dramatic
- Dramatic form subordinated to human interest [Euripides]

Metrical Treatment
- Two sources of Metrical Flexibility
  - Lyric rhythms—declining
  - Rhetorical rhythms—advancing — Rhetorical element has still further gained upon Lyric

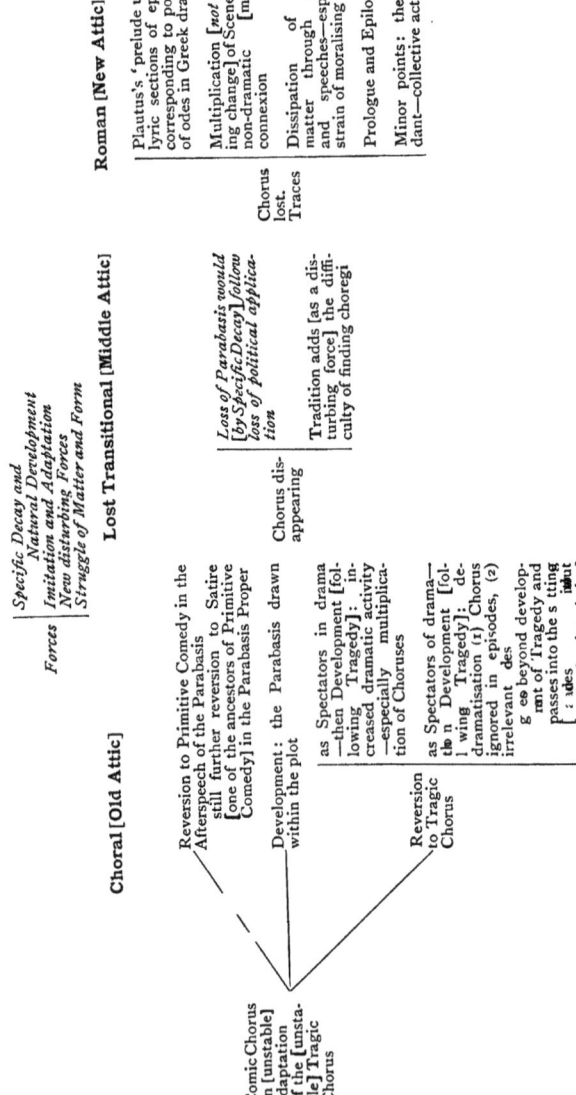

FURTHER DEVELOPMENT IN ANCIENT COMEDY

454

Forces { *Specific Decay and Natural Development* | *Imitation and Adaptation* | *New disturbing Forces* | *Struggle of Matter and Form* }

Choral [Old Attic] — **Lost Transitional [Middle Attic]** — **Roman [New Attic]**

Comic Chorus an [unstable] adaptation of the [unstable] Tragic Chorus

Reversion to Primitive Comedy in the Afterspeech of the Parabasis — still further reversion to Satire [one of the ancestors of Primitive Comedy] in the Parabasis Proper

Development: the Parabasis drawn within the plot

as Spectators in drama —then Development [following Tragedy]: increased dramatic activity —especially multiplication of Choruses

Reversion to Tragic Chorus

as Spectators of drama—then Development [following Tragedy]: dedramatisation (1) Chorus ignored in episodes, (2) irrelevant des g es beyond develop- rnt of Tragedy and passes into the s tting [: ides in ut ws for interludes]

Chorus disappearing

Loss of Parabasis would [by Specific Decay] follow loss of political application

Tradition adds [as a disturbing force] the difficulty of finding choregi

Plautus's 'prelude usage': lyric sections of episodes corresponding to positions of odes in Greek drama.

Multiplication [*not* carrying change] of Scenes with non-dramatic [musical] connexion

Dissipation of lyric matter through details and speeches—especially strain of moralising

Prologue and Epilogue

Minor points: the confidant—collective actors

Chorus lost. Traces

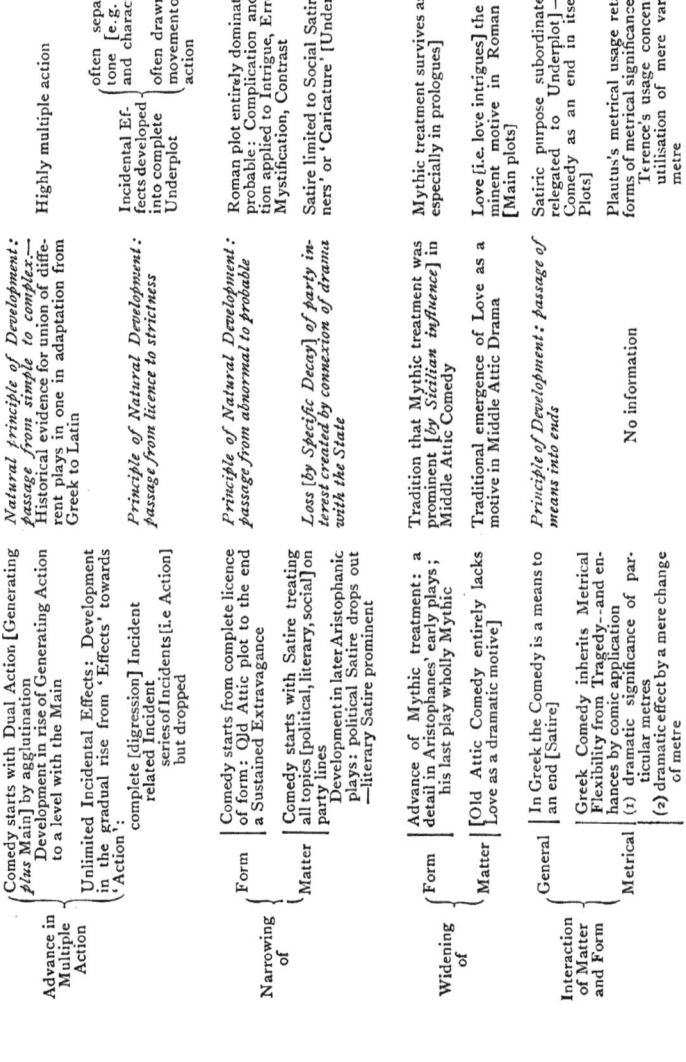

		Content	Natural principle of Development	Result
Advance in Multiple Action		Comedy starts with Dual Action [Generating *plus* Main] by agglutination. Development in rise of Generating Action to a level with the Main. Unlimited Incidental Effects; Development in the gradual rise from 'Effects' towards 'Action': complete [digression] Incident complete related Incident series of Incidents [i.e Action] but dropped	*Natural principle of Development: passage from simple to complex.—Historical evidence for union of different plays in one in adaptation from Greek to Latin*	Highly multiple action {often separated by tone [e.g. manners and character]} Incidental Effects developed into complete Underplot {often drawn into the movement of the main action}
Narrowing of	Form	Comedy starts from complete licence of form: Old Attic plot to the end a Sustained Extravagance	*Principle of Natural Development: passage from abnormal to probable*	Roman plot entirely dominated by the probable: Complication and Resolution applied to Intrigue, Error, Irony, Mystification, Contrast
	Matter	Comedy starts with Satire treating all topics [political, literary, social] on party lines. Development in later Aristophanic plays: political Satire drops out —literary Satire prominent	*Loss [by Specific Decay] of party interest created by connexion of drama with the State*	Satire limited to Social Satire: 'Manners' or 'Caricature' [Underplot]
Widening of	Form	Advance of Mythic treatment: a detail in Aristophanes' early plays; his last play wholly Mythic	*Tradition that Mythic treatment was prominent [by Sicilian influence] in Middle Attic Comedy*	Mythic treatment survives as a detail, especially in prologues
	Matter	[Old Attic Comedy entirely lacks Love as a dramatic motive]	*Traditional emergence of Love as a motive in Middle Attic Drama*	Love [i.e. love intrigues] the most prominent motive in Roman Comedy [Main plots]
Interaction of Matter and Form	General	In Greek the Comedy is a means to an end [Satire]	*Principle of Development: passage of means into ends*	Satiric purpose subordinate [chiefly relegated to Underplot]—rise of Comedy as an end in itself [Main Plots]
	Metrical	Greek Comedy inherits Metrical Flexibility from Tragedy—and enhances by comic application (1) dramatic significance of particular metres (2) dramatic effect by a mere change of metre	No information	Plautus's metrical usage retains both forms of metrical significance. Terence's usage concentrates on utilisation of mere variation in metre

COURSES OF READING

FOR THE STUDENT TO SELECT FROM FOR
FURTHER STUDY

COURSES OF READING

I

THE MYTHOLOGY EMBODIED IN ANCIENT POETRY

As a text-book : Keightley's *Classical Mythology* (Bohn), or Gayley's *Classic Myths* (Ginn).—But the study of the text-book should be accompanied with some working up of the myths in literary form; e. g. Ruskin's *Queen of the Air*, Kingsley's *Heroes* (Macmillan), Lewis Morris's *Epic of Hades*. Several of the tales in William Morris's *Earthly Paradise* are of this nature : e. g. 'The Doom of King Acrisius,' 'Cupid and Psyche.'

These are modern handlings of ancient myths. A specimen of the ancient myth-form utilised for modern thought is the (too little known) *Myths of the Dawn* by Miss Johnson-Brown (Kegan Paul).

II

ENGLISH CLASSICS BEARING UPON ANCIENT LITERATURE

1. Robert Browning's *Balaustion's Adventure* and 'The Love of Alcestis,' in William Morris's *Earthly Paradise*, to be read with the *Alcestis* of Euripides. To this may be added Alfieri's *Alcestis II**. Longfellow's *Golden Legend* handles a similar problem amid Christian surroundings.

2. William Morris's *Life and Death of Jason*, to be read with the *Medea* of Euripides. Several of the tales in his *Earthly Paradise* are classical in their subjects : e. g. 'The Doom of King Acrisius,' 'Cupid and Psyche,' 'Atalanta's Race,' 'The Death of Paris,' 'The Golden Apples.'

3. Mrs. Browning's *Prometheus Bound* (translation from Aeschylus) and Shelley's *Prometheus Unbound*.

4. Ruskin's *Queen of the Air*, Kingsley's *Heroes*, Lewis Morris's *Epic of Hades*, dealing generally with ancient mythology.

5. Milton's *Samson Agonistes*. Swinburne's *Atalanta* and *Erechtheus* (Chatto and Windus). Mr. Todhunter's *Helena in Troas* (Kegan Paul).

6. Homer as an English Classic: *Iliad*, translated by Chapman (in 'Universal Library,' Routledge), or by A. S. Way (or 'Avia,' published by Macmillan). The former is a venerable classic; the latter a masterpiece of translation. *Odyssey*, translated by William Morris, or A. S. Way (Macmillan).

---

* Translation of Alfieri by Bowring, two volumes (Geo. Bell and Sons).

III

ONE OF THE THREE GREAT MASTERS OF TRAGEDY

If Aeschylus or Sophocles be selected, Plumptre's introductions will be found helpful*. If Euripides, see especially Introduction to the second volume of A. S. Way's translation. See also Bishop Westcott's articles on his religious ideas (*Contemporary Review*, April, 1884)—Froude's ' Sea Studies ' in the third series of his *Short Studies*—Mahaffy's *Euripides* primer (Macmillan).—Also, on the whole subject compare Symonds's Greek Poets.

IV

PLAYS IN GROUPS

'Presenting Thebes' and Pelops' line,
Or the tale of Troy divine.'
Milton: *Il Penseroso*

The plays in each group are arranged in the order of the story ; but they are quite independent of, and often inconsistent with, one another.

Legends of Thebes	*Œdipus King* of Sophocles.
	Œdipus at Colonus of Sophocles.
	{ *Seven against Thebes* of Aeschylus.
	{ *Women from Phœnicia* of Euripides.
	Antigone of Sophocles.
	Bacchanals of Euripides.

With this section might be read the *Polinices* and *Antigone* of Alfieri †. Students who are musical might read Mendelssohn's *Antigone* and *Œdipus at Colonos*. (Novello.)

The Tale of Troy and Children of Pelops‡	P *Iphigenia in Aulis* of Euripides.
	Rhesus of Euripides.
	Ajax of Sophocles.
	Philoctetes of Sophocles.
	{ *Daughters of Troy* of Euripides.
	{ *Hecuba* of Euripides.
	P *Agamemnon* of Aeschylus.
	{ P *The Women at the Sepulchre (Choephori)* of Aeschylus.
	{ P *Electra* of Sophocles.
	{ P *Electra* of Euripides.
	P *Orestes* of Euripides.
	P *The Blessed Goddesses (Furies*, or *Eumenides)* of Aeschylus.
	P *Iphigenia among the Tauri* of Euripides.
	P *Helena* of Euripides.
	Andromache of Euripides.

With this section may be read the *Iliad* of Homer [see above : II. 6], the ' Death of Paris ' in William Morris's *Earthly Paradise*, and Tennyson's

---

* See note at end of preface on English Translations.
† Translation of Alfieri by Bowring, two volumes (Geo. Bell and Sons).
‡ The plays marked with the letter P belong to the legend of the Pelops family, a separate offshoot of the Tale of Troy.

Oenone; Alfieri's *Agamemnon* and *Orestes*; Racine's* *Thebaid* and *Andromache*. With the *Iphigenia in Aulis* of Euripides read the *Iphigenia* of Racine; with the *Iphigenia in Tauris* of Euripides read that of Goethe. One of the Shakespearean plays works up this subject-matter into the form of Romantic Drama—*Troilus and Cressida*. [It is very coarse.]

For the Pelops section is specially recommended the *House of Atreus*, by E. D. A. Morshead (Kegan Paul): a translation of the *Agamemnon*, *Choephori* and *Eumenides*.

Legends of Hercules	*Hercules Mad* of Euripides †. *The Maidens of Trachis* of Sophocles. *The Children of Hercules* (*Heraclidæ*) of Euripides. *Alcestis* of Euripides.

To this legend belongs 'The Golden Apples' in William Morris's *Earthly Paradise*.

Legends of Prometheus and Io	*Prometheus Bound* of Aeschylus ‡. *The Suppliants* of Aeschylus §.

With this may be read Shelley's *Prometheus Unbound*.

The Argonautic Expedition	*Medea* of Euripides.

With this is strongly recommended William Morris's Epic : *Life and Death of Jason*.

The Persian War	*The Persians* of Aeschylus.

With this may be read G. W. Cox's *Tale of the Great Persian War from Herodotus* (Longmans).

V

COMEDY

It is difficult to suggest reading in this department until more translations adapted to modern taste are made accessible. [See note at end of Preface.] The Student may select from what plays have been rendered readable, and proceed to Robert Browning's *Aristophanes' Apology*.

---

* English translation in Bohns' series.
† Translated by Robert Browning in his *Aristophanes' Apology*.
‡ Translated by Mrs. Browning in her Works.
§ Translated by Morshead (Kegan Paul).

INDEXES

GENERAL INDEX   INDEX OF PLAYS

GENERAL INDEX

—◆—

INDEX OF PLAYS

₊ *Where* Clarendon *type is used the passage referred to deals with the play as a whole.*

The references in this Index are usually to the footnotes, from which it will be easy to consult both the text and the plays themselves.

TABLE OF REFERENCES

₊ *The Translations in the Universal Library [see note at end of Preface] do not contain numbered lines: this Table gives the average number of Greek lines represented by each page of the English translation.*

THE END